**Also by Jason King**

Kansas Jayhawks: A Year to Remember
Inside the Greatest Season in KU Basketball History

d in the United States of America by Quebecor World, Taunton, MA.
978-0-615-52649-2

photos by Steve Puppe.
and inside design by Beau White.

# BEYOND T

# PHO

Untold Stories from Kansas Basketl
Most Dominant Decade

## by Jason King

with Jesse Newell

Cop
in a
mea
prio

Print
ISBN

Cover
Cover

www.kubook.net
@kansasbook on Twi

# CONTENTS

Introduction

1    Roy Williams 1988/89 - 2002/03    1

2    Luke Axtell 1999/2000 - 2000/01    13

3    Eric Chenowith 1997/98 - 2000/01    21

4    Brett Ballard 2000/01 - 2001/02    34

5    Jeff Boschee 1998/99 - 2001/02    42

6    Drew Gooden 1999/2000 - 2001/02    52

7    Nick Collison 1999/2000 - 2002/03    65

8    Kirk Hinrich 1999/2000 - 2002/03    78

9    Bill Self 2003/04 - present    85

10    Jeff Graves 2002/03 - 2003/04    100

11    David Padgett 2003/04    109

12    J.R. Giddens 2003/04 - 2004/05    113

13    Keith Langford 2001/02 - 2004/05    127

14    Michael Lee 2001/02 - 2004/05    144

15    Aaron Miles 2001/02 - 2004/05    156

16    Wayne Simien 2001/02 - 2004/05    168

17    Nick Bahe 2003/04 - 2004/05    179

18    C.J. Giles 2004/05 - 2005/06    201

19    Jeff Hawkins 2001/02 - 2005/06    206

20    Christian Moody 2002/03 - 2005/06    212

21    Stephen Vinson 2002/03 - 2005/06    218

22    Julian Wright 2005/06 - 2006/07    225

23    Darrell Arthur 2006/07 - 2007/08    234

24    Jeremy Case 2003/04 - 2007/08    248

25    Mario Chalmers 2005/06 - 2007/08    256

26    Darnell Jackson 2004/05 - 2007/08    272

| | | |
|---|---|---|
| 27 | Sasha Kaun 2004/05 - 2007/08 | 279 |
| 28 | Russell Robinson 2004/05 - 2007/08 | 285 |
| 29 | Brandon Rush 2005/06 - 2007/08 | 295 |
| 30 | Rodrick Stewart 2005/06 - 2007/08 | 301 |
| 31 | Matt Kleinmann 2004/05 - 2008/09 | 310 |
| 32 | Cole Aldrich 2007/08 - 2009/10 | 321 |
| 33 | Sherron Collins 2006/07 - 2009/10 | 329 |
| 34 | Xavier Henry 2009/10 | 348 |
| 35 | Mario Little 2008/09 - 2010/11 | 354 |
| 36 | Brady Morningstar 2006/07 - 2010/11 | 360 |
| 37 | Tyrel Reed 2007/08 - 2010/11 | 369 |
| 38 | Josh Selby 2010/11 | 373 |
| 39 | Thomas Robinson 2009/10 - present | 379 |
| 40 | Tyshawn Taylor 2008/09 - present | 383 |
| | Acknowledgements | 391 |
| | Interview Index | 392 |

With a white gold chain dangling from his neck and a baseball cap sitting loosely on his head, Sherron Collins walked into Portillo's restaurant in Chicago and headed straight for the counter. No need to look at a menu.

"Chicken sandwich, fries, water," Collins said as he rubbed his hands together. "Man, I am *hungry*."

Two hours later, Collins' food sat on the table before him, cold and mostly untouched.

It's difficult to eat when you're talking, and for 104 minutes on July 13, 2011, Collins couldn't stop. Whether he was discussing his recruiting trip to Allen Fieldhouse, reliving the crucial moments of the 2008 NCAA title game or describing the scene in the locker room after losing to Northern Iowa, Collins told story after story about his four-year career as a Kansas Jayhawk. Some of his tales were humorous, others tugged at the heartstrings. And a few were downright shocking.

Take-out box in tow, Collins shook my hand as we left Portillo's around 3 that afternoon, nearly two hours after our interview began.

"Hope you got what you were looking for," he said.

I did – and not just from Collins.

Throughout the summer of 2011, 40 players and coaches took part in interviews similar to the one I conducted with Collins. Almost two hours were spent with former standouts such as Nick Collison, Keith Langford, Mario Chalmers and Darrell Arthur. Others such as Brandon Rush, Wayne Simien and Kirk Hinrich were pressed for time – but even those interviews lasted between 30 and 45 minutes.

The final result was 400 pages of the kind of information Kansas fans crave: Untold, candid stories about what it was really like to be a Jayhawk during the most successful decade in program history.

We all saw what happened on game nights, but what transpired in the locker room, in the huddle or during victory celebrations at Lawrence nightclubs? What did the players think of their coaches, their opponents – and each other? Who did they turn to for support? How did they handle pressure? What did they do for fun?

The Jayhawks didn't hold back.

Keith Langford discussed his attempt to transfer to North Carolina, Eric Chenowith revealed why his mother left Allen Fieldhouse in tears after watching his first college practice and Stephen Vinson talked about how the Oregon mascot changed Michael Lee's career.

J.R. Giddens relived his infamous night at the Moon Bar and Jeff Graves discussed his battle to lose weight. Roy Williams gave details about his strained relationship with Al Bohl and numerous walk-ons talked about life at the end of the Jayhawks' bench.

Combined, the interviews lasted nearly 40 hours.

Instead of relaying their stories to you in my words, I decided to let the players speak to you in theirs. The book's conversational tone will make you feel as if you're sitting where I was: next to Collins at Portillo's or across from Drew Gooden in a meeting room at Allen Fieldhouse, fully engaged as they recounted some of the most highly publicized moments in Kansas history while also sharing stories they were never allowed to discuss in college.

Overwhelming as the project often became – I'd rather work in a toll booth than transcribe any more tape – compiling "Beyond the Phog" was also a lot of fun. The 38 players who agreed to be interviewed seemed more than happy to talk. In some ways, I felt as if they enjoyed the conversations as much as I did. I'll never forget Langford holding out his arm so I could see the goosebumps that surfaced as he described the meeting in which Roy Williams informed the Jayhawks he was leaving for North Carolina. Listening as others reflected on various games and moments and hearing about how their lives have changed since college was fascinating. Even standouts such as J.R. Giddens, C.J. Giles and Josh Selby – whose Kansas careers ended on sour notes – were upbeat, friendly and accommodating.

Not surprisingly, longtime media favorites such as Langford, Gooden, Lee, Giddens, Collins, Chenowith, Graves and Russell Robinson came through with some of the best chapters. Then there were guys like Chalmers, Arthur, Simien and Luke Axtell, who have turned into excellent talkers since leaving Kansas, where they were a tad more guarded and reserved. Some of the best stories came from walk-ons. The contributions of Vinson, Brett Ballard, Nick Bahe, Matt Kleinmann and others meant more to Kansas than anyone will ever know.

By the time you complete "Beyond the Phog," you'll be overflowing with knowledge about a program that has won more games (300) since 2001-02 than any major conference school in the country. While some of America's top teams have experienced "down" seasons during the last decade – UCLA, North Carolina, Indiana, Kentucky and Florida have all missed the NCAA Tournament at least once in the past 10 years – Kansas has remained a staple atop the Big 12 standings and in the NCAA Tournament.

This book will provide a vivid understanding of the day-to-day stress and strain involved in maintaining such a dynasty. By the end of the last chapter, you'll have a newfound respect for the players and coaches who made it all happen.

I know I do.

In an effort to most accurately portray their thoughts and feelings, all players and coaches have been directly quoted. Dashes have been used to conceal certain curse words.

The comments expressed by players and coaches in this book do not necessarily represent the view of the authors.

# CHAPTER 1

# 1988/89 - 2002/03
# ROY WILLIAMS

Roy Williams compiled a 418-101 record in 15 seasons at Kansas before leaving to take over at North Carolina, his alma mater, in the spring of 2003. Williams' teams have been to seven Final Fours – the fourth most in NCAA history – and hold the record for most consecutive NCAA Tournament appearances with at least one win (20). Although he never won an NCAA title at Kansas, Williams has captured two championships at North Carolina and was inducted in the Basketball Hall of Fame in 2007.

## IN ROY'S WORDS

If I'd have known how I was going to feel after I told my players at Kansas that I was leaving for North Carolina, I never would've done it. I remember walking into our locker room that day without a real plan. I was just thinking, "Talk from your heart and hope that you can get through it." A few minutes later, when I walked out, I felt lower than I'd ever felt about myself as a human being. I thought I was junk. I thought I was crap – that I was worthless – because I'd just walked into a room and hurt a bunch of kids. No one will ever understand what I felt that day, because no one is Roy Williams. It was just plain awful.

## NO MORE MONKEYING AROUND

One of the unfortunate things about my departure is that it overshadowed what had been a great accomplishment that season by our players. Our Final Four appearance that year was our second in a row, which is something you just don't see very often. As good as those last two teams were, the building blocks for that success actually began the previous season, in 2000-01. We made the Sweet 16 that year, which was big, because the previous three seasons we had lost in the second round of the NCAA Tournament.

The second round losses – especially when they happen three years in a row – can really weigh on a team, a program. We felt like we had a monkey on our back. That year we played Syracuse in the second round up in Dayton. I thought I'd try to relieve the pressure a little bit, so I had our managers go out and buy a stuffed animal, a monkey, so we could use the "get the monkey off our back" theme. I was trying to give them some confidence, but I'm not sure we needed it, because we were pretty good. The year before that was a little more difficult because Nick Collison, Kirk Hinrich and Drew Gooden were all freshmen. We finished fifth in the league and lost to Duke in the second round. But that next year I thought we had a chance to do some good things.

One frustrating thing was that I had three players who were expected to do really well, but things just weren't going smoothly for them. They were all seniors: Kenny Gregory, Eric Chenowith and Luke Axtell. Usually, my players play their best when they're seniors. But I had three guys that were on our preseason poster wearing military garb, and things just didn't go as well for them as we'd hoped. I was really bothered by that, but I was also really proud, because even with all of that stuff, we still had a really good year.

## ERIC CHENOWITH

Eric's sophomore year he was second team all-conference. The summer after his sophomore year – and we didn't know this at the time, but his high school coach and I had conversations about it later – he didn't really put in the effort it took to get to another level. He wasn't focused like he needed to be. He gained a little weight, and it hurt his mobility. To his defense, he tried really hard once school started. But he missed a great deal of time in the summer – and now he had Nick and Drew pushing him. It was a different situation.

I know Eric probably thinks I was hard on him, but I expected more out of Eric. If someone is a second team all-conference pick as a sophomore, you expect him to continue to improve. I pushed him extremely hard, trying to get him to break through – and I'm not even sure I was his biggest problem. His dad was really tough on him, too. I felt like he was really getting a lot of pressure from home. It was hard for him.

I'm not sure if he'll admit it, but I'm pretty sure he saw 11 concerts that summer. How can you see a band that many times and travel around and be a groupie and still work on your game? That's what he didn't do. I pushed him. I was doing it for a reason, because I saw so much from him his sophomore year that I felt like he could – and should – take a step forward. It was just really hard for him. Then when Nick and Drew came, he didn't get as many opportunities.

## KENNY GREGORY

When he was a high school senior, I called and politicked to try to get Kenny on the McDonald's All-American team. He was the last guy chosen. I'll never make that mistake again. I call it "The Kenny Gregory Rule." The McDonald's game was a no-defense, run-it-up-and-down-the-court dunk contest. Kenny is better at that than anybody. He won the dunk contest and then he was named the MVP for the game, too. That put all sorts of pressure and unfair expectations on him to do all these great things at Kansas right off the bat. What people didn't realize, though, that is that Kenny had trouble shooting the ball. Name a great player that doesn't shoot it well. You can't do it. But in that game he was dunking everything right and left. Since then I've never tried to do anything to get someone into that McDonald's game.

Despite all of that, Kenny had a really, really big-time career. Not only did he average between 13 and 16 points his last few years, but he also averaged about seven rebounds (actual number: 7.3) his senior year. And he did it as a three-man. He's still the best rebounding three-man I've ever coached. I've never had another three-man average seven rebounds a game. He was really good at taking the ball to the basket. He got better and better defensively. He just didn't shoot it very well. I shouldn't say Kenny had a bad senior year. He actually had a very good year that year. It's just that people's expectations were so high that whatever he did was never enough. It was a tough situation for him.

## LUKE AXTELL

Luke had a lot on his plate when he came to Kansas. I had to do some things different with him because it had been a turbulent time for him at the University of Texas. I felt like the stress on him was pretty significant. I tried to make sure I didn't add any. But just like Kenny, he also became a victim of people's expectations. I wanted to give him some encouragement the year he sat out (in 1998-99), so we'd put him through a workout before our home games with one of the coaches. A ton of fans, especially the students, would be screaming and cheering for him. He'd make 50 out of 60 3's. It'd be off the charts. I was doing it to give him confidence and to make him feel good and to get him through a tough year. In reality, that set some expectations that were difficult for him to live up to.

There were so many distractions for Luke, but he was a wonderful kid, a kid that I really enjoyed. He never could focus just on basketball. There were so many things going on around him that made it difficult for him.

## GAINING MOMENTUM

We were great against Syracuse. Then we lost to Illinois (coached by Bill Self) in the Sweet 16. Everything that could've gone wrong went wrong for us. Frank Williams was so good for Illinois that day. He just destroyed us. Frank really bothered Kirk. He was a sophomore and Frank was older. So that sticks out. But the other thing that sticks out is looking down that bench and realizing that we were basically going to have everyone back. I knew we were about to get really

good. We had already started to play fast, but with Aaron Miles coming in, we were going to be able to take it to another level. We'd basically have three point guards in the lineup with Aaron and Kirk and Jeff Boschee. It was the perfect formula to play fast.

Kirk was the best runner that I ever coached. The bad thing was that Kirk couldn't push the ball and pitch ahead to himself, because there was only one of him. So we sold Aaron on the idea of really pushing it and being able to push ahead. The other thing was that Kirk was a great finisher and made such great decisions. So not only would he try to score, but he'd make good plays. Aaron was really good at pushing the ball. He'd make great decisions to get it to Kirk and then Kirk would make great decisions. Then our big guys were going to be Drew and Nick and Wayne Simien as a freshman. All three of those guys could run like crazy, too. If it wasn't the best running team that I've had, it was close to it.

## BEST KU TEAM EVER?

We started off the 2001-02 season by losing to Ball State in Maui. But it really didn't bother me, because Ball State played great, and I knew we were still going to be really good. That was about as excited as I've ever been going into a season. It equals how I feel right now about this North Carolina team that has so much potential. We had so many pieces to the puzzle. We had Nick and Kirk and Drew, who I loved. We had Aaron and Wayne coming in. Boschee was back for his senior year.

Everything just fit so well. When I recruit, I'm trying to put together a puzzle. You've got to have corner pieces and you've got to have pieces down the side and in the center. There is no question that that's why I try to do, even to this day. You try to recruit a puzzle that will come together into a beautiful picture.

The 1996-97 team and the 2002 team – the one that lost to Maryland in the Final Four – were my two best teams at Kansas. The 2003 team could've been if we hadn't have lost Wayne. In 2002 and 2003 … I had as much trust in the guys on those teams as maybe any of them. Those teams were very similar to the ones in 1997 and 1998 in how easy they were to coach.

We went 16-0 that season, which is something I was extremely proud of. I still have a picture up in my house that somebody gave me of Quin Snyder and I shaking hands after we beat Missouri at their place for the 16th win. Someone super-imposed another picture so you could see the final score. It was a big win, a heck of a game. To go 16-0 in the conference … I mean, you just don't do that. But that team was special.

Every game I thought we were going to win. When we were down and it was looking bad, I still thought we were going to come back. I just had so much trust in those guys. And again, with Kirk and Nick and Boschee, who was more of a silent leader … it was a group of kids that I just enjoyed being with. It was a confident group of guys that handled themselves really well off the court with the way they represented the university. It was just an easy team to coach.

## MARYLAND LOSS

Losing to Maryland in the Final Four stung, but they were playing with more of a purpose than us. We hadn't been to the Final Four in quite a while. We got to Atlanta and to the arena, and we were looking around like we were mesmerized. Maryland had been there the year before and felt like they'd gotten shafted against Duke. They had a single purpose in mind. That same cast of characters was like, "We're going to win the blessed thing this year." The other thing I remember is that we got off to a good start, but I didn't like it. We were taking shots that I didn't like, but they kept going in. Once those shots started missing, we panicked.

## THOUGHTS ON GOODEN, BOSCHEE

The Maryland game was the last game for Jeff and Drew, who left a year early. Drew was the best offensive rebounder I've ever coached. He was a unique young man. My assistants kept telling, "You've got to coach him. We can't do it. He won't listen to us, but he'll listen to you." I loved that young man to death. I'd step in front of a train for him right now.

Drew's sophomore year, he broke his wrist. He didn't play for seven or eight games. During that time, I made him sit at the top of the bench, right there close to me, instead of down at the end. I wanted him to listen to what we were saying. When he came back he was much easier to coach because he understood things so much more. I loved him. I'd get mad at his actions sometimes, but I'd never get mad at Drew personally, because he was such a wonderful kid. We had a lot of very personal conversations. Each and every month, he matured as a player and matured as a kid.

I had more confidence in Jeff Boschee than any shooter I've ever had. He'd take shots that I would frown upon if it were any other player in my 23 years of coaching. But when Jeff took them, I didn't mind. He took really big shots, too. His freshman year he led us to the Big 12 Tournament championship with a very mediocre supporting cast. He was a coach's dream because he was so confident in what he could do. He worked hard to become better defensively. He went from being the starting point guard to the third point guard. He knew that his niche was putting the basketball in the hole. He could do it as well as anyone.

## 2002-03

I still have a newspaper article in my drawer with a headline that says: "Biggest disappointment of the year? It's Kansas, by far." My last season at Kansas, we started off 3-3. Kirk was hurt, Wayne was hurt ... we weren't healthy. We lost those two games (to North Carolina and Florida) in the Preseason NIT in New York and then we lost to Oregon at Oregon. Most people would've lost to Oregon that year. That was a good team. North Carolina and Florida would've beaten a lot of people, too. I didn't go off the deep end just because we'd dropped a few. I knew that, once we got things straightened out and got healthy, we were going to be really good again. We almost lost at Tulsa when we were 3-3.

Eventually we turned things around, even without Wayne, who only played 16 games. One of the reasons was Jeff Graves. Jeff was really gifted, really talented. I just couldn't get him to buy into the academic side of things. I had to stay on him all the time. But on the court, oh my gosh ... he had such great savvy. And his passing ability, for a big guy, was phenomenal. We're talking about a guy who had 16 points and 16 rebounds in the national championship game. I just couldn't get him to stay out of my doghouse for the academic stuff. He was a gifted young man who was a big-time player at a time when we really needed him.

With Kirk and Nick, it was almost like my North Carolina team in 2009, when I said I thought it was "right" for those guys to win a national championship. I felt like it would've been right for college basketball for Kirk Hinrich and Nick Collison to win it in 2003. They epitomized what college basketball should be about. Unfortunately, it didn't happen.

Kirk, Nick and Drew renewed my enthusiasm and my faith that I could be a college basketball coach. Regardless of what they achieved on the court, they were more important to me off the court. I had gotten so dissatisfied and

skeptical about recruiting and the way things were going. All of a sudden, I found three kids whose families wanted them to be big-time basketball players but also wanted them to get quality educations. They didn't have any bad motives whatsoever. I thought, "Wow! You can still do this with wonderful kids. You can find wonderful kids." That's the thing I remember about those kids more than anything.

Wayne, Aaron Keith Langford and Mike Lee … I loved those guys. They were one of the neatest groups I've ever recruited. They'll be friends forever, they'll be close forever. They were big-time players from the first day they stepped on campus. Aaron and Keith and Wayne played more than Michael, but Michael took the shot that would've sent the national championship game to overtime his sophomore year. They were great kids. There was never any negativity to them. All of them were winners, too. Wayne won a state championship. Aaron and Mike did, too. Keith's high school team was very strong. We were very fortunate to sign Keith, who had initially committed to Ole Miss. For a while we thought we were going to get Josh Childress. I thought he was going to be a big-time player for us, so I was really disappointed when he chose Stanford. Luckily, I saw Keith, and I fell in love with him.

## BAD TIMING

North Carolina's decision to make a coaching change a week before the Final Four really frustrated me – it really ticked me off – because I knew it was going to take away from our players and what they were accomplishing. That bothered me more than anything. That week should've been about my team and those kids instead of what might or might not happen.

After we beat Arizona in the Elite Eight in Anaheim, we flew back to Kansas and landed around 2 or 3 in the morning. I had 17 or 18 messages, and one of them was from Matt Doherty. He said, "Coach, great win. I'm sorry you've had to answer some of these questions, but I think I'm going to be OK. I've had another meeting with (athletic director) Dick Baddour. I think things are going to be fine."

UCLA had been trying to talk to me, too, and I was telling them, "I can't do that right now. I'm trying to win a national championship." I called UCLA on that Sunday before the Final Four and said, "Don't wait on me. Go ahead and move on." I don't know if they would've offered me the job. They made me feel like they would. But that Sunday I was like, "You guys go ahead. I'm the coach at Kansas." I told Wanda, "I'm so happy for Matt." It was a relief. Then a few days later, things had completely changed.

I didn't enjoy the Final Four at all. The only time I enjoyed being in New Orleans was when I was on the court with my team. I told everyone I wasn't going to talk about the North Carolina situation. Even to my closest friends, I was like, "Don't talk to me about that. I'm trying to coach my team." But I could hear people whispering. It was big news. But it was unfair to my kids.

## FINAL FOUR

I can't say the North Carolina situation affected us in the Final Four. We won by 30 points against Marquette in the semifinals and were one shot away from sending the NCAA title game into overtime. That was all because of Kirk and Nick. They led everything.

I remember in Anaheim, we were playing Arizona in the Elite Eight, and it was late in the game. I was talking during the timeout and, at the end, I said, "Anybody got anything they want to add?" Nick Collison said, "Yes! Everyone get your act in gear. I'm going to the Final Four. If you freakin' guys want to go with me, get your ass in gear." I was like, "All right. I don't need to say anything else." That group was just so focused. It was a team that wanted to do those kinds of things. They went off the leadership of Kirk and Nick. But Aaron and Keith and those guys were winners themselves. So I don't think they were distracted at all.

We played so great against Marquette, and it was almost like things were coming too easy for us. I said, "Guys, you don't win a national championship this easy. You've got to be prepared." The Syracuse game kind of reminded me of the North Carolina-Kansas game in 2008 in that Syracuse came out and hit us right in the mouth. Gerry McNamara made six 3's in the first half. But I had so much confidence in that team, we just kept plugging along. We were down by 18 at one point and ended up with the last shot to tie the game.

The biggest thing about that game was our inability to make free throws and the foul situation with Keith Langford. We had Nick and Jeff Graves working the inside game and Kirk on the outside. But Keith Langford was the best player equipped to take the ball to the basket against that zone. And he was also the best-equipped guy we had to guard Carmelo Anthony.

I just remember maintaining our poise after McNamara made all those 3's. We were confident we were going to get it figured out. We never got over the hump, but we would've if we could've made some free throws. We were 12-for-30 from the line.

Kirk ended up passing the ball to Mike Lee for the 3-pointer that would've sent the game into overtime. Hakim Warrick made a great play and blocked Mike's shot. Kirk probably would've been my first choice in that situation to shoot it, and I've heard some people say, "Kirk should've taken that last shot." But Syracuse's defense took that option away. Kirk's a basketball player. He's not the type to force things. He's always been taught to work for the best shot, to pass to the open man. Mike Lee was open. He made the right play. To me, you have to congratulate Hakim Warrick for making a really good block. You've heard me say 100 times that, every now and then, the other team plays a factor in how things unfold, too. In that case, Syracuse did a nice job.

That night was one of the toughest times for me because of all the junk that the North Carolina situation had started, but also because my love for Kirk and Nick and what they stood for. Their pictures should be in the dictionary next to the term "student athlete." They were tough kids, coaches' sons. There was nothing about them that I didn't love. We've won two national championships at North Carolina, but one of the greatest thrills in my life came after that Syracuse game, in the press conference, when Nick Collison said, "That other team may have won the national championship, but I'm happy to have played for this guy right here and to be in his locker room." That choked me up. To this day, that's one of the greatest things anyone has ever said about me.

It was difficult talking to my team that night. Anything you say is inadequate. I just remember Drew Gooden coming into the locker room, crying and hugging me. He said, "Coach, I wish I would've been here."

## AL BOHL

Our athletic director (Al Bohl) was fired after the Final Four. If they'd have done it six months earlier, things might have been different. But by then it was too late. I wasn't the only guy that was unhappy. There was not one freakin' coach on that campus that enjoyed those two years (under Al Bohl). They may not say as much about it, but every damn coach on that campus was talking to me about it. Every coach was coming to me complaining about the athletic director, saying, "Why am I having to do this or that?" For two years, I felt like I didn't have support. For two years, I felt like my boss did not want me to win.

He'd come out and say stuff like, "Roy knows I'm the boss." Well, I never questioned that he was the boss, so why say that? Then he'd brag to people about how Kansas went to the Final Four during his first year here, like he was trying to take some sort of credit for us going to the Final Four. He told me one time, "We've got to sacrifice everything we can to make sure our football program succeeds." I said, "Do you mean to tell me we need to sacrifice what we've got going in basketball?" Then he said it again: "We need to sacrifice everything we can to make sure our football program succeeds." I felt like I didn't have support. I'd have people come and say things to me that he had said. It got to the point where we had a very difficult time talking to each other. During those two years, the only time I was happy was when I was with my team, because every other part of the day was a battle. I knew I was going to leave because I had been so unhappy. It's hard to do something with your heart, body and soul when you feel like your boss doesn't want you to be successful.

The other thing was that my dad was sick and my sister was sick. I didn't want to be the rich little brother back in Kansas sending money. I lost my dad 14 months after I left. I lost my sister a year after that.

I know our kids were hurt. They felt a sense of betrayal. Wayne Simien, who is one of the greatest kids in the world, said he'd given his arm for me, or something like that. He called two days later and apologized. I said, "Wayne, I understand, son." Those kids were great. There were a lot of things said about me calling those kids during the next year. The only time I talked to them was if they called me. Within a week, all of those kids had called me to tell me they supported me. They were phenomenal.

When I turned the North Carolina job down three years before, I honestly thought I would never entertain those thoughts again. I've said it before, but one regret I have is saying, "The next time I have a press conference like this, I'll either be retiring or dying." At the time I wasn't lying. I truly believed that.

## ANOTHER TOUGH TASK

I called all of the guys that had signed with us the previous fall (David Padgett, J.R. Giddens, Jeremy Case and Omar Wilkes) and apologized. I told them I did not plan it, that it was just something that I had to do. I told them Kansas was a wonderful, wonderful place. I was criticized because I went on Pardon the Interruption, and they asked me about recruits trying to get out of their letters-of-intent. I said, "It says in the national letter-of-intent that you're signing with the school and not the coach. It's in bold print." We went to a break. I told Tony Kornheiser and Mike Wilbon during the break, "Maybe they should let a kid leave when the coach leaves, but not let him go to the school where the coach is going." So then they asked me again on the air, and once again I said, "It says on the letter-of-intent that if you sign with a school, you're stuck with that school." People made it out to sound like I was saying those kids were "stuck" in Kansas, like it was a bad place to be "stuck" or something. That's not what I meant. I meant that they were bound. People really blew that out of proportion.

I called David Padgett and told him to stay. Even when he asked about the possibility of transferring to North Carolina a year later, I said, "David, are you sure you'd want to do that?" He went back and told his mother and his father that he didn't think I wanted him, because I was trying to make every case for him to stay at Kansas.

## A NEW START

Just hours after telling my Kansas players I was leaving, I was standing in Chapel Hill getting ready to be introduced as North Carolina's new coach. I was criticized by the North Carolina people because I wasn't all hip-hip-hooray and that kind of stuff during my press conference. They gave me a North Carolina tie to put on and I wouldn't do it. I said, "Hey, I'm not changing my life. I'm coming here to be a basketball coach." I made some North Carolina people unhappy because the school fight song says, "I'm a Tar Heel born, I'm a Tar Heel bred, and when I die I'm a Tar Heel dead." At the press conference I said, "I'm a Tar Heel and a Kansas Jayhawk bred." Our chancellor said it best that night – although no one really listened or cared – when he said it's not immoral to love two institutions, which I really did. But I just wasn't happy at Kansas. Not at the end.

## THE RIGHT DECISION?

I had some buyer's remorse at first – especially when I was getting crap about not wearing the tie or about changing the fight song lyrics. But you have buyer's remorse in just about every situation in your life. What you have to do is live moving forward. You've heard me say tons of times that life can be understood backwards but it must be lived forward.

I went back to Lawrence to pack up stuff, and we went to El Mezcal, this Mexican restaurant that we loved. This little girl and her mother were there. She got up and stuck her tongue out at me and walked out the door. And I'm talking about the mom, not the little girl.

I still tell people it was 15 of the greatest years of my life. I miss Allen Fieldhouse so much. I miss my friends. But I've got to move forward. I would like to go back someday. I don't know if it's time yet. But if you give to something for 15 years – and nobody can ever say I didn't give them everything I had; my heart, my body, my soul – how can I not look back on that with great fondness?

## KANSAS vs. NORTH CAROLINA

When we played Kansas in the Final Four in 2008, we didn't even address all the history and things that happened in the past. My players were never a part of that story. The game reminded me of when we played Syracuse, because Kansas hit us right in the mouth. They went up by 28, but then we cut it to four and had a 3-pointer that went in-and-out.

The thing that beat us in that game was their defense. They were so alert and so aggressive defensively. I was extremely impressed with how good they were. Plus, they made shots, and Cole Aldrich played the best game he'd played all year coming off the bench. Kansas is always very, very good on offense, too. They take good shots. They don't take bad shots. Offensively and defensively, Bill (Self) has got a tremendous plan. I have a tremendous amount of respect for Bill, because he coaches his butt off. He really does. I'm not just saying that. He's done a great, great job there. He's kept Kansas at the top of the Big 12, which I love to see.

I got so much grief from North Carolina people in 2008 when I wore that Jayhawks sticker during the NCAA title game. Well, I wanted them to win. It was an easy deal for me. People said, "You seriously wanted them to win?" I was like, "My God, yes, why would I want Memphis to win?" As much as I hated that we weren't in the championship, I couldn't have been any happier for Kansas.

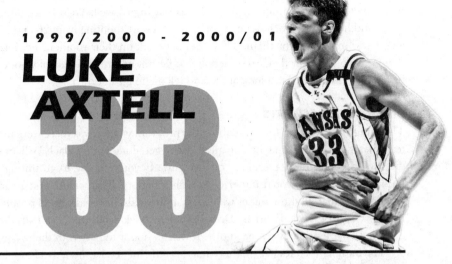

# CHAPTER 2

# 1999/2000 - 2000/01
# LUKE AXTELL
## 33

L uke Axtell transferred to Kansas from the University of Texas in 1998. After redshirting his first year, Axtell's final two seasons each ended prematurely because of illnesses and injuries. One of the nation's top 3-point shooters when healthy, the 6-foot-10 Axtell remains active in basketball circles. In his new business, Luke's Hoops (www.lukeshoops.com), Axtell offers individual and team instruction in the Austin area.

## IN LUKE'S WORDS

When I first showed up at Kansas I brought my share of baggage with me. I had just gone through a very public disagreement with Tom Penders at Texas and, looking back, it was a pretty tough deal for a 19-year-old kid. All I wanted to do was transfer, and all of a sudden I went from being the hometown boy that everyone loved to the fall guy. My family received death threats on our home answering machine. I'd walk across campus each day hoping I didn't take a bullet in the back.

I wanted a new start in a stable program. I'd been burned so badly at Texas. I just wanted to go to a place where I could trust people. Once I visited Kansas, it was a no-brainer for me. I didn't visit anywhere else. Still, once I got there, I kept thinking, "What if these coaches are all about themselves and don't care about the kids?" That had certainly been my experience at Texas. At that point I wouldn't have trusted John Wooden, much less Roy Williams.

## A FRESH START

The summer before my first year at Kansas, I didn't do anything. I decompressed. When I showed up in Lawrence I wasn't in the best of shape, but it didn't take long to get back in the swing of things. After a month or two of practices, I was feeling as good as I'd ever felt. There were times when Coach Williams actually had to take me off the floor because I was playing so well. We'd be running drills, and he'd put the defense in a zone, and I'd start shooting from 26 and 27 feet. I was making all of them. They couldn't work on their rotations because there was no way they'd guard someone that far out in a zone. It actually got to be kind of funny. He'd just look at me and tell me to go sit down.

## CHARACTER COUNTS

The thing I appreciated the most about the program when I was there were my teammates. There was maybe one guy I didn't get along with. Coach Williams did such a good job of recruiting quality guys. If you're going to go through heck with somebody, you'd rather do it with a high-quality person, and I can certainly say that all those dudes were class individuals, just really good people. Kenny Gregory, Kirk Hinrich, Drew Gooden, Nick Collison ... all of the household names that everyone knows. It was an honor to play with them.

Having high character mattered a lot off the court, too, because in Lawrence, if you're a player who is willing to take advantage of your status, you can get whatever you want. People there are falling all over themselves for KU basketball. They'll do whatever they can to bless the players and get close to them. Boosters, business owners, whoever. There's not a question in my mind that, if you wanted to go the wrong route and try to get stuff for free, you could definitely figure out a way to do it. That's why it's so important for the coaches to bring in high-character guys. If they had the wrong coach in there who recruited the wrong guys, it would be a disaster waiting to happen. But it's obvious the coaches who have been there have recruited good kids.

## OUT IN PUBLIC

People used to ask me if it was annoying to always be recognized out in public. I'm sure it could get annoying at some places, but it didn't at Kansas. The fans there had so much heart, and their love for the players was so genuine. It's not like people are looking at you like you're a freak because you're 6-foot-10. They're looking at you with admiration because they look up to you. If you have any perspective, you realize you mean a lot to them. It's one of the few places I can think of where the fans actually care about the players. Of course, we didn't lose very much. If we did they may have had a different tact about them. But that wasn't my experience.

## GETTING ACQUAINTED WITH ROY

Coach Williams knew I had been through a lot at Texas, which is why I think he showed a lot of patience with me my first year there. I definitely tested his limits.

I had a friend on the baseball team that liked to hunt and fish a lot, too, so one morning we went duck hunting right outside of Lawrence. As we were

leaving, he tried to put in a dip as he was driving, and he ran his truck off the road and into this huge mud ditch. We sank in that mud all the way up to our doors. We couldn't go anywhere. Back at Kansas, we had a shoot-around that was supposed to start in an hour. A KU professor drove by, saw us and picked us up. By the time I got to Allen Fieldhouse, they were 29 minutes deep into their 30-minute shoot-around. It would've been better if I didn't show up at all. I was still in my waders when I walked into the gym and, little did I know, I was tracking mud onto the court. I finally stepped out of my waders as Coach Williams was giving his post-practice talk. Then we walked through the tunnel toward the locker room, and Coach Williams was so mad at me that he couldn't even talk. His face was red, and he kept turning around like he was going to say something, but then he'd keep walking. He finally lit into me, but just seeing him try to restrain himself from going over the top was pretty memorable. I had to run wind sprints after practice for the rest of the year while all the other players watched from the sideline, all because I was late to that shoot-around. I totally deserved it, even though what happened was pretty much out of my hands. I always joked with my friend that he was the beginning of the end to my KU career for running into that ditch. I don't know if I ever got out of the doghouse after that one.

## A FEW SECONDS TOO SOON

The other time Coach Williams got really, really mad at me was a year or two later. We had the ball on the last possession before halftime, and I shot a 3-pointer a few seconds earlier than I was supposed to. I was open and I figured

I'd knock it down. I missed it, of course. We went back to the locker room and we were all sitting there. Coach Williams comes storming in, picks up a trash can and chunks it right at my head. It was one of those big, gray 20-gallon trash cans. If I didn't duck it would've hit me in the face. The trash spilled into my locker and all over my stuff. I didn't think it was very funny. I went into his office the next day and said, "You know, Coach, you really don't have to do that to get your point across to me. I understand that I shouldn't have taken the shot." He was like, "You're probably right. I hurt my elbow throwing it, so we're probably even." That was probably the craziest thing I ever saw him do.

I don't remember anyone ever saying anything to me about that after it happened. There were times when everybody was so miserable that it was just like, "Whatever, it's just part of the deal." There is so much pressure on everyone. When you include everyone that watches the games on TV, you're exhibiting everything that you are in front of millions of people. So everybody is pushing themselves as hard as they can all time. It's a lot for the players to handle and it's a lot for the coaches to handle. So people do things that are out of character sometimes, and I think everyone understands. It's a job, and in Lawrence it's magnified because everywhere you go, you're forced to relive what happened that night.

## FRIENDLY FIRE

One of my favorite guys on the team was Jeff Boschee. Both of us were 3-point shooters and, even though we never talked about it, there was a little competitiveness between us. It wasn't out in the open. One time we were playing Michigan State up in Chicago. It was at the very end of the game and we were getting beat. It was obvious we were going to lose. Eric Chenowith set a pick for me and I came off a screen about 25 feet away from the basket. I pulled up off the dribble and made this long 3-pointer. Thirty seconds later, Boschee came down and hit a 27-footer. I was like, "You punk! You stole my spotlight." It was pretty funny. Jeff is a great guy. We got along really well.

## HE ATE WHAT?

Eric Chenowith is from California, and he used to always make fun of me for being a country boy from Texas. He'd always ask me, "Have you eaten this?" or "Have you eaten that?" Once I told him I'd eaten a squirrel, and he thought that was so freakin' sick. He was like, "Man, I'd never eat a squirrel. That's disgusting." Six months later Jeff Carey and I went hunting, and we shot some squirrels and some rabbits. Eric said he wanted to try a rabbit. Well, once a rabbit is skinned and cleaned, it looks just like a squirrel. So I served the squirrel to Eric, and Jeff and I ate the rabbit. We let Eric get halfway through his meal before we told him he was eating a squirrel. He made this face and got so pissed off. Jeff and I were dying laughing.

## OTHER RECOLLECTIONS

I had the pleasure of guarding Kenny Gregory every day in practice. These days, when I teach players how to get to the rim, I'm basically ripping off all of Kenny's moves. I saw them every day in practice. So when I'm teaching spin moves, I'm remembering how Kenny would get me going one way and then spin off of me. He was such an amazing athlete. He'd do stuff, and I'd be like, "Holy cow!"

With Drew Gooden, it was obvious from the moment he got to campus that he was going to be a pro. He started hitting that jump-stop about 15 feet away from the basket and people were just shaking their heads. I remember turning to our assistant, Neil Doughtery, and saying, "This kid is going to be big time."

Kirk Hinrich came to some open gyms the summer before his freshman year, and he didn't look like he was going to do anything. He didn't seem that athletic. He wasn't much of a threat on offense. After a few pickup games I was like, "I'm not sure what this guy is going to bring to the table." But once he moved to campus, it was a totally different story. He just went through the roof as far as confidence and understanding the college game. He turned into an unbelievable point guard who was really good at everything. His progression was really cool to watch. He worked extremely hard.

## A NEW PATH

As a sophomore and junior, I did what everyone else was doing as far as going out and partying and doing the things that college kids do. But then my senior year started, and I wondered, "What's my legacy going to be when I leave KU?" I did some soul-searching. I had a few religious encounters. I got involved with a church and tried to make an impact on the community in a more positive way than I had the first few years I was there. That was my driving force. Like I said, I felt like the people in the community actually cared about us. They cared about me. I felt a responsibility to try to give something back by being a positive influence my senior year.

I started living a different lifestyle. I strayed from the party scene, where I could literally walk into any restaurant or bar and get treated like a rock star. It was an ego-booster that I didn't need any more. Instead I started looking to help change other people's lives. Before, it had been all about me. Now it was about everyone else.

One night in the fall I was talking with Dave Jamerson, a former NBA player that helped me with my journey. He was a big influence on me. I was sharing my story with him and I said, "Why don't I get baptized again?" I was about 5 years old the first time it happened. I wanted to remember the experience and understand it, which wasn't the case the first time. So Dave and I found a swimming pool at some random apartment complex in Lawrence. It was about 40 degrees outside, but we got into the water, and he baptized me. It was so cold in that water, but I'm glad it happened. It was definitely something I'll never forget.

Even though I had made some changes, the reaction on the team was positive. I was so determined to make a stand in my personal life that I probably got annoying at times. I just had a lot of conviction about which direction I wanted to go. The negative feedback was so minimal it's not even worth talking about. Most of those guys had religious beliefs of their own, so this was nothing new to them. I tried to share with guys what I was going through and what I was experiencing. We all respected each other. No one was standoffish with me – and it's not like I was going to be standoffish with someone just because I heard they'd been out drinking or something. That wasn't it at all. I did more than my share of that kind of stuff when I was up there, just at a different point and time.

I definitely had a better work ethic my senior year and I think that had something to do with it. The problem was that I was hurt all the time. I tore up my ankles twice and then my back started to go. No matter how hard I worked, I just wasn't functional.

## BAD BREAKS

Jeff Boschee came up to me in the locker room the day I tore up my ankle for the second time and said, "Man, you are cursed." That's exactly how it felt. I was snake-bitten. I only played 20 games as a junior before I had to take some time off because I was sick. And even before that I never felt right. And my last

year I only played in 19 games because of injuries. In the end my biggest issue was my back. I had two herniated disks that were causing me so much pain that, at times, it hurt to breathe. One time I got off the plane and was literally stuck in the position I'd been sitting in. My legs were straight, but my back was so locked up that I couldn't straighten up from that 90-degree angle I was sitting in. I had to walk around like that for the next hour. I still tried to play with it but, eventually, it just wasn't possible. We played Missouri on my Senior Night, so I got to start. I was half as fast as anyone on the court. They were running around and my body was so locked up that I felt like I had lead weights on my feet. I couldn't keep up at all. It wasn't even close. I met with Coach Williams after the game and said, "Look, I could've very well lost us that game if you had decided to play me more." I told them I had to get my back fixed, and that was it. My Kansas career was over.

## LIFE AFTER LAWRENCE

Even though I was finished with college basketball, I wanted to get back on the court as soon as possible because I still thought I had a chance at a good career. I went to every specialist I could find in the Austin area. Eventually, after some rehab, my back felt good again so I started doing some basketball tours with a group called Champions for Christ. We went through Latvia and Lithuania and Peru and played the professional teams in those countries. My back was doing really well.

But when I came back home, I was playing in a pickup game, and my back completely blew out. I got surgery and that was basically it. I played in Russia for about three months but things just weren't the same. Right now I could go play in an open-gym pickup game full speed and do really well. Then, if I tried it again the next day, I'd be toast. It won't hold up for a consistent amount of time.

I spent a year coaching high school ball at the Hill Country Christian School of Austin. But that was basically it for basketball for a while. I didn't want anything to do with it. After the surgery, it was so tough. I felt like I'd gotten right to the brink of being able to make a living at playing. I was right there and fell just short. I started playing in the second grade and had devoted most of my life to being successful at basketball. When I didn't quite get there, it was heartbreaking. I went into ranch real estate for two or three years and just laid low.

## LUKE'S HOOPS

Right now I'm living the life most people in Kansas probably predicted. I've got a nine-acre ranch in Elgin, Texas – which is just outside of Austin – with a guest house and a barn. We've got goats and chickens, and I fish and hunt a lot. It's nice to be able to escape from the city. I'd always leaned in that direction.

It's everything you'd have expected me to do when I left Kansas. I've got a wife (Monica) and a daughter (Ashlynn, 5) that I adore. There's another child on the way in December.

With Luke's Hoops, I work with kids all over Austin. I've worked with third-grade teams all the way up to high school. I'm coaching the Westlake and Lake Travis High School teams in their summer camps and right now I've got an 8th-and-9th grade team (River City Hoops) that probably has four Division I prospects on the roster. Pretty much anything with offseason basketball, I try to be a part of.

As far as talking to kids and relating to them, I'm very hard on them, but we have a ton of fun at the same time. I tell them it's important we do everything we can to win. But at the end of the day, I want them to walk out of the gym and be able to smile and not feel like they've just gotten beaten up by me. It's just a different balance. It's a different set of priorities. It's got to be about their development more than the win-loss column. I'll test them. I want them to understand that when they get to high school and their freshman coach gets them, certain habits and attitudes won't work. I'll say, "You're going to get absolutely torn apart if you don't get this figured out now." But I'll say that in a way that's matter-of-fact. I'm not in the business of degrading kids. I just tell them, "This is what's going to happen. This is what's coming down the pipe. You'd better get prepared for it now or you're going to have a hard time adjusting once you get to high school."

Sometimes I'll think back to my career and have "what-ifs." But then I go out and try to play in an open gym for two days in a row and I'm quickly reminded why I'm not playing. The frustrating part for me is that I'm in the business of helping kids reach their ceiling. I just wish I could've seen where mine was. If my back wasn't defective, I feel like I know what the answer would've been. But we'll never find out for sure.

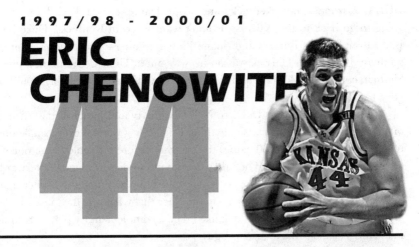

# CHAPTER 3

1 9 9 7 / 9 8 - 2 0 0 0 / 0 1

# ERIC CHENOWITH

## 44

Eric Chenowith is a 7-foot, 235-pound center who played a prominent role at Kansas from 1997-2001. The Villa Park, California native ranks fourth all-time at Kansas for blocked shots and is fifth in rebounding. Chenowith's best season came as a sophomore in 1998-99, when he averaged 13.5 points and 9.1 rebounds. Chenowith probably would've been a first-round pick in the NBA draft after that season, but he decided to return to school, and his career was never quite the same. Chenowith played professionally at various levels before retiring in 2008 because of a back injury. He is now an assistant coach at Villa Park (Calif.) High School, his alma mater.

### IN ERIC'S WORDS

I'm sure Coach Williams would agree with me when I say that I probably wasn't one of his favorite players of all time. I was his whipping boy for a while, and it really wore on me. It affected my study habits, my personal life ... a lot of things. You're trying to do the right thing all the time, but you've got all these pressures and other things going on in your life and you're only a 19- or 20-year-old kid. Playing for him was tough – especially when you felt like he was playing favorites. There were some guys that he never yelled at, ever, and there were some guys that he really rode. I was one of the guys he really rode. I think every coach has their favorites. Now, when I coach, I try my best not to have favorites, just because when I played, I got to feel what it was like on the opposite end of the stick.

### GETTING RECRUITED

For me, it was always Kansas and everyone else. I loved Danny Manning growing up. I loved Larry Brown. I always had this far-off dream of playing at Kansas, just because of the Fieldhouse and stuff. It became a reality when Coach Williams started recruiting me. I narrowed it down to Kansas, Duke, UCLA, Arizona, Utah, Kentucky and Notre Dame. I knew Rick Pitino was going to go back to the NBA, so I didn't want to go to Kentucky. Duke had Elton Brand, Chris Burgess and Shane Battier coming in, so I didn't want to go there. I knew Jim Harrick was on his way out at UCLA. Utah had a great big-man coach in Rick Majerus. If I didn't to go to Kansas, I probably would've gone to Utah.

Coach Williams, Matt Doherty, Neil Dougherty and Joe Holladay … one of them was literally at every single thing I did. They were at every single one of my games. If I played 60 games the summer before my senior year, one of them was at each of them. Then they'd write me some sort of note afterward. They sent me a FedEx package every day, too. They recruited me harder than anyone else. I thought, "I want to go to the place that wants me the most." Duke and Kentucky wanted me, but I felt like I'd be a complementary player. Kansas made me feel like I was their No. 1 guy.

## DECISION TIME

The last day of the recruiting period was July 31, 1996. Coach Williams took a red-eye flight from Florida and then drove to Villa Park High School. He told my coach, "I want to see Eric shoot one free throw, and then I'm done." So at 10 at night, I went down to the gym. He was sitting there, and I shot one free throw. He got up, shook my coach's hand and left. The next day, Aug. 1, was his birthday. Even before I shot that free throw, I had talked to my coach and my dad at length and said, "This is what I'm going to do. I'm tired of the recruiting process. I know where I want to go: Kansas." I didn't want to waste any more of Kansas' time. I wanted them to go recruit more players and spend time with other people.

The next morning I was so nervous to call Coach. I was pacing around. I knew it was the right decision, but I was just nervous to do it. It's like asking a girl to prom. You know you want to ask her, but you still get nervous about it. I called Coach Williams right when Michael Johnson was running in the 1996 Olympics. Coach was watching it, but I didn't realize it. I'm like, "Coach, I just want to wish you a happy birthday and let you know that I want to come to Kansas." All of a sudden he screams out, "Yes! Yes! YEESSSSS!" He's freakin' out and all fired up. I asked him what was going on and he said, "You just committed at the same time this guy won a gold medal. Obviously, my focus was on you, but I kept glancing at the television. It all just happened at the same time, and it's my birthday, too." I had also FedExed him a birthday card.

## WELL WORTH IT

My struggles at Kansas are well-documented. But for everything that went wrong, there were things that were great. Overall I'd say my experiences there were some of the best times of my life. The best part about playing for Kansas was game day at Allen Fieldhouse. You wake up, you go to shoot-around and then you have your pregame meal. Then you'd come home and take a nap. Then I'd walk over to the arena, walk in the same door and say hi to the same people. Instead of walking straight into the locker room, I'd walk out to the court and look at it and take it all in. We're playing here today. Then I'd look at the clock to make sure I was on time. Because if you weren't on time under Coach Williams …

I loved kicking someone's ass and then going out that night. The whole town was so happy. It's an experience that only a few people in the world get to have. There's nothing like playing in Allen Fieldhouse. Now going back as an old guy and watching, it's great seeing those guys carrying on the tradition and continuing to be successful.

## ROY'S ROLE

Coach Williams went above and beyond to take care of his players. The players were always first. When it came to traveling, it was always first class. He really cared about us. He knew that basketball was our livelihood and it was his livelihood as well. Coach wears a lot of hats. He's a coach, a role model, an administrator, a father, a recruiter, a public figure. There are so many things that he has to do. With those things came pressure and expectations. It caused him to be very demanding at times. I learned that on my very first day of school.

## TONGUE-LASHING

The first day of school in August, we had our 12-minute run, where you have to do 6 ½ laps around the track in 12 minutes. C.B. McGrath was a track guy, so he blew everyone away, but I was right there with him. I was in second by half of a lap. T.J. Pugh made a push toward the end. I think he was thinking, "There's no way a freshman is going to come in here and get second," because second was basically winning, since we all knew no one was going to beat C.B. Even though I was flying, T.J. sprinted and caught me and beat me by about 10 feet. I was still proud of my finish, though. I remember it specifically, because Coach Williams had just bought a brand new BMW convertible. Before the race, he said, "After the race, the top three finishers get to ride with me to my house in my convertible." We were going over there for ice cream and our first team meeting. No one could believe that a freshman was in the top three and that he was in the car with Coach Williams on his way to his house. It was kind of a big deal. That's how good of shape I was in. I was ready to roll.

We got to Coach Williams' house and hung out a while. Everyone was having fun, but when we had our meeting, the mood changed. The summer before, I had come to Lawrence for a few days to help at Coach Williams' camp.

I had stayed in Naismith Hall, and the charge was $8 a night. I was there for three nights, so it was $24. My dad knew we were supposed to send in a check, but he forgot. Someone could've made a simple phone call and said, "Hey Bob, you forgot to write that check. Can you send it?" Instead, Coach Williams used it as ammunition on my first day of school. I was so excited that I had done so well on the 12-minute run. I was having ice cream at Coach Williams' house. My dream was coming true. Everything I'd worked for was happening. Then the first thing he did in the meeting was say, "Eric! Did you stay here for summer camp?" I told him yes, and he said, "Then pay your f---ing bill!" I was so caught off-guard. I said, "What?" Then he said, "Did you stay at Naismith Hall during summer camp?" I nodded and he said, "You didn't pay for it! You owe $24 to the university!" I'm like, "I'm so sorry, Coach. I had no idea. Are you sure it's for the dorms?" He said, "No, it's for the freakin' Taj Mahal! Yeah, it's for the freakin' dorms! You're not worth a violation! Pay your f---in' bill!"

That was the first day of my freshman year at my first-ever team function. I was heartbroken. I called my dad and was on the verge of crying. He was like, "Oh my God, I'm so sorry." He FedExed the check the next day. He completely put me in my place. He let me know that he was Roy Williams, and I was just a freshman.

I remember driving back to the Towers with Raef. He knew I was devastated. He was like, "Hey man, I'm not worth a violation, either. Paul Pierce isn't worth a violation. Nobody is worth a violation. Don't worry about it. He's just letting you know that he means business." For the first week of school, I had a pit in my stomach about it. At the end it was a good lesson, because I never took a dollar or a dime or did anything illegal. Ever.

## RUNNING AND RUNNING AND RUNNING AND ....

I remember the first official practice of my freshman year really well, because to this day, it was probably the best practice I've ever had as a basketball player, the best practice of my life. I had been working with Raef, who was a stud, for the previous few months. I was lifting with him and playing against him. I was ready. It was a 3 ½-hour practice. It was a marathon. I was busting my ass in all of the drills. I was diving for loose balls. To this day, in my left hip, I still have little bone fragments from when I dove on a ball and got this big, huge hip contusion. It calcified. But I still have bone in my hip from diving that day. I think about it all the time.

At the end of practice, we had to run three 33s, which is down the court and back three times in 33 seconds. Just running one of them is hard. I made the first one. I didn't make the second one. He was like, "I've got all night. I can blow this whistle a lot longer than you can run. I'll be here all night until you finish these." I missed again. Eventually I threw up and got up and tried to get up and do it again. Then he said, "All right, I'm going to give you a minute to rest. If you don't make it, we're going to come back at 10 p.m. and you're going to try again."

All the guys were standing around me saying, "C'mon Eric, you can do it." I remember looking up in the stands and seeing my parents. They were watching practice because they had been to Late Night the night before. I saw my mom get up and run out of gym, crying. But I stood up, did the drill and finally made the time. Then I just collapsed. I was on my knees. Well, after practice is over each day, everyone is supposed to stretch. So Coach Williams was like, "Get your ass up. Get over there. If you don't get up and stretch, we're coming back at 10 and you're doing it again." I was so exhausted that I couldn't even drink. I was just done.

My parents and I went to eat after practice. We were at Old Chicago. I used to love eating there. But that night I couldn't even eat. All I did was drink water. I had a couple of bites of fries and that was it. I was so dehydrated. What he did to me was something he'd done to every freshman at some point. Players called it "breaking you down." My sophomore year, guys came in, and I warned them and said, "He's going to run you after practice." And sure enough, he did. Jelani Janisse was puking all over the place. Marlon London had a tough time with it. He did it to everyone. It was his way of letting you know, "I am Coach Williams."

I thought it was ridiculous. It's not like we weren't in shape. We had just done an eight-week conditioning program with the strength coach from the Bulls, lifting weights, playing pickup. Toward the end of my career, I was so worried about running at the end that I would kind of pull up at the end of practice and not really go as hard. I wanted to save something for the running. In some ways I think that hurt me. I teach my players all the time to go as hard as you can in every drill and get better every day. There were times when I wasn't getting better every day, because I didn't push myself as hard as I should've, because I wanted to get through the running at the end of practice.

A lot of times, when I'm coaching today, I think about stuff Coach Williams would do that bothered me and I'll do the opposite, because I don't want to be like that. So I use him as an example of how not to do things sometimes. Other times there are things he did that I do use. Every day we come to practice, we're going to work and get better. Every day, he tried to get as much as out me as he could. I try to do that with my players. Again, I wasn't one of his favorites. Nick and Jerod and Jacque and Scot Pollard, they were his favorites. I just wasn't one of them.

## STYLE OF PLAY

When Coach Williams was recruiting me, he said we were always going to run the secondary break and the Carolina, half-court offense. The box offense, with box sets. I loved it the first two years. I flourished in it. Then, before the season my junior year, Coach Holladay was gone for a couple of days. He came back and I was like, "Coach Holladay, where were you, man?" He said, "I went to watch Cincinnati practice for a couple of days because we're going to press like Cincinnati." I was like, "What is going on?" I was a preseason All-American. I thought they'd be running plays to get me the ball. In the past we had run everything through Raef and Paul. I was thinking he was going to do that with me. That year we were really deep, so we started playing 12 guys. We got to where we were subbing guys three and four at a time – and five at a time when Coach Williams was really mad.

I remember one time a player told a reporter, "Gosh, I just can't get into the flow of the game. When you only play 2 or 3 minutes it's hard to get into the flow." Coach Williams came in after he'd read that in the paper and said, "I don't want to hear that s--t. There's no such thing as rhythms and flows. That's a bunch of bulls--t." Coach had always told us that, when we come into the game, don't shoot the ball on your first possession. Get into a rhythm, get a sweat going. So it was a total contradiction. My sophomore year, I was playing 30 minutes a game. My conditioning and my strength training helped me because I'd battle with these other big guys the whole game, and by the end of the second half, they were worn down, they were dead. But I was still going strong. That was stuff I didn't get to use anymore.

Coach Williams never played at a Division I level, so I'm not sure he understood stuff like that. At least not at that time. He didn't understand that, yes, there are flows to games and, yes, players can get into a rhythm. Look at the best teams he's had at Kansas and North Carolina. They all had seven-man rotations. The teams that went to the Final Four after I was there … they were playing seven guys. The Carolina teams he had that won the title were using six, seven or eight guys – not 12.

## BIG WIN

I'll never forget beating Missouri in Columbia when I was a sophomore. We beat them handily (73-61). Ryan Robertson played great. He scored about 30 points. I remember running and grabbing Ryan and hugging him after the final horn. A couple of guys were jumping around and celebrating. It was the best feeling in the world. I remember Coach Williams running over and grabbing me and saying, "Get your ass in the locker room!" He was pissed because he thought I was taunting the crowd. But we were all just hugging because we were happy. He got to the locker room and said, "We don't do that. We don't celebrate like that. I'm so frickin' pissed off at you right now. You just ruined it for me. You ruined the whole thing." I loved playing at Missouri, though. It was a great environment with the Antlers and everything. It's something we looked forward to every year.

## RIGHT CALL?

I had a good year as a sophomore (13.5 points, 9.1 rebounds) and some people wondered if I was going to enter the NBA draft. I talked to Coach Williams about it literally for about 5 minutes. He said, "If you come out now, you'll be a top 20 pick. If you stay and have a good year, you'll be a top five pick." I was like, "OK, that's an easy decision." But then I was watching that draft. I don't think the first big guy was drafted until No. 13, and I was better than that guy. I was thinking, "What the heck? Should I have come out? I could've been a lottery pick." Hindsight is 20-20. I think about it a lot.

## SUMMER SPOILER

The summer after my sophomore year is when things really went downhill. That's when I caught a lot of criticism for going to some Dave Matthews Band concerts. Over a two-year span I think I saw them eight times. They played in Kansas, and I saw them there. Then they came to California, and I went to that one, too. I told Dean Buchan, our media relations director at the time, about some of the stuff I'd done that summer. He passed the information along to a reporter, who ended up interviewing me for a story.

I told him, "Oh, I worked out every morning and then went to the beach. I went to some Dave Matthews Band concerts" and stuff like that. All of a sudden, people were like, "What? You weren't studying film 10 hours a day?" People started blowing the situation out of proportion, saying I was a roadie and that I was touring with the band.

The thing was, I was still working hard – really hard. But I was also a 19-year-old kid in the summer, having fun. I busted my ass 11 months out of the year. I needed a break for a couple of weeks. I wasn't out doing drugs or stealing cars. I was being a kid, having fun. Every time I see Dean, he puts his head down. He says, "Every time I see you, I feel bad that I let that stuff get out. I thought it was going to be a great story about how you had interests outside of basketball, about how you have interest in music and you're creative and all that stuff. It totally backfired. I think about it all the time and I totally regret it." He apologizes every time I see him.

The situation was something I could never recover from. I had an awful junior year. The summer before my senior year, I was a freakin' monster who was working out with NBA coaches and going to Pete Newell's Big Man Camp. I was doing everything I could to get back to where I was as a sophomore, but the damage was already done. Nick Collison and Drew Gooden had really good sophomore years and had surpassed me. I don't blame Coach Williams at all for playing them. It was a missed opportunity on my end.

Even when I turned professional, five years after my senior season, I was in camp with the Nuggets and George Karl was like, "What happened that one summer at Kansas?" I had to tell the same story I'm telling now. It's something I could never shake. I never could get away from it.

The other thing I remember about that time was that the fans were on me pretty hard, too. Thank God it's not how it is now, with Facebook and Twitter and all of that stuff. If it'd have been like this when I was there, I can't imagine how bad it would've gotten. The main thing that bothered me was the student paper. I didn't care what The Kansas City Star or the Lawrence Journal-World wrote. But when a fellow student put something in the "Free For All" section of the University Daily Kansan, that really hit home. That was our home paper, and they were ripping on me. Then again, those weren't the real Kansas basketball fans. The real Kansas basketball fans are the ones who come to the airport after we lose in the tournament, they're the ones who camp out, they're the ones who are at the games. The people that do all that other stuff are just tarnishing the greatest thing that college basketball has, which is Kansas basketball.

## MENTALLY TAXING

I never got to know Coach Williams really well. When you play for him and he kills you for two hours, you don't exactly want to hang out with him and get dinner. I always felt uneasy when I was around him. When he was recruiting me it was rainbows and stars. It was awesome. Then I got there and it was like, "Jeez, dude."

There were times when basketball really started to wear on me. I'd have a bad game, and then I'd be walking to practice knowing I was going to get ripped the whole day. I knew it was coming. It would be on my mind all afternoon, knowing that I was going to get it and that it'd be a tough day.

When I see kids leaving North Carolina now, it doesn't surprise me at all. The Wear twins, who are from Orange County, just left there last season. They're at UCLA now. I know them because they went to Mater Dei High School. I talked to the Mater Dei coach about it before they went there. I said, "Make sure they bust their ass and that they're in shape and that they do everything exactly how he tells them to do it." Sure enough, as soon as school was out, they were gone. They're in for a rude awakening, though, because they're at UCLA playing for Ben Howland. I hear he's tough to play for, too.

## KENNY GREGORY

Kenny was the most explosive athlete I've ever seen. I've played on NBA teams and stuff, but I've never seen anyone jump like him. He would jump through people. He was just so athletic. We went through a lot together. He was my man for four years. I told him at the banquet my senior year that, if people ever asked me who I played with, I was going to say his name first. He was one of my best friends on the team. Kenny was maybe misused a little bit. I thought he was a good shooter, but he needed to work on it a little more. Coach would always yell at him when he shot a jump shot. But I always thought they should've just let the guy play. Kenny didn't get to truly play as much as he wanted to. He didn't have the freedom that he should've had. Now Kenny is in Europe making tons of money and doing great and shooting the ball well.

## THOUGHTS ON DREW, NICK

When I first saw Drew Gooden, I had never seen anyone offensive rebound like him before. He would go up and get hit or get fouled or miss, but then he'd bounce up and tap it in before you could even land to box him out. He was so quick off the floor. Nick was so fundamentally sound. He knew basketball in and out. Coach loved him. I'm sure he would tell you that his favorites of all-time were Jacque Vaughn, Jerod Haase, Nick Collison and Tyler Hansbrough. Sometimes we'd tease Nick. We'd call Coach Williams his dad. We'd say, "Hey Nick, tell your dad to quit getting on me about this or that." In my two years of playing with Nick, I literally don't remember him getting yelled at one time by Coach Williams. That's not Nick's fault. He was a legitimately great player.

I look back on it now, and I had some animosity toward Nick and Drew. Nick basically took my spot. I had some resentment toward him, but it wasn't his fault. He was just trying to win games and do his best and be as good as he could possibly be. Today, when I see Nick … I mean, I still love the guy. I saw him at Kirk's jersey retirement ceremony, and anytime the Thunder comes to Los Angeles, I try to go catch his game at the Staples Center. Nick is a great guy. We had some good times. But it was always in the back of my mind that this guy was better than me, and he took my spot. Now he's a successful player in the NBA, and I never made it. It's something I think about. The cool thing is that, if it was up to Nick, I'm sure he'd have me be in the NBA right there with him.

## JEFF BOSCHEE

I had never played with a scoring point guard before I played with Jeff. He shot it a little too much sometimes. The Kentucky game my sophomore year he shot 18 3-pointers. He was 6-for-18.

There were a lot of good point guards in Jeff's class: Khalid El-Amin, Baron Davis, Earl Watson. Coach Williams went after all those point guards who were studs, and then we got Jeff. The thing was, Jeff was really, really legit. I remember he came to play pickup with us on his visit, and Jacque Vaughn was there. Jeff was a high school senior and he outplayed Jacque. We were all like, "Whoa! This guy is going to be legit." I mean, he clearly outplayed him. No one said anything to Jacque about it, though. Hell, no. Jacque was off-limits. You didn't speak to Jacque. So Jeff came to Kansas and fell in love with shooting a little too much, but he shot the hell out of it, so what the hell, right? I couldn't blame him. When Coach Williams moved him to shooting guard and put Aaron at the point, it helped him out a lot, because it was his natural position.

## JEFF CAREY

When I first met Jeff, he walked into the dorm wearing jean shorts and a polo shirt with Teva sandals and white socks. I was wearing rainbow flip flops, cargo shorts and a white T-shirt. We were polar opposites. He was total Midwest, and I was a total California boy. Our freshman year we were so busy with stuff, we really didn't get to know each other. We were just feeling each other out. But the first day of my sophomore year it was like, boom, we were buddies. We started doing everything together. We'd go to concerts together and go out to eat together. He'd invite me to his family's house at the Lake of the Ozarks. We'd go on double dates. We'd work on our cars together. We were like brothers. Once a year we call each other on our birthdays. If I saw him today, it'd be like I saw him the day before. We'd catch up in five minutes. He knew how hard Coach Williams was on me. There were times I was depressed and miserable, but he was very, very supportive.

## T.J. PUGH

T.J. was one of Coach Williams' favorites, as well. I remember one year the Bulls played an exhibition game at Allen Fieldhouse. We all got to meet Michael Jordan, which was awesome. We all got our picture with him. The Bulls used our locker room. After the game, we went into the locker room and talked to the players. T.J. was always the smartest one out of all of us. T.J. went to Jordan and said, "Mr. Jordan, can I please have your game shoes?" Jordan was like, "Yeah, who cares." He gave T.J. the shoes. We were all happy for T.J. We thought it was the coolest thing ever. Coach Williams got word of it and said, "Oh, no, no, no. We can't do that." So he took the shoes. He said, "Whoever gets Defensive Player of the Year is going to get these shoes at the end of the season." T.J. had always been a great defender. He won the Defensive Player of the Year award – but he didn't get the shoes. To this day, it's still a mystery where those shoes are.

## ASSISTANT COACHES

Matt Doherty was my boy. He recruited the hell out of me. I was closer to him than anyone. When he was there I really felt like he had my back. He'd always stick up for me in film sessions. He'd always have my back in practice. I could go talk to him about anything ... girls, school, family, whatever. I could confide in him. He left to take a great job, and I was really happy for him. But after that things started going south for me. Coach Holladay ... I loved talking to him. He had this southern drawl and this southern way about him that let me know everything was going to be OK. Neil Dougherty was someone I really liked. He was a great X's and O's guy. I thought his knowledge was second-to-none. I've never been around anyone that knew the game as well as he did.

## A GOOD TEAM OFF THE COURT, TOO

One thing no one ever had to worry about with us was NCAA violations. Coach Williams put the fear of God in people. Bob Frederick may have had the title of athletic director, but Coach Williams was really the A.D. He ran that show. It was his baby. It was his thing. He knew everything that was going on in that place. We walked around on pins and needles.

Four or five years after I left there, I heard about people questioning the "graduation gifts" the seniors got from (booster) Dana Anderson after their careers were over. It wasn't a big deal at all. It was $200 or $300. Dana mailed the checks up to the office. Coach Williams knew about it. I lived off-campus and my lease wasn't up until June. My scholarship ended in May. So it helped me pay that June rent. I literally took that $300 and used it to help pay some of my rent, and then I went to the dentist to get my teeth cleaned. What's ironic is that I went to see Dana's son, Justin, who is a dentist in Lawrence. So the money ended up going right back to the Anderson family. I didn't go out and buy a car. I didn't go out and buy a watch. It was totally legal. There was nothing wrong with it. The NCAA was so stupid. They tried to make it look like an improper benefit. Believe it or not, if Coach Williams was recruiting me and said, "You're going to get $300 when you graduate," it probably wouldn't have done a lot to influence my decision. I went to Kansas because I wanted to play for a great program in Allen Fieldhouse. Not because someone told me there was going to be $300 in it for me after four years. Who cares? I didn't even know I was going to get the money until it came.

## POST-KANSAS

I got drafted by the New York Knicks in the second round in 2001. I went to training camp with them, got released and then played in the D-League for Sacramento. I was having back issues, and the American coaches were pretty understanding. But then I went overseas, and we were practicing twice a day. They don't really have the best medical staffs over there. It got to a point where I couldn't perform at a high enough level to keep playing professionally.

It came to a head when I went to Korea in the winter of 2008. I made a move, my legs went numb and I fell to the ground. A few days later the team released me. It's not like America, where they help you get better when you get hurt. Over there they just send you home. I came back to California and talked to a doctor in Marina del Ray. He's the best back specialist in the world. He said I either needed a surgery that would be followed by a year of recovery, or I'd have to retire. He said, "You can't keep going on like this. You're going to hurt yourself more and more." The surgery would've been a bilateral laminectomy. Then they were going to build a cage around my vertebrae. It was obviously pretty serious. I have congenital stenosis, which is the shrinking of the spinal canal. After years of wear and tear, it starts breaking down and shrinking, and the sciatic nerve that goes through there gets pinched. Your legs go numb and you get tingling and discomfort and things like that. I'd played eight years and had a lot of injuries and ups and downs. I decided it was time to move on.

## LIFE AFTER BASKETBALL

As soon as I was done playing, I called Kansas' academic guy, Scott Ward, and asked him how far away I was from my degree, because I wanted to be a college coach, and you can't be a college coach without your degree. I had 19 units left. He put me on a program. I took 10 units out here at Orange Coast College. I actually went to class with 19- and 20-year-olds, which was pretty funny. And then I took the other three classes through KU. I just finished at the end of May (2011).

While I was in school, I needed money because I didn't want to blow through my savings. So I was working for my dad's construction company. We built custom homes in Orange County. I worked for him all day and then went to school at night. I balanced both of those things with working as an assistant at Villa Park High School for the last 2 ½ years now. It's been a good experience because now I've got two years of coaching experience, I've finished my degree and I've gotten a taste of what it's like to work in the real world with a real job as opposed to a fake job.

I played in Argentina, China, the Philippines, Puerto Rico, France. I got to see the world. But there's no place as good as home.

I want to be a college coach. I've already had a couple of positions offered to me, positions like "video coordinator" and things like that. I wouldn't mind starting at that level, but some of them just didn't make sense financially. One of them only paid $18,000, and I'd be in the video room forever. With another year of experience and more networking, I'm hoping I can find a job as a second or third assistant and hit the ground running.

## FINAL THOUGHTS

Scot Pollard said something weird to me one time. He said, "Eric, your career numbers are way better than mine, and I played 10 years in the league, and you didn't. It's crazy to me." I'm fifth all-time in rebounding behind Danny Manning, Raef LaFrentz, Nick Collison and Bill Bridges. That's a pretty good group. And I'm fourth in blocks. I'm pretty proud of those numbers. You don't post those kinds of numbers without a lot of perseverance.

No matter how frustrated I got at times, I always loved Kansas. And I still do love Kansas. I'm sitting in my home office right now, and I've got the chair that I always used in our locker room. I've got my KU degree on my wall. I have a Kansas flag in front of my house. Scott Brooks, the coach of the Oklahoma City Thunder, lives in Corona del Mar during the summer, which is where I live. Every time he walks by he says, "Man, take that damn thing down." I truly love the university and enjoyed my time there. I loved my teammates. I had the best teammates a guy could ever ask for. When Kirk got his number retired, I made sure I was there.

The best part about playing there was the inside jokes we'd have. I could say something right now and you'd have no idea what I meant. But five guys I played with would fall on the ground laughing. We went to Hawaii, we went to Alaska, we went to New York City and Philadelphia – and we did it first class and did it right. Playing in Allen Fieldhouse every day was amazing. That's what made it all worth it. Every minute I had to put up with Coach Williams killing me, it was worth it when I ran through the tunnel.

# CHAPTER 4

# 2000/01 - 2001/02
# BRETT BALLARD

Brett Ballard spent two seasons as a backup point guard at Kansas after joining the team as a walk-on in 2000. The former Hutchinson Community College star appeared in 56 games and played a significant role in the Jayhawks' 16-0 Big 12 record and Final Four run in 2002. After graduating in 2003, Ballard served seven years on the Jayhawks' basketball staff as a student assistant, administrative assistant and director of basketball operations. A Hutchinson native, Ballard is preparing for his second year as the men's basketball coach at Baker University in Baldwin City. He and his wife, Kelly, have two children: Kaden and Brooks.

## IN BRETT'S WORDS

My first KU basketball memory is pretty cool. When I was 9, my dad brought me up for a game. We actually sat in the back of the student section on the north side of the Fieldhouse. We played Kentucky and won 150-95. I was just blown away.

That's the loudest I've ever heard the Fieldhouse. Obviously, for a team to score 150 points in a game, and have the opponent be Kentucky, with Pitino and Williams and all that stuff ... I didn't really know the story lines at that time. I didn't really know what Kentucky was all about. But I think I was floating when I walked out of there.

I came up to KU camp one summer, probably my eighth-grade year. It's funny, because I still have the picture I took that week with Coach Williams. As time has gone on, I've told that story more and more. I joked with Coach Williams about having that picture with him. It's pretty cool to have. Then going through and running Coach Self's camps and seeing all the pictures he takes with those kids — it doesn't seem like a big deal, but for a lot of those kids, that's a picture they can keep for a long time. You just never know who's going to take their picture with you and who they're going to turn out to be.

Another funny story from my childhood is that, at my sixth-grade birthday party, I had a KU cake. We have a picture of it, and it's got No. 3 on it, because I always wore No. 3. I obviously didn't expect to play for KU, especially once I got to high school, but in the sixth grade, I had the cake with No. 3 and Kansas basketball on it.

## COMING TO KU

When I was at Hutch juco, I expressed interest to my coach about coming to KU and walking on. It just so happened that our assistant coach at the time, Eric Duft, had worked some KU camps. So he spoke to Coach (Joe) Holladay, one of the KU assistants, and Coach Holladay had come to watch some of our games late in the season, because he was recruiting at the juco regional tournament.

Chris Zerbe and myself came to KU together, and we got to have individual meetings with Coach Williams in late March of '99. I really didn't know what to expect at that meeting. I kind of just thought, "Well, Coach Williams is just being nice. We're going to come up here and meet with him, and he's going to tell us, 'Yeah, if you come to KU, you might have a chance to walk on.'" Instead he said they were very interested in me as a walk-on and laid out the groundwork for it. Leaving that meeting is probably one of the most exciting times of my life, because I knew I was going to have a pretty good opportunity to be a walk-on. And I felt like, if I just got that opportunity, I would be able to take advantage of it.

One thing that really stuck with me about Coach Williams was, at the time, he said, "If Kenny Gregory and Nick Collison get a steak, you're going to get a steak. If Kenny Gregory and Nick Collison have to run a sprint, you're going to run a sprint." And, for me, that was a way of him tying me in with the program, making me feel like, "Hey, even though you're potentially going to be a walk-on, we're going to treat you just like any other player."

I remember I was staying with some buddies in Lawrence that night, because I had some friends up here. So when I got back to their house after the meeting … it's funny, because that was the day and age before cell phones, so I had to find a land line to call my mom. I said, "Mom, I think I'm going to be a Jayhawk."

## COACH WILLIAMS

People always ask me what makes Coach Williams so good. No. 1, it's how hard he works, and No. 2, he cares about every single one of his players. You would think, "Doesn't every coach?" But he truly cares about each one of his players, 1 through 15.

He's one of the top recruiters out there, and I think a lot of that is how hard he works. He gets out and sees kids. A lot of times coaches, once they get established and once they get at a school like Kansas or North Carolina or Duke or whatever, they don't necessarily go out as much, because they don't feel like they have to. I just think Coach continually outworks a lot of coaches in the profession and gets out and recruits hard, even though he's at North Carolina.

One funny story about Coach Williams: I remember we had just got done practicing, and we were going up to a KU football game. This was when cell phones had just started getting big. I think I was with Boschee, and his cell phone rang. And Coach was in the middle of a conversation with us after practice. I remember Coach Williams saying, "I'll never get one of those things. I'll never get a cell phone." And that was the attitude of a lot of people at that time, not just Coach. It's just funny to think about the coach at North Carolina not having a cell phone in this day and age. It's funny how times have changed.

## KIRK HINRICH

Kirk was interesting because nobody really knew how good he was going to be. I remember even when I first got there, he was good, but if you would have told me when I first got to KU that he was going to be the seventh pick in the NBA draft, I would've thought you were crazy.

Kirk was good at a lot of things. He just wasn't necessarily great at one particular thing. He was a good shooter, but I don't think people knew that he was going to become a great shooter. Sophomore, junior, senior year, he really became a great shooter. And I think just his overall game evolved.

I remember after I got done playing, he'd ask me if I'd come up and shoot with him one night. After we shot for a while, he wanted to play a little bit, so we played one-on-one. I got lucky and beat him 7-6 the first game. I don't know how it happened. And so then he got mad and he won the next two games 7-0, 7-0. He just had that competitive light bulb that would come on. It was on all the time while he was playing in real games, and it clicked on that night after I beat him. He quickly made it known that I wasn't going to win any more games. I think Kirk's one of the all-time KU greats and just did a little bit of everything and impacted the program in so many different ways.

## NICK COLLISON AND "THE WOOD GRAIN"

Nick is one of the most fundamental guys. He's just even-keeled all the time. I never saw Nick get really pissed. I never saw him get over-elated. He just kept the same temperament all the time. He's that way off the court as well.

He used to drive the wood-grain minivan, so that was the funny thing about Nick. He didn't care. He did not care that he was driving a minivan in college. I think that's why people respected him, because that was him. We'd roll around in that thing. I remember on New Year's, we were hanging out and going down somewhere on Mass Street in the minivan.

It was just a funny thing. We liked the minivan, because it had enough room. He always drove, because in a minivan, there were seven seats. We'd get half the team in the minivan if we needed to go somewhere. We didn't mind at all. Nick and I joke now, because I tell him every once in a while, "I think I saw the minivan in Lawrence." He used to call it, "The Wood Grain," because it was blue and had wood-grain panels on the side. And he said he kicks himself for not keeping that car. Now that he's in the NBA, obviously he wouldn't drive it. But I still think he would've kept it, just because. I think he sold it his senior year.

Nick is just humble and low-key. He's not worried about his image. You watch how he plays now in the NBA. He never complains. He plays hard every night. That's just Nick.

## DREW GOODEN

Drew was another guy that, junior year, the light bulb really came on. I think he fought a little bit with Coach Williams and the coaching staff in general. I think he wasn't 100 percent bought in to where he believed and trusted them. It wasn't that he was a bad person, or it wasn't that he was trying to be defiant. I just think that once he completely bought in and realized, "Man, this stuff does work," that's when he really took off. Drew is just funny. He's always talking, and he's always got one-liners and everything.

One funny thing we used to joke about with Drew was that he always wanted to test out little one-on-one moves with you. So he'd be like, "Brett, come down here on the block and tell me how you're going to stop this move." And I'd be like, "First off, Drew, you're 6-9 and I'm 6-foot, so I don't think I'm going to stop anything you're going to do." But he'd always have some new move or some new post move that he wanted to test out after practice. Usually, one of the walk-ons would get dragged down there to guard him for 5 or 10 minutes while he worked on this new move, which was comical in itself.

## WAYNE SIMIEN

Wayne and I were roommates in Maui my senior year. Wayne actually came a couple days late, because he'd just hurt his knee a few days before in practice, so he had to stay back and get treatment.

Actually, I met my wife out there. My wife's sister had been a manager prior to that, so she and her sister were out there in Maui. After our last game, we had a free day, so I got introduced to her then, and we kept in touch. It was crazy. So Wayne, he gives me a hard time, because he always says that since he was my roommate, he's responsible and he should get all the credit for us meeting.

It's been pretty cool to see how he has come about with his faith and his religion. He wasn't as into it when he first got to KU. He's obviously really grown into that and has been able to touch so many people's lives. Now, I joke with Wayne and Aaron Miles. Both are living in Lawrence, and both have kids about the same age as my son. I told them that I'm going to have to transfer school districts, because I said my son's never going to get to play on the basketball teams if their kids are the same age as mine, because they're obviously going to be a lot better.

The other thing about Wayne for me was, "OK, here's this Leavenworth kid." I'd heard decent things about him, but it was like, "He's from Leavenworth. He'll probably be all right — be a decent player at KU." Then he came in his freshman year and obviously, from the jump, it was like, "Wow, this guy can play." Four years later, he was an All-American. He turned out to be pretty special.

## OTHER GUYS

I remember after my junior year, I had kind of played a lot, so going into my senior year, I was thinking, "We're bringing in Aaron Miles. We're bringing in Keith Langford. But if I could beat one of those two out, I'm going to get to play quite a bit." I didn't know much about Keith. But I remember from Day 1, when Keith was on campus, I realized how good he was. He wasn't a highly recruited guy, but he had no fear. Very confident. Keith kept to himself off the court and was sort of a lone ranger. He just did his own thing most of the time, but he was a good guy. Obviously, he had a great career at KU, too.

E-Chen (Eric Chenowith) was funny. Eric, he has that California, surfer-dude attitude a little bit. He says what he thinks. That's Eric. He's going to say what's on his mind. He got criticized a little bit, I think, unfairly from the KU fans, because he had a really good sophomore year, and then, probably didn't play quite as well as people had hoped his junior and senior year. Honestly, I thought Eric put in a lot of time, and I thought that he wanted it. I just think it didn't work out quite as well for him. Eric and I got along great. I thought he was a very solid player for that team that I was on.

Chris Zerbe and I were roommates at Hutch and then we came to KU together. The thing that was funny was, when Coach Holladay came up to watch us play, he really was just coming to look at me. But Zerbe had, like, 32 points in the game that he came and watched. Zerbe's career high before that, I think, was 15. So after the game, Coach Holladay's talking to him, and I'm like, "Man, you're killing me here. You go for a career high when Coach Holladay's here, and now they want you. They don't want me." I was joking with him. But it ended up working for both of us to come up.

Zerbe was a 6-4, 6-5 post guy, so you can imagine what it was like in practice for him, going up against Nick and Drew and Eric and those guys. He got beat up a lot of days. He got tossed around a little bit, but he tried his best. He held his own.

## FINAL FOUR-BOUND

I think the highlight for me from a playing standpoint was getting to go to the Final Four and getting to experience that. Obviously, I wish it would have turned out a little different, but I did get to experience that.

Coach Self and I joke about the KU-Illinois game in the Sweet 16 a lot. In fact, we joked about that game at summer camp, because Drew Gooden was back in town. I was giving Coach Self a hard time. I think Kirk and Nick were in foul trouble. I said, "If they weren't in foul trouble, we probably would have beaten you guys easily." He was like, "Man, I thought we were going to get you guys."

The one thing with Coach Self's teams, especially at Illinois, is you knew they were going to grind and you knew they were going to be physical and you knew they were going to guard. Not that much has changed. His KU teams play a little faster now than his teams at Illinois. But that was one of those teams that we struggled with. They were like Oklahoma that year — a team that was going to slow the pace a little bit and really grind and be physical. That wasn't necessarily the best matchup for us. We obviously had no idea what would transpire a few years later, but I always respected him as a coach.

In the Elite Eight, Oregon was a team that wanted to play our style, and I just felt like that year any team that tried to run with us and play up and down was going to be in trouble. We got going, and they just ran out of gas. I remember Drew and Nick really taking advantage of their big guys inside. They couldn't really keep up.

I remember after the game looking up into the stands and my parents were there. They'd driven up to Madison, Wis., from Kansas. My dad's a teacher and my mom's a secretary, and they'd worked hard, and they'd been KU fans. To me, it was kind of cool for them. I remember looking up in the stands and going, "Can you believe we're going to the Final Four?" because I was almost as excited that they were going to experience it as me.

## MARYLAND GAME

One of the cool things for me was that, at the Final Four, you've got 45,000 people at the practice session. We went live in practice. We were on the red team, and we were joking that this was our Final Four, because we didn't know if we were going to get to play.

Against Maryland, I got in at the end of the first half, then I played the last 3 or 4 minutes of the game. Honestly, I look back on it kind of bittersweet. I still look back at that and think that we were that close to winning a national championship. It eats at me a little bit, but obviously, there are a lot of good memories there, too.

There are two things that I think impacted the game. One was that Kirk was still coming off that ankle injury, which was a couple weeks earlier. So he wasn't

100 percent yet. He really could not move and guard like he was accustomed to. He couldn't guard Juan Dixon. We had to put other guys on him. Keith tried to guard him, and I think Boschee tried to guard him a little bit. And Juan had a big-time game. I'm not saying that if Kirk was healthy, the outcome would have been different, but I do think that would have helped.

And I think the experience of Maryland being there the year before was huge. I just think you look at what KU did the next year, going to the Final Four ... I know they lost, but I just think the experience of being at the Final Four and knowing what to expect is big. Because we got up 13-2, and I think all of us thought, "Well, here we go. We've done this before. We're going to run these guys out of the gym." And they didn't flinch. I think that caught us off guard.

## 2008 TITLE

From the coaching side of it, I really can't explain the feeling I had when Mario made that shot. You're always nervous as a coach until the game's actually over, but for whatever reason, as soon as Mario made that shot, to me, it was almost a sense of relief, because I'd been seen so many KU basketball teams that I felt like were good enough to win a national championship but hadn't. I'd played on a couple of them, then '97 and 2003 and even the early '90s and '86. When he made the shot, there was that feeling of, "We're going to do this."

## LIFE AS A COACH

I use a little bit of both Coach Self and Coach Williams' philosophies. A lot of it is similar, to be honest. A lot of people think Coach Williams and Coach Self are so different. To me, I think they're very similar in a lot of ways in certain things they preach.

We run some of Coach Self's stuff and some of Coach Williams' stuff. I'm a little bit stubborn like Coach Williams in what we're doing, and I think sometimes that's a good thing. But at the same time, I probably treat our players a lot like Coach Self. I try to joke with those guys. We have fun when there's time to have fun, but when it's time to get to work, we go to work.

I'm a lot more nervous now watching KU. There were times last season when I had to turn the TV off. It's harder now — a lot more nerve-wracking than when I was playing or on the coaching staff. I can see what's going to happen before it happens, because I was with Coach and them for so long. I'm probably as big of a fan as they have. But at the same time, I keep everything in perspective. I probably don't get as upset when they lose, because I understand there are reasons sometimes. But at the same time, I still get nervous.

I was fortunate enough to be a KU fan, so I knew how big Kansas basketball was before I got there. But I don't think you understand how big it actually is until you experience it. To me, it was humbling.

I got to experience so many things through my time there. Maybe more so than that, it's opened up so many doors for me. I wouldn't be sitting where I'm at right now if it wasn't for Kansas basketball. I wouldn't have gotten to meet the president. I wouldn't have gotten to be on a national championship staff. I wouldn't have gotten to see all kinds of places around the world. There are so many things I got to experience because of Kansas basketball.

# CHAPTER 5

# 1998/99 - 2001/02
# JEFF
# BOSCHEE
13

J eff Boschee is a Valley Center, N.D., native who owns Kansas' all-time record for 3-pointers made with 388. That figure ranks third in Big 12 history. Boschee was a four-year starter at Kansas from 1998-2002. One of the most popular players to ever wear a Jayhawks uniform, Boschee posted double-figure scoring averages in each of his four seasons in Lawrence. As a senior in 2001-02 he helped lead Kansas to the Final Four by averaging a career-high 13.4 points a game. Boschee is now an assistant coach at Missouri Southern in Joplin. He and his wife, Jamie, have a daughter, Mary Rose.

## IN JEFF'S WORDS

One of the things I remember the most about being recruited by Kansas was when Coach Williams and his wife flew to North Dakota to watch me practice on their anniversary. That day everyone was talking about Jayhawk One – the Kansas jet – landing at the airport. They watched me work out that day, and then Roy came up to watch one of my games in the winter time after I'd committed. He came to our game against Fargo North. I can remember being in the lay-up line when he walked into the gym with Randy Towner. After the game, I can remember coming out of the locker room, and no one had left. Everyone was just standing around, and Coach Williams was with my parents up in the stands. I went up there and gave him a hug and talked to him for a while. I looked over my shoulder, and everyone was staring up at us. And remember, this was an away game. This wasn't even my home gym. So that was pretty cool. I had already committed back in August, so it was neat that he still came up there.

About six months later I moved to Lawrence to start my career. When I first got to Kansas, I'd go out to parties with a bunch of my teammates and everyone knew who they were – but no one knew me. I remember Nick Bradford kept telling me, "Wait until Late Night. After that, everyone is going to know who you are." Sure enough, he was right. I can remember being in sociology class with Marlon London the Monday after Late Night. We started walking up the stairs of this 500-seat auditorium, and all of a sudden people started staring at us and pointing at us. Once that that happened, everything set in. I was like, "Jesus, this is big."

## "A SECOND DAD"

Playing for Coach Williams was the hardest four years of my life, bar none. My freshman year was tough, because I was thrown in with the wolves. I don't think I would've started if T.J. Pugh would've been healthy, because that would've moved Nick Bradford to small forward, Kenny Gregory to shooting guard and Ryan Robertson back to the point. Instead, I was kind of thrown in there, and Coach Williams was a little bit hard on me at times. Sometimes that really helped me, but there were other times when I think it hurt me, especially during the game, when I'd turn the ball over and he'd yell extremely loud where everyone in the gym could hear it. That was tough for me to take as a freshman. Obviously, as you get older, it becomes a lot easier to handle that stuff. He was

just so demanding, but that's what makes him a good coach.

Coach Williams did a hell of a job instilling fear in all of us. For me, my fear was based around two things: extra running after practice, and the fear of letting him down, because I looked up to him so much. I just wanted to do the things he wanted us to do. I didn't want to let him down and get yelled at. Some coaches, you look at them and think, "I'd never listen to a word you say." But other coaches have this aura about them. Some guys just look like a leader. Coach Williams acts like one. What he says, he actually does. He's a great man to look up to. He was like a second dad for us.

Coach Williams joked around every now and then, but it was serious when he was on the court. He yelled and screamed a lot, but other times he used sarcasm to motivate people, which was pretty effective. From my freshman to my senior year, he seemed to get a little more lenient each year. Not just with me, but overall. I think a lot of it was because of the talent level and experience we had my last two years.

## BALDY

My first two years at Kansas I got a lot of attention for being bald. Me and some buddies started that tradition when I was a freshman in high school. It started with a flat-top, actually. But it turned into a buzz cut and then it turned into a buzz cut with a shave on the side. I did it out of superstition, really. Before every game – right after I came home from our pregame walk-through – I'd shave my head, take a nap and get ready for the game. I finally decided to grow it out when I was a junior. It got to be a pain.

Just like I got a lot of attention when I was bald, I also got a lot of attention once I grew my hair out. I remember one time Rick Pitino was on TV and he called me "the Backstreet Boy of KU" or something like that. The guys in the locker room teased me a lot about my female fans. It didn't get annoying. It was flattering, even though most of the girls were teenagers.

## BANNER BACKCOURT

When Kirk Hinrich showed up at Kansas, I don't think any of us realized how good he was. We definitely didn't know he was that athletic. He was really shy at first. He didn't blossom and open up until about midway through his first season. Once he started playing a lot better you could see the confidence just keep growing. He struggled at first, though. I heard from some other guys on the team that he was really unhappy with his playing time and was thinking about transferring. But lots of freshmen go through that.

The game that really stands for him, in my mind, is when we played Duke in the second round of the NCAA Tournament and he went against Jason Williams. He played really well. He proved to everybody and he proved to himself that he belonged on that level.

I think there may have been a little tension between Kirk and me my sophomore year. After the Iowa game, I got benched and Kirk took my spot. I remember coming into practice and seeing my name on the red (scout) squad. Kirk was with the blue team, the starters. It pissed me off. I can remember cussing in practice. Coach Williams brought us all together and started getting on me a little bit for it. At that point, I couldn't care less what he was saying because I was so pissed off. Coach Williams never explained the reasoning behind it. It went unsaid. I was in a shooting slump. Maybe he just wanted to change it up and do something different to see if I would respond. I definitely did. The next game, against Texas Tech, I played 33 minutes, the most out of anybody. But then we went down to Oklahoma State and got our asses beat by 30. I didn't play that much. That was probably the lowest moment of my basketball career up to that point. I felt like the whole team was playing bad. He made a couple of lineup changes, and Chenowith got taken out of the starting lineup, too. I didn't think we were the reason we were playing so bad. The next game, though, I got moved to the two-spot, and we found a good thing with Kirk running the point and me running the two. Kenny Gregory was at the three. It ended up working out but, at that moment, I didn't understand what I'd done wrong. To this day, I still don't think I know why I was the one to get benched. But obviously Kirk had a better career than I did, so Coach Williams made the right choice.

The good thing was that Kirk and I had really good chemistry – and it got even better once Aaron Miles was on team for my senior year. Aaron was a pure point guard, and his ability to distribute the basketball was the best thing that could've happened for our team. With Kirk's and my ability to shoot the basketball, it was fun, because teams had to guard us. They couldn't sink down on Drew Gooden and Nick Collison. It's something that we never talked about, but Kirk and I learned how to play well together. We knew where each other was going to be on the court.

## MAKING IT ALL FIT

Drew turned into a pretty big star when he was a junior but, for the most part, we never really had a kid coming out of high school that was supposed to be the next big thing. You look at guys Kansas had later down the road like Josh Selby and Xavier Henry. So much was expected out of those guys. We didn't have players like that. Nick was a McDonald's All-American but it wasn't like people were saying he was a one-and-done guy. We never really had kids that had a bad attitude toward working and getting better. A lot of that was because how Coach Williams recruited.

Roy would straight-up ask us what we thought of each prospect that came in for a visit. He'd find out who the guy hung out with for the weekend and go up and question them about the kid. I remember Nick Bradford telling me a story about Doug Wrenn, who ended up playing at Washington. He was a five-star recruit coming out of high school. Nick Bradford hosted him, and when Coach Williams asked what he thought of him, Nick said, "No way. The kid is way too arrogant, way too cocky. He wouldn't fit in here." I think that's a good way to do things. What your players think is important, because ultimately they're the ones that are going to have to play with them. It's going to hurt your team if guys don't mesh well.

## FLYING MONKEY

My junior year we beat Syracuse in the second round of the NCAA Tournament to advance to the Sweet 16. It was a big win because it marked the first time in a while that we'd made it past the second round. After the game, Coach Williams brought out this stuffed animal – a monkey – because we'd "finally gotten the monkey off our backs." Well, he brought that damn monkey to San Antonio, too, and he pulled it out during the pregame meal before we played Illinois in the Sweet 16. Right after we got done eating, we were all running around, hitting that monkey and knocking it off each others' backs. Well, Chris Zerbe grabbed the monkey and smacked it so hard that it went flying across the room. It landed in a big platter of lasagna. Coach Williams looked at Chris with the most disgusted face I've ever seen. He said, "Chris! Why would you do that? Why would you hit the monkey that hard?" He just went off on him. He was genuinely pissed about it.

We ended up losing to Illinois in San Antonio. The main thing I remember is just getting beat up. Illinois had a ton of bodies, a ton of bigs. Nick was in foul trouble, and Kirk may have fouled out. It was a physical game and we were getting pushed around. We were too immature for it. Still, even after the loss, it was easy to see that we had the potential to be really, really good the next season.

## SENIOR YEAR

We started off my last season at Kansas ranked No. 3 in the country, but then we lost to Ball State in the Maui Invitational. We had that "Here we go again" feeling. But Coach Williams, after that game, talked to us and said his 1991 and 1993 teams lost their first games of the year and both of them ended up in the Final Four. That ended up being true that year.

For as good as the Big 12 was that season, to go 16-0 was unbelievable. In my opinion, it was the most impressive thing accomplished by a Kansas basketball team until they won the title in 2008. To me, as a player, going 16-0 was a better accomplishment than going to the Final Four, because it's drawn out for so long and you're playing on opposing courts. In the tournament anyone can get lucky and go win six games. It's a shame that some people judge a coach's entire career on how they do in the NCAA Tournament. Granted, it's important to do well in the postseason. But still, look at VCU. They finished fourth in their conference last season, yet somehow they sneak into the tournament, get hot and make it to the Final Four. Now Shaka Smart is the best new coach to come around since Brad Stevens.

Every time we stepped on the court during a Big 12 game that season, most of us thought, "There's no way. There's no way we're going to lose." Our speed and the way we pushed the basketball … Nick and Drew's ability to finish anytime and just catch it and go up with it … Kirk's and my ability to shoot it … Keith and Wayne coming off the bench … we just had so many weapons. Defensively, we were so good at putting pressure on the basketball and getting out and trapping. We were so potent offensively, it was pretty hard to stop us. It was easy to score. We scored so much off of our secondary break and our primary break. The best part about it was the practices were a lot shorter. We were doing well and we'd been through the system for two or three years. That was the year I felt like Coach Williams really changed, as far as just being a lot more lenient with us. He let Kirk and I go a little bit more as far as our shot selection. I think he just trusted us more as a group.

## MR. BIG SHOT

Every now and then I get asked about some of the clutch shots I hit that season in road games against Texas, Iowa State and a few others. I don't know if it's fearlessness or cluelessness, but it's one of those things I've practiced so many times throughout my career. Coming off a screen and catching and shooting is so natural to me. It's like muscle memory. You catch it and, boom, it's up. I don't think there is any added pressure. I'd just done those things so many times that it was almost routine.

If you stand over a putt for too long and think about how weird it feels or about your putter face not being square, you're going to miss it. The same could happen in basketball. That's why I was never thinking, "This is for the game" or "This is for the title."

## HOMECOMING

*(Kansas defeated North Dakota State 108-77 in Boschee's only game in his native state. A crowd of 13,280 – the largest attendance figure for a basketball game in state history – packed Engelstad Arena in Grand Forks to watch Boschee score 23 points on 9-of-12 shooting. A pregame video tribute was played in his honor.)*

The trip to North Dakota was definitely one of the highlights of my career. The whole night was overwhelming. We all lined up before the game, and the announcer was reading off all of my career stats. I couldn't help but tear up.

There haven't been many basketball stars from North Dakota. There have been some guys to go on and play Division I, but no one really went to a big time Division I power like Kansas and succeeded and been part of a team that was filled with stars and known on that high of a national level. No one from there had ever been named McDonald's All-American.

When I was a junior and senior in high school, people came in from all over the state to watch me play, and they followed me when I moved on to Kansas. I had my critics and doubters out there who didn't think I was going to make it and that I'd be back at North Dakota State or North Dakota playing in a year or two. So when I went down to Kansas and won Big 12 Freshman of the Year and was one of the better players on the '98-'99 team ... I think that surprised some people. One thing my brother always told me was, "Act like you've been there before." A lot of that involves the way you treat people. People in North Dakota are so kind and generous. I think that rubbed off on me a little bit. When I go back there and see people, there's never a situation where I act too good for them. I've always tried to be nice and represent the state well and give the state a lot of credit. I'm just a quiet kid, a quiet person from North Dakota that was never really around too much controversy. There has never really a big

controversy in our family or even in North Dakota. It just seems like everybody gets along.

## GOING OUT IN STYLE

My last shot at Allen Fieldhouse is the one I'll always remember the most. It was Senior Night, and there wasn't much time left. The play stopped for a dead ball, and Coach Dougherty called me over and said, "Hey, Coach Williams is about to take you out. You need to get up one more shot." It was our ball underneath, out of bounds. As soon as the ball was handed in, I saw someone – I think it was Chris Zerbe – run to the scorer's table to check in for me, so I knew this was my last chance. We ran the play "24," where I came off a cross screen and came out to the side. When I caught the ball I just stood there for a minute. I didn't even realize how deep I was, but then I realized I was so deep that no one was even guarding me. I took the shot, and when I made it, I was like, "Gosh dang, for me to make that last shot from that far away ... someone was watching over me." That was pretty special to have that be my last basket at Allen Fieldhouse. I played well that game, too. I had 22 points against Kansas State, and we beat them pretty handily.

## FINAL FOUR

I'd worked for years to get to the Final Four, but once it happened, everything just went by so fast. The amount of press that we got was incredible. They actually had a media day for us on our own campus before we ever left for Atlanta. Then, leaving from Forbes Field in Topeka and getting to the Final Four and walking out onto the practice floor ... I've never seen anything like that before. There were 20,000 people there to watch a practice. It was pretty cool.

We were up 15-2 on Maryland, and we were doing a good job on Juan Dixon. Toward the end of the first half, Dixon started going off a little bit. In the second half we tried everything we could. We tried trapping to get back into it, but Steve Blake was at the top of it, just dicing right through it, just throwing it to Chris Wilcox for some easy dunks. Drew didn't have a good game at all. That hurt us quite a bit. The middle of that second half, it felt like that Illinois game a little bit. We were just getting manhandled. Toward the end of the game we made a run to get back into it, but we couldn't get over the hump.

I remember Coach Williams talking to us after the game. He was pretty emotional. I remember Coach Dougherty being really emotional. I remember just sitting at my locker and staring at the ground. I remember walking back to the bus, going to the hotel and just sitting in my room. Jeff Carey was there, but not much was said because it was the last game for both of us. I went to my brother's room and talked to him for a bit. He just said, "Well, what do you want to do now?" He didn't talk to me about the game at all. Every now and then I'll watch a tape of the game when I go back to my parents' house or something. But for the most part I don't like to think about it too much.

People always ask me if the 2002 Final Four team I played on was better than the team that won the title in 2008. My first response is, "Yeah, I think we'd beat them." I'm a competitor. It's human nature to think like that. Our ability to score was just so damn good. Their overall talent may have been a little better than ours. But in my mind, as a team – especially offensively – I think we were a lot better.

## A MUCH-NEEDED BREAK

After the Final Four in 2002 I got invited to the pre-draft camp in Portsmouth, Ark. But I was going to have to leave to go down there two days after we got back from Atlanta. I went into Coach Williams' office and said, "Hey, can you ask these guys if I can skip the pre-draft camp and go straight to the main camp in Chicago?" I just wasn't feeling it. The thought of driving to the airport, getting on a plane and flying to Arkansas didn't seem very appealing at the time. I just wanted to be at home and relax. I was burnt out. So he made the phone call, and they said they weren't going to let me come to Chicago unless I went to Portsmouth. So I made the choice. I said, "Screw it! I'm not going."

After that I didn't touch a ball for three months. The next time I played was at the annual camp game during the summer. Afterward, Coach Williams came up to me and said, "Hey, the Toronto Raptors called. They want you to come to their free-agent camp." What's funny is that Coach Williams had just seen me play. I was out of shape, I couldn't shoot it and I could barely dribble it. I looked at him and said, "Do you honestly think I'm in any shape to go try out for a free-agent camp?" We just looked at each other and laughed. I had worked so hard for four years. I just wanted to be a regular student for a while. I just wanted to spend a year hanging out with my buddies and living the normal college life. It's not like I had never gone out and partied before, but I always had basketball in the back of my mind. I was always thinking, "I've got to lift in the morning," or "I've got to be in the locker room at a certain time." I just wanted time to myself to do what I wanted to do.

Everybody sees Kansas basketball from the outside looking in. They don't understand what goes on behind the scenes. They don't see you when you can barely stand up because you're so friggin' tired from running. In class, they can't sense how worried you are that the coaches are going to yell at you later that afternoon. Every time you go out into public, it's a good thing and a bad thing. There's always someone out there trying to pick a fight with you and bring you down to their level. Just so they can get noticed or get you in trouble.

Right after I got done playing I was out with some friends at the Granfalloon in Kansas City. Some guy intentionally bumped into me, so I said something to him and pushed him a little bit. He yelled, "Boschee, you're a has-been." I had

had a few that night, so I yelled back at him and said, "That's better than being a never-was." Unfortunately that kind of stuff happens to Kansas basketball players all the time. You can always see people pointing at you or snickering as they whisper to their friend. It's usually a fraternity guy just wanting to start something, maybe because he's mad because he caught his girlfriend looking at you or something stupid like that.

## ANOTHER SHOT

After I finished my fifth year of school I played in the USBL for a month. Then I played for a Nike tour team and then I went overseas – first to Greece, then to Iceland. It can get really lonely playing overseas. I went to Greece right after I'd gotten a new girlfriend. We were kind of in that honeymoon stage so it was hard to leave her. I was over there in the middle of Athens, not knowing anybody. There were only a couple of Americans on the team.

We literally practiced twice a day, and each practice was 2 ½ hours. We went hard, too. It was brutal. It was hell. We had a coach who was a tyrant who just yelled and yelled and yelled. It got to the point where I just didn't listen to him anymore. It wore on my body and I ended up having some problems with my hips and my ankles. I made the mistake of telling them that I had hip issues in college, so that gave them an easy excuse to release me since I didn't disclose that before I signed the contract. I had been there for about six months. The pay was good, but it was just wasn't as much fun. Iceland was better. Nick Bradford was about 15 minutes away. He played on a rival team. I got there near the end of the season. I got there in January and stayed until the end of April.

## HANGIN' IT UP

The decision to end my career was tough. I talked to my brother about it a lot before I actually did it. The hardest part is that basketball is something I'd been doing my entire life. In the mornings I always got up, worked out and then went to play basketball. Then I'd lift weights, go home and eat and then go play basketball some more. It was my entire life. Even after I said I had given it up, I was running the academy and thinking, "Maybe there's still a chance. Maybe someone will need me overseas." But I didn't pursue it as hard as I should have if I really wanted to do it. But I was still playing. I was always still working out and staying in shape and things like that.

After I stopped playing, I started doing the Jeff Boschee Basketball Academy while I was an assistant coach at Blue Valley Northwest High School in Overland Park. I worked there for two years and then got the head coaching job at Barstow and continued the academy there. I worked there for three years and after the third year I got the assistant coaching job at Missouri Southern.

# CHAPTER 6

# 1999/2000 - 2001/02

# DREW
# GOODEN

D rew Gooden earned first-team All-American honors as a junior in 2001-02, when he led Kansas to the Final Four by averaging 19.8 points and a national-best 11.4 rebounds. Gooden declared for the NBA draft after that season and was selected No. 4 overall by the Memphis Grizzlies. The charismatic, fun-loving power forward has played for nine NBA teams in nine seasons and is set to begin his second year with the Milwaukee Bucks in the fall of 2011. His No. 0 Kansas jersey was retired at Allen Fieldhouse 2003, ensuring that Gooden will be remembered as one of the best players to ever wear a Jayhawks uniform.

## IN DREW'S WORDS

I've been in the NBA for nine seasons and I've played for nine teams. Still, even at age 29, when I walk down the street or through an airport, people point at me and say, "That's Drew Gooden. He played at Kansas." It's even happened in foreign countries. They don't mention the Dallas Mavericks or the San Antonio Spurs or the Milwaukee Bucks or the Cleveland Cavaliers, where I played with LeBron James for an NBA title. It's always, "That's Drew Gooden. He's a Jayhawk."

Somehow I never knew just how powerful the Kansas basketball brand was when I was in school. I could see that our fans were crazy and that we were a big deal across the state. But once I moved away I realized that people all across the country and even overseas had been watching me play basketball for years. Seriously, everything that happens in Lawrence is a huge deal worldwide. For the rest of my life, I guess people will always picture me in a KU jersey. That's fine with me.

## EARLY MEMORIES

I'll never forget the first time I saw Allen Fieldhouse packed. It was Late Night with Roy Williams in 1990 – my freshman year – and I wanted to show the fans I could play. They knew a lot about Nick Collison and Kirk Hinrich, the other two guys in my recruiting class, but they didn't know a whole lot about me. I wanted to come in and prove that I could play at this level. I was so damn nervous, though. I had the biggest butterflies. I had never played in front of that many people before. I knew the night was going to end with a scrimmage. Once I got out there on the court, I broke the ice and did just fine.

A few weeks later we had our first exhibition game. Nick Collison and I started. I had 12 points, 10 rebounds and eight assists in 19 minutes. I was like, "Wow! I can play at this level!" We were playing against the California All-Stars. They had Ed Cota, the former North Carolina guard, and one of the Barry brothers. Those were big names to me, and I was playing well against them.

Then we opened the regular season against Fairfield. My first basket – my first official two points as a Jayhawk – came on a fast break. Kirk or Jeff Boschee threw it to me on a pitch-ahead. I took one dribble, went up and just dunked on this guy. The crowd went crazy. That play alone gave me confidence. I was like, "OK, now I can feel what this is all about." I went out that night, and people knew who I was. It was on from there.

## HINRICH & COLLISON

Whenever someone asks me about my teammates at Kansas, the first guys I think about are Nick and Kirk. Those are my boys. We'll always be linked because we came in together and grew up together. I was 17 when I got there and they were already 18. One of the funniest things I remember about those guys happened on Freshman Night shortly after the start of school. That's where all the new kids go to Memorial Stadium to learn about all of the chants and fight songs and traditions and things like that. None of us had cars at the time. So when it was time to go back to Jayhawker Towers, we had to walk. Somehow, we went the wrong way and ended up at Sixth and Iowa. We were walking through all these neighborhoods and past all of these houses. Ten or 15 minutes into the walk, I was like, "Yo, are you sure this is the right way to campus?" We walked the opposite direction and damn near went all the way to I-70. We ended up hitting 6th, making a left and then another left on Iowa and walking all the way back to campus.

Kirk was the biggest competitor on the team. I ended up being a competitor, too, but it was because Roy Williams brought it out of me. Diving for loose balls, taking charges, playing tough defense. Just doing stuff that I didn't pay much attention to before I got to Kansas. Kirk was doing that stuff from the first day of practice and Nick did a lot of it, too. I was learning from Coach Williams, and I was learning from them, too. They were a little sharper than me coming in. Basketball was their whole life, with their fathers being coaches and everything. Nick Collison had the best footwork of any freshman I've even seen. I'd study the moves he was making and try to copy them. I'd see how hard Kirk competed and try to copy that. We all used each other.

I remember Nick coming up to me after we played Colorado my junior year. I had a 23-and-15 game or something like that, and it was the fifth or sixth game in a row where I'd put up those kinds of numbers. Nick was like, "Bro, you are ballin' right now. You're on a tear." It was funny, because Nick was averaging a double-double himself. Looking back on it, I don't know how I averaged all those points and rebounds with Nick on the team. I'm being serious. How did I lead the nation in rebounding and score all those points playing alongside Nick, who was putting up damn near the same kinds of numbers as I was? And we were only playing 29 minutes a game. We weren't playing 40. I think about it and I'm like, "Damn, we were good together." We could both pass in the high-low and we could both shoot from the outside at that time. If the guy guarding us left to help with someone else, that team was in trouble. You couldn't block out me and Nick. You still can't do that to this day.

## BOSCHEE

I was in high school when Jeff Boschee started playing for Kansas. I remember watching him on TV when he was Big 12 Freshman of the Year. He had a shaved head and looked like Jason Kidd. Then, once I got to school, I found out Boschee had started going to tanning beds. I guess the Backstreet Boys or someone like that was hot at the time, and they had these little flip-up bangs. Boschee started growing his hair out and styling it just like those boy-band singers. I didn't know who Boschee was anymore. I was like, "Whoa! Is that Jeff?" The more he tanned and the more he kept spiking up those bangs, the more it felt like we had Michael Jackson on our campus. Boschee was like the present-day Justin Bieber at Kansas. He was always the smooth, quiet teammate that all the girls loved.

## LUKE

Luke Axtell was unbelievable when he was healthy. And when I say unbelievable, I mean unbelievable. I just don't think he was in right situation. I can be honest about it now and keep it real. Coach Williams wasn't the right coach for Luke Axtell. The University of Kansas wasn't the right system for Luke Axtell. Luke Axtell was a hell of a player – an NBA-caliber talent, without a shadow of a doubt. He shot it lights out. And when it went in, it was all net. That ball didn't go in any other way. It didn't skim off the back of the rim. It didn't rattle in off the left or the right. It went in the same way every time. It was so pretty. One day in practice Luke caught the ball on the perimeter and tried to take it to the basket. Coach Williams blew his whistle and said, "Luke, I don't want you

shooting anything inside this 3-point line. You stay out here and if you're open, you shoot it." The problem was that Luke had transferred in from Texas where he played for Tom Penders, who was a very high-octane, shoot-if-you're-open, shoot-if-you're-not kind of coach. Luke tried to come in with that mentality, and Coach Williams wasn't having it. He nipped it in the bud really quick. Then Luke got injured a couple of times and couldn't work his way into the rotation. He went from having such a promising career to everything taking a turn for the worse. Eventually I think he just kind of gave up. He sacrificed a lot to come to Kansas, and I don't think Kansas was the right organization for him.

## E-CHEN

Eric Chenowith was a pain in the locker room. But you had to have him around. He had his jokes, and we had ours. If we played hip-hop music one day, he'd have Metallica on full blast the next day. He was a good dude. I love E-Chen a lot more now than I did when I played with him. He tried to be the bully that ran the locker room because he was older. "We're seniors. We have the final say." A lot of people thought Eric Chenowith was going to have an unbelievable college career. E-Chen was a 7-foot-1 guy that was skilled, man. I don't know why it didn't work out for him. There was a time when people thought he'd play 10-12 years in the league just like Greg Ostertag, Raef LaFrentz and Scot Pollard. When we first got there you'd have never thought me and Nick Collison would play in the NBA 10-plus years while Eric Chenowith never completed one NBA season. Everyone gave him a hard time because he supposedly followed the Dave Matthews Band around one summer instead of working out, but I don't think that was it. That was overblown. The bigger issue was that he had Nick Collison and me on his team. Nick and I were playing well, Jeff Carey came in and gave us some good minutes and Eric had his moments, too. But Roy Williams was always going to stick with the players who were playing the best. We had a lot depth, and sometimes it was hard to stand out.

## KENNY G

Kenny Gregory was my roommate in 102C at the Jayhawker Towers. My freshman year Kenny led us in scoring and I was second. My sophomore year we were neck-and-neck. I just remember apartment 102C was always the thing. We always wanted to have the most combined points of any roommate duo in Jayhawker Towers. We felt like we had to carry the team. It wasn't cockiness because we weren't cocky guys. It was just something we knew we had to do. Sometimes you'd look up in the stands and see people holding signs that said "102C." Kenny was a good roommate. He never washed any dishes, but he was a good guy to talk to. We'd stay up all night and just talk about life and situations. He was a spiritual guy. My last year there I roomed with Bryant Nash, and he never said a word. He's a D.J. down in Texas now – D.J. Nasty Nash.

## OTHERS

When I was a junior, I spent a lot of time hanging around the freshmen, guys like Aaron and Jeff Hawkins and Mike Lee and Keith. We nicknamed Aaron and J-Hawk "The Soap Sisters" because one time we caught them kicking the soap bar back and forth in the shower. All of those guys were a lot of fun. I thought it was my job to talk to those guys and tell them what to expect and be there for them, just like Lester Earl and Nick Bradford had been there for me.

## BORDER WAR

Missouri was the game you hated to play, but you had to play it. If you won that game there was a huge sense of relief, because there was so much pressure, so much buildup. That was like a championship game in itself. In 2002 we had to play them in the last game of the year on the road to stay undefeated in the Big 12. We barely pulled that one off. I remember Aaron Miles dribbling the ball down the court with about 30 seconds left on the clock. We were up by three points and, for some reason, he shot a pull-up jumper early in the shot clock, and Missouri got the ball back. Coach Williams called a timeout and said, "As soon as they inbound the ball, foul them!" That way they couldn't get the 3-point shot off. Keith Langford went out there and was hacking away at Clarence Gilbert, just trying to take his arms off completely. But the refs didn't call it. He finally shot the 3 and it probably should've been a three-shot foul, but the whistle didn't blow and we got out of there with the win, which gave us a 16-0 record in the Big 12. Going undefeated would've been a big deal no matter what. But it was especially huge that year because the league was so strong. I'm not sure the Big 12 has ever been as strong as it was that year. Texas, Texas Tech and Oklahoma and Missouri were all in the top 25. Iowa State was always in the mix, and overcoming that Hilton magic in Ames was so, so tough.

## A BIG RIVAL ... LITERALLY

One guy I wasn't very fond of in college was David Harrison, the 7-footer from Colorado. We played them three times in 2002, with the last time coming at the Big 12 tournament. We were supposed to meet at midcourt and shake hands after our names were announced in the starting lineup. They announced his name and he walked out to midcourt and waited for me, but when they announced my name, I walked straight into our huddle and left him standing out there all by himself, looking stupid. He deserved it, though. That's one thing I would never take back. He had shown so much hatred toward me leading up to that game, and I couldn't understand why – especially since I had tried to encourage him earlier in the year. I told him a bunch of positive things. We beat Colorado in Lawrence, but David had a decent game. He was obviously mad that they lost, though, so I went up to him after the game and, "Don't worry about it, man. You're a hell of a player. Keep working hard and you'll do great things." He said, "Thank you, thank you." Then the Big 12 tournament rolls around, and I start reading all these comments from him in the paper saying, "Drew Gooden is soft. He gets all the calls," and "Drew Gooden is overrated." He even called me "Drew Pudding." I hadn't done anything to him. I hadn't even seen him since the last time we played them. When the time came for me to shake his hand, I mean ... how could I? Everyone in the stands knew that stuff was out there. They should've announced the lineup in a different order, where someone else had to meet him at midcourt to shake his hand, because I sure as hell wasn't going to do it. But I'm glad they set it up like that, because after he embarrassed me in the paper, it gave me a chance to embarrass his ass in front of thousands of people. I guarantee you he remembers that s--t. I would never take that back. I was able to talk to him and get to know him a little bit when he was in the NBA. He turned out to be an OK guy. But I couldn't stand him in college.

## BEST KU TEAM EVER?

My first two years at Kansas were solid, but the 2001-02 season is the one I'll always remember the most. We had the 16-0 Big 12 record and, of course, the appearance in the Final Four. Kirk, Nick and I were all juniors. Having that kind of experience set our team apart, because all the other talented juniors and seniors across the country had left for the NBA. We were playing against freshmen and sophomores and a few seniors that weren't as good.

Me and Kirk and Nick were the nucleus of the team, but we also had Jeff Boschee, who was a third-year starter at shooting guard. Then we had a freshman point guard in Aaron Miles, whose presence allowed Kirk Hinrich to move to the three-spot, where he could score a little more. Then we had Keith Langford and Wayne Simien, who were helping us. We even had Brett Ballard making a contribution.

We averaged 91 points a game that season, which led the country, and were absolutely killing teams by 30 or 40 points. What was strange was that we actually started the year off by losing to Ball State in the Maui Invitational. I remember that game because it was so hot in that gym. We were all cramping up. At first I started cramping more than anyone. I was telling people, "I'm locking up, I'm locking up." They kept telling me to drink fluids. I thought it was just me. So I kept playing and drinking and drinking. Then Nick went down and rolled over in pain. Then Aaron Miles caught a full body cramp on the last play of the game. Patrick "Action" Jackson crossed Aaron over on the perimeter and drove into the paint. Nick and I went up to block his shot but he tucked it back down and rolled it right off the backboard. I was like, "No! Not us! We've seen this kind of thing happen to other teams, but not us." That loss hurt us. I felt so bad. That was Aaron Miles' first collegiate game. It was on TV. I didn't know how he was going to bounce back. Keith Langford didn't do much that game. Simien was hurt. Afterward we were all like, "This s**t can't happen again."

We were ranked No. 7 when we lost that game, but a few months later we had climbed all the way to No. 1. It happened right before we played UCLA in Los Angeles, and I think we let it get to our heads a little bit. We were on the cover of Sports Illustrated and, when we were in California, Fox Sports sent a limo to our hotel to pick me up so I could go on the "Best Damn Sports Show." I was doing all the Hollywood stuff. It was all new to me. I still came ready to play the next day, but UCLA beat us. Matt Barnes had an unbelievable game, and Jason Kapono was there. Their fans rushed the court. I just remember struggling with their zone. Ball State had used a zone to beat us, UCLA did it, and Holy Cross almost beat us playing zone. Oklahoma always gave us fits playing a make-or-miss zone, and then Maryland did, too. When teams went to zone, it hurt us. We were a high-octane offensive team. We were almost like the Phoenix Suns except we played defense. The zones slowed us down. When we couldn't score on the secondary break we had to run a high-low, stagnant offense. Our goal was to run, and most of the time we did.

It was just amazing how fast we were. Usually when a player scores a basket, they'll flash his picture across the screen as he's running back down the court to play defense. But anyone who scored against us didn't get their "TV moment" because we'd take the ball out of the basket and get it down the court so fast that the cameras didn't have time to adjust. Think about it: We had three point guards in our starting lineup. We were so fast. Who could stop that?

By the time Big 12 play was in full swing, we honestly believed we couldn't be beat. There was no doubt in our minds that we were going to win every game. It got to the point where we weren't even running plays anymore. We had so much confidence in one another that we could make one pass and everyone knew what to do next. If a play was called, so be it. I'd say we scored two out of every three baskets on our secondary break. But if we didn't score on the secondary break, we were going to get it some other way. Nick or I would grab an offensive rebound and set things back up. He'd get a high-low pass from me or vice-versa. We were working every angle.

## FINAL FOUR FRUSTRATIONS

We lost to Maryland in the Final Four in Atlanta. To this day, I still haven't watched a tape of the game. It's been on TV a couple of times, but I haven't seen anything. I played one of my worst games at the wrong time. I blame so much of it on the fact that I got caught up in everything except for the game itself. There was too much going on leading up to it. Everyone was in my ear. Are you leaving? You could be the No. 1 pick. Adidas has a big contract waiting for you. Nike has a big contract waiting for you. Upper Deck will do this-and-that for you. Even when people aren't talking to you directly, word gets to you. Kansas had a contract with Nike at the time, and Nike people were bugging me all week to wear these new Vince Carter shoes. They hadn't even been released yet, but they kept bugging me to wear those shoes even though I'd been feeling good in a different style of shoe throughout the whole season. Now, in the biggest game of my life, I'm playing in some futuristic, spaceship-looking Vince Carter shoes. They were terrible. By halftime the insole was starting to detach and it was coming out of my shoe. I'm not saying that's the only reason I played bad. But it was definitely a distraction. I still have that shoe in my house in my trophy case so I'll always remember it as the shoe I wore in my only Final Four. The damn insole is still sticking out of it.

Even though there was a lot going on I still thought I'd be able to focus and have a good game. You look at my numbers and see 15-and-9 and think, "OK, he had a decent game." Well, no, I didn't. It was one of the worst games I ever played at Kansas. I just wanted to cry. I didn't cry, somehow. But I wanted to. I got in foul trouble early and took myself out of the game. I was like, "There's no way I'm fouling out of this f---ing game." I started walking over to the bench in the first half and said, "I've got to come out." Roy agreed. I was seriously thinking, "If I foul out of this game I might kill myself." I remember being on that bench thinking, "Oh my God. No. This can't be happening." I got my third foul with about 14 minutes left in the second half. When I came back in, we were down double digits. The last points I scored – and my last collegiate basket – was a 3-pointer, of all things. It didn't mean anything. There were only 20 seconds left when I hit it.

After the game – and even today – people said we lost because we got out-toughed, because Maryland was more physical than we were. It's true that Chris Wilcox had the best game of his college career against me, but our stat lines were basically the same. Lonny Baxter did some good things. But that's not why we lost. It was Juan Dixon – Juan Dixon! – who beat us. You want a story line from that game? Juan Dixon is the only choice. He had 19 first-half points, he got us out of our rotations, and he helped free up guys like Baxter and Wilcox for easy baskets. We'd go to trap Dixon, and then Wilcox and Baxter would end up with the ball wide open under the basket for a dunk. He made them look like Shaq. Dixon ended up with 33 points that game – a career high. It was destiny for him to win that game. We couldn't change that. I remember him hitting a 3-pointer right before halftime. We had him trapped in the corner with two dudes, and he still made it. I passed him on the way back to the locker room and said, "Damn Juan, calm your ass down." He just said, "Keep playing hard, man. We'll see what happens." Maryland ended up winning the championship game against Indiana two nights later, but our game against them was basically for the championship. We had the two best teams.

After the game that night I went to eat with LeBron James and his sidekick, Maverick Carter, in the revolving restaurant at the top of the Westin in Atlanta. LeBron played for the same AAU program that I had played for growing up. He was about 15 at the time. LeBron was like, "Damn, do you really think that loss is going to hurt your draft stock that bad? Do you really think you're not going to be one of the top picks now, just because of this one game?" I was like, "I hope not. I don't know what's going to happen." I just felt like s**t. LeBron kept saying stuff like, "They beat you guys with the zone and by running Flex." I was thinking, "How the hell does he know that as a 15-year-old?" You could tell back then that he really watched the game and understood it. Because he was right, they beat us with the zone and the Flex.

## OPPORTUNITY KNOCKS

Everyone had an opinion on whether I should enter the NBA draft after my junior year, including Roy Williams. He told me to leave. I knew it was the right thing to do because I was going to be a high pick (Gooden went fourth overall to Memphis), but it was still tough. The NBA was my biggest dream, but I still wanted to win a championship, too. If I came back with Nick and Kirk I knew that we weren't going to lose a game. I told myself that in my head: "If I come back, we're not losing any basketball games – at all! We're going to go undefeated, win the championship and then go to the NBA together." I also thought about finishing school because I was almost done. My mom had always told me how important that was. I just didn't want to let people down. I wanted people to be happy for me. That's what was tough. I didn't want fans thinking I gave up on them. I was more worried about what people were going to think about me than anything. I was 20 years old, and there was a lot of stuff going on in my life. But I made the decision to leave, and it was a decision I would never take back. I'm glad I made it. I've had a great NBA career.

## WILLIAMS vs. BOHL: ROUND 1

A few months after I was drafted I came back to Lawrence for a little while. I went into the weight room to work out one day, and one of the new football strength coaches came up to me and said, "You can't be in here." I was like, "Ummm, OK." So I went up to Coach Williams' office and asked him, sarcastically, if he knew of a gym around town where I could go work out. I told him what happened, and Roy marched me into Al Bohl's office. He was pounding his hand on the table saying, "The basketball program is one of the main reasons we have all these nice things here. This guy gave his blood, sweat and tears to this school, and he's going to work out here whenever he wants. And the same thing goes for any of my former players!" Roy was really hot. Really hot. There weren't any problems after that. I worked out there whenever I wanted.

## TEARS

Even though the NBA season was still going on, I was able to go to New Orleans to watch my guys play Syracuse for the NCAA title in 2003. Tracy McGrady was with me because we were teammates in Orlando at the time. That night was so painful. When we lost, I cried. That was the only time in my career when I've all-out bawled, and I didn't even play. That's how hurt I was. If we'd have won that game I'd have felt like that was my championship, too. It wasn't a deal where I felt like I cost them by leaving early and not being on the team anymore. There was no guilt or anything like that. I just felt hurt because all of those guys were still my teammates. Nick, Kirk, Wayne, Aaron, Keith. Less than a year ago I was right there with them, and now it was like, "Yo, we're back!" If they would've won that game, I was going to have a ring made for myself, too, because I would've felt like I put work in for it. If the school wouldn't have gotten it for me, I would've found a place to have one made, and I wouldn't have had any problems showing it off, because I felt like a part of that team. Those were my guys, and that's why I was so hurt. I went into the locker room and saw their faces. It just killed me. I couldn't take it. I walked into one of the bathroom stalls, shut the door and started crying. I was crying more than Nick and Kirk. I was so hurt. I was more hurt then than I was when we lost to Maryland, because this was two in a row. To fight so hard to get back to that point and then to lose in that fashion ... it was rough. To this day Nick and Kirk won't even talk to me about it. Nick takes it the hardest.

## THOUGHTS ON ROY

I hated to see Roy leave Kansas, but we all have to make tough decisions in life, and he did what he thought was best. I respect him for that.

Roy was an extension of my father away from home. He did a great job of being an authority figure in my life when I really needed guidance. He did two things for me. He pushed my body to a point where I never thought it could go. There were times when I thought I was going to die because I was so tired. He also brought out the competitor and the toughness and the "no-let-up" in me. That's why I'm still playing. That's why I'm the man I am today on and off the court, because of what he instilled in me. We had to walk a straight line at Kansas. We couldn't do any knucklehead stuff off the court. As young men, we needed that kind of discipline. I look at Roy Williams as a second father.

I still keep in touch with Roy, although he's probably one of my busiest friends. He sends me a message before the beginning of every season wishing me luck. I see him on the AAU circuit because he's recruited some of the players on the AAU team I sponsor. But it's tough to have an everyday conversation with him. Think of how many kids he's coached. There are hundreds of guys he's coached that want to talk to him. He's going to be remembered like a John Wooden or a Dean Smith. He's that good. So for Roy Williams to still sit down with me and talk like we're as close as we were when I was 17 and 18 years old ... I'll always be thankful for that. It's special for me.

## ONE BIG FAMILY

The cool thing about the NBA is that I'm always running into guys that played for Kansas. Whether it's Brandon Rush or Darnell Jackson or whoever, I make it my business to find them during the pregame warm-ups or afterward to congratulate them for making it to the NBA. I give them my contact information and tell them if they ever have questions or need anything to get at me. You've got to look out for people that went to your school – especially a school like this, with so much tradition and high standards. You've got to show the love.

I was lucky enough to play with Kirk when we were both with the Chicago Bulls. It was cool to be sitting there on an NBA plane flying back from a road game, playing cards with a guy you've known since you were 17. That's special. I enjoyed the days I played with Kirk. The night Kansas won the NCAA title in 2008 I was with Kirk and Joakim Noah in Miami. We had a game there the next day, so we couldn't make it to San Antonio. We went to Wet Willie's on Ocean Drive in South Beach and watched it at the bar. We were probably the only two Kansas fans in there. And, remember, we had two Dukies on our team (Chris Duhon and Luol Deng), so there had already been a lot of trash-talking during the week. Watching the game in 2008 I was like, "It's finally our turn. It's finally our time." That was one of the best college basketball games I've ever seen in my life. And I'm not just saying that because it involved Kansas. That was literally one of the best basketball games I've ever watched.

## LIVING THE DREAM

I've had a great NBA career. I've played with future Hall of Fame players and Hall of Fame coaches. And being able to get to know fans in all these different cities has been fun. I definitely have a lot of "contacts" in my cell phone. If I'd have spent all my years in one city I don't think as many people would know who I am as much as they do now. I walk through the airport and pass by five or six gates in a row where it says Los Angeles or Dallas or Orlando or Memphis. I've played for each city, so sure enough, when I walk past those gates, there's always someone saying, "I remember you with the Mavs" or "I remember you with the Bulls." It makes me feel good.

The high point of my career was probably playing with LeBron in Cleveland, because I was on the same court with the best player to ever touch a basketball. Cleveland went from an organization where there were 1,000 or 2,000 fans in the stands each night to a team that drew sellouts all the way up to the NBA finals. A lot of that was because of LeBron, but I felt like I helped build that, too. I put the work in and helped the team get to where it needed to be. All of us felt that way. It was a good group of guys.

I'm not married and I don't have any kids. I don't own homes all over the country. Why buy a big house in these big cities when I'm just going to live by myself? I usually just get an eight-month lease with some rental furniture in whatever city I'm playing in and then spend the offseason at my home in Orlando. I'm from the Bay Area in California, and my dad is still there, so whenever I'm out west, his house is my house.

## GIVING BACK

Whenever I go back to Kansas and walk in the gym I'll peek up at my jersey in the rafters. They've moved it a little more toward the corner (laughing) but it's still there. Seeing it gives me goosebumps. So much has changed, though, with all of the upgrades and renovations at Allen Fieldhouse. I get lost walking around in there sometimes. It shouldn't be like that. I need to go back more often. All of us do.

I want guys that played for Roy to come back more and be more active. It's normal when there's a coaching change for some guys to not come back as much. But it doesn't have to be that way. I'm trying to bridge that gap and be a leader. I want to get the older guys who played for Roy to come during the offseason just like the guys who played for Bill Self. There are a lot of great guys that have come through this program, and there are a lot of people around here who would love to see them again. I'm willing to do whatever it takes to give back to this organization and doing whatever I can to bridge that gap.

I'm at the point in my career now where it's time to come back and start helping Kansas. I started off by helping my high school and then my AAU team, but Kansas was a big part of my life, too. I realize that now more than ever.

# CHAPTER 7

# 1999/2000 - 2002/03
# NICK
# COLLISON

Nick Collison is the second-leading scorer in Kansas history with 2,097 career points. He starred in Lawrence from 1999-2003 and led the Jayhawks to the Final Four in each of his last two seasons. The Seattle Supersonics selected Collison with the 12th overall pick in the 2003 NBA draft. Collison is still a key player for the franchise, which has relocated to Oklahoma City. Collison's No. 4 jersey was retired one year after his graduation and now hangs from the Allen Fieldhouse rafters. He averaged 14.8 points and eight rebounds during his four-year career and earned first-team All-American honors as a senior, when he also chosen National Player of the Year by the NABC.

## IN NICK'S WORDS

My first few years in the NBA, there were a couple of times when I thought, "Man, I'm glad I went to Kansas." From a fundamental standpoint, I was as well-prepared as I could've been, more so than most guys I've seen come into the league. Everything you can do on the court, I was taught to do the right way. I was coached on things over and over again and forced to repeat things until they became a habit. That's why I've been able to do well in the league, because of my habits and what I bring every day. I'm able to do certain things on the court now without even thinking, simply because they come so natural after all the times I repeated them during practice at Kansas.

The biggest thing I developed at Kansas was a standard of effort and a grasp of how hard you have to play all the time. Coach Williams showed us that playing at a high level takes a new kind of dedication and work we never knew existed. It became the baseline for how we prepared and how hard we played. Being able to play really good teams in college and being in an atmosphere where the only thing that was important was winning … that was huge, too. There are a lot of players in the NBA that were never in that type of situation. At their school, the focus may have been on something else, but at Kansas we were trying to win every game.

For guys that never went to college or guys that left school really early, the NBA might be better for skill development, because you're developing against better competition and more athletic players. But college helps you with so many intangible things. For instance, if you're the star player in college and you don't play well, your team is probably going to lose, and that's going to be a very negative thing for you. You're going to have to hear about it when you walk through campus and be embarrassed about it. They're going to talk about you on TV and the coaches are going to be angry with you and you're going to have hard practices. That's a lot of pressure for an 18- or 19-year-old. You also learn how to deal with teammates when things don't go well and how to handle adversity. College helped me with those things. Those are things you can't really measure, but they're important in an NBA season and an NBA career.

## THE ROAD TO LAWRENCE

I was a junior in high school the first time I went to Kansas and saw the campus. Raef LaFrentz was dating the sister of one of my best friends, Mike Roelfs. I came down with Mike to watch a game and someone told the KU coaches that I was a good player. At that point they weren't recruiting me yet. I went to watch a practice, and Coach Williams came over and said a few words. He was really honest with me. He said, "Nick, we've never seen you play. We don't know much about you. But we know some schools like Iowa are looking at you. We're going to start keeping in touch with you and we'll send a coach to see you practice." I thought that was pretty cool. He didn't have to take the time to come talk to me, and when he did he didn't feed me any lines. He was honest. I respected that, because that's not always the case in recruiting. They sent a coach to practice and liked what they saw. They started recruiting me, and by the state tournament that year, he had offered me a scholarship.

## REPETITION, REPETITION, REPETITION

Some people say Coach Williams' players are too programmed and that they don't have enough freedom. But I can't imagine anyone being any better at teaching a guy the correct way to play than Coach Williams. People always ask me, "How did you guys run so well? Your up-tempo game … how did you get so good at it?" It wasn't like it was some new scheme that no one had ever heard of. We did it well because it was preached and harped on and corrected every single day. If one of our guys didn't take the ball out of the basket and inbound it quickly enough, Coach Williams would blow his whistle and correct us. We kept doing it until we got it right. He just doesn't just let things slide. He's really good at coaching every phase of the game.

His organization extended off the court, too. He wanted everything done a certain way. His itineraries for us were made out down to the minute. At team meals, the seniors went through the line first, then the juniors, sophomores and freshmen. Most programs wouldn't even think about something like that. Maybe it didn't help us win a game. I don't know. But I think being organized really sets a tone that carries over throughout the entire program.

## FOREVER LINKED

My transition to college life and college basketball was a lot easier because of Kirk. We were both from small towns in Iowa and the sons of high school coaches. When we were seniors we shared the state's Mr. Basketball award and we played on the same AAU team. I'd known him for a long time.

As close as we were, Kirk and I were competitive with each other, too. It's not something we really talked about. But I didn't want him to think he was tougher than me in any drill or that he was playing better than me at any time. I think he felt the same way, too. When we started playing together at age 16, we were at an age where we were trying to get recruited. We were trying to make a name for ourselves. That carried over into college.

We raised each other's level of play and competitiveness. There were a lot of pickup games where we'd really get into it. Of all the guys on the court, he was the one who I didn't want to beat me. It was almost like a brother thing. Guys that have brothers understand what I mean. You're the closest guy to him but you'll also do the worst things to him because you're so competitive and you want to beat him. We had that going on in college. Sometimes it was spoken. Sometimes it was unspoken. But I think both of us wanted to live up to what the other one was doing. I think it was good for us.

When Kirk was getting recruited to come to Kansas, Coach Williams told him that he'd probably back up Jeff Boschee for three years. After that Kirk really came close to going to Oklahoma, because they were telling him he could start and play all the time. At the end of the day, he saw how cool of a place Kansas was and how great the program was. And he always had confidence he could play.

Kirk is the kind of person that can always come up with a reason to have a chip on his shoulder. You'd never know it by keeping up with him in the media, because he's not the type to publicize it by saying, "I feel like it's me against the world." But he always finds a way to psych himself up. He still does it in the NBA. I won't say who he talks about, but there are certain guys in the NBA who have done something to motivate him, to give him a reason to try to get after him. He'll feel slighted or that he's not getting the credit he thinks he should. He always keeps it quiet, though. He knows he plays better that way. At Kansas, he probably used that stuff Coach Williams said about him being a backup to

Boschee as motivation. He loves Coach Williams and wanted to play for him more than any other coach, but that drove him a lot.

When Kirk got to school he struggled a little bit. The first half of his freshman year, he had a tough time. He wasn't playing as much or as well as he wanted to. It was just the typical stuff a freshman goes through. But he kept working hard and, again, using certain things as motivation. I was a McDonald's All-American, and he wasn't. Kansas recruited me sooner than him. With our freshman class, people were talking about Drew and me more than him. All of that stuff fed into his motivation. By the end of the year, he was starting and playing great. By the end of his sophomore year he was first-team All-Big 12 and he probably would've been a lottery pick if he'd have come out after his junior year.

It's really neat to see how well everything turned out for him. He deserves everything he has because it came through hard work. Kansas fans will probably always link me with him. The rest of the country will probably forget about us. I was really fortunate to be able to play with one of my best friends.

## A CLASS IN CHEMISTRY
When Kirk moved into the starting lineup it didn't cause any tension between

him and Boschee. Jeff continued to play really well. It's not like he lost his starting job. He just slid over and started making some huge jump shots for us. It helped his game because he's such a natural shooter. Kirk is more of a natural point guard because he handles pressure better. I think it really helped Jeff's game. His senior year, he was unbelievable. Jeff's senior year, Kirk had to play small forward so Aaron could play point guard. So he got moved, too. They just wanted to put the best guys on the floor. Kirk and Jeff both deserve credit for switching positions so we could get our best players on the floor. Kirk is a point guard in the NBA but his junior and senior year at Kansas he played small forward. A lot of guys would be upset about having to do that. But all they cared about was winning. I didn't sense much tension at all between those guys. It speaks to their character, and it's just what everyone was about, which was trying to win.

Because everyone had that attitude, my junior and senior seasons were a blast. It was so much fun. However it looked, that's how fun it truly was. We didn't have many issues at all. We had a close group of guys. It may hurt him sometimes, but one thing Coach Williams tries to do in recruiting is sign guys who he thinks will mesh really well together. Sometimes he'll miss out on a guy because he's waiting on a guy that he really wants to get. He's not trying to stockpile talent and just hope that it meshes well together. When you do that it can create problems, because you have really talented guys who aren't getting to play. On most of our teams, it was fairly obvious who was supposed to play what role and it worked out really well. We never had too many guys that were unhappy, because it was fairly obvious who should be starting and who should be coming off the bench. It gave people a role that everyone accepted. Our chemistry was really good. We also just had really good guys, really fun guys. My last couple of years we had a younger group with Aaron, Keith, Jeff, Wayne and Michael. But we all got along really well. They were fun guys to hang out with.

## THOUGHTS ON TEAMMATES

Even though my junior and senior seasons were the most memorable for me, I had a chance to play with some really good players those first two years, too. Eric Chenowith was a little stubborn but he had a lot of ability. He had a fairly good career for who he was and what he did on the court. He would've liked for things to go better for him, but he had a good career. He's one of the leading shot blockers in school history and he played on some good teams. I do think maybe the way we played – the fast, up-tempo style – might not have been the best thing for him. If we could've played more of a half-court game it would've suited his abilities more. Eric can move, especially for a 7-footer. But his size and what he brought to the team didn't always mesh with the style of play. That might be why things didn't work out the way he wanted them to. I always really liked Eric, though. He was really nice to me. As an older guy he was always trying to help out. I still talk to Eric from time to time. He's at peace with his career. He loves Kansas. He loves Kansas so much. He goes back a lot and is as big of a Jayhawk supporter as any of the former players.

Luke Axtell was a big-time talent, but I'm not sure Luke truly liked basketball. He was really good at basketball. But I don't think he loved it. It's a tough position to be in, because you have the talent to play and you go to school and everyone expects big things from you. When I was with him I don't think he loved playing. The amount of work you have to do in college is really different. The intensity of it all can wear on anyone. With me, even as a young kid, I always knew in the back of my mind that I wanted to play. I wanted to be a pro. That's what I wanted to do when I grew up and I was always working toward that. There were a lot of times when it wasn't necessarily fun. It's a lot of work. Even when it's fun in college, it's a lot of fun in a different way. You're competing at a really high level and you're playing in front of unbelievable fans and you're getting the most out of your abilities. But it's not like going to the park and playing with your buddies like you did in high school. It's still fun to play, but at that level it's a lot of work, too, and there's this whole pressure dynamic that makes it different. As it relates to Luke, if he didn't have that passion to get him over the hump, it was probably really tough. It was probably tough for him to have all that pressure and all those expectations when, deep down, he wasn't into it as much as he once was. I'm not sure if he would say that, though. Only he knows what he's feeling at the time. I always thought he was a really smart guy, a deeper guy. There is probably a lot more to Luke than the rest of us. He's into a lot of stuff. He's well-rounded. Basketball wasn't the only important thing in his life. With the rest of us, that's all we cared about.

## THE TIME IS NOW

The motto at Kansas is that, every year, we're playing to win the championship, but I don't think we felt like we really had the team to do it until my junior year. There was a different feel with that team, a lot more talent, a lot more experience. Jeff, Drew, Kirk and I had been through enough that we felt like the older guys. We had experience, and we were just really, really focused on winning it all.

We also had a really good freshman class coming in. They were joking around all the time and hanging out together. At first they were a little annoying, because they were always playing jokes. They put maple syrup on my door knob a few times and leaned a couch up against my door. But they were always in a good mood, always super-positive. They were all confident and cocky in some ways. But there was never a negative arrogance about them. They fit in really well and gave us a lot of energy. You had Wayne, who had more of a stable personality. He liked to have fun, but he was an old soul compared to the rest of them. Keith was kind of like that, too. Aaron and Jeff were like little brothers, always clowning around and having fun with Michael Lee, too.

## IT'S ALL GOODEN

Drew and I met at a high school all-star game, the Capital Classic in D.C. He and I were totally different. I was from a small town. I was pretty shy because it was one of my first times away from home. Drew has always been so outgoing and bold. I really got along with him. It was cool that we did, because we came into a situation where we could be competing for a lot of things, whether it was playing time or press or accolades or whatever. We did a good job of saying, "We're here to try to win and improve and go to the NBA." Drew is so inclusive. He'll talk to a guy on the street that he doesn't even know. He's not a moody guy or anything. He's just so positive.

Drew struggled a little bit in his first year. I was further along than he was in terms of understanding what Coach wanted. He'll probably admit that I had had more coaching in certain fundamentals of the game. That was stuff he hadn't picked up yet. He was always more talented and he played extremely hard. He always played with a lot of effort, but that first year Coach had to rein him in a little bit. He had a tough time that first year. We struggled by Kansas standards. But he did a good job of fighting through it. By the next year he was fine and, when we were juniors, he was so confident that by the end of the year he thought we couldn't be beat. A lot of people felt that way.

My personality is a little different. My inner monologue doesn't work that way. I was always that guy that was always saying, "Man, we're struggling with this-and-that" or "We struggled in practice yesterday. I don't know how we're going to play." With that team I was really confident. I thought we could play with anyone and beat anyone. Still, I was always the cautious one, and Drew was the outspoken one. Kirk and I have that same dynamic, too. I'm cautious and he's like, "Screw it! Let's go."

## MAYHEM IN MAUI

I'll never forget cramping up in that loss to Ball State in Maui. That was terrible. I guess it was just dehydration. I sweat more than anyone. Our equipment manager when I was in Seattle with the Supersonics started as a ball boy when he was 13. He'd been in the league for 28 years. He said the only guy he's seen sweat more than me is Patrick Ewing. I've always been a sweater. Being in Maui for two days prior to that game and walking around ... my body just got dehydrated. We didn't do anything different as far as trying to hydrate before the game. That was probably a mistake. They probably told us to drink more fluid, but I didn't do anything different. In that gym, with it being 90 or 100 degrees or whatever, I probably just sweated to the point of dehydration. I've had times at AAU tournaments where I've played three games in one day. I'd feel cramps coming on and just fight them off. But this was different. My quad cramped, up and I couldn't bend my leg. That muscle was just locked. I'd try to get rid of the cramp by stretching, but when I pulled my ankle back to do a quad stretch, my hamstring cramped up. My whole body cramped. It was just a nightmare. I didn't know what to do. I couldn't move. I just laid there and waited for someone to help me. It was something I'd never experienced before.

## BOSCHEE THE BOMBER

Jeff had a great senior year that season. Off the court, he was really cool with everybody. He would hang out from time to time. But he wouldn't usually be in the big group. He had a girlfriend and some friends from back home that he hung out with a lot. But he was always really cool with everyone and was in on all the jokes in the locker room. But when we all went out, Jeff sometimes went out with other people. He probably just got tired of all the juvenile jokes and wanted to get away from them from time to time. But to say he was an outsider is inaccurate. Because when we were together he got along with everyone. We wouldn't have gone 16-0 in the Big 12 in 2002 without him. The reason that team was so good was because of the versatility of those three guys in the backcourt and their willingness to pitch ahead to whoever was open. For Drew and me to play well inside, we needed Jeff to help space the floor. We needed teams to be face-guarding him so we had space to operate inside. He played great. He hit big shots. He wasn't afraid to take them. He was fearless.

## FINAL FOUR vs. MARYLAND

We went 16-0 in the Big 12 that year and only had three losses going into our Final Four game against Maryland. It was a weird game. When we started off on a 13-2 run, and everything was going right. It's funny, though. I see teams get off to a big jump like that in the NBA, and it never lasts. I don't know what it is. The same thing happened with us. Everything happened so easily at the start of that game. All of our shots were falling. Then Maryland started playing better, and we went the opposite direction. What made them so tough was that they executed so well. They ran the Flex offense with screen after screen after screen. Juan Dixon was going off, and we couldn't figure out how to stop him. Chris Wilcox was big for them early because he was blocking shots. Our inside guys had really been aggressive at going to the rim all season, but him blocking those shots affected us a little bit and got us away from what we did.

I was crushed when we lost. At that age, your world view isn't what it should be. You think all that matters in the world is that you lost in the Final Four. It's tough to deal with. We felt like we didn't play that well, which was frustrating. Everyone was watching the game. We didn't know if Drew was coming back and Kirk really considered leaving. The future was up in the air.

## DECISION TIME

I looked into entering the NBA draft after my junior year. The feedback I got was that I'd be a mid-to-late first round pick. I just didn't want to risk being a second-round pick and not getting a guaranteed deal. Part of me was happy they didn't say I'd be a higher pick, because then I would've had a decision to make, and I didn't want to do that. I really wanted to be at school. I loved being at school. I really wanted a chance to try to win again. But if I would've had an opportunity like Drew to go in the top five or 10, I probably would've gone. It would've been tough, but it's a choice I probably would've had to make. Kirk had a more difficult decision to make. A lot of people were saying he'd be a mid-to-late lottery pick. Looking back on it, he probably risked a lot by coming back to school.

## SENIOR YEAR

My last team at Kansas – the one that played Syracuse for the NCAA title – wasn't very deep compared to some of the other teams I played on. We really had a really good top five and a solid top seven. I thought we practiced well. I thought we were prepared going into the year. But we had a stretch early where we lost to North Carolina, Florida and Oregon in less than two weeks. We were 3-3 and just didn't look very good. It was probably good for us to get out of the spotlight. We lost three games, and people quit paying attention to us. We could just play. We got that embarrassment and fear of failure out of the way. We could just start over and go play.

## THE X-FACTOR

Because we had lost Drew to the draft, we knew we were going to really need Jeff Graves to step up and be a factor. He had transferred in from a junior college and was really overweight at the start of practice. We were frustrated because we didn't have a lot of guys, especially in the paint. We needed him to play. I made some comments about him in the press because I was a little upset. Knowing what I know now, I realize it probably didn't do any good to say anything publicly. But at that time, in my opinion, I didn't think he was going to be able to help us.

Jeff definitely proved me wrong. He turned it around and got in shape. He's a real talented guy. He had a ton of ability and a really good feel for the game. He was huge for us down the stretch. We wouldn't have gotten out of Anaheim and the Sweet 16 if we didn't have Jeff Graves. He was the key to our season and to our Final Four run. If he didn't start playing well and improving, we wouldn't have done much at all. He deserves a lot of credit for sticking with it. I'm sure it was tough on him. It was his first year at Kansas, and everyone was dogging him. He probably just didn't realize what he was getting into at the start. That happens to a lot of guys. It's about more than just walking in and playing basketball. Coach is really going to test you. Everyone thought he was going to quit and not be able to do it. But he kept his confidence high and came through in the end.

## KUDOS TO KEITH

When you look back at both of our Final Four runs, Keith Langford played a huge role in each. It's funny, because Josh Childress was the guy in the 2001 recruiting class that Coach Williams really wanted. Chuck Hayes wanted to come, too, but he ended up going to Kentucky because he got tired of Coach Williams waiting on Josh's decision. When Josh announced he was going to Stanford, it was a bummer because we didn't know who we were going to get. We signed Keith, and no one knew anything about him. I remember watching him play right away in a pickup game and really liking his game. He has such a unique ability to get to the rim. The pace to his game is really good. That's something you can't teach, a feel for the game, a feel for how to score. He's a lot like James Harden on my Oklahoma City team now. Just his change of speeds and stop-and-go, that explosive athleticism while keeping your body under control. He was different than all our guys because he could really create his own shot and make plays and give us instant offense. Basketball-wise, he was a piece we definitely needed.

## GETTING TO THE POINT

I really loved almost all the guys I played with. I've got nothing but good things to say about all of them. But Aaron is one of my all-time favorites. Aaron is a natural leader. Even though he was a young guy coming into an older team that had been really successful, he was talking and trying to lead. But he was willing to listen, too. He was the reason why we were able to change how our team played. When you think about it, we had the guys back from the year before, but when you put him in the backcourt with Kirk and Jeff, we could play up-tempo even more. He was a major game-changer for us. There are not enough good things I can say about that guy. When you talk to him, he's genuine. He's concerned with how your family is doing. He's had a really good career. He had a chance to play in the NBA and probably could've gotten called up last season if it wasn't for his knee injury. But he still sounds so positive. He's just got a really good perspective on life and what's really important, which is his family. There aren't a lot of young guys that have that kind of perspective, but he's always been like that. He has his priorities in order.

## BEAST MODE

Toward the end of my senior season I was playing as hard as I possibly could and was putting up some pretty good stats. I had 16 rebounds in our Senior Day game against Oklahoma State, and then I put up 33 points and 19 rebounds in the Sweet 16 against Duke. Against Syracuse I had 21 rebounds. I had always played hard but, those last few weeks, I just found something extra. It's easier in a tournament-type setting, where you know you're done if you lose. When you can see the end it's easier to give everything you have in those games. I think

that's the mode I was in. It was a heightened level of focus and awareness and all those things. Everything is heightened at the end of the year in the NCAA Tournament. People always told me to lose myself in the game. I think that's what I did.

## COMING UP SHORT ... AGAIN

We felt really good going into the championship game against Syracuse, especially after things had gone so well against Marquette. We were a little concerned with Syracuse's style of play, though. We were a really good basketball team when we could run and play up-tempo and attack the basket and get to the rim. When we had to play half-court, we struggled – particularly on that team, more so than the year before. We didn't have the shooters. We were a little more reliant on me inside and Kirk on the perimeter. We had a higher number of eggs in one basket. Still, we felt good. We felt like we should win.

Once the game started, they came out and got all over us. They were 9-for-11 from 3 in the first half. That's really tough to bounce back from. It seemed like everything went wrong that night. I don't think we played tentative, but we didn't play well. We couldn't get our up-tempo game going. A lot of that was because we weren't getting stops. We were taking the ball out of the net almost every trip. We had a tough time scoring. It was that way all year. We were a really good team, but we didn't have a ton of shooters. Kirk shot the ball well, but he was trying to get to the basket a lot. Keith was trying to get to the basket, and Aaron was trying to get to the basket. You had Jeff Graves and I camped out inside. Our spacing wasn't great that game. We had to have really good spacing and perfect execution to get shots, because they really weren't guarding us on the perimeter too much.

The other thing was that, all year long, we relied on our defense to force turnovers so we could get out on runs and get easy baskets. It wasn't happening that game. Syracuse was also really talented. They had length at every position. The way they played that zone was difficult. They covered a lot of ground. They had a ton of good players. Carmelo Anthony is obviously extremely talented and deserves all the credit he gets. But Gerry McNamara and Kueth Duany are the ones that killed us by hitting all those 3-pointers. In the end we couldn't overcome it and we lost (81-78).

## FREE THROWS COSTLY

For years that game really bothered me. No matter who it was, I didn't want to have any conversations about what happened that night. Now I'm a 30-year-old man. I'm a father who has things in perspective. I'm at peace with it now. That's not to say it doesn't still sting. It does, especially in March. I don't watch a ton of college games, but during the NCAA Tournament it always hurts a little. It's unbelievable how many times I've thought, "If I hit four more free throws, we win a championship."

I had a good game other than the free throws. *(As a team, Kansas was 12-of-30 from the foul stripe. Collison went 3-of-10.)* I struggled at the line pretty much my whole college career. I was about a 60-percent shooter at the line. I just never had a lot of confidence there, particularly late during that season and then in the tournament. I just didn't feel comfortable. In every other area I felt like I was in a zone. I was playing as hard as I could possibly play. But at the line I felt uncomfortable. I didn't know where the ball was going to go. It wasn't like I was scared to shoot them, but free throws are all about confidence. One miss can turn into two or three if your mind isn't right. Since I've been in the league, I've changed my stroke a little bit. I think it would've helped me back then. I used to bring the ball up from my waist and shoot it. Now I set the ball first. My stroke is a lot shorter. I'm much better now.

At least one day a week I try to shoot 100 free throws. I usually hit between 80 and 90. You don't know how many times I think, "God, couldn't I just have gotten four of these back in 2003?" But, hey, that's who I was at the time. I was a good college player but not a very good free-throw shooter. I'm at peace with that. I just wish I could've been hot that day. Everything would've been totally different.

My memories from college aren't just from that game, though. I made a lot great memories and had a lot of great times in school. Fortunately I had a chance to play in that game and another Final Four the previous year. Still, it would've been a pretty sweet party in Lawrence and New Orleans that night if we'd have won.

## LIFE AS A PRO

When I got to the NBA, the one thing I really wanted to do was stick around a long time. I think I've done a good job of figuring out how to stay on the floor. I'm able to affect the game in a lot of ways. Every time I'm out there I'm trying to do something to help us win. Defensively I've gotten a lot better as my career has gone along. I'm not necessarily putting up a lot of big offensive numbers.

In college I was counted on to score a lot more. I was doing a lot of different things on the offensive end. Here that's not the case. I'm not as talented of a scorer as a lot of the other guys, so defense is something I'm able to focus more on. My niche in the league is as a good defender. Experience has really helped me a lot defensively, how to defend certain situations and recognize when they're coming and being prepared for them. The game is a lot slower for me now than it was when I first got in the NBA. I'm comfortable with what I do in the league. There's definitely a place for it.

## A WINNER ONCE AGAIN

It's a good feeling driving to work each day knowing that you've got a good chance to win. I've been on some teams where you drive to the arena and you know you're probably not going to win the game. It's just a totally different feel. Road trips are better. We've got a good group of guys that get along well.

It's such a different outlook when you're on a playoff-type team. It definitely feels like a job, but it's a lot of fun, too. I just feel like I'm extremely fortunate to be able to play. It's hard work, though. It doesn't feel the same as it did in college or high school because of the length of the season. Plus, when you do it for so long, it's a lot harder to go really hard in the offseason. Finding motivation to do that is one of the most challenging things about being a professional. Your body doesn't feel as good anymore because of injuries or whatever. But being on a winning team makes all the difference in the world. It makes things go faster. It makes coming to work each day more of a pleasure. Everybody is happier when you're winning. Just like at Kansas.

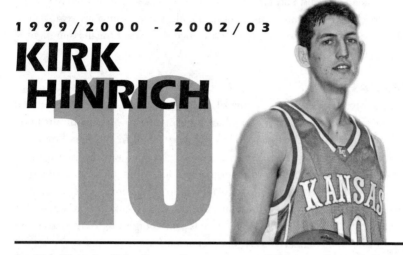

# CHAPTER 8

## 1999/2000 - 2002/03
# KIRK HINRICH
**10**

Kirk Hinrich will be known forever as one of the best players in Jayhawks history. The guard from Sioux City, Iowa, led Kansas to back-to-back Final Fours before being selected by the Chicago Bulls with the No. 7 overall pick in the 2003 NBA draft. Hinrich was part of a 1999 recruiting class that also featured Drew Gooden and Nick Collison, his close friend and AAU teammate in high school. He became a full-time starter as a sophomore and, a year later, help spearhead one of the fastest offensive attacks ever in college basketball. Hinrich now plays for the Atlanta Hawks. Hinrich and his wife, Jill, had a daughter (Kenzie) in 2008.

### IN KIRK'S WORDS

I was happy for Kansas when those guys won the title in 2008. But at the same time, in the back of my mind, I couldn't help but think, "Man, I can't believe we didn't win one, too." That's one thing I've learned about the NCAA tournament: The best team doesn't always win. The tournament is great for college basketball, but sometimes it takes a little luck to win it all. My senior year, we smashed Marquette in the semifinals. I felt like we were playing as good as we had since I'd been in college. But then we had a really rough first half against Syracuse – and we missed 18 free throws. One bad night, one bad half, and our dream got ruined. I don't have any regrets, though. I wouldn't trade my experience at Kansas for anything.

### BECOMING A JAYHAWK

The story of how I ended up at Kansas is kind of crazy. I was initially headed to Iowa State, but when Coach (Tim) Floyd left I decided to decommit and re-open my recruitment. It all happened so fast. I had just gotten to Orlando for the

17-and-under national championships and, all of a sudden, people were after me really hard. Kansas saw me as a guy that had potential. Coach Williams knew I had tools, but I wasn't an upper echelon recruit. I wasn't a McDonald's All-American or anything like that. But Nick and I were on the same AAU team, and he had watched Nick so much that he'd seen plenty of me, too. I guess he was sold. Oklahoma wanted me, too, and I knew they were going to be good. But I didn't want to go Oklahoma and end up at home, watching Kansas play for the NCAA title. I just wanted to go to the best place I could, the place that gave me the best chance to win a championship. That place was Kansas.

## WELCOME TO LAWRENCE

Life became a lot different for me when I showed up at Kansas. I remember when I first got to campus, Nick and Drew were the big recruits and I was just the "other guy." Boschee had just had a great year. No one was expecting much from me. I used that as a motivating factor, because I felt like I had so much ground to make up from the start. People back in Iowa were probably wondering if I was going to be any good. People at Kansas didn't really know who I was. I didn't have any hype. I felt like an underdog. I just wanted to prove people wrong.

I've always been like that. I've always been super-competitive. It bothers me when people doubt me. And because it bothers me, it's made me a much better player and put me in the position I'm at today. I can't really explain it. I probably get it from my parents. They're both really competitive. I always grew up playing against older guys, where I had to be tough and really compete to survive. It was something that was just instilled in me at a young age.

I always enjoy the game within the game. The matchups, getting to play against good players, responding to critics. For some reason, I always felt like people doubted me. I always believed I was good enough, like I was better than people who were supposedly better than me. Every time I played, I wanted to show the world or whoever was watching what I could do.

I liked playing against Kareem Rush, because it seemed like every time we were about to play Missouri, he was always in the paper, running his mouth. I love it when guys start talking. I revel in it. I don't say much, but once I get out there I'm ready to go and compete as hard as I can.

I think actions speak louder than words. Talk is cheap. Of course, if you ask my friends growing up, they'd probably say I was as cocky as anyone they knew (laughing).

## SHAFTED

I've always been the kind of guy to play with a chip on my shoulder. The turning point for me came after my freshman year, when I tried out for the USA Select Team. I didn't make the team and Drew and Nick did. There were guys who played my position who made the team that I thought I was better than. I remember going home and saying, "Man, something has to change." I'd always worked hard, but at that point I felt like I was going to give everything I had to prove that I could play at a high level, that I was good enough to play in the NBA someday. I was a man on a mission from that point on. I took it to another level after that.

## KIRK & NICK, NICK & KIRK

People at Kansas always associated me with Nick, and vice versa. And that was great. He's a good guy to be linked to. We're really close today, much closer than we were when we walked on campus, when everyone thought we were best friends or related or whatever. I'm really good friends with a lot of the guys I played with. But I've known Nick since we were 16 and playing in AAU ball. We've always been able to relate to each other and talk about stuff. We were both really excited to go to Kansas. We blossomed as players and played on good teams. Being able to go there with him, we'll always look back on those times as the good ol' days. I'll always remember going up to Allen Fieldhouse with him late at night – just the two of us – to play one-on-one. We'd get super-competitive with each other. We didn't argue too much, though. When Nick gets mad he gets kind of quiet. He doesn't say much to you. So there wasn't too much talking going on back and forth. We were just going at each other hard.

## THOUGHTS ON BOSCHEE, GOODEN

Jeff Boschee was the starting point when I got to Kansas, so things were pretty competitive between us in practice. Obviously, I wanted to play, and so did he. I love Boschee. He's a great guy. He's one of the better teammates I've ever had. Even though we were competitive with one another, I don't think there was any ill will or anything. We're still good friends. I don't talk to him very much these days, or at least not as much as I would like to. It just kind of happened that way. Boschee just cared about winning, period. He didn't care if he was playing the point or the two. The year we had that great team, his senior year, we had great chemistry, and it was because of guys like Boschee.

With Drew, you knew something was going to happen every day to make you laugh. He kept things loose. He had a unique personality. But you also knew that, when it was time to play or practice, Drew was going to bring it, because he was super-competitive. He wants to win, so he's going to play hard. That's what you love about him.

I played with Drew in Chicago and, even though we'd been out of college for a while, it was more of the same. I think he had a bet with DeShawn Stevenson to see who could grow the longest beard. When he finally cut it off, it looked like his chin disappeared. He's been through the ringer. He's been on a lot of different teams and traveled a lot. But on game days, you know he's still going to give you 10 rebounds and he's going to do a lot of dirty work. He's a solid pro. He's had some injury problems and he's bounced around a little bit. But he's still one of the best rebounders in the NBA.

## "OUR TEAM"

By the time Drew, Nick and I got to be juniors, we felt like it was our team. If we lost, it was our fault. We took that responsibility seriously. We went to practice every day and tried to set a good example. Our mentality on the road was that winning on the road was so much more fun than winning at home. It was just the challenge of it. To us, the best sound in the world was the dead silence we'd hear after we beat a team in their own arena.

That's the way we were all year. Our whole junior season, we almost felt invincible, like no one could beat us as long as we played a solid game. It was like we knew were going to go out and score 100 or 105 points or 90 points or whatever every single time. We could just score. We played really fast and we had so much confidence. We had the two best big men in college basketball that year and we had Boschee, who doesn't miss when he gets open looks. The style of play, playing fast … it was just hard for teams to keep up with us. It really didn't matter that we were small on the perimeter because we had such good big guys inside.

## RIVALRIES

It was always really important for us to play well against Kansas State and Missouri. We knew how bad our fans wanted us to beat them – and we wanted it, too. Coach Williams always told us that our streak against Kansas State was going to end one year, but that it doesn't have to be today. We took that rivalry very seriously. By the time we got there Missouri had emerged as a pretty good team, but Kansas State was still trying to get going again. We knew every time we stepped out there we were going to get every team's best shot, especially Kansas State, because we knew how bad they wanted to beat us.

The Missouri rivalry was pretty nasty. There were a few incidents I can recall that made it that way, at least for me personally. The whole week before the game, I'd get prank calls from the Antlers. Some of them were pretty vicious. My junior year, my parents were going into the Hearnes Center, and they had to walk by all the students who were lined up, waiting to get into the game. The students actually started throwing stuff at my parents. That made beating them that day even better.

## LAUDING LANGFORD

Aaron and Wayne weren't the only freshmen playing big roles for us my junior year. Time and time again, Keith came up huge. He hit that big 3 to help us beat Nebraska in Lincoln. We wouldn't have gone 16-0 without it. He also played

great in our regional against Illinois and Oregon. Keith could get to the rim on anybody and finish. If we would've had a one-on-one competition, Keith probably would've won. My senior year, he was great. He's definitely an NBA-quality player, without question. The problem is that scouts are always trying to pinpoint a certain position for someone. Keith may not have a set position, but they should still be able to look at him and say, "This guy can ball. We'll find a spot for him." That he's the highest-paid American playing overseas isn't a surprise at all. I always knew he was going to do his thing. He can get to the hole on anyone. He's athletic. He just had that kind of game. He was incredible.

## FINAL FOUR – ACT I

It's hard to explain our game against Maryland in the Final Four. We had beaten some good teams (Holy Cross, Stanford, Illinois and Oregon) to get there and we were rolling early. Then everything just went south. I don't know what it was. Maybe it was because it was the first time we'd been on that big of a stage. We started taking some really bad shots – and Juan Dixon was on fire. Juan is like a little water bug out there. He has good range, he's a great cutter and he has a knack for finishing at the rim. He never stops moving. He was really a unique college player. The other problem for me was that my ankle was jacked up that game. I had hurt it in the first round against Holy Cross and it was still giving me problems two weeks later. I was wearing an ankle brace that felt like it was up to my frickin' knee. I wasn't close to 100 percent that game. After we lost, I remember walking out of the locker room and throwing that ankle brace in a trash can. I never wanted to see it again. We might have been looking ahead a little bit. I don't know. We were young kids. It was really weird feeling after that game. We didn't know if we were going to have the same team back ever again.

## DECISIONS, DECISIONS

Not many people realized it, but I considered leaving after my junior year. I actually considered it pretty hard there for a week or so. I remember going back and forth about it. I was at the point where I felt like I really wasn't ready to leave. I loved playing at Kansas. At the same time, I felt like it was a good window of opportunity for me, because I was projected to go in the first round. I thought about it really hard. I talked to guys like Ben Miller, one of the assistants that I was really close with. I talked to Coach Williams. They didn't put any pressure on me to stay. They were straight shooters. They said if I left they'd be really happy for me, but that they'd really miss me. The reason I came back was because I felt like we had unfinished business. We worked so hard every day to win a championship. I wanted to give it another shot. I felt like we had a good enough team to get a championship for Coach Williams and for ourselves.

## FINAL FOUR – ACT II

With Boschee gone and Drew leaving for the NBA, we struggled a little bit early my senior season, but it didn't take long for us to come around. The year before, we were more talented. But our last year, after the way we started that year and with everything we went through, it enabled us to come together and gel at the end of the year. When we were in the NCAA Tournament my senior year, that was the best we had ever played as a team. At least until we played Syracuse.

Wayne getting hurt earlier in the season may have hurt us. But I don't know if he would've made much difference in the title game. We still would've missed 18 free throws so we still wouldn't have won. That's what was so frustrating. We knew we were better than Syracuse. We just didn't show it. We missed free throws and got in a hole in the first half.

I've put it behind me now. But for four or five years, I tried to make sense of it and I never really could. It bugged me a lot. When you lose a game of that magnitude it sticks with you for a long time. We felt like we were the better team. But 18 free throws … it's pretty easy to explain. We were down by 20 points in the first half and still fought to get back into it.

I passed the ball to Mike Lee at the end for the 3-pointer to force overtime. Some people may think I should've taken the shot myself, but I feel like I made the right play. There was still time left – and Mike was wide open. Hakim Warrick just came over and made a hell of a play on it. I still think our team that year played about as close to its potential as any team I played on there.

The next week was when Coach Williams decided to take the North Carolina job. It was obvious to me what he was going to do. I didn't blame Coach Williams. I just felt bad for the guys that were still there. I didn't really want to go to the meeting when he told everyone. But I went because I respected Coach Williams too much. I wasn't mad at him but I just felt terrible for Aaron and Keith and Wayne and those guys.

Coach Williams has been great to me ever since I left. Every year now, before my first home game, there's always a fax on my chair from him that says, "Best of luck on the upcoming season." I talk to him once or twice a year. If something happens, you can count on him. Once you leave you know you have his support. You appreciate him but he also appreciates your work, too.

## FINAL THOUGHTS

Coming out of high school, the reason I came to Kansas is because I wanted to go to the best school I could where I felt like I had a chance to play. At Kansas I felt like I'd have the opportunity to compete for a championship every year. Even though we never won it, I don't look back on things with any regret. I had the opportunity to play for such a stand-up, honest guy like Coach Williams, who helped me develop as a player and a person.

Staying the extra year in college, not leaving after my junior year – even though I came back to get my education and win a championship and only accomplished one of those two things – I just felt like that whole year really helped me mature. Coach Williams was really demanding. But at the same time he really cares about his players. Looking back on it now, the farther away from it you get, the more you appreciate it.

# CHAPTER 9

# 2003/04 - Present

# BILL SELF

Bill Self replaced Roy Williams as Kansas' head coach in April of 2003. The Jayhawks won the 2007-08 NCAA title under Self, who has also led the program to seven straight Big 12 championships. In his last 13 years as a head coach, Self – who has also coached at Oral Roberts, Tulsa and Illinois – has won 11 conference titles. Self entered the 2011-12 season with a record of 237-46 in eight years at Kansas, including a 107-21 mark in the Big 12. He was chosen National Coach of the Year in 2008-09. Thirteen of Self's Kansas players have been drafted, including nine in the first round. Three others have made NBA teams as free agents. Self and his wife, Cindy, have two children: Lauren and Tyler.

## IN BILL'S WORDS

I remember the first meeting I ever had with the players after I took the Kansas job. All of the guys gathered in a conference room up here in our coaching offices, and everyone was great. We had some laughs, and I told them what my theory was on some different things. It got to the point where everyone was relaxed enough to where Keith said something like, "Hey, can we wear red uniforms every now and then?" It went from serious to light-hearted. The only player who was being standoffish was Wayne. He didn't participate or talk. He just sat there and kept quiet until the very end. All of a sudden, he piped up and said, "I've got a question. What did you tell the players at Illinois when you left?" He had apparently been thinking about that throughout the whole meeting.

I told him that I told my Illinois players that I wasn't choosing to coach other players over them. I was choosing to be at a place that I thought was better for my family over time. I told them that if they were happy I was leaving, sad I was leaving, mad, confused … any emotion was fine. Any emotion was understandable, because basketball was a really big deal there, too.

## STICKING WITH A SYSTEM

Coaches can't coach different styles than what they believe and know. Roy ran motion offense, but the big thing with Roy was that they were very, very good in transition and they scored quite a few points off of their primary or secondary break. I never emphasized that like Roy emphasized it.

Our first teams didn't play as fast as Roy's Kansas teams, but we also didn't have the same personnel. It's easier to play faster when you've got Hinrich and Collison and some of those guys. We didn't have that exact same personnel. So we didn't play as fast as the guys probably thought we should play, but that wasn't who I was.

The first two years were a struggle at times. We had our moments. The first year we weren't very good early on. I remember going out to Nevada, and Kirk Snyder and those guys just killing us. Stanford beat us. Stanford ended up being a No. 1 seed. They were really good. Instead of calling it a struggle, I would describe it as pieces not fitting. There were square pegs in round holes. A lot of it was stubbornness on their part – but probably on my part, too. I could've done things to appease them, but that wasn't something I was interested in.

## THE VETERANS

Aaron, Keith, Wayne and Mike were a unique bunch. They probably thought I didn't respect their past accomplishments as much as I should've, and I probably thought they were spoiled. Those guys were all good, though. Aaron and Wayne were the rocks. They were the best in the locker room.

Aaron is like Eddie Haskell from Leave it to Beaver. Smiling all the time, really nice guy ... but you know he's got something up his sleeve. He's got as good of a personality and is as fun to be around as anyone I've ever coached. He was great for our team. He loves Kansas. He loves to compete, and he loves winning. Assist totals, won-loss record ... he had an unbelievable career here.

Keith was a problem at times, but I liked Keith. I loved his competitive spirit and I loved him on game night. I loved a lot of things about him. The only thing I didn't like about coaching Keith was that things became so frustrating for him health-wise, and I didn't know how to help him. He played his whole senior year on one leg. He didn't have the same bounce and explosion. He knew it, and that really, really frustrated him. When he hurt his knee against Oklahoma his junior year, I don't think he ever got it back. Then he had the microfracture surgery in the offseason that we didn't tell anyone about. It takes about a year to fully recover from that stuff. He was never himself his whole senior year.

Mike Lee and I butted heads big time. I told Mike, "God dang, you should leave. I can't coach you." I remember saying to Aaron, "Is Mike Lee a good kid?" Aaron said, "Oh, coach, he's the best kid." I said, "Is he stubborn? Has he been bad with me?" And Aaron said, "Oh yeah, he's been bad with you." I said, "Then how can you tell me he's a good kid? Because I only see it through my

own eyes, and he's been a real pain." That was early on, though. It turned out Mike Lee was more than just a good kid. Mike Lee was a stud. What made him so good as a person was that exact same stubbornness. That was an attractive quality. Mike was so stubborn. He had to get the last word in on any argument. He should've been an attorney. If he thought he was right, he'd keep fighting you until the bitter end. If you got on him in practice and he thought you were wrong for doing it, then he had a hard time ever forgetting it. A lot of times, I'd get on him on purpose, just to mess with him to see how he'd react. It'd get under his skin. You look at Mike Lee, his senior year, he was our best player against Bucknell. He became an important player for us. He got a lot better.

## JEFF GRAVES

Graves was really a good player, but I had to suspend him for a couple of games for not being very responsible. We had to hide his car from him for about a month. We knew it'd be much easier to keep tabs on him if he didn't have a vehicle. So we took his keys, gave them to a manager and told him to park Jeff's car on the very top floor of the parking garage next to Allen Fieldhouse. We figured he'd be too lazy to walk all the way up those steps looking for it. Even if he had a spare set of keys, he wouldn't be able to find it. We told him we took his car. We said, "Jeff, you're being a jerk, so we're taking your car." He asked us where we put it, and we said, "It doesn't matter. It's in a safe place." He was OK with it.

Jeff kept saying that he had this sleeping disorder called narcolepsy. He said that's why he was having a hard time getting up for class every day. We said, "Jeff, you may be right. So this weekend, on Friday and Saturday night, we're going to check you into Lawrence Memorial Hospital. We're going to have them run a whole gamut of tests so they can find out what the deal is with your sleeping disorder." As soon as he realized he wasn't going to be able to go out and have fun on Friday and Saturday night, he was like, "Oh no, no, no, Coach! I'm fine. I'll be OK." We were like, "Jeff, this is going to be for your own benefit. You need to get checked out." He was like, "I'll be OK, coach. I'll be fine."

I knew Jeff from when he visited Illinois. I liked him a lot. He's a lot of fun. He just didn't have great focus. But when he was playing well, we were tough to beat. He came on strong right at the end and helped us get to the Elite Eight. It was good that we got that far in my first year, but I don't know if I'd say we were pleased, because we were a call away from getting back to the Final Four. We were in overtime against Georgia Tech and clearly had the momentum, but then Keith fouled out on this call that … I mean, gosh almighty, it was a (bad call). Then they made a couple of plays after that to beat us.

## DAVID PADGETT

I was OK with David leaving. I went to David a few weeks before he decided to go and said, "Hey David, I'm hearing you and your family are thinking about leaving. That's fine. But if you care about your teammates at all, you'll let me know soon, so I can go sign somebody else." I said, "I don't want you to leave, but we've got to cover ourselves if you do, and there are a few guys out there who are still available." The only thing that bothered me about him leaving was that he told me after the spring signing period started. But I was OK with him leaving. I think it was a family decision. That's fine. I didn't recruit him. I didn't know the family very well.

It really hurt our guys when David left. We were preseason No. 1 that next year. But we knew we had some holes. It was a big loss when we lost David. We couldn't replace him.

## 2004-05

There was a ton of hype surrounding my second season, because Wayne, Keith, Aaron and Mike were seniors. We started 20-1 that year, with the only loss coming to Villanova in Philadelphia. It was a complete blowout. We were supposed to come back that night after the game, but we got snowed in, so we ended up having about a three-hour meeting at the hotel. They didn't like me that night, and I didn't like them. I was so disappointed, because we quit in that game. But I had to somehow put it behind us, because we had already started league play. I hammered them pretty good that night. I showed them tape, which I found out later on was an NCAA violation, because you can't show them tape of a game on the same day that you played it. So I think I got busted for that. We were just awful that day, though. But that was a coming-out party for Villanova. People forget, but Villanova had more pros than we had. They had Randy Foye and Allan Ray and Kyle Lowry and Curtis Sumpter and Jason Fraser. They had more guys that played in the league than we had. But we had the better team, I thought.

The loss that set us back more so than the Villanova loss happened a few weeks later, against Texas Tech in Lubbock. We were 20-1 overall and 10-0 in the Big 12. In my opinion, we won the game. We had the game won until the questionable travel call on Aaron Miles in front of their bench with about 8 seconds left in double overtime. (Note: It appeared Miles was fouled as three Texas Tech defenders attempted to strip him of the ball after Miles rebounded a missed shot. Kansas led by two points at the time. Texas Tech retained possession on the travel call.) Then a guy that had never made a 3-pointer (Darryl Dora) hit one to beat us at the end, 80-79. That was a big loss for us, because right after that, Iowa State came into Lawrence and upset us. Then we lost at Oklahoma, our third loss in a row. We still had a chance to win the league outright, but Missouri beat us at their place in the last game of the year when Keith got hurt, so we had to share the title.

I think we had been living on borrowed time. I don't think we were ever that good. But because the kids were tough and experienced, they figured out ways to win games. Eventually it just caught up to us. Go back and look at our wins that year: Vermont could've easily beaten us the Fieldhouse. South Carolina could've, too. That was the game when C.J. Giles made a basket for the other team. Somehow we found a way to beat Georgia Tech and Kentucky without Wayne. Eventually, everything just took its toll. We got tired, and the big thing was when Keith got hurt. Keith was awfully good.

## BUCKNELL

Looking back on it, I wish I would've handled Keith differently. Keith wasn't supposed to play against Bucknell. We didn't have any indication that he was ready. But Keith announced to the media the day before the game at shoot-around that he was going to play, despite the fact that he had told us that he was absolutely, positively out. He had told us he was done, at least for that game. He hadn't practiced in two weeks. We had prepared to play without him. But once he told the media he was playing, what were we supposed to do? He was a senior, one of the best players Kansas had had for the previous three or four years. We didn't start him, but we played him. He wasn't effective, but how could he have been? He hadn't done anything. He wasn't healthy. He hadn't practiced in two weeks. That was a scenario I'd never been in before.

Mike Lee kept us in the game. Then the guy for Bucknell made a lucky hook shot from the middle of the lane off the glass to beat us. Then Wayne got a great look at the end and just missed it. It was a shot he makes 60 or 70 percent of the time. My opinion is that we were obviously better than Bucknell – but we weren't a lot better than Bucknell. Without Keith being healthy and the way we were playing at that particular time, we were kind of on a downward spiral. We were definitely better, but we weren't a ton better. As coaches, we knew that.

They played matchup zone, which is something we'd struggled against. It was a good matchup for Bucknell.

## BRANDON RUSH

We lost Wayne, Keith, Aaron and Mike after that year. Then there was the big mess with the J.R. Giddens situation. So we ended up losing our best five players. Plus, we had no momentum. Zero. We couldn't get out of our own way off the court. We had a miserable summer. After the Moon Bar fight, I put a curfew on the guys for the whole summer. They weren't allowed to be out at a bar. For a college kid, that's rough. You can't go anywhere that your friends are going. They didn't like it, but that's OK. I had to do it.

Later that summer, in July, I was sitting over at Okun Fieldhouse in Shawnee recruiting, and I overheard a conversation between two dudes. I didn't even know who they were, but I heard one of them tell the other that Brandon Rush was a qualifier. We had heard all along that he wasn't going to be a qualifier. I'd never talked to Brandon. I didn't know him. I made a call and, out of the blue, Brandon called me back a few days later when I was at lunch at Set 'em Up Jacks in Lawrence. He said, "Yeah, I'll come visit." I said, "What will your mother and grandmother think? I've heard they hate Kansas." He said, "Yeah, they do." So I called them, and they were great. They said, "We don't like Kansas." I said, "Hold on a second. I'm new. You don't know me. I don't know you. Think about how good this could be. Just think about it." They bought in. Brandon came and visited and fell in love with it. He really liked Mario. The next thing you know, he was coming to Kansas. It was probably the least work anyone has ever done on a recruit.

The next step was to get Brandon eligible. We had to go through the NCAA Clearinghouse to make sure everything was OK. It took them a while to figure things out, but they did figure it out. The delay was that there was a school he had attended in Kansas City that was closed down. We had to get documentation from that school, and it just took a while.

Brandon was the best teammate I think we've had since we've been at Kansas. I don't think there's anyone that's ever said anything negative about Brandon Rush. Ever. Everyone liked him. The guys that didn't play, the guys that did … he respected everybody. He never put himself above anyone. Everyone respected his athletic ability, obviously. He was a great kid. Quiet, but fun and mischievous. He'd come up to me in practice and say, "Coach, run such-and-such play and watch Mario. He has no idea what he's doing. He'll screw up." So I'd run it just so Brandon could laugh at Mario.

As talented as he was, Brandon had never really been coached before he got here. He didn't have a clue when it came to X's and O's. When he came on his visit, I put in a tape, and I said, "Brandon, I want you to watch this and tell me why you think this team got scored on. What happened here?" He said, "Coach,

I have no idea." I said, "You can't tell me what breakdown occurred?" He said, "Coach, I have no idea." But he became the best defender we've had since we've been here. He was unbelievably bright, basketball-wise. He just needed to be taught. He picked everything up really quickly. He was so conscientious and he wanted to please so bad that he took great pride in learning and knowing. He didn't want to be one of those kids that would blow things off.

## JEFF HAWKINS

Even with a team loaded with freshmen, we ended up winning the Big 12 title and the Big 12 conference tournament title that year. No one ever talked about it, but one of the main reasons we did so well was Jeff Hawkins.

I love Jeff Hawkins. Hawk is a stud. He's one of the most fun kids I've coached since I've been here. If you remember, I suspended him for a month before his junior year. I put him through crap and he just kept coming back for more. The thing that got lost on Jeff a little bit was how good of a player he was. You're talking about a guy that went 4-for-5 from 3-point range in the 2006 Big 12 championship game against Texas. The thing I'll remember the most about Hawkins is this: He was starting for us when we started out 3-4 his senior year, which is when Mario and those guys were freshmen. We weren't playing well as a team, but he actually wasn't playing bad. Still, he was catching all the blame for us not being good as a team. People thought it was because he was playing and Mario and Julian weren't. So many people made it sound like everything

was his fault, and it wasn't, because those freshmen weren't ready. I'll never forget him coming to me once he thought Mario was ready to play more. He said, "Coach, I think it's time you start the young fella." That just shows you what kind of kid and teammate he was.

## C.J. GILES

We liked C.J. We loved coaching him. I hated to let him go right before his junior season (in the fall of 2006), but the truth of the matter is that he knew the deal. We weren't going to tolerate him making any more poor decisions. He was a sweet kid, a nice kid, a good teammate. It was a sad deal.

I had suspended C.J. that fall for being late to a meeting or missing weights or something. The very first day he came back to practice, there were a bunch of NBA scouts in town to watch us work out. They told us afterward, "C.J. Giles is the best pro prospect in here by far." And that was on a team that had Shady, Brandon, Mario, Sherron, Julian, Darnell, Sasha and those guys. That was his last practice. The incident with the girl happened that night, and we had to move on. *(Note: Giles was issued a citation for misdemeanor battery on a 20-year-old KU student, prompting his dismissal from the team.)*

## FINAL FOUR

When we got to San Antonio in 2008, I put the team on lockdown. We went to a team function on Wednesday night in San Antonio. But after that, they weren't allowed to leave their hotel room floor. We had times set up where their parents could come to their rooms. But they couldn't leave to go see their parents. I didn't want them out amongst the people. I didn't want them down on the streets. I had talked to other coaches who had been there about the best way to handle the situation, and most of them said to quarantine their guys. So we quarantined them. We had a room upstairs where they could have snacks and play video games. They could hang out there, but they couldn't go down into the lobby or anything like that. We had police that wouldn't allow anyone up to their rooms.

I thought we were pretty loose. We practiced for 18 minutes on Sunday before the game. And I remember Bob Knight telling me we went too long. He was at an awards ceremony I had to go to Sunday night. He said, "How long did you practice?" I said, "Eighteen minutes," and he said, "That's too long. I told you not to work them out. Keep them off their feet." But our guys were so ready to play.

## NORTH CAROLINA

All season long, our guys wanted Carolina. Once the brackets came out, they were hoping Carolina kept winning. After they advanced to the Final Four, we were hoping we could hold on and beat Davidson so we could play them in the Final Four. That couldn't have been a better scenario for our guys.

I don't think I ever said a word about Roy to our team at the Final Four. Before we left for San Antonio, Roy called me and said, "Let's make sure we handle things right this week." I'm thinking, "Coach, I'm going to handle it right. I always handle it right." But he didn't say it in a bad way. He just said, "Hey, there are a lot of questions that are going to be asked about the past. Let's just make sure we're on the same page." I said, "We're positively on the same page."

North Carolina had a great team that year. It was the same team that won the national championship the next year. They were the No. 1 overall seed in probably the most stacked Final Four in recent memory. I thought Ty Lawson was just unbelievable. Some people worried that we may come into the game tight, but we were just the opposite. We had been tight the week before against Davidson. We were loose as could be in the Final Four. Those kids were so ready and so hungry. I've never had a team play that well for 12 minutes in a row.

## JOHN CALIPARI

Beating North Carolina put us in the title game against Memphis and John Calipari. I came to Kansas as a graduate assistant in 1985, right after John had left to go to Pittsburgh, so I knew John. It wasn't some major relationship, but we knew each other. When I was at Tulsa, we played St. Joseph's on the road in Philadelphia. John was an assistant with the Philadelphia 76ers that year. He came and talked to my team after the game. We won that night, and he came in the locker room and said, "You guys have no idea what you just did. My best UMass teams couldn't win here." He and Coach Brown were supposed to be at the game together. Coach Brown couldn't make it, but Cal came anyway and then did that for us afterward. He was great. He's a good coach, a great coach. He gets his teams to play hard, and they guard. That was especially the case with his Memphis team that year. Those guys guarded. But we did, too. Those were probably two of the better defensive teams that have played for the national title in a long time. We couldn't score on them. Their length was a killer with us. They had good players with Chris Douglas-Roberts and Joey Dorsey. Those guys were tough, but not as tough as the NBA MVP (Derrick Rose).

## THE GAME

The night before the game, I just watched tape all night with our staff. We talked about what plays would work in certain situations. We came up with a script of the first five or 10 plays we wanted to run. But really, there really wasn't much that went into it.

More than anything that night, I was thinking about what I wanted to tell the guys before we ran out onto the court. I don't think I wrote anything down, but I rehearsed it in my head. I wanted it to be meaningful.

We got off to a terrible start. It was 7-2 or 6-1 or something like that. But after those first few minutes, we really controlled the first half. But we only went into halftime up three or four when we had probably played better than that. They controlled the second half, totally, until the last 2 minutes.

People always ask me what I did to keep us focused when we were losing late, but I don't think it was me. I think what helped them was losing to Bradley and losing to UCLA. Russell and Sasha and Jeremy and Darnell had been on the bench when we lost to Bucknell. And most of our kids had been through some stuff off the court. I've always loved coaching kids that have done something where the odds were stacked against them. We've had guys that have come here where, on the surface, everything looked fine. But when you really get down to it, if these guys weren't tough, they'd have no shot to be here. We had a lot of those guys on that team. To see how they persevered when the deck was stacked against them tells you that they may have something that a lot of people don't.

There were a bunch of things I was proud of that night. Our body language never changed. We never pointed fingers at each other. Shady made an unbelievable 18-footer when we were down by seven. I remember telling them after that, "All we need is a steal and a big play." All of a sudden, Sherron stole the ball and made a play. It wasn't like it was unbelievable coaching.

## MARIO'S SHOT

After Mario's 3-pointer, I haven't seen myself react on tape in any other way except, "Get back! Get back!" Because it's easy for guys to start celebrating and get caught off-guard. But if you watch the tape, Mario makes his shot, and then everybody runs back, points to their man and defends the way they were supposed to defend. There was no jubilation, no celebrating. It was great. Then the horn went off, and our players came into the huddle and said, "It's over!" I was like, "Guys, it's not over." They said, "Coach, it's over!" Then the next three possessions were the best three offensive possessions we had all year. Unbelievable. You can't execute better than that.

Mario had the biggest set of kahunas when it came to those types of plays. Mario Chalmers was the best kid to coach, because he has no memory. He can't remember any bad thing that happens. He only remembers the good stuff. So he could go 3-for-15 and leave the arena thinking, "Man, they couldn't guard me tonight."

## DARRELL ARTHUR

Shady was a freak – an absolute freak athlete. Very competitive. He was never the rebounder we thought he could be. We thought he could be a great rebounder. I don't know if his conditioning was great. He got tired too quick. Still, we've never had a big guy that could run like Shady. We haven't had a big guy that could slide his feet like Shady. When NBA people would come watch our practices, I'd tell Shady, "Go guard the point guard, and pick him up full court." The guard couldn't get it past halfcourt.

Shady was the best player in the national championship game. He had 20 and 10. That's how he should be remembered: Darrell Arthur was the best player in the game when we won the NCAA title. Better than Derrick Rose, better than anyone.

## DARNELL JACKSON

We've had a lot of success stories, but Darnell, as much as anyone else, sticks out. It's incredible what he and that family went through. It's incredible the way he persevered. Look at him now. He's in the NBA. He's been there for three years. Who would've thought that would happen when he first got to school? I'm proud of my home state, but Darnell didn't even make all-state in Oklahoma in high school. Everyone makes all-state down there. When he was here he was driven, and he tried really hard. After the NCAA stuff and after his mother and grandmother got into that accident, he recommitted himself. For a while, we were always nervous that he was going to quit. He tried to one time when he left in the middle of the night and went home. He just needed to be talked to. He didn't want to quit. He had so much guilt on him. He felt like he shouldn't be off playing basketball when his whole family was struggling so bad back home. He thought he should've been back there helping them in some way, shape or form. What he didn't realize was that the best way he could help them was by staying in school.

## SHERRON COLLINS

Sherron was the best point guard, talent-wise, that we've recruited, just from a raw talent standpoint. He's a great kid. He beat all odds. I still think he should be playing professionally and making a lot of money. He had an unbelievable four years for us, and he was certainly our leader the last two. The only reason he didn't start for the team that won the national championship is because he broke his foot. He missed six games early, and he had a great attitude when he came back. He knew what was best for the team, so he came off the bench. He doesn't get enough credit for making a couple of big plays in that national championship game. Without him we would've had no chance to win it.

He was pretty easy to coach once he got rid of his stubbornness. He was one of the most stubborn kids I've ever been around. But it was a good kind of stubbornness in a lot of ways, because he spun that stubbornness into a situation where it was a competitive advantage for him. I don't think I'd want it any other way. He was fun to coach. I knew he'd go to battle every night we played.

I really didn't know what Sherron was going to do after his junior year in regard to the NBA draft. I didn't think he'd be a first-round pick. He had had some knee issues and stuff. His logic for coming back was good. He had a good senior year, although he probably didn't have the kind of senior year we'd hoped he'd have from an individual awards standpoint. But he was the quarterback of a team that went 33-3.

One thing people didn't know about Sherron is that he couldn't lift weights, because whenever he lifted weights, he gained weight. So we spent a lot of time with him doing extra cardio and all that kind of stuff. He was so stubborn that he thought he could play just as well at 220 as he could at 200. We had to drill him and drill him and drill him. His freshman year, he thought he had all the answers. I told him flat-out, if you don't lose this much weight in this amount of time, I'm not going to play you on national television against Boston College at home. He ended up losing all the weight, but he didn't do it in a healthy way. He didn't follow the plan we laid out for him. He'd just say, "I'm not going to eat today," or whatever. But he lost it, and he played in the game, but I hardly played him because he was awful. He didn't have any energy. After the game, he was mad that I didn't play him. I was like, "You're mad at me? You're the one that let your body go. That's not my fault. That's your fault." He was so mad when he left the locker room. He went home for Christmas, and I thought, "I'm not sure he's even going to come back." But he went home for Christmas and he lost more weight, because he was in the gym and he was eating right. I knew right then how much he cared. From that point on, for the most part, he did a really good job of taking care of himself. When we finally got him down to 200, he was almost unguardable.

## MORRIS TWINS

I love Marcus and Markieff, but when they first got here, they'd be the first to tell you that they threatened to go home 20 times. And these were guys that were playing minutes for us. If we hadn't have lost all those guys from the championship team, they wouldn't have played minutes. But they got playing time, and they learned about everything it took to be a major-college athlete. They improved about as much as anyone I've been around, in large part because they learned how to work and how to push themselves and how to take their body to places it had never been before.

If they'd have come back for their senior seasons, Marcus would've been a favorite to be a first-team All-American, and Markieff would've challenged him for Big 12 Player of the Year. I really think that they're both that good. Instead they entered the NBA draft, which made total sense. Draft night was a neat deal, because the entire time that they were there … you just can't imagine how, in a span of seconds, their lives changed immediately. That's what was so cool. There have been a lot of sacrifices made by a lot of people to put them in the position they were in.

## SIGNING PLAYERS LATE

*(Note: Some of the most high-profile players during Self's tenure – Brandon Rush, Darrell Arthur, Xavier Henry, Josh Selby and Ben McLemore – haven't signed until the spring or*

*summer before their freshman year.)*

I wish that we could get our work done before the early signing period. It'd be great to get them all committed and locked up, but that hasn't been how it's worked here as of late. A lot of kids are making their decisions so early that we haven't had a chance to get them here on campus. Kansas isn't the easiest place to get to for kids coming from the coast. Secondly, when you're trying to recruit the best, other big-time programs are trying to recruit those guys, too. We've signed our fair share, but we've missed on some guys, too. That's one reason we've had to go into the spring semester so much lately, because we've missed on some guys. But guys like Ben McLemore, we felt like we were going to get Ben the previous summer. Josh Selby, we were confident about getting him the previous fall. Even though they didn't sign or commit publicly, we felt really good about our chances with them. We waited on them because we felt like we were in good shape with them.

## COACHING HIGH-PROFILE, NBA-CALIBER PLAYERS

I never feel any pressure when I'm coaching a kid who is supposedly good enough to play in the NBA, mainly because I don't make any promises when I sign them. I want them all to do well. We don't tell recruits, "We're going to build this around you and we're going to put the focus on you." We tell them all, "You're going to be given an opportunity, and we're going to do what's best for our team. But if you play like we feel you're capable of playing, that's going to be best for us, and we'll utilize you." Every coach wants to see his most talented guys perform the best. At the same time, we're not playing to keep guys happy. We're playing to win.

I loved seeing Xavier and Josh play well, because in all honestly, when Xavier and Josh were at their best, it was best for our team. If Josh hadn't have been injured, he would've been one of our best players. But with injuries and suspensions and missed practices, he never really had a fair chance. With Xavier, the vast majority of the time, he was playing 30 minutes a game, because that's what was best for Kansas.

Those kids are under a lot of pressure – but all of our kids are under pressure. The kids in our program that aren't projected to be lottery picks are under pressure, too. I don't mean that in a bad way. It's a good thing. There's pressure to play at Kansas. There's pressure to play at North Carolina and Duke. There's pressure to play football at Oklahoma and Texas. You've got to deliver. That's what history and tradition says is supposed to happen. There is obviously pressure there, but with those kids that are expected to be lottery picks, they've had pressure put on them subconsciously with everyone telling them what they should be and what they should do and how high they should go. They can't help but let it get to them a little bit. I thought they both handled it well. Josh didn't struggle because of pressure, though. It was because of health.

## FRUSTRATIONS

One thing that can be difficult at Kansas is that we don't have a recruiting base. Our recruiting base is elsewhere. When you have to go into somebody else's backyard and beat them on their homegrown players ... that's hard. I wish we could recruit three kids out of the Kansas City area every year. That's how the majority of the schools do it. Duke and North Carolina are national recruiters, but there are a lot of good players in that state. UCLA has players in their area, so they have a home base.

The other thing is that you're under the microscope. Sometimes you make simple decisions that are best for your team, but when you do that, the media are all over it so much and it gets so much publicity that it brings more negative attention to your program than positive. Case in point, we suspend a kid for two games for not acting right. That's what you should do. But nationally, the story becomes, "What's wrong with the character of the kids at Kansas?" That shouldn't be the case just because a coach made a decision to help his team. We should be able to handle our guys without it being so scrutinized. Sometimes, the issues simply aren't that deep. At Illinois, I didn't start Frank Williams, the Big Ten Player of the Year, for a couple of games. All you have to say at Illinois is that it was a coach's decision. Here, things like that get dissected so much on the Internet and by the bloggers and things. They want to read into it more than what it is.

We've had two major incidents since we've been here – the Moon Bar fight and the fights between our players and the football team. One of them was serious, the other one wasn't serious, but it could've have been serious. The fight with the football team got so much national attention that it made people view our program as something that it wasn't. We're preseason No. 1, and all anyone wanted to talk about was the football incident, which was totally unfair. I've never questioned the character of our guys. But whenever you suspend a guy or whenever you bench someone, the character of our guys comes into question. It shouldn't be that way. That's one of the toughest things for me to deal with as a coach. But that's what happens when you play at a place where the attention is so strong.

One thing I believe is this: You shouldn't complain about the negative attention you get if you're going to relish in the positive attention. You can't say, "I want all the attention" and then pick and choose when you get it.

## NCAA TOURNAMENT LOSSES

We've lost four NCAA Tournament games to mid-majors: Bucknell, Bradley, Northern Iowa and VCU. When you don't have a ton of time to prepare – in some case, it's only one day – those things can happen. I know, because I've coached at places like that. Those schools can beat Kansas. They can beat Kentucky. They can beat Carolina and Duke if the draw is right. Unfortunately, we've had three of our worst performances of the year in those games. The

Bradley game didn't bother me quite as much, because we were so young, and they were really good.

The Northern Iowa game ... I was a little nervous, because I knew how good they were and how sound they were. I was very nervous for the Bucknell game, because we weren't a good basketball team when we played Bucknell. We were a tired team with a bunch of holes, and they played matchup zone, and we struggled against teams that did that because our outside shooting was so inconsistent.

The two that hurt the most are VCU and Bucknell. The VCU game was more hurtful to me, because it was set up for us to go to the Final Four. The Bucknell game, nothing was set up for us. That was in the first round of the tournament. Northern Iowa, even though we were a No. 1 seed, it wasn't necessarily set up, although maybe it was going to get that way.

But against VCU, everything was set up for us. If we win, we're in the Final Four and we're playing a No. 8 seed (Butler). They were really good but, again, it was a No. 8 seed. I know I always say seeds are overrated, but that was a team that we could've beat. If we would've won that game, we'd have been favored in the championship game no matter who we played (Kentucky or Connecticut). So the VCU loss really hurt. They were really good, and we were really bad. We shot it miserably. We turned it over. Markieff Morris is an excellent player, and he had seven turnovers in the first half. Brady and Tyrel, collectively ... one of them led the league in 3-point shooting and the other one had been in the top 10 for three years. But in that game we were 2-for-21 from behind the arc. As coaches we didn't do a great job by any means. It was a total team effort. We didn't come to play, and we let them get comfortable. You can't let that happen.

I was really hurt by the loss initially, like we all were. Then the hurt becomes anger. Then you strap it up and get back after it. That's where we are right now.

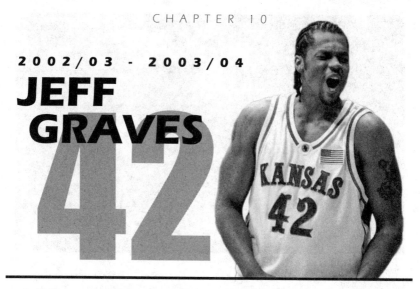

# CHAPTER 10

# 2002/03 - 2003/04
# JEFF GRAVES
## 42

J eff Graves played just two seasons at Kansas after transferring from Iowa Western Community College, but his career in Lawrence was a memorable one. Filling in for an injured Wayne Simien, Graves was the X-factor behind the Jayhawks' march to the 2003 NCAA title game, where they fell 81-78 to Syracuse. Graves scored 16 points and snared 16 rebounds in the loss. He considered entering the NBA draft after the season but instead chose to play his senior year under new coach Bill Self. Graves got off to a rocky start in his final season, but he hit his stride just in time to lead Kansas to the Elite Eight. A native of Lee's Summit, Mo., the 6-foot-9, 260-pound Graves has played in the NBDL and for numerous organizations overseas.

## IN JEFF'S WORDS

I had a bunch of Division I coaches recruiting me before my sophomore season at Iowa Western Community College, but when it came time to pick a school, I narrowed my list down to Kansas and Illinois – or, as some people saw it, Roy Williams and Bill Self.

I took my official visit to Illinois a week or two before I flew back home to visit Kansas. As I was leaving Champaign, the last comment Bill Self made to me was, "Hey now, don't go back to your hometown and get wined and dined and sign with Roy-Boy." I was like, "OK, I won't." But sure enough, I went to Kansas, got wined and dined and signed with Roy-Boy. Self called me a few days later and said, "Graves, you big son of a bitch, if we play you, we're going to double-team you. You won't even touch the ball." He was laughing and joking about it. He was cool, a good sport. Then what do you know … a year later, he's the coach at Kansas. I thought, "OK, this coach recruited me. He knows me. We'll have a good relationship. It'll be a more of a relaxed environment around here than it was under Roy."

I was wrong.

## WEIGHT ISSUES – THE REAL STORY

When I showed up at Kansas before my junior year, it was no secret that I was overweight. I knew everyone was upset with me. All throughout the fall, people gave me a hard time about it and cracked little jokes. After a while it started to piss me off, because I didn't have any control over it. I almost lost my life in a wreck. I literally almost got run over by a semi, an 18-wheeler. The newspapers said I had some sort of minor concussion, but it was much more than that. No one ever realized that I had been in a major, major accident.

It all happened as a friend and I were driving back to Lawrence from Lee's Summit around 8 on a Sunday evening in early September of 2002. We were on Interstate 70, and I was passed out in the passenger seat. I woke up and saw that my friend – the driver – was passed out, too. I started shaking him and saying, "Wake up! Wake up!" I guess I freaked him out, because he woke up and lunged forward, and all of his weight mashed down on the gas pedal. We did a 360 in the middle of the highway and hit both guardrails before skidding into a ditch on the shoulder of the road. My seatbelt snapped, and I ended up in the backseat. I hit my head on the window. I had a goose egg the size of a baseball on my head. When I got out of the car I was dazed. I staggered to the edge of the shoulder of the highway and this semi almost hit me. The driver started honking his horn, and I stepped back just as I was about to get side-swiped. The wind from the semi was so strong that it blew me back and knocked me off my feet. I was out of it. I ended up in the back of an ambulance.

## JEFF GRAVES: TRACK STAR

For the next couple of weeks I couldn't do much of anything. When I finally started feeling better I stepped on the scale and it said I weighed 293 pounds. I was like, "Oh my God. How did I gain all of that weight?" Before the wreck I was about 260.

Coach Williams wasn't happy. He said a bunch of negative things and told the media I wasn't an official member of the team yet because I couldn't pass his preseason conditioning test, which was 6 ½ laps around the track in 12 minutes. Nick Collison even made some comments in the paper questioning my desire. I hung all of those quotes up on my wall and used them for motivation.

Over the next two months I lost about 50 pounds. I felt like a marathon runner. I was getting up at 6 in the morning and running all the way to Massachusetts Street and back. The crazy part about it was that Coach Williams was running with me. Each and every morning, he got up and ran with me until I was finally in good enough shape to pass that test. Looking back on it, the transformation I went though was pretty amazing. I did a complete 180, and it was all because of Coach Williams. I felt like I got to know him really well through all of that. That's why I was so hurt when he left. I looked at him like a father figure. I'm not close with my dad. I told Coach Williams about how I was raised by a single black mom with no male role model and implied that I needed his support. I needed a good pat on the back from time to time. I told him I can accept criticism and punishment when I do something wrong – but I probably won't do a lot of things wrong if I get some encouragement every now and then.

## PLAYING FOR ROY

Coach Williams was always pretty intense, but sometimes, when he got really mad and chewed someone out, it was tough not to laugh. There was one day in practice when we were running a play where we were supposed to set a screen for Kirk so he could shoot. But instead Bryant Nash got the ball and shot it himself. Coach Williams was so mad he was shaking. He was fumbling with his whistle, trying to get ahold of it so he could put it in his mouth. When he finally did he blew it as hard as he could for what seemed like 10 or 20 seconds. Then he said, "Everybody, meet our new All-American. Not Kirk Hinrich – but Mr. Bryant Nash!" Then he really lit into him.

I got it pretty bad one day, too. Practice had just ended, but most of the players were still on the court, putting up extra shots. But I had gotten my extra shots in before the workout, so I went into the locker room and started eating these brownies that were in my locker. Someone had made them for me and given them to me that day. All of a sudden I turn around and Roy is standing there with his jaw dropped and his arms dangling at his side. He said, "Graves, what the hell is going on in here? Everyone else is out there shooting, and you're in here eating a flippin' brownie!" With my mouth full of chocolate I was like, "Sorry, Coach." Then I ran back out to the court and got some extra shots up. I thought since I lost all that weight I deserved a few brownies. I guess he didn't agree.

## IN THE SPOTLIGHT

In a lot of ways, playing at Kansas is like playing in the NBA. Everyone knows who you are. They're watching your every move. You have to be careful with everything you do and say. Even then – even when you're careful – there are still going to be false rumors about you. I hardly ever drank when I was at Kansas. I just wasn't much of a drinker. But I still liked to go out and be a part of the nightlife scene. I'd be like Chad Ochocinco, just standing there with my orange juice and cranberry drink, and people would think I was drinking alcohol and label me as a "partier." Not once did I ever show up to a practice smelling like alcohol. I knew how to have a good time without drinking.

Another time someone started a rumor about me getting arrested, which wasn't true at all. My brother, Robbie, and I were driving down K-10 back to

Lawrence, and he got pulled over for speeding. He had a warrant out for his arrest because of an unpaid parking ticket or something. The officer told him, "I've got to bring you in." We were all standing outside the car and I said, "Officer, before you take him to jail, could you help me get to practice? I'm about to be late." So the officer put Robbie in the back of the patrol car and then let me drive Robbie's car to practice. He gave me a police escort all the way to Allen Fieldhouse with my brother cuffed in the backseat.

## MEANWHILE, BACK ON THE COURT ...

Once I lost all that weight I could feel myself getting better and better. I was banging with Collison every day in practice – he's got the best footwork of any big man I've ever faced – and I could see all the hard work I had done with Roy was really paying off. Before practice, during practice, after practice ... I was going hard all the time. I was so obsessed that my friends outside of basketball were asking me if I was crazy. That's what it takes, though. When Wayne Simien hurt his shoulder midway through the season, I was ready.

It sucked that I ended up getting my big break because Wayne was injured and out for the year. It's never good when something like that happens to any of your teammates, especially a good guy like Wayne. But I seized the opportunity. Wayne was out. We didn't have many big men. It was time to step up my game. By the time we got to the NCAA Tournament, I had been putting up double-doubles and really felt confident. We beat Duke in the Sweet 16 and then I played really well (13 points, 15 rebounds) in the Elite Eight against Arizona. The next week, we beat Marquette so bad in the first game of the Final Four that all of us were looking at each other saying, "Dwyane Wade who?" We were playing so well. That's why I still can't believe we lost that last game.

## SYRACUSE

The main thing I remember Coach Williams telling us all season long was to "leave everything on the floor." I don't think we did that against Syracuse. I don't think Nick and Kirk played their best. Maybe they were distracted, maybe they were nervous because they were seniors and everyone expected them to do something big. Whatever it was, I know it wasn't intentional. But something wasn't right that night. Nick missed seven free throws. I hadn't seen him miss seven free throws all year long in practice. Kirk shot almost 50 percent from 3 that year but he was only 3-for-12 against Syracuse – and then he's passing to Michael Lee at the end instead of taking the big shot himself. We designed that play at the end for him. It would've been a tough shot because he had a defender on him. But he could've made it. He'd been making them all year. But instead the ball ends up in Michael Lee's hands. What was that about? What was going on? I didn't understand it. There was just something weird about the whole thing.

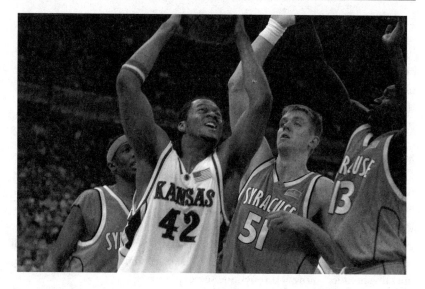

I went off once we got back to the locker room. I threw a trash can. I said, "That was some bulls**t. We talked about leaving everything on the court. We didn't do it." It was a highly emotional time for everyone. We just all showed it in different ways. Some people were quiet, some were crying. Others just sat there looking at the ground. I had put all of my blood, sweat and tears into that season. People can't say I slacked off. I busted my ass every day. I ran after every practice. Some of that was because I brought it on myself. But all of it helped me in the long run. I balled out that game: 16 points, 16 rebounds. No one can say I didn't give it my all. When we were done, I wanted to walk right back out there and play another game, right then and there. I was like, "Make them give us a rematch."

My life probably would've been a lot different if we would've beat Syracuse. I told my mom before we played that night that I was going to declare for the draft if we won. Most of the mock drafts at that time had me going in the first round. If we didn't win, I was going to go back for my senior year for her. Winning that night would've changed a lot of people's lives forever. Keith was going to leave, too. It's strange to think about how things may have turned out for me if the score had been reversed.

Still, overall, I'll always remember that week – the Final Four – as the most fun time of my life. It's something no one can ever take away from me. Thinking about it gives me chills to this day. Getting police escorts everywhere made you feel like the president. The crowd was so big and so loud. Coaches tell you to lose yourself in the moment, and everything on the court will come like second nature. It really does. I didn't hear anybody. I was talking to myself in my head.

In some ways, eight years later, that game still pisses me off. I was happy when the 2008 team won the championship, but in the back of my head I was thinking, "That could've been us." At the same time, I've got a daughter now that's 2 ½. She's changed my whole perspective on life. I don't really have any pent-up anger or frustrations anymore. If anything I'm just thankful to have had a chance. We didn't win the championship, but we played for it. That's something to be proud of, too.

## ADIOS, ROY!

A week after the Final Four, Coach Williams told us he was leaving. Wayne and some of those guys seemed so shocked. They must've had their eyes closed because, to me, it had been obvious the whole week just through the way he was acting. He kept singling out Nick and Kirk when he talked to the team and wasn't showing everyone else quite as much love. Roy and Wanda were sitting behind Jeff Hawkins and me on the plane back from New Orleans, and I kept telling J-Hawk in my fake Coach Williams voice, "He's-a-leavin! Ol' Roy and Wander are-a-leavin' us, J-Hawk!" At the time I couldn't understand why someone would stay somewhere all of those years, build something so great and then just leave. But looking back on it now, I can understand exactly why he left. I'm not mad at him for it. Like I said, I appreciate Coach Williams and what he did for me.

## BIG MISTAKE?

For me personally, Roy's timing couldn't have been any worse. It's easy to see now that I should've entered the draft after my junior year. I had that big championship game, I was playing well and my name was hot. The problem was that I didn't have anyone to tell me about sports agents or testing the waters. I didn't know how any of that worked. No one told me about anything. People can say, "You were your own man. You should've looked out for yourself." Maybe, but there was obviously someone there advising guys like Nick and Kirk and Wayne. How come I wasn't getting any help? At that point in time, I never felt like anyone cared enough about me to give me that kind of advice. People couldn't wait to criticize me or throw me under the bus for being late to a practice, but once I turned things around and did something good, no one was there to help. I just wish I would've been given more information about how I could leave or declare – or at least explore the option. I just wanted to be on equal footing with everyone else.

## BUTTING HEADS WITH BILL

I was actually kind of excited when Kansas hired Bill Self. I thought he was cool during the recruiting process the previous year and figured it'd be a good situation for me, but that season turned out to be pretty difficult.

Coach Self told me all the things I needed to hear at the beginning: "You're going to be a senior. We're going to make this all about you. You'll have plenty

of opportunities to shine. If you come back you'll get to do this and that." A lot of things were said and promises were made. But then someone else (David Padgett) started getting the things I was promised. Coach Self will probably say that I brought it all on myself by being late to practices and stuff. But I mainly started doing that once I realized I wasn't going to get what was promised to me. As a young man, a young athlete, I needed that support and backing. When it's not given to you, it feels like someone is stepping on your back. Eventually you just turn your shoulders away from that person because you feel like they don't care all that much.

## BOOT CAMP

We really started to find out how tough Coach Self was during Boot Camp right before the season. Everyone hated it – especially me. We had to be on the court by 6 a.m. – and I'm not a morning person. There were times when Coach Dooley was outside my room, pounding on my door for me to wake up. I had the deadbolt locked so he couldn't get inside. Another time they had the assistants and the managers walking all across campus trying to find me in the middle of the day, but I was in the locker room the whole time, passed out in the corner because I was so tired from everything we'd done that morning.

Here's a story no one has ever heard: You know how we had that Jayhawk emblem right in the middle of the locker-room carpet, the one no one is supposed to even step on? Well, one time I was in the locker room all by myself after Boot Camp. I was lying there, so tired and so worn out that I felt sick. All of a sudden I was like, "Uh-oh!" I leaned over and threw up, and some of it splattered onto the Jayhawk. There was nothing I could've done. It came so fast that I couldn't hold it. I ran and grabbed some towels and got down on my hands and knees, scrubbing until it was all gone. No one ever saw me. No one ever knew.

## 2003-04

I hurt my knee the summer before my senior year and was getting cortisone shots before every game. I probably should've redshirted, but when I brought it up to Coach Self in December, he said it was too late. As players we weren't having nearly as much fun as we'd had the year before under Roy. Self was trying to put his system in, and most of the guys weren't buying into it. That was also the year J.R. Giddens came in.

J.R. was pretty arrogant. One time I got into it with him in the locker room. I grabbed him and slammed him up against the wall and said, "You need to stop with all this cockiness and arrogance. People already know who you are. This is KU. You don't have to make the brand name. The brand name speaks for itself. You don't have to do all this extra showboating and stuff." I think most people liked J.R., though. He wasn't a bad guy.

For a team with a new coach, we actually ended up having a decent year. We finished second in the Big 12 and made a nice run in the NCAA Tournament. The game I remember the most is our win against Alabama-Birmingham in the Sweet 16. Mike Anderson was their coach, and they had just beaten Kentucky in the second round. Everyone was talking about how fast they were and about how we were going to struggle against their "Forty Minutes of Hell" defense and their press. We weren't worried at all, though, because Coach Self had us prepared. The day before the game, he made our starters practice against eight scout team guys, eight defenders at once. Their whole job was to trap us and swarm us and steal the ball. It was five-on-eight. When we got on the court against UAB the next day, it was easy. We destroyed their press. Coach Self is a good coach. He proved it that game.

We lost to Georgia Tech in overtime two days later. I still can't believe we lost to that team and that big, goofy center, Luke Schenscher.

Even though I finished the season strong, I still didn't have a good enough year to get drafted. I remember a month or two later, I was up at Allen Fieldhouse with a friend. We went into the basketball offices and ran into Coach Self. I had a bad outlook on things at that time. I didn't know what I was going to do. I told him, "I regret not leaving after my junior year." He looked at me funny and said, "Not leaving? Where were you going to go?" I told him I would've been a top 10-15 draft pick that year. He scrunched up his face and made his expression like he couldn't believe what I was saying. He was like, "Jeff, you wouldn't have been a first-round draft pick." I still can't believe he said that to me. It hurt. I had 16 and 16 in the NCAA title game. I was in tip-top shape. I knew what people were saying. I knew what I could've done.

## BOUNCING AROUND

Not long after I left Kansas, I tore my ACL in an all-star charity game with a bunch of local celebrities in Kansas City. I sat out a year and then started taking advantage of some opportunities. I played summer league ball with the Los Angeles Lakers a few times and went to camp with the Spurs at the same time that Keith Langford was there. I've been close a few times but still haven't made it. I've been in the NBA D-League in Idaho, which was rough because even the top D-League players only make $25,000 or $30,000.

I've also played in Turkey, Slovenia, Croatia and Latvia. Most overseas teams pay pretty well. In Turkey I was making $25,000 a month. It's definitely a culture shock, though. When I first got on the airplane to go to Turkey, the smell was absolutely terrible. I thought maybe it was the plane, but I stuck my nose outside the door and everything smelled fine, so it was obviously the people inside the plane. Some people don't wear deodorant over there. The Americans on the team would make fun of the Turkish guys. We teased them that they took shower pills. They would walk into the shower and do a 360 to get their hair wet and then walk right out – without soaping or anything. We were like, "Man, do you guys just take shower pills that magically get you clean?" I've had fun in most all of those overseas countries, though. The key is to be open-minded and embrace the culture. There's no reason to be arrogant or cocky.

I tore up my knee in Croatia and had to have surgery again. I've had three knee procedures in the last 2 ½ years and am finally ready to come back. I've still got a lot of basketball left in me. I'll have to start out overseas, but I still think I can play in the NBA. I've played against some of the big centers like Tim Duncan. They're great players, but they're string beans. I can hold my own against them physically, but it's all up to me.

One thing I've learned is that who I am isn't enough. Saying I'm Jeff Graves, the guy from KU who played in the national championship game, isn't going to get me anywhere. I need someone else backing me, someone in my corner, just like so many of the other players have. A Golden State Warriors scout told me, "Jeff, it's not about who you are, it's about who you know." The NBA is political, just like everything else. No one there cares that I went to Kansas.

I know one thing, though: I'm proud of it. I had some good times there and some bad times, but all of them combined helped make me who I am today. The best part about Kansas isn't the basketball. It's the friends you make and the relationships you build just because you're a Jayhawk. I kick it with Lester Earl all the time, and I didn't even play with him, but we click because we're KU guys. We're family. I made a lot of memories in Lawrence. A lot of things happened and it all went by so fast. It's an experience I'll be thankful for for the rest of my life.

# CHAPTER 11

## 2003/04
# DAVID
# PADGETT

D avid Padgett is a 6-foot-11 McDonald's All-American who was signed by Roy Williams in the fall of 2003. Padgett, however, never got to play for Williams, as the coach left for North Carolina the following spring. Padgett played in 31 games for Kansas during his one season under Bill Self in 2003-04. He averaged 6.5 points and 4.5 rebounds in 19.2 minutes for a squad that reached the Elite Eight. He is best remembered by Kansas fans as the player who hit the game-winning shot to beat Missouri in the final game at the Hearnes Center. Padgett transferred to Louisville after the season. He averaged 11.8, 9.5 and 11.2 points during his three seasons with the Cardinals. Padgett played briefly overseas and is now an assistant coach at IUPUI.

### IN DAVID'S WORDS

I found out Roy Williams was leaving Kansas on ESPN. It was my senior year of high school and I had signed with KU the previous fall. I was sitting at home and either my mom or my dad called. They were at work and they said "Turn on the TV." It was obviously the big story. I was a little disappointed that I didn't get a phone call before the announcement was made, but I didn't have any hard feelings or anything.

Roy ended up calling me that night. I didn't speak to him because I was pretty upset. But I called him back a day or two later, and he pushed me pretty hard to honor my commitment to Kansas. He wasn't trying to steer me in a different direction. He didn't say, "Hey, you should think about coming to North Carolina." He didn't do any of that. He said, "I still think you need to honor your commitment and go to Kansas. Obviously you get along with the players really well. It's still a good fit for you."

## A PLACE IN KU HISTORY

When I hear people talking about the greatest rivalries in college basketball, the same ones always get mentioned: Duke-North Carolina, Kentucky-Louisville and a few others. I was only at KU for one year, but I can say with confidence the Kansas-Missouri is right there in that mix.

My most memorable game at Kansas came when we played at Missouri in the last game of the regular season. It was also the last game Missouri would ever play at the Hearnes Center. The thing I remember about that trip is that we had a police escort going to the hotel. Being a freshman, I was like, "Wow, what's going on here?" I had never seen anything like that. And I'm pretty sure someone snuck in the hotel and set off a fire alarm in the middle of the night before the game. The atmosphere at the arena was crazy. It was electric, which was fitting because it was a hell of a game.

It was back and forth the whole way. The score was 82-82, and we had the ball with the chance for one final shot. We were either going to win the game right there or we were going to go to overtime. The play was for Keith to freelance and try to get a basket. He got the ball at the top of the key, but they double-teamed him. When that happened, I made a cut, because it was my defender that went and helped. Keith passed it to me. I caught it on the baseline and I knew I had to shoot it quick. I turned and got it off before the horn sounded. Arthur Johnson tried to block it and almost did. It was a line drive shot. I don't know how it went in, but it did.

The next few days I remember walking around on campus and a bunch of people coming up to me and telling me, "Great shot! Congrats on the win!" It was a huge deal to beat Missouri – but that year it may have been even bigger. Even when we played them at home at Allen Fieldhouse and their players walked onto the court, it wasn't just a normal boo. Our fans really didn't like them. They genuinely despised them. It was an atmosphere of hatred.

## GOOD EXPERIENCE

I had a good time during my one year at Kansas. A lot of people talk about how some of the returning players were frustrated because they were playing for a new coach. But I'm sure there was frustration on the other side, too. Coach Self was trying to implement his style, which had been very successful for him. But he also had guys who had been to two Final Fours and were used to playing a certain way. All in all we still had a pretty good year. I remember playing in the Elite Eight and what a great experience that was. Sure, there were some tough times. But there are tough times everywhere. People just needed some time to get used to each other.

Jeff Graves and I competed for a starting job. He and I actually got along really well. At first he may have been a little bothered because I was coming in, and his spot wasn't guaranteed. He had kind of waited the year before, too,

playing behind Nick Collison. I always figured I'd handle my business, he'd handle his and whoever earned it at the end of the day would get the starting nod. I ended up starting 20-something games that year. There were times when I would play well and he wouldn't and vice versa. It ended up working out fine.

We had so much talent on that team. Aaron had started in two Final Fours. He ran the show. I enjoyed playing with Wayne quite a bit. I felt like we played well together. I was a pretty good passer, and he was obviously a very good post player. We fed off each other. It was a good situation because I could just come in and play and not have any pressure on me. There were three or four other guys out there who were going command the majority of the attention. J.R. Giddens struggled a little bit to adjust to the college game compared to high school. In high school, guys are allowed to take 30 shots a game, whereas college is more structured. But by the end of the year we all started to figure each other out pretty well. The whole team was pretty close on and off the court. There weren't a bunch of different cliques and groups. Everyone seemed to have a pretty good relationship with one another. They were all good guys and easy to be around. We turned into a pretty good team.

## TRANSFER

Throughout my senior year of high school I couldn't wait to get to Kansas. I was excited about playing for Roy Williams. They made it to the national finals the year before and I was looking forward to playing a big part in helping them get back there. When Roy left, one of the things I was most disappointed about was that I might have to go through the recruiting process all over again. It wasn't something I really enjoyed. It wasn't too bad the second time around, though. As soon as Coach Self got the job he came out and visited with myself and my parents. After that I really didn't look anywhere else. We felt good about our meeting with Coach Self, and I had spoken to some of the other guys who were coming back and the younger guys who were in my class. We decided that we wanted to make it work.

Unfortunately, after playing there for a year, I didn't think the situation was a very good fit. I didn't have any hostility toward any of the players or coaches. I just felt like, to be successful as a player, I needed to go somewhere else. It was tough. I'm sure some of those other guys will say the same thing. You get recruited to play for a coach who uses Style A and then you end up with a coach who uses Style B and it's not for you. It wasn't personal. It was all basketball-related.

It wasn't a deal where I was like, "I don't believe in high-low so I'm not going to stay here." It was more about the way Coach Williams coaches and the success he had had with post players, whether it was Nick or Drew or whoever. He was somebody I wanted to play for because I thought he'd give me the best chance to be successful. It was a basketball decision. If I had to go back and do it all over again I'd do it the same way.

I told Coach Self, and it became public with about a month to go until the end of school. I didn't want to wait until the summer, because that was going to screw up their recruiting. I didn't want to be there for a month knowing I was going to leave without them knowing. That wouldn't have been right. I flew out to Reno one weekend and came back on a Monday and told them. It wasn't easy going to school there for a month because everyone knew. But I figured that was the best way to handle it.

I caught a lot of heat for my decision. There were some people who weren't happy about it, probably because they didn't understand. I never held a grudge or anything. It's not like I turned on the TV after I left, watched Kansas play and rooted for them to lose. It wasn't like that at all. They have passionate fans that really love their basketball. The fact that they didn't want to see me go means that they liked me as a player. I chose to take that as a compliment.

## NEW HOME

When Coach Williams found out I was leaving Kansas he tried to recruit me a little bit, but I just wanted to get away from the whole thing. Every time I've run into him or spoken with him since then, it's been fine. When we played North Carolina my senior year he said nothing but great things and he wished me luck.

I found a great home in Louisville and I had a great relationship with Coach Pitino. Sometimes things just work out certain ways for a reason. I got to go to a Final Four, even though I couldn't play that year, and I played in another Elite Eight. I met my wife, Megan, in Louisville, and Coach Pitino and I are still very close to this day. Kansas has obviously had a lot of success. Even though it didn't work out, the experience I had at Kansas was a good one, on and off the court.

# CHAPTER 12

# 2003/04 - 2004/05
# J.R.
# GIDDENS

J.R. Giddens is an Oklahoma City native who played for Kansas from 2003-05. He averaged 11.3 points as a freshman and 10.1 points as a sophomore but was kicked off the team following a highly-publicized bar fight in Lawrence in May of 2005. Giddens and five others were stabbed during the brawl. Giddens then transferred to the University of New Mexico, where he earned Player of the Year honors in the Mountain West Conference in 2007-08. The Boston Celtics selected Giddens with the 30th overall pick in the 2008 NBA draft. He played in 38 games in two seasons with the Celtics and New York Knicks and has since spent time in the NBDL and overseas.

## IN J.R.'S WORDS

Once I transferred to New Mexico, the main thing I missed about Kansas was the fans and how much they loved basketball. One night my senior year, my friend called and said, "J.R., you've got to come over to my house right now. This girl is over here and she doesn't believe that I know you. She goes to Kansas, but she's in town visiting her friend. She wants to meet you." It was a little after midnight, but I went over there. As soon as I walked into the room, this girl looked broke down in tears. She was even shaking a little bit, like she was in awe or something. I gave her a hug, and she just held me there for a while. She wouldn't let go. Later on I told my friend that a lot of Kansas fans were like that, although that's probably the craziest thing I remember – other than running through the tunnel at Allen Fieldhouse and having girls slap their picture in my hand with a phone number on the back and a message that says, "Call me."

## SMITTEN WITH ROY

Even though I played for Bill Self, I was actually recruited to Kansas by Roy Williams. The main thing I remember about Roy was the aura he had. His overall presence was so commanding when he walked into the room. He reminded me of the guy in the Fantastic Four with the flame around him. When Roy Williams called me over to his house and cooked me waffles with whipped cream and sausage, I definitely had to commit to the Jayhawks. I committed later that night. I was obviously in awe of Roy Williams.

During the recruiting process, my dad and I asked Roy about the North Carolina job. We wanted to know if there was a part of him that still wanted to go back there. He said he'd been offered the job many times before, but he wasn't going to go. He said he'd walked around Kansas and dipped his feet in the water fountain and thought long and hard about it. He knew Kansas was where he wanted to be. I can't fault him, though. Things change. Something could've happened within in his family or in his life that caused him to make that decision. Me not having all the details, it wouldn't be fair for me to judge him.

## DECISIONS, DECISIONS

I slightly considered trying to get out of my letter-of-intent and re-opening my recruitment once Roy left. I was at the Michael Jordan Capital Classic, and people were talking about how he was leaving. I was like, "I just talked to him. He's not leaving." Then I see on ESPN that he's gone. It was a very frustrating time. But with Bill Self being an Oklahoma guy and me being from Oklahoma, I figured things would work out well. I remember asking him a specific question. I said: "I feel like I'm a pair of shoes that you inherited. They'll do the trick, but is this the pair you wanted?" He said, "If I could pick a pair of shoes, J.R., this is the one I'd pick." I was happy with that comment, so I went to Kansas. From there we built an "interesting" relationship.

## MIKE & KEITH

When I first got to Kansas I had a hard time fitting in. Coach Self was a defensive coach, and I had a hard time adjusting to playing tough defense. I had some teary nights in that Allen Fieldhouse locker room. The guys treated me well, though. I ended up taking Mike Lee's position, but he was still very important to me that year from a big brother standpoint. If I subbed in for him it wasn't like he didn't want me to do well. He'd be like, "J.R., go out there and play hard! Kill!" He was always talking to me, always making adjustments for me. My transition into the starting lineup was a lot easier because of people like Mike and Wayne and Aaron, but I'd say mainly Mike Lee. That tells you a lot about the character of Mike, a guy that was older and hoping to play professionally one day. Some hot rod came in and took his position, yet he still made it a point to be my friend.

Then there was Keith Langford. Keith was my hero. I was in awe of Keith Langford when I got to Kansas. I knew he wore No. 5 because of Jalen Rose, and I knew he went to North Crowley High School in Texas. He's still my favorite college basketball player. The first time I hung around him, he sneezed. I was like, "Wow! Keith Langford sneezes?" That's how in awe I was of him. He said Roy Williams always told him, "You can do whatever you want to do out there as long as you get to the basket." That's why he's such a phenomenal driver.

Keith and I had a big brother/little brother relationship. I told Coach Self that I wanted to be paired up with Keith for every drill so Keith and I could get better. With him being such a phenomenal driver, he made me look silly a lot. I got a lot better defensively because of Keith. He busted my head every day. With Keith it was a dogfight every drill. If there was a loose ball, we were going to fight each other until one of us had it. Sometimes they'd have to separate us for the rest of the practice, but that's the kind of mentality Coach Self wanted.

## "GET HIM OUT OF HERE!"

Where I was from, high school basketball was like AAU basketball. We didn't have any offensive structure or defensive schemes. Players just went out there, made plays, got buckets and blocked shots. I had to learn a lot of little things about basketball at Kansas. I was always a good athlete, but now I had to become more of a cerebral player. That was the hardest part for me. Coach Self was such a firm coach. One day I tried to strip Wayne Simien, and he knocked my teeth through my lip and I got a concussion. I remember waking up in tears and Coach Self screaming, "Get his ass off the court! He's soft! Get him out of here!" I'm standing there teary-eyed with a concussion and could barely even walk. Coach Miller came over and just hugged me and said, "It's OK, J.R." I just broke down. Those first few weeks were rough, especially considering I came in at 170 pounds and other guys weighed 210 because they lifted weights all the time. I hadn't even lifted weights yet.

## GIDDENS FOR 3

Coach Self used to give me supreme confidence when I was a freshman. That's why I was shooting the ball so well. He was like, "Shoot it every time you're open, every time you touch it." We'd be in practice passing the ball around the perimeter, and a chance would come for me to pass it into the post. He'd be like, "I don't even want you to pass it. Just shoot it." So I did. The other coaches were like, "What are you doing? Why aren't you running the play?" Coach Self would say, "I told him to shoot it." He did a lot of things to help me mentally and keep me on track that first year.

I got really hot toward the end of the season. I was our second-leading scorer the last 18 games. During one stretch I think I made 50 out of 100 3's or something like that. The negative was that everyone just wanted me to shoot it all the time. I never really shot the ball like that in high school. I was more of a driver, but sometimes you get on a team and you find a niche. I guess 3-point shooting was my niche at Kansas. That's what they needed at the time, a new Jeff Boschee with a little more athleticism.

One game that stands out to me from my time at Kansas was when we played UAB in the Sweet 16. We ended up winning by 30 or 40 points, but the preparation for that game is what I remember the most. UAB ran that 40 Minutes of Hell, full-court press that had been giving everyone trouble. They had just used it to beat Kentucky, who was a No. 1 seed. To get ready for the game, our starters practiced against seven or eight guys all week. Just getting the ball down the court was a challenge. By the time we got to the actual game and only had to face five guys, it was like child's play. We smacked them pretty good in what turned out to be a very easy game. A guy from Oklahoma City named Richard Jones played for UAB. We were rivals, so it felt good to look at him on the bench as we were killing his team.

## TRIALS AND TRIBULATIONS

Making the Elite Eight was great but, overall, Coach Self's first year was a struggle for everyone. He wanted to prove to everyone in Kansas that he was the right man for the job. He had to be politically correct, and he also had to be the leader of our team. So it was a struggle all season, because when a coach is nervous like that, they're going to do everything they can to make sure you win.

During finals week we were having two practices a day. We had to be on the court at 4:45 a.m. ready to go with football pads. We had helmets and shoulder pads and no mouth pieces. It wasn't too bad for me because I played football. But for people like Keith Langford and Moulaye Niang ... they didn't know what to do. Every time we made a turnover, we had to run. It wasn't easy because we were playing regular basketball but we had helmets on. If someone throws you a pass and you drop it, we had to stop and go into some sort of hitting drill. Those workouts were really violent. And like I said, it was during finals week. I had tests to study for. We'd get up and hit each other for two hours, then go take finals, then have a regular practice and then stay up all night studying.

## NIGHTLIFE

If you're not careful, the way you get treated at Kansas can be very dangerous. You go from being a high school student to a college rock star overnight. It's a lot of fame for someone that isn't used to it, especially someone coming from a strict household. I was on my own, and everyone was treating me like a hero. I had a lot of maturing to do, a lot of growing up to do. I wouldn't say it went to my head, because I was very confident in high school and got a lot of the same treatment I got at Kansas.

At Kansas you couldn't even go into Wal-Mart or Denny's or do simple things without people coming up to you and talking. Every time you went out to experience the Kansas nightlife, no matter who was with you – even if it was 20 people – the bar owners would let you skip the line, and then they'd take care of you and your friends all night. It was a whole lot of power and fame for a young kid. And I think it did go to some people's heads. Think about it: You're a 7-foot guy who hasn't been considered popular or cute your whole life. Now you're at a place where girls are just throwing themselves at you. You're thinking, "Man, I couldn't even get a girlfriend in high school." I'm not talking about David Padgett or Sasha. But I know David and Sasha both very much benefited from the nightlife. We used to always joke with D.P. We'd say, "David you don't have to work for girls. You're 7-foot, so they just come and talk to you because you're tall. They'll say, 'How tall are you?' and then you're set for a great conversation for the rest of the night. You don't even have to do anything. You're 7 feet, so they know you probably can't dance, and they don't even care."

We all liked to get out and have a good time. In terms of nightlife, it was truly a wonderful experience at Kansas – besides getting stabbed. The knife part, I didn't like so much. Other than that, everything was cool.

## FIRING BACK

There were times I probably acted a little cocky just because I felt like I didn't have to appeal to the masses. If somebody didn't care enough to get to know me, then why should I care? Let's be real: You're a young African-American in a predominantly white town, and white girls are interested in you. Some people aren't going to like that. They're going to shout crazy things. Other times guys would be like, "Hit a shot, J.R." and stuff like that. Because you have so much status given to you, it's hard for it not to go to your head. You want to talk back. You'll say some arrogant things when you're attacked. If someone screams, "You're not s--t" or tells me I suck, I'll be like, "Whatever, come to the game and watch me kill tomorrow" or "Watch me from your TV."

I call people like that "couch haters." Most people that hate like that are people who are sitting on their couch trying to be a coach while they're watching on TV. As a fiery young man, I liked to shut up any doubters or anybody that had anything bad to say about me. I wanted to prove them wrong, so I was immature in the way I reacted. I didn't handle things the way that I should have. If I had to do it over again, I'd be more professional about it. I always want to hold on to the confidence I have. But back then I probably exerted it in the wrong ways.

## ALMOST A GONER

I wanted to leave after my freshman year, but I had to have two surgeries – one on my foot and one on my knee. I definitely think I needed the one on my foot, but the one on my knee ... I'm not saying they were trying to keep me in school,

but they did a whole lot of things that were interesting. Before the end of my freshman season, I wasn't even practicing. I just wore a protective boot and only played in games. Coach Self was telling everyone, "J.R. has to come back next year because he has to have two surgeries. And I'm like, "Wow – I didn't know I had to have two surgeries."

## MORE THAN A SHOOTER

My sophomore year was horrible. Bill Self knew there was a good chance I was going to leave for the NBA, because he knew I had thought about leaving after my freshman year. He used to tell me, "Every time you dribble the ball, you're losing money." I was like, "People are running at me. I have to pump-fake and go around them." My friend, Stephen Graham, played for Oklahoma State. He told me the scouting report was, "When J.R. Giddens gets the ball, run at him as hard as you can and jump, because he's not going to dribble." So even when guys were closing me out, they had no responsibility with me off the dribble. The word got out because they were passing that information down to every team they played, because everyone wanted to see Kansas get beat. I told Coach Self that I couldn't get my shot up and that I needed to pump-fake and at least put it on the ground a few times. Coach Self and I were really having some conflicts. I was missing all these shots – at one point I was 6-of-36 from 3 – and he wasn't treating me like the golden boy anymore. He was frustrated with me. He didn't want to run any more plays for me. He was yanking me in and out of the game.

It was a frustrating year for me. I'm more than a shooter, but that's all he wanted me to do. I was trying to get to the NBA and feed my family because we were poor. All he would say was, "If you're worried about what the NBA thinks instead of what I think, you're not going to play." I was like, "Damn, I'm just trying to play basketball. I've got people running at me full speed. I can't even get my shot off. Why can't I dribble it a little bit?" My head was so messed up that year. I was missing shots, and I wasn't very strong in the weight room, and people were trying to bully me every possession. Coach Self was all over me about it. He was complaining that I don't bench-press enough. It was a nightmare. I went from being the golden boy that could get away with anything to him taking everything away from me. It completely shot my confidence, and I didn't have the sophomore season that I should've.

## BUCKNELL

I took our first-round loss to Bucknell really hard. It was in Oklahoma City, and I only had two points. My family was there, and Coach Self and I were bumping heads the whole game. My freshman year he would let me react to what the defense was throwing at me. But now he had taken all of my freedom away. During that game I kept telling him, "Coach, they're calling out the play before I ever get the ball." They were out there screaming at each other, "Giddens is coming off the screen, and he's going to get it here or there!" I told Coach Self that I needed to be able to play basketball and not be a robot, or we were going to lose.

My family was in the stands. They don't know much about basketball. They were yelling, "C'mon, J.R. Hit a shot!" To lose to Bucknell and to play that bad in front of my family ... I mean, you saw me after the game. I was an emotional wreck. I couldn't even talk. I felt like everything was my fault because I knew I was the X-factor. I played like s--t, and we lost to Bucknell in one of the greatest upsets in NCAA history. My mind was thrown a curveball. I didn't think we could lose.

When you play for Kansas and you lose to Bucknell, you don't want to go to class. Those fans are going to let you know about it. Some of those people are like, "You f---ing suck," the minute you walk through the door. Then you'll probably have a guy that bet his whole paycheck on the game. We lost, so now we're his worst enemy. Fans are fair-weather. That's just how it was. It was a very hard transition after we lost.

## THE MOON BAR: J.R.'s SIDE OF THE STORY

The night I got stabbed, I was in the club wrestling with Jeff Hawkins. I chased him around the pool table and then into the back room, the karaoke room. I got him in a headlock and, all of a sudden, some white guy (Jeremiah Creswell) walked in and punched me. J-Hawk and I froze and were like, "What's going on?" The security threw the guy out of the bar, and I left a little while later, too. I went to go drop off some friends and then I came back. They were going to let us and the KU calendar girls come back in and have a nice little time after hours, once the bar had closed and they had cleared people out. Some Chiefs players were supposed to be there, too.

When I got back, I made a call to have someone come unlock the door. Well, the guy that had punched me earlier (Creswell) was standing near the front door. As I was getting out of the car he was going ballistic. He had his shirt off, showing his tattoos. He called me the n-word about 50,000 times. He and I squared up, and I gave him a couple of good shots and knocked him down. Because he had been screaming the n-word before we got into it, a bunch of black guys that I didn't know came up and got involved. They didn't like hearing that word from a white guy, either. That's the only reason all those other guys came up and jumped in, because he was white and he was using the n-word. When they came up and started hitting him, they bumped me out of the way. I actually grabbed one of the guys by the shoulders and tried to move him out of the way so I could get back in there. That's when I felt myself get hit. It felt like someone had just football-kicked me in the back of my calf. The pain was so bad that my body just went into shock. Still, I had no idea that (Creswell) had used a knife until I pulled up the leg of my pants. There was blood everywhere. I was like, "Oh my God, my leg is split open." He had sliced my artery. Five of the other guys got stabbed, too. I got to a hospital as fast as I could. Coach Self was up there after I had surgery. He was like, "You f---ed up. You really f---ed up. I can't help you."

## WHO STARTED IT?

People said I instigated that fight. Man, I didn't instigate that fight. That guy was probably on hallucinates. Two weeks later he got arrested for (allegedly) threatening his mom and his uncle with a knife. They recorded his phone conversations from jail and someone said, "Hey, do you know you stabbed that superstar guy J.R. Giddens from Kansas?" and he was like, "I don't care who that n----- is. He's lucky I didn't have my big knife." He was just trying to start trouble. That's why I was so mad at Jason Whitlock. We're both African-American, and he's over there writing in the paper about it being racist between white guys and black guys? The only reason those other guys jumped in is because the white guy was screaming the n-word at a black club where the people were predominantly black. That's not a smart thing for a white guy to do.

Plus, I was a Kansas Jayhawk. You can't just fight a Jayhawk like that without people trying to jump in. I saw Jason Whitlock at the NBA's Rookie Orientation, and they wanted me to speak to him. They wanted me to have an intervention with him, and I was like, "There is no reason to even speak to that man." He was old enough to understand my situation. Yeah, I was immature and I went through some bad times. But I was out there trying to feed my family and get drafted like the next man and he was doing nothing but bash me during the worst part of my life. That's a man. Kick somebody when they're down. That's a real man. Way to kick me, Jason Whitlock.

I wanted to give my side of the story, but no one would let me do it. Bill Self was threatening me. He said if I said anything, he was going to throw me under the bridge to the NBA. We all did crazy things at Kansas that he'd find out about from time to time. He was like, "If you say anything, if your mom says anything … I'm going to make you look bad." So I had to shut my mouth. *(Note: When informed of Giddens' comments, Self denied that he threatened to make disparaging remarks about Giddens to NBA scouts, coaches and administrators.)*

## DREAMS DASHED?

Any thoughts I had about leaving for the NBA ended when I got stabbed. After that I knew I wasn't going anywhere. If anything, I was trying to figure out if I was ever going to play basketball again. I think that's why they made me leave Kansas. The doctor said I would walk with a limp for the rest of my life. He said I was going to come back 50% and I wasn't going to be able to play basketball anymore. I'm not saying Kansas threw me out like a battery. But they get McDonald's All-Americans every day. They weren't going to let me stay around campus and be Moulaye Niang.

Micah Downs was coming in. Bill Self used to always tell me, "Micah is coming in, and he's better than you." He would just say little stuff like that, and I was like, "Dang, man, you're not even for me, are you?" I wanted to stay at Kansas but I felt like they just pushed me out the door, especially after getting stabbed. I was like, "I'm sitting here worried that I'll never play basketball again, and you guys are over here talking to me in an inappropriate manner? I'm 19 years old. You guys are supposed to my college coaches. Instead, at the first sign of trouble, you guys are turning your back on me?" I felt like it was everyone from the coaching staff to the people up there in the offices. As a 19-year-old who was immature and didn't understand life, I took that really hard. I left the office in tears when I knew I was leaving.

I remember that day really well. I walked out of there on crutches, crying. I'd been interrogated for about seven hours for three days straight. Then those guys did that to me? A few weeks before that, I had to move out of my dorm at the Towers. I was staying with Josi Lima, my girlfriend at the time who played volleyball. Bill Self was telling my teammates not to have any contact with me. Darnell Jackson and Jeremy Case were two of my best friends, and they weren't even allowed to talk to me. Aaron Miles was done playing, so he came over. He was the only person who came and saw me. I was like, "Dang, I'm 30 feet from where I used to stay, and you guys can't even come over here and see me?" I'm stabbed and laid up and don't even know if I'm going to play basketball again. That was very kind of Kansas basketball and Bill Self, to tell people to stay away from me like I was a team cancer.

## PAINFUL PROBLEM

When I was in the cast, I wasn't even allowed to wiggle my toes. When you sever your soleus muscle, it can't be sewn back together. You have to let it fuse back together on its own. That was the most painful process. I tried to cut through my cast a couple of times because it would just spasm up, and it would cramp. I would have a cramp in my leg for three hours and I'd be sitting on the couch crying in pain for about 23 hours of the day. I couldn't walk for two months.

Once I got out of my cast, I couldn't even feel my foot. My whole leg felt strange. They told me it would probably be like that for the rest of my life. A lot of times I couldn't get any information about what was going on with my leg. They even tried to keep me out of the training room at Kansas because I heard the trainers weren't supposed to help me. I was like, "Dang, I don't have any insurance. You guys know I'm an inner-city kid that's poor." The doctors had given me this rehab stuff to do, but KU wouldn't let me do it there. Luckily the KU trainer, Bill Cowgill, was a good guy who must've felt bad for me or something. I'd sneak into the training room at 5 a.m and learn how to walk again on the underwater treadmill with Bill Cowgill. It was shear pain. My Achilles needed to be stretched. I couldn't walk. I was like a 6-foot-5 baby. Bill was like, "J.R., I don't care what they tell me. I'm going to make sure I give you the best chance to rehab this injury." It was very nice of him.

## PAYING THE PRICE

For getting stabbed, I was charged with misdemeanor battery and put on probation for a year. I had to be drug-tested and piss-tested for a full year. They said if I had any alcohol in my system I'd go to jail. I'm like, "How do you get stabbed and then you get a year of probation? That makes no sense at all." Kansas did all of that. They painted everything. The police were telling me the whole time that I wasn't going to get into trouble, and that I had done nothing wrong, which I hadn't. All I did was get into an altercation, and I got stabbed. It was unfair. Being an athlete, it was on ESPN and highly publicized, so the judge was under pressure to penalize me.

Still, I was like, "Let's be real here. I'm 19 years old, everybody in the club is drinking under age, they give us free drinks everywhere we go. I got into an altercation – which is something college kids do all the time – but because I got stabbed, you're going to act like I'm the bad sheep and I'm doing something different than anyone else in the program?" That's the picture they tried to paint.

## BOOTED

Here's how my career at Kansas ended, and I'm going to hit you with the real, man. Coach Self told me he would back me as long as my story about what happened that night stayed the same. But he said that if I changed my story I'd be off the team. Looking back, I feel like it was some sort of a ploy to push me out of the university.

Lew Perkins had hired people to come in and investigate the situation. Not the police, but private investigators. I'd be in my dorm room on all kinds of medication, and I'd get a call saying, "If you want to stay on this team, you need

to come down and talk to these guys right now." They'd hold me in this room for four or five hours at a time. I was literally about to break out into tears. I was like, "Man, can I have some water? Can I have some food? I'm not a criminal. I haven't done anything." One of the investigators kept telling me, "I'm a big fan of yours. I'm trying to help you out. If you say these certain things, we're going to be able to help you. We want you to be able to come back to Kansas and play." I kept sticking to my story, but it was getting out of hand. They questioned me for hours and hours for two or three straight days. I wasn't trying to be an assh---, but I was getting frustrated. I said, "Listen, man, I've said it three or four times. You have a tape recorder right here. You can rewind what I said and listen to it. Why do you keep asking me to tell the same story again?" He was like, "I'm old. I'm going to need you to repeat it." But I kept telling him, "You've got a tape recorder. What is your issue with me?"

I'm convinced Lew Perkins hired them to get after me. He hired them to get me out of that university. Plus, besides those guys, I was getting interviewed by the real police, too. I was probably spending seven hours a day answering questions. I finally changed my story because they said it would help me if I said certain things. But then Bill Self was like, "You changed your story. I told you not to do that. I can't help you now." That's when I broke out into tears. I knew what he had done. I was like, "You got me. You did that on purpose." I knew he had f---ed me. I was like, "It's cool. I'm going to make it without you. I appreciate all the opportunities you and Kansas have given me." But when I walked out of the room I was crushed. I loved Kansas to the core and I always will. I felt like I was treated unfairly.

*(Self had this response to Giddens' comments: "That's as big of a lie as there ever was. I told J.R. I would support him as long as he told me the truth. I said, 'Tell me the truth. I can deal with the truth. But if you lie to me, and I find out later that you lied, you're gone.' When the police – not the investigators, but the police – kept questioning him later on, and he came clean, he walked into my office and I said, 'You know what our deal was.' And he said, 'Yes I do. I know I've got to go.'*

*"He hadn't been forthright and honest. After all the investigations had taken place, the police came back and said, 'Hey, we know what happened. Do you still want to stick to your story?' He said, 'You're right. That's what happened.' He had been misleading them the whole time.*

*"I didn't think it was right for me, especially with him being hurt, to immediately kick him out without knowing the truth. To get to the truth, it took most of the summer. I'm not saying who did or didn't start that fight. But we know what happened. The whole thing could've been avoided. When someone brings so much negative attention to something as big (as Kansas basketball), you want to stick with them, but there's also a point where you have to say, 'We can only stick with you if you level with us and tell us what's up.' I had his back. I didn't run and hide. I just told him, 'If I find you're lying to me, you're gone.'*

*"He needed a change of scenery from us and we needed a change of scenery from him. There were no hard feelings from a personal standpoint. I hated what we went through, without question. But it was good for his life to go to New Mexico, and it was good for Kansas basketball for him not to be here.")*

## FAMILY AFFAIRS

After I got kicked out of Kansas I went back to Oklahoma, but I had nowhere to go. My family turned their back on me for a while. I could tell my dad was frustrated, but it was more my mom. We were going through a hard financial time, and everyone expected me to be in the NBA by then. We were still living in the inner city and not doing well. Money was tight, and everyone was looking at me to be the hero. That's the way I had always talked to my family: "Don't worry, I'm going to the league. I'm going to get some money, and then we'll be in a better financial situation." But it didn't happen. We were poor as s--t. There were car notes and electrical bills and people had been counting on me to help. But I couldn't do anything because I was sitting on the couch, stabbed and laid up. I could feel their frustration more and more each day, so I left and moved in with one of my friends, who let me use his couch. He and I were literally living off the food stamps he was getting from the government. Every day, I just prayed that I could come back.

## A NEW OPPORTUNITY

The main thing that got me through that time was that my cousin happened to be a masseuse. My cousin would come over to my friend's place every day and rub my leg until I learned how to walk again using my crutches. I'd take three steps forward and then three steps back with both legs on the ground and the crutches under my arm. Before long, I was on the phone with college coaches telling them I was going to be OK.

For the next few weeks I sat on the couch all day with my leg in the air, talking to schools and swearing that I would bounce back. I'd tell them that the doctors were wrong and that I was going to play again. I found out about this later, but when I went to New Mexico, the trainer told people he didn't think they should sign me. I had literally started walking again the day before the trip. I had been holding off all my visits because I couldn't walk, but now I was telling them that I could. They got me in the training room and looked at my leg and said, "Whoa, that's pretty nasty. Can you stand on your tippy-toes?" I couldn't even lift my heel off the ground but I was trying with all of my might. The trainer looked at the coach and said, "Man, this isn't good." I just thank the Lord New Mexico needed a player of my caliber and that they took a chance on me.

I know the New Mexico players doubted me at first, though. They were like, "You're the big, bad J.R. Giddens?" They all knew I was really hurting emotionally, though. I was like, "Dang, I suck. I can't run and jump right now. I'm trying to hoop so I can get some jack. I'm not a 4.0 student. I'm not going to medical school. I need this. This is my life."

My family went ballistic when I told them I was going to New Mexico. It wasn't some big-time program. They didn't even know where New Mexico was. But I really felt like New Mexico rolled out the red carpet for me. As you can see, first round ... everything worked out.

## A FRESH START

I redshirted for a year at New Mexico, and then things really started going in a good direction. As a senior, I was the Mountain West Conference Player of the Year and I showed people what I knew all along at Kansas – that I was more than just a shooter. I hit 74 3's my freshman season at Kansas. I hit 25 as a senior at New Mexico but I led the conference rebounding (8.8), ranked fourth in scoring (16.3) and was in the top 10 in assists (3.1), steals (1.4) and blocks (1.1). My game is more of an all-around game. You shouldn't expect a guy with a 43-inch vertical to sit there and shoot 3's every possession. That's why I was mad at Bill Self. He was forcing me to shoot 3's all the time.

## ACHIEVING A DREAM

The 2008 NBA draft was a magical night. It was one of the best nights of my life. I had a low-key party in New Mexico with my coaches and my teammates.

My agent played a joke on me that night. I was actually supposed to go 28th because Memphis had said they were going to pick me. So after that didn't happen and then I didn't go at No. 29, I was over there holding my AAU coach's hand saying, "Is anyone going to draft me?" I was having a little pity party. Then my agent called and said, "Hey I don't know about Boston. They can go either way." Boston had actually called him and told him they were going to pick me at No. 30, so he was just teasing me. I figured out he was lying when they called my name on television a few seconds later. My friends tackled me. It was a great moment – especially after all I'd been through. People can never take that moment from me.

I was proud of myself for fighting back. I've always had a big heart, and I've always had the same motto: If I've got my back up against the wall, I won't be the guy with my hands bracing my face. I'm going to come out swinging. And that's the way I work now. That's why I know I will be successful, one of the best in the league, because besides Kobe Bryant and probably a few other people, I don't think there are too many people who work harder than me at my craft. It's just going to stay that way until I can't run anymore. I like to say I'm the underdog's underdog. When life is tough for me, I feel like I perform my best.

I have the utmost respect for Boston, and I thank them for the opportunity that they gave me. Things just didn't work out. As a young guy going to a team that just won a championship, it was very hard. They already had their lineup. They were confident in the players they were going to play that season. Being there for two years, I didn't feel like I was given much of a chance to compete and show those guys what I could do. I don't really feel like I got a fair handshake in all of that. I'm very confident I'll make it back to the NBA. I'm in the gym every day.

## ONCE A JAYHAWK, ALWAYS A JAYHAWK

Kansas is a big reason why I'm the man that I am today. I love Kansas with all of my heart. I wish them the best. I still cheer for them. I have no problems with Bill Self or anybody on their coaching staff or any of their fans. I just wish people would know that I'm always going to love them unconditionally and I hope the true Kansas fans will love me unconditionally, as well. I want them to know that I made a mistake and I'm sorry for it, but I just wish certain people wouldn't have turned their back on me, because I bled Jayhawk blue. I was the most faithful Kansas person out there. I knew I was going to Kansas when I was 15 because Roy Williams came and offered me a scholarship and told me I was going to be his secret project. I only went on one official visit, and that was to Kansas. I knew where I was going. I put on Twitter the other day that I love Kansas and I always will. I hope some people saw that, because I meant exactly what I said. I will always love Kansas.

# CHAPTER 13

# 2001/02 - 2004/05
# KEITH LANGFORD

Keith Langford ranks seventh on Kansas' all-time scoring list with 1,812 career points. The Fort Worth, Texas, native wasn't all that heralded when he arrived at Kansas in 2001, but he ended up impacting the Jayhawks' program just as much as highly touted classmates Wayne Simien and Aaron Miles. The always-outspoken Langford was at his best when the lights were the brightest. He had a knack for slashing to the rim and making big shots. After stints in the NBDL and with the San Antonio Spurs, Langford took his game to Russia and is currently regarded as one of the top American players overseas. Langford married Brittany Herman on Aug. 6, 2011.

## IN KEITH'S WORDS

I was 17 when I took my official visit to Kansas. On all of my visits, my mom would tell the coaches, "Keith is young. He doesn't need to be out doing this or that." Bless her heart, she was just being protective, but it probably played a role in the way some of my visits went. There wasn't a whole lot of partying going on.

I can honestly say that my trip to Kansas was the worst of all my visits. I got to Lawrence the night before they played Emporia State, so there wasn't much the guys could do anyway. I had dinner with Kirk. He drove a Rodeo at the time. He took me to Burrito King and we hung out and made small-talk for a while. Then we back to the Towers, and I chilled with Drew and met some of the other players. I really didn't know who these guys were because I didn't follow college basketball that closely. I slept in Drew's room that night and woke up and did some stuff with the coaches the next morning. I had fun hanging out with everyone, but I really didn't do anything special – at least not until I went to the game Saturday night. That's what did it. I had never seen anything like it before. Even though they were only playing Emporia State, the place was packed. The fans were chanting, "We want Langford! We want Langford!" At that point, I was like, "I need to come here."

The other thing that got me was Roy Williams. He had a very powerful presence. I didn't know much about college basketball, but I knew who he was. I'd seen him in "He Got Game." I knew he was famous and I enjoyed being around him. He didn't promise me that I'd get a certain amount of playing time or make any other sort of vows about what would happen once I got there. But he did say he could guarantee me one thing: A fair chance. At that point, I'm 17, I'm the hottest thing back in Ft. Worth, and I'm looking at Kansas' team thinking, "All they've got are these two white guys, Boschee and Hinrich, playing my position. I'm good to go. I'll come in here and set the world on fire. It'll be easy." Plus, I liked everything: the school, the fans, the coaches and players. I didn't commit that day, but I was pretty certain Kansas was where I'd end up.

## UNDER THE RADAR

Of the five guys in my recruiting class, I was probably the one people knew the least about. Aaron was regarded as the top point guard in the country and Mike Lee was his best friend. Wayne Simien was a McDonald's All-American who had grown up just down the road, and Jeff Hawkins was a local star, too. I'm sure when I signed people were thinking, "Who is this guy?" It didn't really bother me, though. I didn't understand how it all worked at the time. I didn't know there were recruiting rankings and I didn't realize how big of a deal it was to be a McDonald's All-American like Wayne. At the time, if someone would've said, "Not many people know who you are," I'd have said, "Why would they?" So, no, I didn't have a chip on my shoulder or feel like I had something to prove. I was just glad to be there. After all, it was almost a fluke that I became a top-flight, heavily recruited player in the first place.

My best friend was one of the top players in the Ft. Worth area back in high school. Wes Grandstaff – who coached Team Texas, one of the best AAU programs in the country – saw one of his games and asked him to come to a try out. My friend didn't want to go by himself because he didn't know anyone, so he asked me to go with him. So I'm at this practice with some of the best players in the area, and I end up dunking on Jason Maxiell, who had a good career at Cincinnati and is now with the Detroit Pistons. Wes came over and asked what my name was. He wrote it down and contacted me later, and that's how I ended up on Team Texas, which led to me signing with Kansas. Shady (Darrell Arthur) eventually played for them, too.

## MISSISSIPPI MISSES

Before Kansas even came into the picture, I thought I was going to Ole Miss. I actually committed to them before I ever went down there. When I finally took my visit, I realized I'd made a mistake. I thought Texas was about as southern as you could get. But Oxford, Mississippi … goodness gracious.

We had to literally stop my dad from fighting someone down there, because he got called "boy." We had been out to eat with the coaches, and we were following them in our car back to their offices. A few cars got between us, so we got separated. The coaches had already pulled into the parking lot when we got to the arena, so we had to explain to the security guard what had happened. We told him we had just had lunch with the coaches and were supposed to tour the facility with them. The guy was like, "Do you have any sort of pass you can show me?" My dad was like, "No, my son is here on an official visit. He's going to play basketball here." The security guard still wouldn't let us into the parking lot. Finally, my dad said, "Hey, man, we're from Texas and we're just trying to …" The guy cut him off and said, "You're in Mississippi now, boy." My dad just lost it. He was trying to get out of the car, and we were grabbing him and holding him in the seat, trying to stop him from getting out of the car. He started screaming, "My son isn't coming to this school! He's not coming here!" That's not the only reason I backed out of my commitment, but it was definitely a factor. I had never seen anything like that before. It was crazy. It all worked out for the best, though, because I re-opened my recruitment and ended up at Kansas, the place where I was supposed to be all along.

## GETTING ADJUSTED

From the moment I met them, Drew and Nick and Kirk made it understood that they were ready to win. When I first started playing in pickup games and doing the individual workouts, I thought, "They're not going to be able to blame me for anything. I'm going to hold my own. I'm going to carry my weight." I was trying to work to the same standard as those guys were. They were really going at it.

Off the court, the freshmen were really immature that first year, especially that first summer. We got on the older guys' nerves a little bit, but they handled it great. Once we pulled a couch to the outside of Nick Collison's room. We stood it up straight against his front of his door and knocked. He came to the door and opened it. Once he started moving the couch out of the way we were standing there with buckets of water, which we threw all over him. The amazing thing was that he stood there and took it and said, "I'll get you back." But he never tried anything. We ragged on each other, too. We used to call Aaron and Jeff Hawkins "The Soap Sisters" because Mike caught them in the shower one day playing soccer with a bar of soap.

## IT'S ALL GOODEN

I remember the first time I saw Drew play during a pickup game. I had never been around someone that tall that could do the things he was doing. I remember calling my friends back home and saying, "We've got this tall guy, man … he can do this, he can do that. Watch for Drew Gooden when we play this year. He's going to the NBA." I was just so impressed with him. We played one-on-one in the Fieldhouse a few weeks before the start of practice, and he was giving me all these tips and pointers. Being so young, I was trying to soak in everything he said. I figured he really knew what he was talking about. Then, once we got to work with Roy in a practice setting, it turned out everything Drew told me was wrong. I never gave him a hard time about that, but I should've.

One time Roy kicked Drew out of the gym. The team wasn't practicing very well that day and he wanted to make an example out of Drew. About 5 minutes later, I ran back to the locker room to use the bathroom. Drew was sitting in the hot tub with his hands behind his head and his feet propped up out of the water, just twiddling his toes and relaxing with this big goofy smile on his face. I thought, "Man, this dude doesn't have a care in the word." I went into the stall and all of a sudden I heard this assistant coach − I think it was Coach Miller − screaming, "Drew, what are you doing? Coach Williams wants you back on the court now! Get out there! Hurry! Hurry!" Drew ran back on the court all wet, still wearing the tights he had on in the hot tub.

The other funny thing about Drew was that the guy who gave him the most trouble in practice was a walk-on. Chris Zerbe was only 6-foot-5, but he could really play − especially against Drew. He could use that butt of his and swivel around anyone. Hook shots, scoop shots, whatever. He went right at Drew. He wasn't scared. Guys like Zerbe and Todd Kappelmann … practice was their time to play, their time to shine. We had a lot of respect for those guys.

## MAUI OWIE

My freshman season started off on a down note. We played in the Maui Invitational, and one of the biggest memories I have of that trip is losing to Ball State in the opening round of the tournament. Aaron cramped up at the end of the game and got crossed over for the winning basket, and the guy that beat him was named Patrick "Action" Jackson. Mike Lee busted Aaron's balls about that for the rest of the season. Mike and Jeff Hawkins were always on the red (scout) team in practice and Aaron and I always ran with the blue team (starters and key reserves). So whenever Jeff was guarding Aaron and giving him trouble, Mike Lee would yell, "Get him, Petey! Get him Action Jackson!" It was hilarious. Aaron would get mad because he was so competitive, but he'd be laughing at the same time. It was a running joke that every time someone got the best of Aaron, we'd make an Action Jackson reference.

## LOSING TO MARYLAND

We went 16-0 in the Big 12 my freshman year but lost to Maryland 97-88 in the Final Four. Maryland's team was built just like ours. But when they went to

their bench they had a little more experience. They just wore on us. They were big and they ran their offense to a "T." It was a gradual attack. They kept doing everything right. They kept setting screens. They kept blocking out. They were getting back and playing transition defense, which most teams had a hard time doing against us because we were so fast. It was just real methodical. They just caught a great rhythm. I only scored eight points and didn't play that well. For most of the season it was comforting knowing that I didn't have to play great for us to win. We had so many good pieces. I could've been terrible, and we could've ended up in the same position at the end of the year. If I played great it was just a bonus. That's one of the reasons I did so well as a freshman. I was relaxed. Still, I wish I would've been more of a factor in that last game.

As a freshman at that time, part of me was satisfied with just getting there. Being younger, you think, "We're going to be able to do this again easily." I took it for granted. After we lost to Syracuse the next year, it sunk in more that it's not going to happen all the time. Just getting there two years in a row was very rare.

## RESPECT FOR ROY

Most people don't know this, but we had a lot of recruits take visits here, guys that are in the NBA right now, that Roy turned down. He would talk to us after their visit and ask us if we thought the guy would be a good fit. That was Roy's thing: It wasn't always about getting the highest-rated recruits. It was about getting guys who were the best fit for what was going on. Kris Humphries came on a visit and tried to commit. He really wanted to come here. But no one on the team liked Kris Humphries. He was arrogant. He told everyone he was going to come in and be the leading scorer as a freshman and that we'd all have to take a backseat to him. We were trying to be respectful and not say anything. But he was an absolute jerk. It was tough, because Roy was really excited about him. Kris Humphries was a big deal. He was a one-and-done or a two-and-done kind of player. Roy wanted him to commit on his visit. But we told him, "Coach, you can't bring this guy in. You can't do it." You'd figure Roy would say something like, "Let's work on him," or "Let's give him another chance." Instead he told Humphries, "Sorry, but you can't come." Bill Self did the same thing years later with Terrence Williams.

For all the respect we showed Roy, he always made it a point to show respect back. He treated everyone in his program really well. The coaches would never eat before the players. And when it came to getting in line for food, the seniors would always go first – then juniors, sophomores, freshmen, managers and then coaches at the very end. They treated everyone from top to bottom the absolute same. Drew would get the same amount of attention that Chris Zerbe would get. It was incredible. His morals and his ethics and the way he conducted himself ... we would never catch him being a hypocrite. That was big with us.

Another thing was that, with us, you never had to worry about any sort of NCAA violations or rule-breaking. Roy always emphasized that he was going to do everything he could to help get us money. He was going to squeeze every dollar he could out of our scholarship checks. He was going to help us get our Pell grants and find camps for us to work at during the summer. He'd always say, "Don't do anything to break NCAA rules, because we're going to make sure you have a way to make money." He was great about that. The fact that we stayed out of trouble also goes back to the character of guys he brought in. Like I said, it wasn't always the top 10 guys. It was the guys who were the best fit.

## ROY ON THE RAMPAGE

When Roy was angry it could turn into borderline rage. A few times he got so mad that he had his vertigo issues. He actually fell down on the court one time because of it. Another time Roy actually tried to fight Jeff Graves. We were in the basement of his house about a month before we started workouts in the fall of 2002, Roy's last season. We were working really hard, so every now and then he'd have us over to his house and have a barbeque or something. One time, after we ate, he had us down in the basement talking about expectations and stuff. He started getting on Jeff about how he was overweight and about how he was letting the team down. Jeff had really been struggling. He was out of shape – partly because he'd been in a car wreck – and he couldn't cover the required distance on his 12-minute run. Roy was really tearing into him. I looked over at Jeff and he was sucking his teeth, frownin' up and getting all mad. Then Roy goes over to a closet, opens the door and says to Jeff, "I don't think you're very tough. Get up and let's meet in the closet. Only one guy is going to come out, and it's going to be me because I'm tougher than you." No one said anything because he was being serious. Jeff just sat there and didn't do anything, didn't respond. After it was all over and we left, I asked Jeff what he thought about all of it, and he said he really wanted to drag Roy in that closet and show him how tough he was. Did he seriously want to hurt Roy? No. But he didn't like being called out like that, especially when it involved getting physical. When you look at Jeff Graves and you look at Roy, it's pretty obvious who would've won. Roy kept on him that whole semester, though. Sometimes he'd blow his whistle out of the blue and say to Coach Holladay, "Coach, we can't practice today. Jeff Graves is too fat."

## TAN MAN

I only played with Jeff Boschee for a year, but he was one of a kind. You talk about a rock star ... women loved him. After games he was in and out of the shower pretty quick. He'd get dressed and get out of there. He didn't waste a lot of time hanging around and talking. But he cared about the team so much. One time we were on a road trip, and Aaron looked out the window and saw Boschee tanning at the hotel pool. The funny thing was that he was trying to tan the underside of his arms, so his arms were out to the side, turned up all awkward and funny. We were upstairs in the room just going crazy. We joked around with Drew, Nick and Kirk but, for the most part, we left Jeff alone. He was all about winning, though. You weren't going to break his focus.

## OPPORTUNITY LOST – AGAIN

When we went back to the Final Four my sophomore year, most of the talk centered on Roy instead of our team. Everyone wanted to know if he was going to take the North Carolina job. Roy tried to address it with us a little bit. He would just tell us to focus and stay in the moment and little things like that. It was almost like he was giving us the same answers he was giving to the media. He never came out and told us, "Hey, I'm not going anywhere." He didn't reassure us that everything was OK. Still, that's not the reason we lost to Syracuse.

It's tough not to think back to that night and wonder how history may have changed if we'd have won that national title. Jeff Graves and I had gotten really close that year. He was having a tough time with Roy, and I was in his corner more than anybody. Before the game we made a pact that we were both going to enter the NBA draft if we won the title. We were looking at mock drafts and we were both on there. Some of them had Jeff going in the first round and me in the second. Others had it vice-versa. We were like, "Hey, if we win this, we're getting out of here. It doesn't matter what happens with Roy. We're gone." Had Mike hit that shot to put us into overtime, had Gerry McNamara not hit six 3's in the first half … who knows how history would've been different? There were so many what-ifs that night. What if I hadn't have fouled out? What if we had made our free throws? To this day, one of the toughest things for me to do is watch that game. There's no doubt in my mind that Mike would've hit that shot if it hadn't have been blocked by Hakim Warrick. Mike had a great tournament that year. He was so motivated that whole postseason. Just watching him grow from a guy that everyone thought was a throw-in with Aaron to a guy who was on the court in the crucial minutes of the NCAA title game was really neat. He was all heart.

The postgame locker room was a sad scene. I remember Drew Gooden coming in there and hugging Roy and crying right in the middle of the locker room. All my teammates were staring at the ground in shock. I was thinking, "Am I really going to leave these guys?" But I was also thinking I had done all I could do in college basketball. I scored 19 points that night on the biggest stage possible. I felt it was time to move onto something else. If that's how it ended for me, I was going to be OK with it. I was still really disappointed, though, because we all expected to win, especially after the Marquette game. They were one of the hottest teams in the country and we had just killed them. After that I didn't think there was any way we were going to lose. I guess it wasn't meant to be.

## A SUDDEN GOODBYE

We didn't see Roy at all from the time we left New Orleans that night to the day we saw him in the locker room back at Kansas. Man, I'm getting goosebumps just thinking about this. We were all sitting in our chairs in the locker room. A lot of people were laughing and cutting up. Most of us didn't think there was any way he was going to leave. But then I looked over at Kirk, who was sitting right next to me. He was absolutely stone-faced, playing with his hair and staring at the ground. I said, "What's up, man? You all right?" In a really low voice, Kirk was like, "I already know what he's going to say." It was like a movie, because the minute those words came out of Kirk's mouth, the door swung open and the assistant coaches walked in. Roy came in last. I was like, "Oh s--t. He's gone." He gave us the, "This is the hardest thing I've ever done," speech. A few hours later, I turned on ESPN and saw him getting off a plane in North Carolina. That day changed a lot of people's lives forever.

After Roy left we all stormed out of the locker room and into the parking lot. There were cameras everywhere. I said, "I didn't come here for this s--t." We drove off, and then ESPN and all these other national media outlets started calling and e-mailing me. I have no idea how they got my number or

my address. They were saying, "We'd love to let you tell your side of the story. We can do it live." I never responded to anything. I actually had to change my e-mail account. I started hearing stuff about Mark Turgeon coming here and Mark Few. I told people I was leaving. I didn't think there was anyone they could've hired that I was going to like.

## BUTTING HEADS

Right before they hired Bill Self, I called Roy and said I wanted to come to North Carolina. He said, "Keith, you know I'd love to have you, but there's a lot going on right now. Just see who they bring in, and if it's that bad, we'll go from there." Then they hired Bill, and he sat me down and gave me the whole spiel about how important I was to the program and stuff. I ended up staying.

Things between Coach Self and I were tense from the get-go. In December of my junior year we played at Nevada, and Kirk Snyder just killed me. He was really good. Before the season I had said a bunch of stuff in the media about how I was mad that some of the preseason magazines had Snyder ranked ahead of me on the "best slashers" list. I was being borderline arrogant and I shouldn't have done it. A few days after the game, I was dogging it in practice a little bit, and Coach Self made a comment about Kirk Snyder "sticking it up my ass." He dropped a couple of other comments on me after that, and we ended up having an exchange. It wasn't good. It wasn't healthy to do that in front of the whole team and coaching staff. That was one of the low points of the year.

At that point I was ready to transfer. I had my AAU coach and my mom contact the Kansas coaches over Christmas, but they refused to give me a release. They talked to me, and I agreed to say. That's when things kind of went downhill. It was tough after that and a lot of it was my fault. I was stubborn about a lot of things. I take 70 percent of the blame. I was comparing everything we did with how we did it under Roy. I thought, "Why does everything have to do a complete 180 when we had so much success doing things the way we did them under Roy?" I knew inside that we were going to be Self's guinea pigs, an experiment for him as he installed his system. It felt like our legacy and our careers were going to take a hit, because there was no way we could win a national championship with a first-year coach. That's not a slap in the face to him and his abilities and it's not me saying I tanked the season. In my heart, I just thought it was only a matter of time before Self got his guys in, guys that fit his mold and his philosophy.

Another time, during my senior year, we lost to Texas Tech in double overtime in Lubbock. Going into that game we were 20-1 and 10-0 in the Big 12. I actually played really well in that game. I didn't think there was anything he could say to me. But he said, "You don't care about winning. You just want the camera to show what shoes you have on after halftime." If you remember, I was superstitious and always changed my shoes at intermission. I'm thinking, "Yo, I just played my ass off. What are you talking about?" At that time I was still rebellious and I acted out. Looking back on it now, I totally understand what Coach Self was trying to do. If you attack the leader or the team or one of the better players, the other guys will know to get their butt in line, too. But I wasn't thinking like that back then.

## OFFICIALLY SCREWED

When you consider all we went through my junior year, it was actually pretty impressive that we got as far as we did. We came one win away from our third straight Final Four – and we would've made it if it wasn't for Jim Burr, the official. You always hear announcers talking about what a great ref he is, but anyone who watches the games knows that's not the case. He knocked me out of the Georgia Tech game in the Elite Eight 2004 by whistling me for my fifth foul. It was a terrible call, and it marked the second year in a row when I fouled out of the last game of the year at a time just when I was really heating up

Against Syracuse the year before, Josh Pace was dribbling the ball down the court, and I had my arms out to the side. He tripped and fell right into me and the ball rolled out of bounds. They called a blocking foul, and I was done. The Georgia Tech call was even worse. For (Jim Burr) to make that call – a charging call in transition, on the opposite end of the floor at the beginning of overtime – was unbelievable. I spun around Isma'il Muhammad, and he flopped. I hadn't even crossed midcourt yet. (Burr) was trailing the play and was literally about 50 feet away when he blew his whistle. There was another ref standing right there and he didn't call anything. I had killed Georgia Tech in the second half. There was no way I was going to let us lose. I just had that mentality. I made a comment to the media after the game about how bad the call was. The NCAA was going to suspend me before my senior year, so I had to apologize. Well, actually, the school wrote up the letter, and I just signed it. I don't understand why he's still a ref. If he wouldn't have called that foul, Kansas would've gone to three straight Final Fours. I've never talked to Jim Burr. That's probably a good thing.

## NICE SHOT, J.R.

One reason we were even in that game against Georgia Tech was J.R. Giddens. He had one hell of a year as a freshman and hit a huge 3-pointer with 17 seconds left to force overtime. I liked J.R. There was a side to him that a lot of people didn't understand. J.R. lived down the hall from me. After my first knee surgery, I was sitting on the couch with my legged propped up, and J.R. walked in with a toast-and-egg sandwich with grape jelly on it. He made it in his room and brought it down to me without me even asking. Then he wanted to know if there was anything else he could do. I was surprised, but I probably shouldn't have been, because J.R. was a good teammate. J.R. wanted to fit in so bad and wanted to be great so bad. I just think he approached it the wrong way. But he was a good kid, a genuine kid. When you get here as a freshman and everyone is kissing your ass, it takes a certain kind of person to handle it the right way. Honestly, we all take advantage of it at certain points. But I think he got overwhelmed by it a little bit. Still, what happened with him was a shame. He was a good person. He fit.

## HIDDEN GEM

I would've loved to have seen what kind of career Jeremy Case would've had if Roy Williams would've stayed at Kansas. Things with him would've been totally different. Jeremy Case would've been like Jeff Boschee. He had that same kind of game. He was a heady player who was smart and played good defense. He could shoot the hell out of the ball. It would've fit right in with the way we were playing. I'm sure Roy was thinking the same thing when he recruited him. Bill Self's style just wasn't for Jeremy.

## MAN OF FAITH

Another good thing about our junior year was that Wayne Simien finally got a full season to show what he could do. Wayne had only played about half of the season in 2002-03 and missed the Final Four. And he played through a lot of injuries as a senior, too. He wouldn't have admitted it then, but Wayne got a little tired of some of the names people would call him. He'd get on the Internet and see people referring to him as "Wheelchair Wayne" and things like that. That kind of stuff hurts. He was never 100 percent healthy. I did everything I could to take his mind off of it. Once he got older and found his faith, that kind of stuff was easier for him to deal with because he was in such a happy place.

Wayne was a completely different person his last two years at Kansas. He spent some time away from Lawrence the summer before his junior year. When he came back, it was like someone had flipped a switch inside of him. He threw away all of his rap CDs and took the rims off of his truck. Then he moved out of our apartment. He said, "I have to live a different lifestyle and surround myself with people who are men of God." I resented that. We had been so tight since the time I'd gotten here. Because we were all still pretty young at the time, some of us didn't understand his decision. We were like, "Wow! Are you serious? What's going on?" He explained it to us and shared what he was so excited about. I just don't think we understood at the time. I even apologized to Wayne years later. I opened up about it. I'd found my own faith. I apologized to him. During that time, we were living that rock star lifestyle. None of us wanted to give that up. When he did, our little clique went from five players to four. I don't think it changed anything on the court. We still had good chemistry. But off the court it was a little awkward. We'd be on the bus laughing and joking and talking about each other, but Wayne would be sitting there with his headphones on and his Bible out. If he had a turnover, he'd say, "God bless" instead of "Godd---." Sometimes girls would come into the gym to watch us play pickup. Once they walked in, Wayne would stop the game and go put his shirt on. We probably didn't handle it well. You mock what you don't understand. You resent it. Thinking back on it now, I realize how mature that was for a 20-year-old to change his lifestyle when everything from women to fame is easily accessible to you. The dude had blinders on. It was absolutely incredible. And I say that in a good way, not a bad way.

## MESSAGE BOARDS

I don't think people understand how big of an effect message boards have on players. We're already our own biggest critics. You can go out and ask 100 fans what they think about Keith Langford, and if eight or nine of them say, "He's a jerk," that's what I'll remember the most. I know we get a lot of perks and get treated well, but at the end of the day, we truly care about basketball and winning and making fans happy and representing the school well. To be demeaned by people who supposedly love Kansas basketball feels like a slap in the face. That's why you may see players act like jerks from time to time.

Sometimes my mom would get on those message boards and post things. She's the reason I even started looking at them. I had no idea about them at first. She'd try to get me to use things people posted as fuel and motivation. But it got to the point where I was like, "Yeah, but you're writing stuff, too, mom! Why are you doing that?" I can understand a parent wanting to defend their child. But it gets to a point where you're not a kid anymore. You're a man. You have to deal with the criticism. I'm a huge Cowboys fan. I love Tony Romo to death, but as soon as he throws an interception I'm ready to trade him for

Donovan McNabb. So I understand their passion. But sometimes people went a little overboard.

## INJURIES

After the Oklahoma game of my junior year, I started having some pain in my knee. I got an MRI and found out I needed microfracture surgery. From January until the end of the year, I played knowing I was eventually going to be operated on. I just got injections before every game, and my practice time was minimized.

The day after we lost to Georgia Tech in the Elite Eight, I came back to Kansas and had the surgery. The recovery is typically four to six months, but I came back a little early. We had that Canada trip the first week of September, and with all of the new freshmen coming in, I thought it was important that I play. The decision was obviously a bad one, because after that trip I had to have the same surgery again. I thought about redshirting that season, but Aaron, Mike, Wayne and I had all come in together, and we wanted to leave together, so I decided to go ahead and play even though I wasn't 100 percent. I was overweight when the season started because I hadn't been able to do much. I just wasn't feeling like myself. I felt like I'd made a big mistake.

## OFF THE COURT

Injuries weren't the only issues I faced during my senior year. Obviously this never became public, but I got a girl pregnant, and we decided to have an abortion. It was a serious deal that added to the pressure that I was already feeling. I got some people to help me out and talk to me before the final decision was made. It's not something I'm proud of, but it's real. It happened. I'm not going to pretend it didn't. I was never in trouble for any rules violations at Kansas. I was never arrested and I never had anyone accuse me of rape. This was something that happened that was a mistake. It's a mistake a lot of athletes make. I dealt with it and I learned from it. If it happened to me again, it's something I would handle differently. It's something I wouldn't do. The school was there for me. Coach Self was there for me. He said he wasn't going to pay for anything or help with anything or give me advice on which option to pick. But he made sure I got advice from the right kind of people to handle the situation. I know people may have different reactions to this and I understand. But the purpose of a book is to put everything out there, and this was something I had to deal with that maybe people can learn from.

## BITTER END

I sprained my ankle really bad early in our game at Missouri, which was the last regular season game of the year. They gave me a couple of injections so I could go back in and try to play. Those injections ended up being very costly – both for me and for Kansas.

Here's what happened: The next day or two, I started having these really bad back pains. I was like, "Man, I don't know what's going on, but I feel like crap." I didn't practice at all and, for some reason, I couldn't go to the bathroom. My stomach was starting to swell. On about the third night, the pain was getting really, really bad. It was really intense. I called our trainer, Bill Cowgill, around 2 in the morning. I said, "You've got to come get me. Something is wrong. My back is hurting really, really bad." He told me to meet him at the training room. I told him to come pick me up and he said, "C'mon, Keith. Just meet me there." So I started walking and, by the time I got outside, I couldn't take it anymore. I collapsed and was literally crawling on all fours. Luckily, of all people, Greg Heaggans, one of our football players, was just getting back to the Towers in the middle of the night. I didn't know where he was coming from and I didn't care. He put me in his car and drove me over to the training room.

Once Cowgill saw me he took me over to the clinic on campus and they hooked me up to an IV. The next day they put me in the hospital. By then my stomach was really, really big and the pain was bad. Eventually the doctor came in and said, "Your kidney isn't functioning right but we don't know why." They finally realized it was a delayed reaction to the medicine I took at Missouri, the injections. I had an allergic reaction to them. I missed the Big 12 tournament and was still really weak when I came back for the Bucknell game. I didn't even start that game, probably because I hadn't practiced for a single minute. I wanted to play, though, because all these people who didn't know what was wrong with me were saying, "Why doesn't Langford just suck it up? All he's got is a stomach virus? He can't play through that?" No one ever knew the real story of what happened.

I did some warm-ups and some shooting, but when I didn't start I just figured I'd just cheer on my teammates and mentally prepare to play against Wisconsin in the second round. Then a point came in the game where Coach Self kind of looked at me. He didn't say anything, but it felt like he was telling me, "You might want to check in. This might be it." That was the feel I got from the look he had in his eyes. The whole game is a blur to me now. I don't remember my stats or what happened. I just remember being out there but not moving very well. I caught a lot of hell for not performing well in that game. It was just tough to go out like that.

## "BASKETBALL PURGATORY"

As tough as things were at the end of my college career, they got even tougher the next couple of years. For the first time I didn't have a very good grasp on what I was going to do. I didn't know where my career was going. It was very uncomfortable for me. I was in basketball purgatory. I played in the D-League my first year after college and realized that getting to the NBA wasn't going to be easy. I turned down several offers of $200,000 and $300,000 to play overseas right off the bat, but after a year in the D-League, I was $70,000 or $80,000 in debt because I'd taken a big loan from my agent, part of which I used to buy a maroon Hummer right after I got out of school. After a year in the D-League, I didn't have any choice but to go overseas. I ended up signing for about $150,000 with a second-division team in Italy. I struggled quite a bit socially over there and just wasn't happy. I came back and got an apartment in Texas and had no plans to go back to Italy. I had a little money left over from paying off my agent but I spent most of that during the summer. I remember my lease being up and not wanting to go back to Europe. So I crammed all my belongings into the Hummer, drove over to my girlfriend's place and stayed there with her and her roommate for about two months. I was just waiting for my next move, trying to figure out what was going on. I probably had a couple hundred dollars in the bank. It was crazy.

Three days before NBA training camps started that year (2007-08), I got a call from the Spurs asking me if I wanted to come down. I went and played pickup with their guys a few times and went to a couple of workouts. After that they said, "We'd like for you to join us in camp." I played well in camp – Jeff Graves was there, too – but they said they weren't ready to keep me on the full-time roster, so they sent me to their D-League team in Austin. The head coach was Quin Snyder, who coached against us when he was at Missouri. Quin was great. He was so cool. When I first met him, I didn't really know what to expect because of the whole Kansas-Missouri thing. But there was a mutual respect there. He showed a lot of admiration for me. He put me in a position where I could do some good things. He understood where I was at in my career. He'd tell me what Coach Popovich and R.C. Buford – the Spurs coach and general manager – were saying about me. He's good friends with those guys. I ended up getting a call-up to the Spurs. I was in great shape and really started getting into a nice rhythm like I was back in my good years at Kansas. But then they released me after I'd only played in two games. At that point I made up my mind that I was going to make as much money as I could and further my career in Europe. I finished off the season in Italy and went back the next year and won a championship. I was named the MVP of the Final Four. After that things really started to take off. Out of nowhere, the contracts started skyrocketing. In June of 2009, I signed a two-year deal for $2.6 million per year with a Russian team: Khimki, Moscow Region. This summer (2011) I was given a new, four-year deal by the same team for $2.3 million per year. That contract makes me the highest-paid American player in all of Europe. It's something I'm pretty proud of.

## LIVING IN RUSSIA

Typically, if you're on one of the good Russian teams, you can make a little more than you can anywhere else. Moscow is nice, but it's pretty far away from everything, and the weather is an issue. If you have a $700,000 deal in Madrid and a $700,000 deal in Moscow, which one are you going to take? That's why they have to pay a little more in Russia.

I've adjusted to Russia completely. The team has done a lot to make things easier on me. I have my own driver that works for me from 9 in the morning to 11 at night. I have a nice apartment that overlooks the city. They give me business class tickets to bring my family over during the year. As far as eating, if you get homesick, they have Chili's, Dunkin' Donuts, Burger King and KFC. There's a lot of stuff like that right around where I live. It's incredible the way it's set up. The nightlife is nice. My wife and I spent time in Bologna, Italy. Both of us think Moscow is better, hands down.

## WHAT'S NEXT

People ask me all the time if my goal is to get back to the NBA. My answer is "not at all." The league minimum is right around $470,000. The NBA takes about 48 or 49 percent of that money. My first paycheck from the Spurs was $38,000. I had a little over $20,000 left when all of the money was taken out. I was making the league minimum, and other guys are going over to Europe and making $250,000 and not getting any taxes taken out of it. So it was basically the same. One difference, though, is that a low-level guy in the NBA spends a lot of time around his rich teammates. He'll be out clubbing every night. He has to pay for his car and his apartment in the city where he plays – plus payments on his house in his home town. It shouldn't be shocking that a lot of guys who play in the NBA end up going broke.

The other thing is that I want to play. Physically, these are the best years of my life. I'll never be as good of a player as I am in my 20s. I want to spend those years on the court, not on the bench.

I'm a little bit different of a player than I was at Kansas, mainly because I'm completely healthy. I've got a trainer in the offseason. I understand what it takes now to keep my body right. I've taken my game to a whole different level. Now I play more like an actual guard as opposed to a guy who takes a couple of dribbles and then slashes to the basket. I'm doing a little bit of everything, whether I'm playing the point or the two. I'm playing the pick-and-roll really well. I understand the game so much better now from a mental standpoint.

## LOVING SELF

If it weren't for Kansas, I wouldn't be where I am right now. I had to go through some struggles after college before I could look back and fully grasp what the school has done for me and my family. I have a genuine appreciation for the growth I went through there – and an appreciation for Coach Self.

Coach Self taught me there is more than one way to do things right. I

spent all this time thinking that Roy's way was the only way. Looking back on it, I never had any adversity under Roy, from dealing with him as a coach or disputes over playing time. It all went really smoothly. But there's no way I would've been able to get through the past five or six years if I didn't get such a good foundation from Coach Self. From being cut several times to almost being broke to having to play in Europe ... what I went through with Coach Self helped prepare me for that stuff. Everything from his boot camp to him pushing me and staying on me all the time, I needed that. I hadn't had that in my life until I met him. There's no telling if I would've crumbled after college if not for Bill Self.

## ALL-TIME GREAT

A lot of the guys I played with – guys like Nick and Kirk and Drew and Wayne – have had their jerseys retired. Sometimes I wonder if I'll have mine retired, too. I tried to shy away from it for a long time, but I can't help but think about it. Do I want it? Yes. I feel like I should at least be considered. There aren't many guys that did what I did at Kansas. I think I'm one of the 10-15 best players that have played there. At the very least, it should be brought before the committee who decides. All the numbers should be broken down. It would definitely mean a lot to me.

Even if it doesn't happen, I'll always be proud to be a Jayhawk. The other day I was back in town eating in the restaurant of the Oread Hotel. A wedding party came through and all of them stopped and stared at me. They were just in awe of the fact that I was sitting there eating chicken fingers. It made me feel good. There is no other place like Kansas. There is nowhere else I would've rather gone.

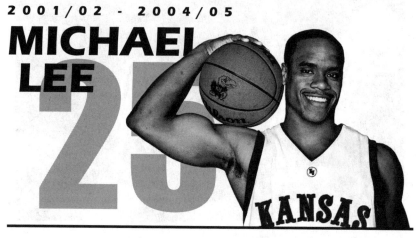

# CHAPTER 14

## 2001/02 - 2004/05
# MICHAEL LEE

Michael Lee arrived at Kansas in 2001 along with Aaron Miles, his high school teammate and best friend. A role player early in his career, Lee eventually became an integral part of the Jayhawks' rotation. The Portland, Ore., native was on the court during the most crucial moments of Kansas' loss to Syracuse in the 2003 national title game. The following year he helped lead the Jayhawks to the Elite Eight. Lee was a graduate assistant on Kansas' 2008 national championship squad. The 2010-11 campaign marked his first season as a full-time assistant at the University of San Francisco, which is coached by former Jayhawk Rex Walters.

### IN MICHAEL'S WORDS

A lot of people thought Aaron and I came to Kansas as a package deal. I can see how it may have looked that way to people on the outside. Aaron was the McDonald's All-American that everyone wanted, and I was his best friend. What people don't realize is that I actually committed to Kansas before Aaron and that, for a while, Aaron had all but decided to go to Arizona. He had the time of his life on his visit to Tucson. Gilbert Arenas was his host. Gilbert is a clown, a silly guy just like Aaron. They had a lot of fun. We never sat down and talked where I said, "Aaron, I'm going to Kansas. Do you think you'll come with me?" Still, I'm sure our coaches thought that, if they got me, they'd have a good chance to get Aaron. They never mentioned it me, though.

Oregon did. Ernie Kent wanted us as a package deal. He wanted me to come in with Aaron and redshirt. That's not how Kansas approached it. They were following Aaron and they saw what I could do. They initially wanted Daniel Ewing, but he ended up going to Duke. Coach Williams said, "Mike, we've seen what you can do. We know what you can bring to the table. We want to offer you a scholarship, period." I think they brought me in because they legitimately thought I had a chance to play. I remember being on my visit with Aaron and Josh Childress and Jamal Sampson. We were in a room with Drew Gooden and he said, "What do you think? Do you like it so far?" I was, "Oh yeah. I'm going to come."

## YOU WANT ME TO DO WHAT?

Early during my freshman year, I gave some thought to leaving school, mainly because Coach Williams asked me to redshirt after the first week of practice. That threw me off. I was really prideful. I went back to the locker room and started asking Drew and Nick and everyone what they thought I should do. They didn't have much advice for me, but I just needed to say something to somebody. At the time, I took it as, "They don't think I'm good enough." But what they were really saying was, "You're more than good enough but you're not quite ready. Give it some time." I wasn't mature enough to look at it like that. Sometimes I wonder what would've happened if I'd have taken that redshirt. My life may have taken a different turn if I'd played another year with Coach Self.

## EARLY MEMORIES

We started off that season with a loss to Ball State in Maui. I remember watching the scout tape for that game. I was sitting by Lewis Harrison, and we looked at each other like, "These dudes are good!" They were fast and athletic – and it didn't help that the heat got us. Nick kept cramping up and then Aaron cramped up right as Patrick Jackson got by him for the winning basket. Some people were saying Aaron faked the cramp because he got beat. He didn't fake anything with the game on the line. Aaron wouldn't do that.

After that game Coach Williams was so mad. When you lose a game under Coach Williams you're scared to death. You don't know if he's going to run you. You don't know if he's going to scream. You prepare for the worst. I remember Aaron was lying on the bench in the locker room with a towel over his face. Coach Williams saw him and started turning red. He yanked that towel off of Aaron's face and said, "Sit up! You need to hear this!" He was livid. He ran us the next morning. He found a high school gym where it was about 300 degrees. We practiced and then he put everyone on the baseline – even all of the assistant coaches. He said, "Everybody is going to run – and I mean everybody!" All of a sudden Coach Holladay was out there jogging a little bit. Coach Dougherty was running, Jerod was running. It was crazy, especially considering we had a game later that day.

One of our other losses that year was at UCLA. I was so nervous that game because I had a lot of family there. I was hoping I'd get in the game but, once I did, it didn't last long. I played terrible. Coach Williams put me in, and I literally ran over Rico Hines. They called a charge on me, and Coach Williams took me right back out. I can laugh at it now, but it wasn't funny that day. I'm sure he was thinking, "I can't play this guy. I can't play him." After that game, I felt so bad because I wanted my parents to be happy. I felt like I'd let them down. I can still remember my dad coming up to me after the game and saying, "Son, whether you play 1 minute or 20 minutes, we're going to support you the same. It doesn't matter. You've already made us proud."

## A PLACE IN HISTORY

I'm not a big Kansas historian that knows everything about the last 100 years of basketball in Lawrence. But I can't imagine there have been many – if any – teams at KU as good as the one we had in 2001-02. We had some horses. We were ranked No. 1 in a bunch of statistical categories and we had the best offense in America. No post player could run with Drew. Nick Collison was a sure bet any time you gave him the ball. You had Aaron handling the ball, which took some responsibility away from Kirk so he could score. Then there was Boschee. It felt like he shot about 80 percent from 3-point range that year. At one point I thought, "We're unbeatable." Everything just clicked. We passed the ball so well. We shared the ball and got up and down the court so fast. We were blowing teams out by 30 and 40 points. I was having the time of my life, and I wasn't even really playing that much.

The other thing was that our chemistry was so good. It could've been a bad situation since there were a bunch of new guys on the team, but the veterans wouldn't let it happen. When we first got there Drew took us under his wing. Every time Drew went somewhere we were there with him. Kirk kind of kept to himself because Aaron and J-Hawk got on his nerves so bad. They'd glue pennies to his door and put big mattresses in front of his door. They drove him crazy. But overall we all fit off the court, and on it, guys like Aaron and Keith and Wayne were really contributing.

Keith was a hell of a recruit for Coach Williams, a hell of a find. He was under the radar a little bit. He didn't have a lot of hype. But I remember after the very first practice or pickup game, guys on the team were walking around saying, "Man, Keith is a pro." He came in kicking everyone's butt. The first week of practice, me, Wayne, Aaron, Keith, Bryant Nash and Hawkins ... we beat Nick, Kirk, Drew, Boschee and Jeff Carey. It was just a 5- or 10-minute game, but we won. I'll never forget that.

It was tough to lose in the Final Four that year because we all felt we had the best team in the country. But Maryland was a very mature team, a good team. Those guys complemented each other well. We came out on fire at the start of that game. I was like, "Man, we're about to run them out of the gym." But then I looked at Juan Dixon on the Maryland bench during one of the first TV timeouts. We were beating them 13-2, I think, and he was just settling everyone down. He was so calm. You could see it in his eyes. The rest of the guys were calm, too. From then on, they played well.

## ANOTHER CHANCE

When we got to the Final Four the next year (2003) we felt like we had the best team in the country once again – especially after we absolutely killed Marquette (94-61). I was fortunate enough to guard Dwyane Wade in that game. He actually had a bad game against us. Still, that dude was amazing. He was strong. He was explosive. I remember one time I was guarding him, and he hit a turnaround jumper from 17 feet off the backboard. No one at the college level is supposed to be doing that.

When we played Syracuse two nights later for the title, Gerry McNamara made six straight 3's in the first half. Psychologically, we were like, "Man, what's going on?" It was almost out of our control. We looked like we were about to get blown out of the water. One thing about Coach Williams is that his teams always fight back. We knew we were going to make a run. We'd done it earlier that year at Oklahoma. But we just ran out of time. We didn't shoot it well from the line, and then Keith fouled out. He was the only guy we had that could penetrate that tough Syracuse zone off the dribble.

## BLOCKED SHOT

Even though we were down by almost 20 points, we still had a chance at the end to send the game into overtime, but Hakim Warrick blocked my 3-pointer with a few seconds left. To this day, I'm still convinced it would've gone in. I just took too much time to get it off. I hate talking about it because I still play it back in my head. Each time it ends with me screaming to myself, "You idiot! Shoot the damn ball!" I'm not sure what I could've done different. Maybe I should've

pump-faked. I saw where Warrick was. I knew the time and score. I was set up good for the shot. I just took too long to shoot it. It meant a lot to me that Kirk threw me the ball. I didn't want to let him down. We'd lost to Colorado earlier that year on the same kind of play. Kirk passed me the ball for an 18-foot jump shot. I missed, and we lost. So it meant a lot that he still had that kind of confidence in me. Kirk could've taken the shot. But he was pretty far behind the line and, somehow, two guys closed on him, and I was on the left wing, wide open. But as soon as Kirk left his feet, Warrick started coming my way and made a play on it. I was hurting for a long time after that one. In a small way, I probably always will be. That's just the competitor in me.

After that game I crawled under a table with a curtain around it. I didn't want anyone to see me. I didn't want anyone to find me. I didn't want anyone to talk to me. That was a real quiet locker room. When you look back, you've got to be proud of what we accomplished. We played our ass off. We had no reason to hang our heads. But at that time, it was a dead silence.

## SAYING GOODBYE

I never thought in a million years that Coach Williams would leave Kansas. It didn't make sense to me. But I wasn't thinking about his situation. Dean Smith is his mentor. His family is there. That's where he went to school. I wasn't thinking about any of that. I was just thinking, "I'm still here. Aaron Miles and Keith Langford and Jeff Graves are coming back. We're going to make another run." I remember him walking into the locker room. His face was swollen. He looked like he'd been crying for hours. I looked at him and thought, "There is no way this man is about to say what I think he's going to say." But then he said it. Actually, he couldn't talk. He couldn't get it out. He was too choked up. For a while he just stood there and cried. When he finally said, "I've decided to go to North Carolina," he just kind of waited to see what everyone's response was going to be. The room was just quiet. I'm not sure he said anything else after that.

About a week later, Coach Williams came back for the team banquet. Beforehand all the families and parents were standing around talking. I was standing by him near the door to the auditorium. He was leaning up against a wall and he didn't look too good. I said, "Coach, are you all right?" and it almost looked like a sense of relief came over him. He was thinking everyone was against him and mad. He just patted me on the back and whispered, "Yeah Mike, I'm OK."

I don't hold it against him. Lots of coaches dream about coaching at their alma mater – especially when their alma mater is one of the best programs in the history of college basketball. Before he's a coach, he's a father, he's a husband. I'm sure that played into it, too.

## FIRST IMPRESSIONS

The first time we meet Bill Self, he looked like he hadn't slept in three days. His shirt was untucked. His tie was loose. He was just really cool. That's what everyone was saying: "This guy is cool." Coach Self was like, "We're going to have fun, and I'm going to have fun. We're going to run. We're going to push the ball. We're going to do what you guys do best." He really loosened us up.

After a few months, though, you could really see that he was going to change some stuff around. That's understandable. He was a new coach and wanted to do things his way. The problem was that we were still trying to do things our way. Under Coach Williams, we were programmed. We were programmed to do certain things a certain way at a certain time. We had our whole itinerary written out on the first day of school. It was day and night when Coach Self came in. I was very stubborn. They called me "the locker room thug" because I was always complaining about something. At one point I told the media there was a tug-of-war going on between the coaches and players. Coach Self sat me down and said, "What are you trying to say?" We had a lot of those meetings.

At the end of the day, he wanted to win. Kids size up coaches real quick. If we felt like he was a bum or that he didn't have his stuff together, we wouldn't have given that man respect. But he absolutely wanted to win. He was coaching his tail off, too. Even with all of our problems, he still found a way to make things work that first year. We were seconds away from going back to the Final Four with a team that wasn't buying in every day. Coach Self coached his ass off.

## JEFF GRAVES: THE GOOD AND THE BAD

Coach Self had a rule in Boot Camp that if anyone missed a class, we'd have to do extra running. Graves was notorious for missing class. Someone would drop him off in front of the building, he'd walk in – and then walk out the back door. At the end of Boot Camp each day, Coach Self would get the class attendance report. One day he was like, "All right, it's time to run for J.G." We already had to run five 17s – a 17 is when you sprint the width of the court, sideline to sideline – as part of the normal routine. On top of that we had to run extra ones because J.G. missed class. Making it worse was that the drill is timed, and of all people, J.G. couldn't make the time. Each time he didn't make it, Coach Self would make us run it again. It happened over and over. Bryant Nash got so mad that he walked out of the gym. At some point, I took my shirt off and started screaming and cussing at J.G. He was bent down trying to catch his breath, and I was standing over him with my fists balled up saying, "Man, if you don't pick this s--t up ..." I wanted to knock his head off. I think Coach Self wanted me to hit him. No one was trying to stop me. No one told me to calm down. Jeff never said anything back. As mad as I was, I could never hit one of my teammates. I love J.G. But he was so selfish that day. We were running because of him, and he didn't even look like he was trying. The coaches had to put up with it, though. They had no other choice. When Jeff was playing his best basketball, we were a completely different team. So they kept running Jeff like a gerbil on a spin wheel. Every day after practice he'd run. At one point he started running sideways because he was so tired.

I also remember how Jeff drove this nice big Escalade. We'd roll down the window, turn up the music and drive around campus listening to the soundtrack from "Training Day." He loved that Escalade and he was always taking it back to Lee's Summit. Sometimes, while we were practicing, Coach Self would have the team managers steal Jeff's keys and hide his car all the way across campus, where he couldn't find it for a while. That kept him from going home all the time.

## WHO STABBED J.R.?

J.R. Giddens was also on Coach Self's first team. He had been signed by Roy and still decided to come once Roy left. The best way to describe J.R. is Jekyll and Hyde. Some days, he could be the best teammate in the world on and off the court. The next he could be very tough to deal with because he was very cocky, very arrogant. None of us were like that. One day he'd be joking around and getting along with everyone, the next day he was like, "I'm better than you." He'd come into practice and tell the walk-ons, "Y'all might as well get off the court now, because you're not going to be playing during the season." That didn't sit well with people. The thing people don't know about J.R. is that J.R. tried so hard. He worked so hard. We'd run sprints and do other stuff, and he'd want to win every drill. He never took a drill off. He was always in the gym. He worked his tail off. In a lot of ways, he was misunderstood. He felt like a lot of people were out to get him. A lot of times I didn't feel sorry for him because he brought stuff on himself. But he was still my teammate. We all hung out and went out to dinner and had a good time.

I remember a lot about the day J.R. got stabbed at the Moon Bar. Earlier that afternoon we were playing pickup games and, for whatever reason, J.R. just lost it. He got mad about something and stormed out of the gym screaming. He was so mad that he was actually crying. Something was wrong that day. He had some issues. I was like, "Whatever, no big deal. He'll be OK." After pickup that day, no one really saw J.R. He wasn't hanging around The Towers. When I went to the Moon Bar that night he was already there. J.R. got into it with some dude, and they threw the guy out. After that, I left and went home. A while later, I got a call saying he'd been stabbed. I went to the hospital, and the same girls I saw J.R. with at the Moon Bar were sitting in the lobby. I was mad at them for letting it happen. I was mad at everybody. It was just a crazy situation. It was almost spooky. I don't know what he did to instigate that situation. It was almost surreal. I was like, "This dude just got his calf ripped open." Looking back, I feel like I should've said something when he walked out of the gym that day. Something obviously wasn't right with him, and it just escalated into what happened that night.

## AARON'S ANTICS

Aaron loved to go around campus squirting people with water guns. We'd get into Jeff Hawkins' car, and Aaron would put on a Halloween mask. He'd see someone walking, roll down his window and say, "Excuse me, can you help us find so-and-so?" As soon as the person took a step closer to the car, Aaron would get them with the Super Soaker. One time someone was smoking. He asked the guy to come over to the car and he said, "Don't you know that smoking causes cancer?" The guy said, "Yeah, I know," and Aaron was like, "Here, let me help you." Then he just drenched the guy and put out the cigarette before we sped off. You're not supposed to drive through the main part of campus in the middle of the day. If you do they write down your license plate number and send you a ticket, so J-Hawk would put mud on his tags to cover the numbers up.

Aaron was a clown. Whenever he had a class in one of those big auditoriums, he'd bring a pillow and go to sleep in the back row. The teacher couldn't see that far back. J-Hawk did it, too. Another thing we liked doing was playing Texas Hold 'em down in Christian Moody's room. Aaron wanted to have his own little identity, his own little costume like the poker players on ESPN. So he'd come down wearing some sort of bathrobe and a headband and he'd play entrance music as he came into the room. I don't know if he ever won a game. We played spades on the back of the team charter plane all the time, too, and he always lost. Then, as we got off the plane, Moody and Stephen Vinson would steal stuff. Granola bars, fruit, cookies, Gatorade. There was so much food. They'd bring extra backpacks and load up their bags as they got off the plane.

## WWE – KANSAS STYLE

For some reason, we always used to have wrestling matches on the road. I don't know why. One time, we were playing at Texas Tech in Lubbock my sophomore year, and at the hotel a few hours before the game, I started wrestling J-Hawk. It only took about 3 seconds to put him on his back. Then I started picking on Keith. I was saying, "C'mon Keith! You're from Texas. You're tough. Let's go." He got the best of me, though, because I didn't have any shoes on. I couldn't get any traction, you know (laughing). Everyone was gassing it up, and Keith ended up putting me in a submission hold, and I couldn't do anything. He had my neck locked up. He finally let me up and I was like, "Man, my neck hurts." Aaron was rolling around on the ground, holding his stomach because he was laughing so hard. I was like, "It's not funny, man. My neck hurt. We've got a game tonight. This isn't good." I couldn't tell the coaches what happened. How could I explain that? We got to the arena, and I asked our trainer, Mark Cairns, for some Flex-All and told him it was for my knee. He gave it to me, and

I went into the bathroom stall and rubbed it on neck. Then we were going over the scouting report right before the game, and I was still twisting and turning, trying to get my neck right. Aaron and J-Hawk were just sitting there snickering. I never messed with Keith again.

## SNOWED IN

My senior year we started off 20-0, but we weren't running away from anyone. We weren't playing like the No. 1-ranked team in the country should be. We'd had some scares. It all caught up to us when we played at Villanova. That was one of the worst nights of my college career. I just found my old journal. I wrote a lot about that game because I was so pissed off. We were wearing our new red, white and blue Jordans. No one else in America had them. And we were wearing our red jerseys. Ever since that game Coach Self has not been fond of those red jerseys. He doesn't like them. We actually had a good walk-through the night before. But we just got our butts kicked. Mike Nardi, Curtis Sumpter, Allan Raye … they gave us a total ass-kicking. Then we got snowed in. We sat in a hotel room for about eight hours that night watching film. Coach Self was on a roll. He told us how he felt about each and every one of us. We were tired, falling asleep. I don't even think they let us eat. It was the worst trip in history.

## WOUNDED WAYNE

Just like in previous seasons, Wayne was never 100 percent our senior year. After a while it got tough to watch. The first time I met Wayne was at a hotel in Durham, N.C., when I went to watch Aaron at the McDonald's All-American game. Wayne was hurt then, too. He couldn't play because his collarbone was all messed up. Wayne was always a great teammate. He was a better person than he was a player. For his career to be plagued by injury … it just wasn't fair. I was always like, "Why Wayne?" If Wayne would've moped around all the time and said, "Woe is me," it would've been even harder to watch Wayne go through that. But he was always upbeat.

Wayne always had his own workouts. He would do arm rotations, and me and J-Hawk would joke and say, "What is Wayne doing? He just came into the weight room for 15 minutes and left. We've been here an hour and aren't even done yet." He'd go to the trainer and get his treatment and stuff. He didn't have to practice all the time once Coach Self got there. We needed him for the games. That's why our offense worked. Throw the ball to Wayne and get out of the way.

The summer before our junior year, I was at home in Portland, and Wayne called me and said, "I've dedicated my life to Christ." I thought that was cool. I had grown up going to church. But I didn't know the extent of the changes he was talking about until I got back to school. He did a full 180 right away. He was carrying his Bible with him everywhere and quoting scriptures. I was like, "This guy is serious right now." He didn't push what he was doing on anyone. He just did his own thing.

## NO! NO! NO!

Nothing went well when we played Bucknell in the NCAA Tournament my senior year. They had a good guard named Charles Lee that just kicked my butt all over the place. I had a decent game (18 points), but it didn't matter. They matched up well with us, and we were not on our best game. By halftime, I was thinking, "We've just got to get through this game. We're not going to win going away, but we've got to find a way to get through it. Then we can regroup, and everything will be fine." My freshman year we had a really close first-round game against Holy Cross, and then we started cruising. I figured something like that would happen again this time. Unfortunately, it didn't work out like that.

I remember throwing that ball into Wayne all the way down the court for the last shot. He'll make that shot nine times out of 10. From my angle it looked good, but the ball bounced off the rim, and their team rushed the floor. I walked straight back to the locker room and into the shower. I started banging my head on the shower wall. I kept saying, "No! No! No!" I didn't want to believe it. After all we'd accomplished in four years, that wasn't how we should've gone out. I felt so bad for our fans, for the university. Coach Self didn't know what to tell us. We'd been to two Final Fours and made a good run to the Elite Eight. What do you say? He didn't say too much. It was a quiet locker room. People still call it one of the biggest upsets of all time.

## MOVING ON

After my last year of basketball I had a conversation with Mark Mangino about joining the football team. I still look back and wonder if I made a mistake by not doing it. A few months later the Chiefs called me, then Pittsburgh. They just wanted to see if I had any interest in trying out. They weren't offering me a contract or anything, but they wanted to get me in for a workout.

Instead I ended up signing with the Harlem Globetrotters, mainly because they were the ones who offered me the most money. If I would've gone back for my second year, I would've been paid $120,000.

It was a great experience, but it wasn't basketball. Anyone that knows me knows I'm not a showman. That's not what I do. I actually got fired from the Globetrotters. They sent me a letter in the mail to tell me. That's how they were conducting business at the time. Nobody called or anything. They just mailed me a letter that said, "Send us our stuff back."

I didn't have much going on at the time. Aaron was over in Poland and he said, "Mike, come over here." There was a younger team over there – not the same team Aaron was on – and they let me work out with them. They had a try-out, and I made the team. I was just trying to find myself. Once the season was done I was ready to come back home. I couldn't speak the language. I lost so much weight because the food was bad. The first day I was in Paris I got a speeding ticket, and my car got towed. I got a call to go back to Paris the next season, but I didn't want to go. I wasn't going back across the water.

To bide my time, I went to play with the Salina Cagerz. Then I got hurt so I needed to find something else to do. I drove up the road to Kansas' camp in June. I heard that Nate Mast, the graduate assistant, was leaving and, a few days later, Coach Self offered me his position. That was the summer of 2007. At that time I wasn't even thinking about going into coaching. But then we won the national championship that season, and Coach Self sat me down and said, "What would you think about becoming a full-time assistant somewhere?" I thought it was a good idea. Coach Self started telling me how to dress and what to say in interviews. He went to bat for me. He made sure I got out there and got noticed. I took the job at Gardner-Webb – about 40 miles west of Charlotte – because of what Coach Self and Coach Williams said. They both said the same thing in a different way, that it'd be good for me to get out on the road and recruit and learn the ropes at a young age. I was only 25 at the time.

There is a lot of stuff that goes into coaching. It's more than just showing up and being on the court and recruiting. Coach Self said, "You'll find out if this is what you want to do." I made $19,000 a year for two years at Gardner-Webb. After my second year, my boss, Rick Scruggs, got let go. Then Rex Walters at San Francisco reached out to me. It was a no-brainer. I like what I do. I need to be around people and be active and travel, and I enjoy watching basketball. I don't like being in the office. I can't stand the paperwork and the office stuff. But overall I really enjoy what I do.

## KANSAS INFLUENCE

At Kansas, I got to see what a well-run program really looked like. Now that I've been away I've been able to see the issues that can arise when you don't have a "program," per se. Not having everyone on the same page, not having your alumni and your boosters involved and not having a strength coach and academic adviser that are specifically for basketball. At Kansas we had resources that were second to none. That doesn't happen everywhere. At Gardner-Webb our guys got about two pairs of shoes for an entire season. At Kansas, players would go through two pairs of shoes every couple of weeks. Now, when we're at the drawing board talking about things we may need or things we should do, I can say, "Here's what we did at Kansas, and it absolutely worked."

When I'm coaching I use stuff from Coach Self and Coach Williams. If I ever get the opportunity to be a head coach, I want to be a mixture of both of those guys. I love what I learned under Coach Williams and, from an individual standpoint, Coach Self took my game to a new different level. Under Coach Williams we ran a system: Get the ball inside, if it comes back out, get the ball to Aaron, etc. We were programmed. With Coach Self, if you were a guard, you'd better be able to handle the ball. I became a much better ball-handler under Coach Self. We did a lot with individual skill improvement. Coach Williams is a perfectionist. Coach Self is more of a players' coach. In the huddle, he's like, "Guys, what do you see out there? Aaron, how are they guarding you?"

One time we were playing Nebraska, and they had a player named Joe McCray. We got into a scuffle on the ground. He kicked me, but they gave me the foul ... it may have even been a technical. I was so mad. I went into the timeout and I said, "Coach, I didn't do anything. He kicked me." I was so mad that I almost teared up. Coach just said, "All right, Mike. We'll get him back for you. We'll get him back. Here's what we'll do." I think he drew up some play where McCray had to run through three or four screens. Coach Self was good with that kind of stuff.

I was more of a fit for Coach Williams' system, though. Coach Self probably wouldn't have recruited me to play his kind of basketball ... coming off of ball screens, penetrating and kicking or finishing in the lane. That wasn't my type of game, but I did the best I could. With Coach Williams, I was more of a glue-guy. I'd come into the game, bring some energy, dive for loose balls, guard bigger guys, feed the post, that kind of stuff. I was a role player.

## A PLACE IN HISTORY

I look back on my time at Kansas with no regrets. I was fortunate to be on good teams with good players. If the nation ever knew my name, it was because of them. I loved those dudes, each and every one of them. They were the best teammates a guy could have. I wouldn't trade those experiences or memories for anything.

I can only imagine what the college game would be like – how much better the product would be – if everyone would stay for four years like we did. I'm as proud of that as anything.

# CHAPTER 15

# 2001/02 - 2004/05
# AARON MILES

aron Miles was the headliner of a banner 2001 recruiting class that also featured Wayne Simien, Keith Langford, Jeff Hawkins and Miles' childhood friend, Michael Lee. A Portland native, Miles was Oregon's Gatorade Player of the Year as a high school senior. He was a four-year starter at Kansas who led the Jayhawks to two Final Four berths and an appearance in the Elite Eight. Miles, who has played in the NBA and overseas, holds the school and Big 12 record for assists with 954. He and his wife, Mikki, have two sons: Aaron Jr. (Deuce) and Adonis.

## IN AARON'S WORDS

Other than Kansas, the main college I considered was Arizona. The reason I didn't go there was because everyone was telling me that Lute Olson's wife was ill, and he was thinking about retiring. That was also the year Coach Williams had turned down North Carolina and decided to stay at Kansas. That was right before I committed. I was like, "He's not going anywhere." He even told me during recruiting, "Aaron, I don't have any intentions to leave. I don't want to go to the NBA, and the only college job I ever thought about taking, I just turned down." I felt safe and secure with that. I didn't think there was any way the North Carolina job would come open again two years later. But sure enough, it happened, and he left.

I'm not mad anymore. I love Coach Williams. But obviously, initially, it was like, "Man, eff him. We're going to win the championship without him." Those were my thoughts. I wanted to win a championship for myself and my family and my teammates and my school. But I always wanted to show Coach Williams, "Yo, you should've stayed with us." Instead it was reversed. He won a championship at North Carolina my senior year. That was frustrating to watch, especially because all of the components he had on that team, he would've had with us. But I don't think players were a factor in his decision. His 2009 championship ... I was happier for him then, because Kansas had just won the championship the year before.

## WELCOME TO LAWRENCE

I came and visited Kansas for Late Night and was hooked. Late Night was dope. The students had these big sheets with our jersey numbers on them, and they carried them around the gym and then brought them to us to autograph. There were five of us. It was me, Mike Lee, Jamal Sampson, Josh Childress and maybe J-Hawk. I was supposed to be at Midnight Madness that night at Arizona. But Josh Childress and I were good friends, and we wanted to go on our visits to Arizona and Kansas at the same time.

I talked with Coach Williams and he was like, "Aaron, I won't promise you that you'll start, but I'll be surprised if you don't play a lot." I was appreciative that he was truthful with me and didn't promise me anything. He said if I come in and work and do what he thinks I can do, then he wouldn't be surprised if I started.

Mike committed during the visit, and I was pretty sure I was coming here, too. But I wanted to get a few more visits in. I wanted to see Arizona up close and see if I got a different vibe. I'd loved Arizona since I was a kid, mainly because Damon Stoudamire went there, and he's from Portland. I think every guard from Portland wanted to go there for that reason. So when Arizona started recruiting me, I was excited. I was like, "Oh yeah!" They had Mike Bibby and Jason Terry. I had Jason Terry's jersey back in high school. I think I might've even worn a Jason Terry jersey on an unofficial visit to UCLA. I didn't do it intentionally. I just didn't think about it. It was one of my favorite shirts. I had a good time on my visit. Gilbert Arenas was my host, and we hit it off. But besides the uncertainty surrounding Coach Olson, there was the fact that Arizona had Jason Gardner. He was going into his sophomore year, so I wasn't sure what my situation would've been like if I would've went there.

In the end I went with my heart. I called Coach Williams and said, "I'm calling to let you know that I've decided to go to Arizona." He was like, "Well, Aaron, I would've loved for you to come here, but you've got to do what you feel is best for you. We would've loved for you to have been a part of this, but good luck with everything." After that I said, "Coach, I'm just playing. I'm coming to Kansas." He started laughing and just let me know how happy he was.

## BFFs

Another big reason I chose Kansas was because of Mike. I always thought that wherever Mike ended up, I would go there, too. I wanted us to be able to stay together. That's something that I had always prayed for, and it came to life for us. We could've easily gone to a lot of small schools together, but when I prayed I was like, "God, I want to play with Mike at a big school." I talked to all the schools that were recruiting me and said, "I'd like to play with Mike." But everyone said they didn't have another spot open. But I kept praying and a few weeks passed and people started committing elsewhere. The No. 1 recruits for some schools started falling through. That's how it happened at Kansas. When a few guys opted to go elsewhere, a spot opened up for Mike. I thank God for that.

People have always speculated and said that Mike wouldn't have played at Kansas if it wasn't for me. I just tell them that he was always on their list. He was just down a little further. So initially they weren't recruiting him. But after a couple of players turned them down, he was the next one on the list. It was a blessing for him and for me.

## K-FREEZE

Even though we were in the same recruiting class, I didn't know Keith at all when we first got to school. I had played against him in AAU and I remembered he was cold – a nice, smooth lefty. Still, initially, I was thinking there were a couple of recruits out there that were better than him. But once we started playing pickup in the summer, I was thinking, "Yo, this dude is about to get it started." He was cold. He could score. He has a knack for scoring. He still does. But I didn't know him very well and I didn't know Jeff Hawkins very well.

The very first weekend we were on campus, we were in the Horejsi practice gym, and Mike and I played Keith and Hawkins two-on-two. If you talk to Keith now, he might tell you that he and Hawk didn't care for us initially. When they were together that day they'd look at us, and you could tell they were thinking, "Man, screw these dudes." On my end, I'm thinking, "Cool. These are our teammates. Let's go and play." But I think they might have been thinking that I was cocky because I came in so highly touted. Keith and I talked about it later on, and he said his thought that day was, "Let's bust their ass." Who won? I honestly don't remember. But it was definitely competitive. After that we started hanging around all the time. We were all in the same classes during the summer. We just bonded.

It took a few months before people on campus really knew who we were. Before Late Night we'd walk around and people would look at us like, "Hmmmm, he looks like he could be an athlete." To be honest, the majority of the African-Americans on campus either play basketball or football. So when people saw us, they always asked what sport we played. After Late Night, people were like, "That's Aaron Miles. That's Keith Langford. That's Michael Lee and Jeff Hawkins." It changes your whole swag. It's inevitable. When people know who you are, your swag just changes, man. You've got more confidence.

## THOUGHTS ON DREW, KIRK

I looked up to Drew because he had been around a few years. All of those dudes were like big brothers to us. Guys like Drew, Nick, Kirk and Lewis Harrison. Drew and I were roommates throughout that whole season on the road. We had hella conversations about all types of stuff. Basketball, women, school, everything. Some nights we would stay up so late. All of the freshmen wanted to hang with Drew, and he wanted to hang with us because he was still a young kid at heart. He was a young clown at heart.

Kirk was a dude that, when he first met you, he'd be like, "What's up?" And that'd be about all. There weren't any long conversations early on. But once he got to know you, you became boys. That was your boy. You'd laugh, you'd joke, whatever. Kirk just liked to feel people out first.

All players think they work hard, and to some extent they do. They may work harder than the next man. But there is always somebody else working harder than you. On our team that guy was Kirk. He just knew how to keep going and going. It seemed like he just didn't get tired. He just kept pushing himself. In the weight room, it would surprise you how strong he was and how hard he worked. I looked up to that. Coach Dougherty always said, "If you keep going to the gym with Kirk and attach yourself to him, you'll do fine here."

Kirk is surprisingly athletic. In other words, if you look at him, you aren't going to think he's fast and strong and athletic. So it's a surprise. It was a surprise to me when I first got here. You're thinking like, "Oh man, he's probably slow." But when I got out there, he was guarding me and I couldn't go by him. And then when I finally did he was so strong that he'd hit me and bumped me off my path. It was hard to guard him, too, because he was so fast and so good at changing directions. He can obviously shoot the ball great. He doesn't have all that New York, street-ball, Sherron Collins-type handle, but he's got a great handle on the ball. In transition, he goes so fast, and he's so strong that when he hits you with his body, he's creating space.

## "THE PERFECT MIX"

The first game of my college career, we got beat by Ball State in Maui. I took the loss really hard. I had just made a jump shot on the baseline with about a minute left. They passed it to me, and I was about to shoot it again, but the ball slipped out of my hand, and they called a travel. The ensuing possession is when I cramped up, and Patrick Jackson got by me for the game-winning basket. I felt the cramp coming on 3 minutes earlier. But I was like, "Man, I can't come out of the game. I've got to fight through it." Obviously, after it was all over, I looked back on it and thought, "Damn, should I have come out?" It was tough at first, but I always thought there was a chance the game would be on the line again at the end of the season, maybe in the NCAA championship or something, and then I would knock down the shot. That was my thought process.

Even after that game, I didn't think anybody could beat us. I felt like we couldn't be beat that year. There were obviously going to be some tough games, but I just thought our overall team was too good, too deep. We played D and we ran. I didn't think anybody could match us in that area. And we had the best big man tandem in the country along with one of the best guards in Kirk. I didn't see how we were going to lose.

The best part was that our chemistry was so great. We were all talented guys who worked really hard. Everyone pushed each other in practices. You had people that had been there, so you had experience, and then our freshman class added the youthful part to it. We balanced it out. We kept it from having that go-to-work, professional feel. You knew when we came around there was going to be some fun to it. When you watched us play, you saw us jumping up and down and cheering and hugging each other. That was genuine. We had a lot of love for each other. I always felt like it was the perfect mix.

## AND A FRESHMAN SHALL LEAD THEM

Even though I was a first-year player on a team full of future lottery picks, it was my job as the starting point guard to be a leader on the court. I've always been vocal. I've been back to my high school a few times to check out their team, and there are a couple of freshmen there that are pretty good, but they don't talk on the court. I'm like, "You have to talk. You have to be a vocal leader." I tell them that as long as they work their ass off in practice, and people can see that they're working hard, they have the right to speak their mind if it's for the good of the team. You shouldn't hold back, because your teammates are going to respect what you say because they see how hard you work.

I think that's something my teammates respected about me. I believe they felt like I practiced hard all the time. If I had been a lousy, lazy dude trying to say something, people would've been like, "Man ... whatever." But I earned the right to say something. I was never too afraid to speak.

## PLAYING FOR ROY

I loved playing for Coach Williams because I loved the style of play. I loved getting up and down the court, and I loved how he ran his practices. Punctuality is key for him. He comes out with a practice plan, and he sticks to it. If he says practice starts at 4, you're on the court stretching from 4 to 4:15. From 4:15 to 4:19, you're doing a shooting drill. From 4:19 to 4:21, water break. From 4:21 to 4:30, press offense versus defense or whatever. He stuck to it. If the clock went out before we finished a drill, he'd stop and say, "OK, we'll work on that more tomorrow," and then we'd move on to the next one. But practice was always fun. We kept it competitive.

## LOSING TO MARYLAND

We got off to a really good start against Maryland in the Final Four. Kirk hit a 3 in transition, and their team was panicking. I looked over and saw Juan Dixon put his hands up. He was like, "Calm down, we'll be all right." The next thing you know, he went for 33 on us. He was my teammate overseas a few years ago. We talked about it. He talked a little noise low-key, but he wasn't too bad about it. He could've really rubbed it in, though, because he was torching us. He was coming off those Flex screens and hitting jumpers. I was like "Coach Williams, let me guard him. I can guard him. Let me do it." I got on him and they ran a Flex cut, and he hit a jumper right on me. After that it was like, "OK, switch back."

Later, we started coming back. We were pressuring full court and causing turnovers. I remember I got a steal and I jump-stopped to shoot it near the top of the key. But at the last minute, I passed it, and the refs called a travel on me. We were only down by five at the time. That just killed us right there. Coach Williams looked at the tape later and said I didn't travel. There was only about a minute or two left. We had been down by almost 20, but we had clawed back and scratched back. That play took the wind out of us.

That year I always felt like we were the best team followed by Duke, Maryland and Oklahoma. I thought we were the four best teams that year. Not Indiana, who made it to the title game. When Indiana beat Oklahoma in the semifinal right before our game, I was like, "Oh, this is ours." We're about to beat up on Maryland. I just felt like we matched up well. I thought Kirk was better than Juan Dixon. I knew Juan was good, but I thought Kirk was underrated at the time. Boschee was better than whoever was guarding him. I thought I was better than Steve Blake, Drew was better than Wilcox, and Collison was better than Baxter. I guess now I can say we were even. But at that time I didn't think we could be beat. But I'm sure they didn't think they could be beat, either.

## ROUND TWO

Going into my second year, we were just as confident about our team – but now we were sophomores. We had lost a couple of key components – actually, big components with Drew and Boschee. But we still had a good core of guys coming back. Plus, we were adding Jeff Graves, and B-Nash was growing up. We just knew we were going to win the championship that year. But part of winning the championship is luck. No matter how good you are, things have to fall into place for you.

We had to play Duke in the Sweet 16 in Anaheim that year. Duke wasn't even a factor to me. They didn't have Jason Williams, Mike Dunleavy and Carlos Boozer. They just weren't a factor. They had Chris Duhon and Daniel Ewing. J.J. Redick was a freshman. Luol Deng was a freshman. But they were young dudes. They didn't have enough experience to go very far. Chris Duhon was the only one with experience.

Arizona, on the other hand, had some good seniors with Luke Walton, Jason Gardner, Salim Stoudamire and Channing Frye. Then there was Hassan Adams and Andre Iguodala. We had lost to them earlier that year at Allen Fieldhouse in a game we were winning by 17 points. I just felt like they got on a hot streak. Salim caught on fire that first game. That's why they won. Since they had already beaten us that year, I felt like we were going to kill them in the Elite Eight. They really couldn't play with us. I figured we'd smash them really bad the second time around. They ended up hanging around, but we stuck it out and won (78-75).

Jeff Graves played really well that game (13 points, 15 rebounds). Coach Williams had been on him hard all year. I remember Coach telling a couple of us, "Don't worry about Jeff. I'll take care of him." I think he did a good job with Jeff. Jeff got a lot better. Being punctual was one of the things that Jeff struggled with a little bit. But he came around. Jeff was obviously really talented when he got to Kansas. But by the end of the 2003 season, he was on top of his game. He was in shape. He could run for days, he was athletic, he could play good defense because he was so big and strong. He had everything. He was a hell of a player for us.

We didn't celebrate too much after we beat Arizona. You enjoy it, but you have to remember there's a bigger picture there. My freshman year it was fulfilling to get to the Final Four, but the Final Four wasn't the goal I had in mind. I wanted to win the national championship. People at the airport were waiting for us to come home that night. It was a great feeling, but I was already looking ahead to New Orleans.

## HELPLESS FEELING

The main thing I remember about the national championship game against Syracuse was Gerry McNamara hitting six 3's on us in the first half. I caught a couple of them right in the mouth. After a while I was like "DAAAAMMMNNNN! He hit another shot?" I was right there with a hand in his face. It was just one of those things. Some players just catch that fire. It wasn't like he was even trying to penetrate. It was just straight, pull-up transition 3's. He hit six 3's in the first half. I was like, "C'mon, man." After that I felt like I had to guard him as soon as he crossed half-court.

I still thought we would be OK because I knew we had one of those teams that was resilient and knew how to fight. I never thought anybody would give up. I thought we would fight all the way back, even though we were down by about 15 or 17. I was like, "Man, they've got to start missing, and we have to capitalize." We made a great comeback. The thing that hurt the most was Keith fouling out. He was our best penetrator. He was able to penetrate that zone better than anyone else.

Mike Lee had his shot blocked at the end. He took the loss hard, but we all did. The loss was hella hard. How do you deal with getting all the way to the championship and then losing to a team that you felt you were better than? We had plenty of times we blew that game before Mike's shot got blocked.

## MOVING ON

When I was in high school, I went through a coaching change. We had gone to the state tournament my freshman year and, after the season, there was speculation that our coach was leaving to go to a different school. So me and a couple of my teammates went up to him and were like, "Yo! You leaving?" And he was like, "Man, I ain't leaving. I ain't going to leave you all." And then a week later, he left. So when this situation came up I decided to go ask Coach Williams. I went to his office and said, "Coach, there's all this speculation. What's your plan?" He said, "Aaron, to be honest with you, I'm torn right now. I don't know what to do." I looked at him and said, "Coach, I want you to stay. Hopefully you'll decide to stay." He just said, "I don't know what I'm going to do." So when he called the meeting and walked into the locker room all teary-eyed and stuff, I knew what the deal was. I thought about getting up and walking out. It crossed my mind. But then I respected that he at least came and told us. Still, I was really pissed off.

## BILL SELF

The first time I met Coach Self, I thought he was a really good dude. He came in and said all the right things about how we were going to have fun and about how we were going to run. He said all the right things to keep us around. He said we were going to play a similar style of basketball. But we didn't. Hell no, we didn't. Coach Williams wanted to score 100 points and hope the other team had 99. Coach Self wanted to score 1 point and hold you to 0. We would play in the 50s. Coach Williams wanted to get up and down the court and outrun you. Do you remember that Oregon game in the Sweet 16 where they had us on All Access? At halftime, Ernie Kent told the Oregon players, "I know you guys are tired, but they're more tired than you." That was kind of funny, because we weren't tired at all. We wanted to keep running. That's how Coach Williams wanted to play. It was just the opposite under Coach Self, which was kind of frustrating at first. We had the personnel to run under Coach Self. We had Mike Lee and J.R. Giddens, who did really well as a freshman. Jeremy Case, Omar Wilkes, me and Keith all loved to run. And in terms of our bigs, Wayne, Jeff Graves, B-Nash and Moulaye were all used to running. Padgett could run, too.

It wasn't just a tough first couple of months. It was a tough two years. Even the second year was hard. There are a lot of ways to skin a cat, but when you don't like how you're being told to skin it, you're going to fight about it. You're going to do it your way. We ran whatever he called. But it was a tug-of-war.

## VOICE OF REASON

I didn't like everything Coach Self did and I didn't like everything Coach Williams did. But they're the coaches, and you've got to do what they say. If we were going to be successful, we had to buy into their system. I felt like a couple of players were upset with Coach Self because of the whole situation, but I was more upset with Coach Williams for leaving. I was like, "Forget Coach Williams. Let's buy into Coach Self and go out here and prove Coach Williams wrong." That was my thinking. "Let's go out here and prove that Coach Williams should've stayed with us."

Other players were upset with the situation so much that it affected what they thought about Coach Self. But as long as we were all butting heads, we weren't going to be that successful. If the coaches and the players aren't on the same side, there is only so far you can go. I tried to talk to guys about it, but everybody is human. They've got their own feelings and thought process. I was just hoping that it was eventually going to change, although I knew it wasn't going to change overnight for anybody.

## SENIOR YEAR

Eventually, I felt like the tables were turning in Coach Self's favor, and that people were buying into what he believed. We had a good freshman class that came in. I thought our sophomores were pretty good, as well. We had all these seniors who had been to two Final Fours and an Elite Eight. We had the perfect team. I always look back at all the teams that won championships, and they all have a good point guard, a good wing and a good post. I compared our team that year to Michigan State's championship team in 2000. I was like, "I can be the Mateen Cleaves. Keith is Morris Peterson. J.R. Giddens was the Jason Richardson-type, real athletic. Mike Lee was like Charlie Bell. Wayne Simien was Andre Hudson."

It didn't happen for us, but we had the pieces. We just didn't fully commit to Coach Self once again. We didn't buy into it. Obviously some injuries hurt us, and losing David Padgett during the offseason did, too. That was big. That was huge. It hurt us a lot more than people remember. David would've been a sophomore. His freshman year he averaged something like six points and six rebounds. In the high-low system he would've been great. He had a high basketball IQ. It was mind-boggling to me. He probably would've come close to a 10-point, 10-rebound average his sophomore year, and the next season, with Wayne gone, he'd have been the man. I don't know why the hell he would leave. Was I mad at him? Hell yeah, I was mad at him. Plus, J.P. Batista wanted to come here, but we didn't have a spot for him. He signed with Gonzaga, and then the next day, David announced he was leaving. If David would've stayed he'd have probably been in the NBA right now. I'm not saying we would've won the championship, but we would've had a better year.

## BUCKNELL

If you look back at the previous few years, the first round game in the NCAA Tournament was usually tough for us. There was Holy Cross my freshman year and Utah State my sophomore year. I figured we'd beat Bucknell by about seven points. We had started the season 20-0. But then we lost to Villanova and then we lost to Texas Tech. Once we lost to Texas Tech, everything went downhill after that game. It was nasty after that. It was bad. You could just feel everything tearing apart. Coaches vs. players … all that stuff. We tried to get things going again. The seniors met and talked before the tournament, but it didn't help.

The main thing I remember about the Bucknell loss is just how I felt after it, when I was in the locker room. You start thinking about all the games that you've played throughout your career and how everything is over with. You have no more chances to win the national championship. When you're a freshman and you lose, you're like, "OK, I can win the championship next year or the year after. We'll be cold. Once it's all on me, we're going to do it." But once it's all on you and it doesn't happen, you're like, "Damn, I'm never going to play for the University of Kansas again. I'll never win a national championship."

## A TASTE OF THE NBA

I didn't get drafted after my senior year but I ended up making the roster for the Golden State Warriors. I played a half-year and got cut on Jan. 5. From there I went to the D-League and played the remainder of the year in Ft. Worth with Keith.

The following year I was planning to go to camp with the Portland Trail Blazers. I flew out there from Kansas City on a Thursday and took my physical. Then on Friday I was supposed to have a mini-press conference. I thought everything was cool. But when I got to the facility, the GM was like, "Man, we were trying to contact you before you got here. We're not going to be able to sign you because the doctor said your foot isn't all the way healthy. You're not 100 percent, and Nate McMillan only wants 15 guys in training camp, and he wants a guarantee that they're all healthy."

It was a pretty big letdown. That was going to be my chance. I had a great shot. All summer long I had been back in Portland playing pickup with those guys and doing really well. Even though the contract was only going to be guaranteed for training camp, I thought I had a great chance to make the team, because they needed a third guard. I could do some things a few of the other guys didn't do. Nate McMillan seemed to like me a lot. I thought I was going to be perfect for them. Unfortunately, though, I had hurt my ankle at a mini-camp in Chicago earlier that summer. The last game of last day, I went up for a layup and came down wrong. When I took that physical in Portland, I guess I wasn't all the way healed.

That was one of the toughest times for me. Getting cut with the Warriors hurt a lot. That was my first time ever getting cut from anything. But the second time, because I had played so well in the summer league with Chicago and Seattle that year, I felt like I was on top of my game more than ever. Then I got hurt.

For some odd reason I felt embarrassed. Coming from Portland, I felt like everything I did was for my family and my town. And that town has always supported me and showed me love. I felt like I let Portland down by getting hurt and not making it. It was a tough time because everyone knew I was supposed to go to camp with them. It had been in the paper that I was coming. People kept asking me, "Are you excited, man? I hope you make it." So when I got cut, I was hurt and stressed out and maybe even borderline depressed. I actually went away for about a week. I just wanted to rehab my foot and get away. I didn't want to deal with people asking me what happened.

## MAINTAINING FOCUS

After I dealt with everything that happened in Portland, I eventually came back and went to church. It was there when I felt like God was telling me that everything was going to be OK. It hurt that I didn't get to sign with the Blazers, but there were some great opportunities for me overseas. I spent the next season in France and then went to Spain the following year. After that I spent two years in Greece with two different teams. Playing overseas was a great experience for me. The only tough part was being away from my family. My oldest son, Aaron Jr. – we called him Deuce – was born in 2008. I didn't get to be there for the birth. That was tough. I played for Reno in the D-League this year because my youngest boy, Adonis, was born in November, and I wanted to be there for it.

I tore my ACL on Jan. 5 and have been rehabbing ever since. Once I'm healthy, I'll probably go back to playing. That's the plan, at least.

The good thing is that I've been able to spend a lot of time in Lawrence lately. My wife and I live here. It's great to be around the Jayhawks again. I enjoyed my time at Kansas. I just wish we would've won the title one of those years. Then I would truly be satisfied. I'm really happy with where I'm at and what I've done, but winning a championship would've taken it over the top.

# CHAPTER 16

# 2001/02 - 2004/05
# WAYNE SIMIEN

Wayne Simien is a Leavenworth native who received first-team All-American honors as a senior in 2004-05, when he averaged 20.3 points and 11 rebounds. His No. 23 jersey was retired at Allen Fieldhouse in the spring of 2011. Simien was selected with the 29th overall pick in the 2005 NBA draft by the Miami Heat, where he won a national championship during his rookie season. Simien retired from professional basketball in May of 2009 to work in Christian ministry on college campuses. His organization, Called to Greatness (www.iamctg.org), continues to thrive.

## IN WAYNE'S WORDS

My sophomore year is when I started taking unofficial visits to Kansas. The first game I came to, Nick Collison and Kirk Hinrich were there. I remember sitting next to them, and we were talking about being from small Midwest towns and playing AAU ball against guys from Chicago and Los Angeles and New York. We said, "Yeah, it'd be cool to go to a high-profile school like this and show everyone how well small-town guys can play." A few years later, there we were, all on the court together at Allen Fieldhouse. It was obviously pretty cool to be able to play with them.

## THE OBVIOUS CHOICE

Roy Williams probably never had an easier time recruiting a player than he did with me. Going to Kansas was a no-brainer. UCLA was a distant, distant second, just because I knew some guys that had gone there like Earl Watson and JaRon Rush. And I knew Steve Lavin. But they were so far off of my radar compared to Kansas it wasn't even funny. We had KU yard ornaments in our front lawn. Jayhawk flamingos, flags ... we had it all. I was like, "Mom, you've got to take these down. What if another coach wants to come to the house for a visit?" She was like, "Nope, you're not going anywhere else anyway." She was right. My high school coach, Larry Hogan, went to Kansas. My AAU coach, Lafayette Norwood, coached there. And Neil Dougherty, who was a mentor to me, was the main guy who recruited me. Neil was my cousin through marriage. My mom's sister married Neil's brother. His whole family lived about 10 blocks away from me in Leavenworth. The park that I grew up playing in was named after his grandfather. The Dougherty family was a staple in Leavenworth.

Roy never came to my house when he was recruiting me. He didn't need to, just because we were in Lawrence so much. So there really aren't any memorable recruiting stories. His wife's waffles were phenomenal on my recruiting visit. I do remember that. Wanda could make some waffles. They were slammin'. It was up to you to add the powdered sugar and syrup and strawberries. But they were phenomenal.

Before I started getting recruited, I didn't go to a ton of games at Allen Fieldhouse growing up, but I watched a bunch of games of TV. I wasn't a huge college basketball fan growing up, but I liked the Jayhawks. I didn't go to my first game there until the seventh grade. That was tight. I went with my best friend, Nicholas Sanders. It was an exhibition game against Furman. It was funny, because years later, Nick signed with Furman, and I signed with Kansas on the same day.

## ROY WILLIAMS

I'm glad I had such an easy situation with Kansas being right down the road, but I didn't like the overall process of being recruited. The coaches who would come up and try to sweet talk me and stuff ... I had distaste for them. They'd call and visit my school and come to games and talk to my coaches. They'd make promises and talk down about other schools. That didn't sit well with me. It's funny, because I can actually remember another college coach saying, "Don't go to Kansas. Roy is going to leave. Bill Guthridge is on his way out at North Carolina, and Roy is going to take his place." I just thought, "There's no way." Coach Williams was a straight shooter, straight as an arrow. He never promised me anything. He was honest. That was consistent with how he coached once I got there. Nothing ever changed, from the beginning to the end.

I remember I scored 27 points in my first exhibition game. It was cool, but I was still doing the same freshman stuff the very next day in practice. Coach Williams was ripping me up and down. He'd say, "You didn't run one play right out there last night!" The first big home game I ever played in, against Wake Forest, I had a double-double. It didn't matter. He was right back on me the next day. He could really get on a player, but he did it in the right way. He could get on a guy to the point where, if his mom was sitting in the stands watching practice, she'd be OK with it. I respected him for that.

## 2001-02

My very first year at Kansas, we had a heck of a team. The practices were probably the most competitive practices I've ever been involved with. The players we had there and the atmosphere that was cultivated there and the expectations ... that was a crazy year. Being able to come in and play right away was a bonus, too. That team had an interesting mix of freshmen like me and Keith and Aaron and upperclassmen like Nick, Kirk and Drew. We meshed well together, though. I think the reason we meshed is because we could all play. It wasn't one of those situations where the freshmen came in as prima donnas. We weren't promised anything. We came in and just played. We proved ourselves on the court. We still knew our role, though. Aaron was starting, and Keith and I were getting tons of minutes as the sixth and seventh men. But we still knew our role as freshmen. We were respectful of the upperclassmen. We knew our assignments when we came in. We put in the work during the games and then we carried the upperclassmen's bags afterward ... all the general stuff. But we still had the expectation of performing on the court.

## DREW & NICK

It was a lot of fun playing with Drew. Drew was big-time. He was preparing and carrying himself like a pro before he ever got to the NBA. His work ethic was like you'd see in a professional, just his approach to the game and his preparation. Drew was a stud at knowing his strengths, but he was always conscious of the things he needed to work on. He was an extremely versatile player when he was here. That was something I always watched and recognized. He was a pretty good leader, too. A lot of people saw him smiling and joking around. But there were some times he really stepped up in the huddle and let his leadership shine. Obviously, he did a great job of leading by example. But he did some things vocally, too.

The other thing about Drew was that he was very coachable. I saw Coach Williams jump his butt pretty good a few times. Some guys don't respond to that very well. But Coach Williams and Coach Self are masters of knowing how to motivate guys differently. You jump on Drew differently than you jump on Boschee or Keith. But both of them are masters of drawing the best out of guys. That's why there have been times when they've had teams that people thought wouldn't be successful, but they overachieved because those coaches are able to get the most out of their guys.

Nick Collison was the guy who really took me under his wing. Nick did that with a lot of players. Drew was the guy who wouldn't let you settle. He'd challenge you. He'd push you. Nick was the guy you'd have conversations with. He was the guy whose room you'd go to for a conversation about the game that night or about problems you might be having on the court. He was the guy who would pull his headphones off and drop his magazine when you sat next to him

on the bus so he could talk to you if you were frustrated. That was his niche.

We ran through the Big 12 that year. The Big 12 was good. Because of the shot we took from Ball State early in the year, I think we were always on our toes. That was pretty sobering. It was always in the back of our minds. We knew that a less-talented team could beat us if we didn't come ready to play. Cramps or no cramps, that shouldn't have mattered. We shouldn't have lost to Ball State.

## INJURIES

I struggled to stay healthy throughout my career. I only played in 16 games as a sophomore, when we went to the NCAA title game. I watched us lose to Syracuse from the bench. I missed some big games as a senior, too. There was never a "woe is me" attitude, but it definitely got frustrating, to the point where I was like, "Man, not again!" But there was never any resentment in my heart, because every time I played, I played as hard as I could. There was no insecurity on my part about what people were saying and what people thought. Frankly, it didn't matter, because I was harder on myself than any of those other people. I'd always wonder if it was better for the team for me to rest or to practice. My junior year, Coach Self would say, "I want to sit you out against Pittsburg State." I wanted to play, whether it was Pittsburg State or Michigan State.

## SAYING GOODBYE

I was shocked and I was hurt, as we all were, when Coach Williams left. I was especially hurt, though, because when I injured my shoulder against UMKC my sophomore year, there were people advising me to sit out the rest of the season and to have surgery. I still would've been able to get a medical redshirt. But I was like, "No, we're getting ready to do this. We're getting ready to win a national championship." Roy and I had some in-depth conversations about it. He didn't pressure me, but I definitely didn't want to let him down and I didn't want to let the team down. We had something special. I had known him since sixth grade. I was hurt, but I got over it.

A few days after he made his decision, I thought it was important to call him and bury everything instead carrying any resentment and bitterness into the next season with the next coach. I know there was some tension during that next season about former players contacting Coach Williams. But my contact with him was only about that. I can't speak for the other guys. I don't know what their conversations were like. For me, it was just a matter of calling him and wishing him luck.

## TIGHT BOND

I had a really close bond with my recruiting class: Keith, Aaron, Mike and Jeff Hawkins. A lot of people forget that Jeff was in that class because he redshirted the first year. But he was right there in the mix with all of us. We all experienced a great four years together. We really bonded and became really close, especially with the coaching change. We were all hurt when Coach Williams left. A few guys talked about transferring and going to different schools. But the five of us came together and made a commitment to stay and finish strong. We wanted to compete for more Big 12 titles and national championships. Had it not been for our bond, I don't think we would've stuck around. As well as we did on the court together, I took so much pride in saying that all five of us graduated. That's pretty rare in college basketball. These days, things are cool. I married Jeff Hawkins and his wife this summer. Keith just got married and I keep in touch with Mike Lee and his coaching career. I see him at Final Fours. Aaron lives here in town. Our families spend time together. We go bowling and hang out at practices together. The thing that I value the most out of my college career isn't necessarily the wins or the accolades. It's the relationships I was able to make, especially with those four guys.

## LIVING A LIE

When you go on a recruiting visit, it's not uncommon to see things get wild and crazy. But once you sign with a school and get to campus, you realize that life can be like that every night. It's up to you.

I definitely got caught up in that lifestyle my first few years at Kansas. I was partying, I was drinking, there were girls, I was smoking (marijuana) ... just doing a little bit of everything. I hadn't been involved in any of that kind of stuff back home. I didn't smoke or drink or party in high school. But when I got here, I figured, "Hey, I guess this is the way it's supposed to be done." It was college life. When you see 20,000 other college kids around you doing the same thing, you just figure, "Hey, this is just the way that it is. It's the way it's supposed to be."

One night, after we beat UCLA when I was a sophomore, I went out and celebrated. I was in a bar, and a drunk guy walked up and said, "Man, I wish I had your life." When he said that, I felt like I'd been punched in the face. It may have looked like my life was great with wins and Final Fours and NBA draft projections and stuff. But he didn't know that, inside, I was a wreck. I left the bar, went back to the Towers and cried myself to sleep that night.

All the stuff I was pursuing – wins, notoriety, fame, the NBA dream – none of it satisfied me. I was gripped by fear and insecurity. I was afraid of not performing well. I was afraid of getting injured. I was afraid of what people might think about me. I was one of the biggest, strongest guys on campus, yet I was walking around afraid and insecure. I didn't want to live like that anymore.

In the midst of all that, I just started searching for something greater to live for other than just myself and basketball. That's all I had lived for the previous 15 years of my life. None of it was really making me happy.

## MAKING A CHANGE

I ran into some Christian college students on campus. They began to tell me about Jesus and his life and all the things he had done for me. Then, as I began to spend more time around these people, I really started observing how they lived their lives. I saw how authentic they were and how full of joy and excitement they were. It started to appeal to me, because I never knew you could be a young person and live the way they were living. They were having sober fun and they were in the right kinds of relationships. They were living in purity and saving themselves for marriage. All of that was foreign to me. As I listened to the things they were telling me about Jesus and as I watched them live their lives, my eyes opened and my heart opened. I was like, "That's what I desire. That's what I want."

In July after my sophomore year, I was rehabbing because my shoulder was all jacked up. I wasn't going to Nike All-American camp or anything like that. I couldn't play pickup or work camps. I was rehabbing off by myself, which was probably a good thing, because the wheels in my heads were turning as I connected with these folks.

That summer, I went down to Texas for a conference for Christian athletes. A friend invited me down for it. I wasn't going to go because it was during finals week. But my teacher moved my final up that week. Then I was going to back out because the plane ticket was too expensive. But my parents said, "Hey, we'll pay for you to go." So it ended up working out. I went down there and was around college athletes who were living for Jesus. It was exciting. I became a Christian, and my life had been transformed ever since.

When I came back, I got connected with a church here in Lawrence. I had older men coaching me on what it meant to be a Christian. They taught me how to read my Bible and how to pray and how to serve other people and how to stay away from temptation. I'd eat dinner at their houses and sit back and observe how they handled their marriages and how they parented their children. It was incredible.

## ON-COURT WORSHIP

When it came to basketball, all of a sudden I had a freedom that came from not feeling like I had to perform for the fans or to meet my own expectations or to achieve my dream. It was difficult for me at first. Starting out my junior year, I had thoughts of quitting. It had nothing to do with the coaching change. I really just struggled with how to compete. I didn't know how to compete because of this new transformation that had taken place in my life. Before, I had only played for selfish reasons. I had just wanted to dominate my opponent by any means necessary, whether it was cheap shots or talking crap or doing anything else to get by.

In the preseason, I wasn't any good. I was soft. Coach Self was calling me out. I was wrestling with these things. I was driving to our second preseason game, and I stopped at the light on 19th and Iowa. I remember talking to God at that stoplight. I was like, "Lord, if you don't show me a different way to play this game, then I don't want to play it at all. I'll quit. I'll leave school and become a missionary." That's literally what I thought. It wasn't the right mind-set to have.

In that short drive from 19th and Iowa to the parking garage at Allen Fieldhouse, the Lord reminded me of this teaching that Jesus had in The Parable of the Talents. The way the story goes, there was this master, and he gave talents to his three servants. In this case, the word "talent" meant the same thing as money. He gave one of the servants five talents of money, another one got two talents and the last guy got one talent. The servants with five and two went and multiplied their talents and, thus, had a return on their master's investment. The other servant took his one talent and buried it in the ground and hid it. The master came back and praised and honored the ones that had done something with their talent and multiplied it. And he ended up giving them more. The one who hid his talent … the master was upset with him. He rebuked him and called him lazy and worthless.

The Lord spoke to me – and I realize it may sound funny saying the Lord spoke to me, but I'm cool with saying that, because He did – and He said that if I was to quit basketball, it'd be like burying my talent in the ground. I just said, "Lord, you've got to show me a different way to play." He said, "Play to worship me." All of a sudden, I wasn't concerned with my performance any more. I wasn't concerned with my team's performance. Playing basketball just became an act of worshipping the Lord.

There was such a freedom that came from playing that way. It was the most fun I had ever had playing basketball. I wasn't insecure. I wasn't afraid of getting injured or of losing. It was awesome. I kept playing. I thought I was a better leader because of that. I was definitely a better player because of that.

## REACTION FROM COLLEGE TEAMMATES

For a while, my teammates thought it was just a phase. They figured I'd get over it. Then it became real to them. It was cool, because the majority of those guys were able to witness a real transformation. It was radical, like night and day. Some guys were with it. Some guys weren't with it. Some guys asked about it. Some guys didn't care. Some guys were really supportive of me. But it was real.

The coaching staff really didn't know much about it. They were in the transition phase. They probably thought I had always been like that. They probably thought I was always the guy who was on time, the guy who was trying to be harmonious in the locker room, the team player. But in reality, I had never been like that before. Before then, I was always short for words. I didn't like crowds. I'd shoot a basketball in front of people, but give me a microphone and I'd be terrible. But because what had taken place in my life was so awesome and so real, I wanted to see that take place in other people's lives. I was out preaching in the middle of campus, telling anyone who would listen what had happened with me. That's what I was getting encouraged and excited about.

## REACTION FROM NBA TEAMMATES

Being in Miami was good from a basketball standpoint. I was excited to be there and live the NBA dream and play with players that I grew up watching: Shaq and Alonzo Mourning and Gary Payton and Dwyane Wade. But from a faith standpoint, it was pretty difficult moving into city like Miami, being young and single. The word had gotten around the locker room that I was a Christian. People found out about some of the things I'd done ministry-wise on college campuses. There was a huge skepticism about how long I'd be able to keep up that kind of lifestyle, especially being in Miami and in an NBA locker room. It was very intimidating. Guys were making jokes and taking bets on how long it would take before I was in the strip clubs or hanging out in the bars or chasing girls. The first couple of weeks were pretty rough. But as time went on and I continued to live my life for the Lord, they continued to see the type of guys I surrounded myself with. I didn't have an entourage of old high school buddies or a girl on both shoulders. I had 40-year-old pastors coming to pick me up at the hotel when we were on the road. I had A.C. Green coming to have lunch and dinner with me. As they began to see that throughout the season, it showed that I wasn't going to make any compromises. At that point, the guys actually started to encourage me. When I started dating my wife, I shared with them that I was living pure and that my wife and I were going to wait until we got married to share our first kiss and to be intimate with one another. It really blew a lot of those guys away. But as it went along, they started to cheer for me and encourage me. I thought that was really nice.

## BILL SELF

There was some resistance when Coach Self first got to Kansas. But it wasn't a resistance to the man. It was a resistance to the way of doing things. We had been so successful prior to the coaching change. It was hard to receive a completely different style of play when we'd just gone to back-to-back Final Fours. It had nothing to do with personalities or the coach himself. It wasn't bad at all, though. The transition to the style of play, like in any coaching change, was difficult. That happens whether you were a successful or a terrible team before. There was a little stubbornness on our part. We wanted to do things the way we'd done them before. It wasn't volatile, though. My attitude was, "Whatever it takes to win." I was coming off an injury that caused me to miss the national championship game. I just wanted to get back there. The transition for me wasn't difficult. The high-low offense played to my favor, because I was getting touches. I didn't have any issues with that. More of my energy went toward managing the locker room.

## FINAL GAME

Everyone is always going to remember how my college career ended. I missed the game-winner against Bucknell. Not only did I miss it, but the play before that, the Bucknell guy banked in a running hook shot over me from about 10 feet away. That was my man. So not only did I miss a shot, but my man scored on me to win the game. I was fine after the game, though. That's the freedom I was telling you about, dude. I knew I had given it my all and I was content with that.

That's not to say I wasn't disappointed. I was mainly disappointed for Coach Self, because I knew he was going to take a lot of heat from that loss. I had agents calling me. I knew I was going to have the luxury of moving on to the next step in my career. I was going to the league. But Coach and the rest of the team was stuck with that. Still, when I looked in the mirror, I knew I'd given everything I had. I don't have any regrets about my career.

My college experience exceeded my expectations. It was phenomenal in every sense of the word. But I really feel like the best years of my life are still ahead of me. It breaks my heart when I run into guys and all they can talk about is what happened at Kansas and how it was the best years of their life. It was a great time. It really was. But I'm more excited about what's ahead.

## NOWADAYS

Right now I'm a full-time campus minister. My organization is called "Called to Greatness." I work with a lot with KU students, but I also travel around to other college campuses. I minister to college students. I do it through one-on-one mentoring, and I do it through small groups of six or seven people. We talk about life and the Bible. We'll also have big campus meetings where 100-120 kids from all across campus get together. I do some stuff with the athletic programs, too – mainly football and basketball. And I preach in churches sometimes.

I also have a sports ministry. We host sports camps and leagues and teams for younger kids in the third grade all the way through high school. We'll teach them Biblical principles through the sport we're coaching them in. I do that mainly in the summer. During the fall, spring and winter, my focus is on the college campuses.

I want to see people go through the same kind of transformation I went through here, whether it's with a student-athlete or an international student from China. It's been great to be married to a woman who has that same vision. My wife, Katie, and I do campus ministry together.

The campus ministry that reached out to me at Kansas ... there was one like that at Florida State, where she went to school. I got to know her campus pastor after he moved to Miami when I was playing for the Heat. He and his family were the only Christian family I knew in Miami. I basically lived with them. I had an apartment and everything, but being 22 and single in Miami is tough, so I basically lived with them. Katie came to visit them a lot, and that's how I got to know her. We met in August, started dating in January, got engaged in February, and married in July. We've got three kids: Selah, 3; Rael, 2; Simon, 1.

## PLAYING DAYS OVER

I had some injuries during the two years I was with the Heat that kept me from reaching my potential. When I got traded to Minnesota in the fall of 2007, I had just had surgery a few weeks earlier, a scope to clean some things up. So I couldn't perform and compete for a spot. They cut me even though I was still under contract. I spent the year rehabbing and was headed to Atlanta for training camp in 2008, but they called me a few weeks before camp started and said they were going to go in a different direction. It was completely out of the blue. We had some other teams that had been interested in me, but we were committed to Atlanta.

After that happened, my wife and I talked. We knew that I was nearing the point where I wanted to wind down and go into ministry full time. She had lived in Spain when she was a young girl and her father was in the Navy. I had a good opportunity there, so we said, "Hey, let's just go on an adventure and move to Spain for a little while." I played well, and the team did pretty well. I was one of the leading candidates for league MVP. But then my cousin, Sean, who lived with me growing up, got really sick. He had been diagnosed with cancer right before we went to Spain. He was living with my mom. She wasn't telling me how bad things were getting. Then I came home from practice one day in May, and my wife was bawling and weeping. She had been talking to my mom. The doctor had said Sean's cancer had progressed pretty rapidly and that he only had a few weeks to live. We packed up our things and came back with a few

games left in the season, so I didn't get to finish up in Spain. Sean moved in with us. He made it for a few more months, and then he passed away in July.

At that point, I retired from basketball. It was something I'd been thinking about anyway. Once I got back on campus and started spending time around the guys, I didn't want to leave again. Called to Greatness, which I started my second year in Miami, had been growing. I'd be at practice, but I'd be thinking about that.

I don't play basketball anymore. I have zero desire to play. I enjoy coaching. I enjoy being around the game. I might whip on some guys in HORSE every now and then. But as far as getting out there and playing ... nah. I'm all good. That part of my life is behind me now. I love what I'm doing now. Not a day goes by where I wake up and don't love what I'm doing. There's never been a thought of, "Man, should I have kept playing? Did I make the wrong decision?" There's never been a bit of envy as I watch NBA playoffs or hear about guys doing well overseas. I never think, "Man, I wish I could be doing that." I'm doing what I love. I couldn't be happier.

# CHAPTER 17

**2003/04 - 2004/05**

# NICK BAHE

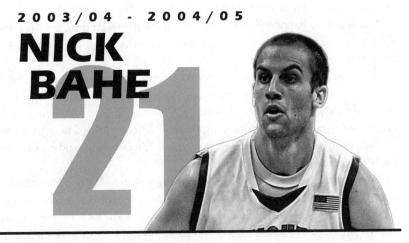

N ick Bahe spent two years as a preferred walk-on at Kansas from 2003-05 before transferring to Creighton. He was a Jayhawk during coach Bill Self's first two seasons as head coach, which included an Elite Eight run in 2004 and a first-round loss to Bucknell in 2005. Bahe graduated from Creighton with a degree in journalism and is now in his is in his second year as a talk show co-host for radio station "1620 The Zone" in Omaha. He also broadcasts games for the Creighton Bluejays radio network.

## IN NICK'S WORDS

My interest in KU probably all started with Kirk Hinrich. He was my favorite player in high school. Watching him play, I always felt like I saw a little bit of my own game in some of the stuff that he would do.

I always watched him play on TV in my basement with my brother. KU was consistently on Big Monday on ESPN, and we would always break it down. It was right when TiVo was coming out. You could rewind things and say, "Oh, look at him here. Look at his feel here to come off this screen," or, "Man, look at him fight through this ball screen," and, "Look at this vision."

I loved Kirk's competitive nature, but he did it in a way where he wasn't a jerk. And I loved how good of a defender he was. He could guard anybody, from Kareem Rush to T.J. Ford.

## LASTING MEMORY

My favorite thing ever that happened to me in college basketball happened when I was at KU. It was my freshman year. We had a young man, he was probably 7 or 8 years old, and he had a brain tumor. He was from Kentucky, and he wanted to come watch a game at Allen Fieldhouse, and the doctor didn't give him very long to live. That was one of the last things he wanted to do.

This kid comes, and he's so full of life and he's such a nice kid and his parents are there. He hangs out with us at practice. He eats pregame meal with us. And it just so happened to be the Richmond game. And we go out there, and if you remember right, they hit a little runner with about 1 second left, and Richmond upsets us at home.

After the game, we're in the locker room and we're all upset, and in walks this kid, and he's just sobbing. Just sobbing his eyes out, and he's distraught. I can remember Coach Self kind of stopping and saying, "That's what's important. This is just a game. That's what's important." It really helped us get over the loss, as we all were more concerned then about consoling him and making him feel better than feeling sorry for ourselves.

A year later, we go play at Kentucky at Rupp Arena. We win an emotional game there. Mike Lee stepped up. Keith Langford actually got a concussion at the end of that game and had to leave and go back to the locker room. We win a tough game against Rajon Rondo and those guys, and I can remember going back to the locker room and in walks the kid, the same kid that watched us lose to Richmond. He walks in with the biggest smile I've ever seen, ear-to-ear. The locker room just explodes. We all explode, and we attack him and we're hugging him, and he's excited.

Then about a week later, we get a phone call, and Coach Self tells us that the kid had passed away. So it just was amazing, the full journey of the whole year. That kind of summed up the power of Kansas basketball. It was amazing. I know it was a sad story, a sad ending, but it was one of the most amazing things to experience over the course of the year, through the vehicle that is Kansas basketball.

## COACH SELF

I had a unique situation with him coming in just because here I am, I'm a walk-on, there's nothing really contractually binding me to the university. I commit to Joe Holladay and Roy Williams and then Coach Williams goes to North Carolina. Well, that puts a person like me in jeopardy, because you don't know if the next guy believes in walk-ons. I had developed a relationship with the previous coaching staff, and I felt like if I did some things right on the floor, I could see some minutes by the time I was a junior.

When Self met with me after he accepted the KU coaching job, I think I was quoted in some of the papers as saying it was the most impressive 20 minutes of my life. The guy sat down, he's charming. He can charm you. He charmed my mom. He said all the right things to my dad. And most importantly, he said everything I wanted to hear. He cited different times when he was at Oral Roberts and Tulsa and Illinois when he played walk-ons, because that's something that was important for me, and that's something Roy had done. That takes some guts for a coach to do. If you put a walk-on on the court, and it doesn't work out, they don't blame the walk-on, they blame the coach.

When I was at KU, Self would have a rule where you had to go check in to his office every day, even if it was just for a second. Some coaches, they only know how to talk to you about basketball. The cool thing about him is he would talk to you about anything. He would talk to you about your girlfriend, he would talk to you about a movie you saw. That just builds that relationship, when you feel like he cares about you as a person — that if you would ever break your leg and never be able to play basketball again, he wouldn't toss you out like yesterday's trash. You would still be important to him. I think that's rare in college basketball, and it was something I always valued.

I remember one time we went to a volleyball game together, and he was asking me about my love life and if I had a girlfriend. Then he was telling me a story about how for a little bit, he and Cindy were having a rough time at Oklahoma State. He was just joking about that and how he realized how stupid he was to ever not be with her. So that's cool. He would open up about his relationship with his wife, then you'd be able to go over to his house and have barbecues with him and his family. You felt like you were talking to a friend, but some guys don't know how to turn that off. Then, when you got on the court, there was still that respect level.

I can remember, we were at Oklahoma getting ready to go over film the night before the game, and we were all kind of messing around and talking, and I started doing a Coach Self impression, and in walked Coach Self. The room got quiet. And he said, "No, let me see it. Let me see it." So I did my coach Self impression, and he's laughing. I was kind of putting on a little mini-standup act for the whole team, and he was loving it.

## KEITH LANGFORD

I lived with Keith Langford, so obviously, you build a relationship with the guy you live with. You talk about a guy that played more video games than anybody. Unbelievable. I can remember, I had a buddy coming down for our home game against Oklahoma. Keith was sitting there playing video games. I told him, "I'm going to head over to the Fieldhouse a little early and get some shots up." I walk out the door, and Keith's still sitting on the couch playing video games. I was like, "All right man. I'll see you over there. Let's get this win tonight." And he's like, "OK."

My buddy who was hanging in my room was there that weekend. Ten minutes goes by, 15 minutes goes by. All of a sudden, the game's getting close. My buddy goes out and says, "Keith, you realize you've got to get over to the game?" He said, "Oh yeah. Oh yeah."

Keith also loved the show, "Martin." We had TiVo, and we would record that. It was funny to always listen to him rewind different lines and just be howling laughing at different stuff, because you'd hear that TiVo rewind noise and go back to the same line. He'd play that same line in a Martin show six or seven times, laughing harder and harder and harder every single line. The video games and how much he would die laughing at Martin were two things that I remember most about Freeze.

## HOMECOMING

My most memorable game at KU was probably the game at Nebraska my freshman year, just because I was able to get in there and knock down a few shots. I know we lost, but I was getting heckled like LeBron when he went back to Cleveland in that game. I didn't realize people cared that much. They were chanting, "Traitor" any time I was in the game, and when I touched the ball, they were booing.

One of the funniest stories was after the starting lineups, I'm walking back to the bench, and our bench is right in front of the student section. I don't know how they nailed this, but actually the chair I was going to sit on had a piece of paper that was facedown. And I grabbed it and flipped it over, and it says, "Seat reserved for Nick Bahe." And the student section's right there, and they're laughing at me and pointing at me and screaming.

And you almost have to laugh. I don't care how much that may hurt your feelings or whatever. That's funny. I had a good laugh at that. So that made it feel good to get in there and knock down some shots and try to shut them up a little bit. It was too bad we weren't able to win that game. For a kid from Lincoln to go back to Lincoln and get booed, it was a surreal experience.

## BAHE, BAHE SHEEP

I remember feeling like I really arrived as a player when I finally had my own campout group. I think I was, "Bahe, Bahe Sheep." It's just amazing. I don't even play, but there's a large group of people in the student section that like me, chose me as the name of their group. But I just hope everybody understands that however amazing you think it is … "Man, I wonder what it would be like to be Sherron Collins or to be Stephen Vinson?" It is 100,000 times better than you would ever imagine, and it's all because of the fans.

## BUCKNELL LOSS

That was one of the most surreal nights of my life. To be honest with you, I think you can ask any of us … I knew we weren't playing well as a team. Granted, I'm just a walk-on, but I did feel like I had a pretty good feel when we were going to play well and when we weren't. We had lost at Texas Tech on a last-second shot late in the season on Valentine's Day, and I felt like we never really recovered from that game. Keith was really beat up. His knee was bothering him. To me, he was kind of the engine that made us go. He wasn't healthy.

I honestly remember having a bad feeling going into the game. The whole

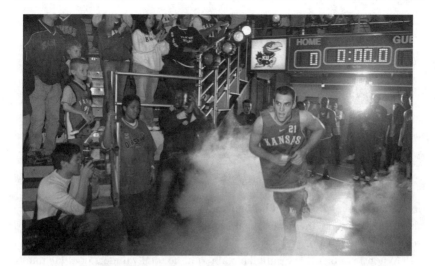

time, you kind of kept feeling like, "OK, they're going on a run. But Wayne's going to get it going. Aaron's going to make some plays. Maybe Keith will find a way to get it going. J.R. Giddens will start knocking down some shots." You kept waiting for our run to come, and it never came.

I can remember going back to the locker room and sitting there. Silence has never been so loud. We sat there in complete silence for 15, 20 minutes before the media had to come in. I say I had a feeling that we weren't going to play well, but it didn't change the shock of it. It didn't change the fact that we were pretty dang good that year. We had a talented team, and we felt like we had an opportunity. That was those guys' senior year. There was nothing that could be said. You had a feeling, but it didn't change the fact that it hurt and it just shocked us all.

My road roommate was Aaron Miles, and having to watch him that night and the next day before we went home, that was painful. He was just shocked. He was really quiet. He was very stand-offish, just kind of staring off into nothing. Just spacing off. That night was one of the most difficult lives in my athletic career, and in large part because I had so much respect for Keith and Aaron and Wayne and Mike, and to see those guys hurt, that hurt me. We were on the wrong side of history that night.

## TRANSFER DIFFICULT

I will say that the decision to leave Kansas was probably, to date, the hardest thing I've ever had to do. I can remember, the last thing Coach Self said when we got back to the locker room at Allen Fieldhouse after the Bucknell game — we got back to Lawrence the next day — was "I want everybody to make sure they come in and say goodbye to me and let me know what your plans are for spring break." And everybody went in, but I knew I kind of had transferring

in the back of my mind, and I didn't know what to say to him, so I didn't go in there. He called me the next day and said, "What's the deal?" I think he could tell something was up.

When I confessed I was thinking about it, he totally understood. He totally tried to convince me to stay. But when I said I wanted to go, there was nobody that was peddling my name harder than Bill Self. He was calling schools and trying to help me out. I'm forever indebted to Coach Self.

You hear about people transferring, and you think, "Oh, they must have been unhappy there." I was the happiest guy in the world there. I really was. I loved being able to walk over to Allen Fieldhouse for practice and put on that jersey. I remember during every national anthem, I used to look up and look at all the jerseys hanging, and you'd look at Pierce and Manning and Chamberlain. Even during the games, I'd be like, "This is unbelievable that I've had the honor to put on this jersey with these types of people." So when you have to give up all that, it's hard.

A lot of the guys, they weren't upset with me, but they took it hard. I remember Russell was difficult to talk to about it. Russell was a guy that I tried to go out of my way for to make feel comfortable when he first got to Lawrence. Because I respected Russell's toughness so much, it was hard to tell him that I was going.

He took it harder than I thought he would. I told him right outside the weight room that I was going to transfer, and he just got quiet. I could tell it was bothering him.

Those guys, I remember when they came in 2008 when they won the national title, the first round of those games were in Omaha at the Qwest Center. It was my senior year at Creighton, and we were playing in the NIT. We were playing Rhode Island at home in the first round. Russell and Jeremy and those guys, they came to my game.

Talking to my mom and dad, they said any time I scored, the most excited guy at the Qwest Center was Russell Robinson. He would stand up and kind of put his arms out like, "Yeah, that's my boy."

The senior class (above) of Jeremy Case, Rodrick Stewart, Sasha Kaun, Darnell Jackson & Russell Robinson and a talented group of underclassmen won the national title for Kansas in 2007-08.

Darrell Arthur, Mario Chalmers and Brandon Rush (right) all entered the NBA draft after the championship season.

Sherron Collins and Cole Aldrich (above) stayed two more years.

Kansas is always in the mix for the country's top prospects. These four recruiting classes were all highly regarded.

(from top) The 2005-06 newcomers were Micah Downs, Rodrick Stewart, Brandon Rush, Julian Wright and Mario Chalmers.

Joining the team in 2004-05 were Darnell Jackson, C.J. Giles, Sasha Kaun, Matt Kleinmann, Russell Robinson and Alex Galindo.

Keith Langford, Michael Lee, Wayne Simien and Aaron Miles headlined the 2001-02 class.

Future first-round NBA draft picks Nick Collison, Drew Gooden and Kirk Hinrich were freshmen in 1999-2000.

Wayne Simien (top left), Michael Lee (right), Keith Langford (bottom left) and Aaron Miles (bottom right), appeared in two Final Fours for Roy Williams (top right) before playing their last two seasons under Bill Self.

(clockwise from above) Jayhawk big men Cole Aldrich, Drew Gooden and Nick Collison were all NBA lottery picks.

Kansas has had two one-and-done players. Xavier Henry (above left) and Josh Selby (above right) left Kansas after their freshman season to pursue the NBA. Others such as Brandon Rush, Mario Chalmers and Darrell Arthur (below with Darnell Jackson, left) also turned pro before their senior seasons.

Kirk Hinrich (above) keyed Kansas' up-tempo attack under Roy Williams. But the Jayhawks would've never reached the 2003 NCAA title game without Jeff Graves (left). Drew Gooden (bottom right) sparked Kansas to a 16-0 Big 12 record and Final Four berth in 2002. Jeff Boschee (bottom left) made a school-record 338 3-pointers.

(clockwise from top left) Point guards Aaron Miles, Russell Robinson, Sherron Collins and Kirk Hinrich all played in the Final Four. Talented as they were on the court, the four players will also be remembered as some of the greatest leaders and example-setters in school history.

C.J. Giles (left) and J.R. Giddens (below) had loads of talent, but off-court issues led to their dismissal from the team. Eric Chenowith (bottom left) ranks fourth on the Jayhawks' all-time list for blocked shots and is fifth in rebounding. Darnell Jackson (bottom right) beat some tough odds to make it at Kansas and, eventually, in the NBA.

(clockwise from bottom left) Tyshawn Taylor, Julian Wright, Sherron Collins and Keith Langford were among the country's top slashers during their time at Kansas.

Instead of point totals, headlines and individual awards, Kansas players are most proud of the team chemistry and air of selflessness that has been a staple in the program throughout the last decade.

(above) Brandon Rush, Mario Chalmers, Sasha Kaun and Sherron Collins. (right) Collins, Russell Robinson and Darrell Arthur. (bottom) Nick Collison, Aaron Miles, Jeff Carey, Bryant Nash, Chris Zerbe, Michael Lee, Brett Ballard and Lewis Harrison.

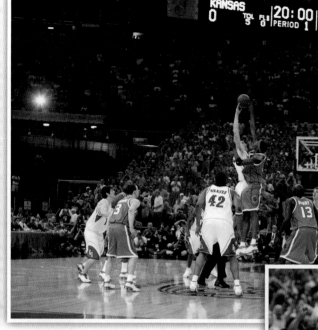

Kansas has played in three Final Fours and
two national championship games since
2001-02. Mario Chalmers' (right) clutch
3-pointer in 2008 helped Kansas defeat
Memphis for its first NCAA title since 1988.

(left to right above) Tyrel Reed, Jeff Boschee and Brandon Rush are among the top long-range shooters in Kansas history. Russell Robinson, Jeff Hawkins and Jeremy Case (bottom left) were also dangerous from beyond the arc.

Kansas' run of success under head coaches Roy Williams and Bill Self has been remarkable. But assistants such as Joe Dooley and Kurtis Townsend (top, flanking Self) and Danny Manning (left) have played a major role, too.

Thomas Robinson (left) is carrying on the tradition of great Jayhawk big men that can run, rebound and score such as Darrell Arthur (top left), Wayne Simien (top right) and Sasha Kaun (below).

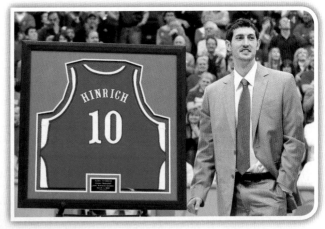

Senior Day and jersey retirement ceremonies always provide memorable moments at Allen Fieldhouse. (left to right, top to bottom) Max Falkenstien retired in 2006 after broadcasting KU games for 60 years. Kirk Hinrich and Wayne Simien had their jerseys retired.

Sherron Collins left Kansas as the school's all-time winningest player. Jeff Boschee's final basket at Allen Fieldhouse came from well beyond the 3-point line. The Class of 2006 featured Stephen Vinson, Christian Moody, Moulaye Niang and Jeff Hawkins.

Kansas won seven consecutive
Big 12 titles from 2005-11.

Tyshawn Taylor (left) and Thomas
Robinson (above) will try to make it
eight straight in 2011-12.

# CHAPTER 18

# 2004/05 - 2005/06
# C.J. GILES

C.J. Giles is one of the most talented players to wear a Kansas uniform during the Bill Self era. The 6-foot-11, 240-pound Seattle native was one of the top shot-blockers in the country, had a nice midrange shooting touch and ran the court extremely well for a player of his size. Giles, however, was involved in a series of off-court incidents that ultimately led to his dismissal in the fall of 2006. He transferred to Oregon State and was kicked off the team after playing in just 10 games. Giles then entered the 2008 NBA draft but was not selected. He has played in the NBDL and overseas.

## IN C.J.'S WORDS

I picked Kansas for all the wrong reasons. Part of it was because my parents went there, and part of it was because I heard it was a party school. I wasn't looking at the tradition and the fact that it had a great basketball program. I didn't care about any of that. I just thought it would be a nice escape from Seattle, where I wasn't doing much of anything. Every school I visited, I never asked myself, "Can I play here? Can I succeed here? Is this the right place for me?" I just wanted to have a good time. Instead I ended up making a lot of mistakes. I was running around in a grown man's body acting like a little kid, learning by trial and error.

## TROUBLED PAST

My life before I got to Kansas wasn't easy. I went through a lot of stuff when I was young. When I was around 7 or 8 years old, my mom started using crack. She tried it for the first time right when crack hit the streets, right when it was becoming big. No one knew at first how powerful it was, but she found out firsthand. She was hooked. We moved in with my grandmother, and my mom stayed in an upstairs room, off in the corner. She hardly ever came out. She'd stay in there for three or four days at a time and then come out and ask for $20. Once she got the money she'd leave for a little while, come back and go straight back up to that room. It happened like that over and over again.

With my mom out of the picture, my dad had to take care of my younger brother and our two sisters. He wasn't a good father to us. I mean, he put a roof over our heads most of the time. But he wasn't around, he wasn't there. He was working all the time, and whenever he wasn't working, he was going out with chicks – and I mean multiple chicks. It seemed like every one of them was named "Lisa" or their name ended with "lisa." Basically he was just out having fun and bouncing us from neighborhood to neighborhood during elementary school. We must've changed schools four or five years in a row. No one was watching over my brother, Malcolm, and I. My sisters were older so they didn't do much with us. We basically did whatever we wanted, whatever we felt like. We didn't go to school very much. We just walked around in the streets all day. No one seemed to care.

Even though I messed up a few times over the years, I didn't get into nearly as much trouble as some of my friends. One of my boys tried to pistol-whip someone, and the gun went off by accident. The guy he shot died. Another one of my best friends is in jail for 20 years for doing a bunch of different stuff. Basketball probably helped me avoid that kind of life. I didn't even start playing until my junior year of high school. I had transferred the previous year to Rainier Beach, the top basketball school in Seattle, but I had to sit out because people thought they had recruited me. It sucked getting caught up in all that political stuff.

## THE ROAD TO KANSAS

Along with it being a fun school, one of the main reasons I went to Kansas was because of Kurtis Townsend, who I had known for a long time. Kurtis had been recruiting Rainier Beach players for years, guys like the Rodrick and Lodrick Stewart and Jamal Crawford. When Kurtis was at USC, I committed to USC. When he left for Miami, I signed with Miami. When Miami's coach got fired after my senior year and Kurtis wound up at Kansas, I got out of my letter of intent and signed with Kansas. I always liked Coach T because he was straight up about everything. We still talk off and on to this day.

The other thing about Kansas was that my parents both played there. That's where they met. My dad won a national championship at Independence (Kan.) Community College and then signed with KU. But he tore his ACL during preseason workouts his first year in Lawrence. He redshirted that year and then played the next two seasons. As a senior he did OK but not great. I think that always bothered him. (Chester Giles played in 28 games and made 17 starts for Kansas in 1979-80. He averaged 4.1 points and 3.7 rebounds.)

When I first got to Kansas I was doing some really good things. At times I was killing it on the court. Wayne Simien got hurt, and I started in his place when we beat Kentucky in Lexington. I had 10 points in that game and six rebounds. A few weeks later we were 20-0. Even though the season ended with that loss to Bucknell, I was finally getting some confidence. I'd turn on ESPN and see myself dunking all over people on the highlights. I was like, "I can play ball at Kansas. I can excel on this level." My dad apparently thought the same thing. He saw me living his dream – and he wanted to be a part of it.

The next year he left my younger brother all by himself out in Seattle, hopped in his car and drove all the way to Kansas. He found a place to live in Eudora and, from that point on, I went on a downslide. He just kept hovering around and pumping all this stuff into my head. "You need to enter the draft after this year. You're doing this wrong. You're doing that wrong. Tell Coach Self to run more plays for you." It got to the point where I wasn't even listening to him, but he was still in my ear. I couldn't focus at all.

When I didn't answer the phone, he'd text me. When I didn't answer the text, he'd send another one. It just went on and on and on. He never came at me with, "How was your day? How was school?" It was always about basketball. Every single thing had to be about basketball. A year earlier, when I was a freshman, I found out (from doctors) that I can't deal with a bunch of stuff on my plate. When there's a lot of stuff on my plate, there's a good chance something important is going to fall off. I was already having trouble focusing because I was trying to juggle a lot of things at once. When my dad came down he just added more to it. I was listening to him more than Coach Self because I felt like I needed to please him because he was my dad. I was really confused. That's why I started slipping off in school. That's why I wasn't as focused as I needed to be in practice. I was just totally off-balance. Like I said, he was trying to fulfill his dream through me. But when I was little he wasn't around, because he never thought I'd amount to anything. No one did.

## THE FINAL STRAW

I made it through my sophomore year and was hoping to do good things as a junior, but I never got the chance. I wasn't doing well in school and had missed some practices, which caused Coach Self to suspend me for the first semester. Then I had the incident with the girl in Jayhawker Towers, which was basically the last straw. *(Giles was issued a citation for misdemeanor battery on a 20-year-old KU student.)*

Here's what happened with that: That girl was being used by everyone. I was using her, too, but I was actually trying to be nice to her at the same time. That night she wouldn't leave my room. I asked her to leave, and she just wouldn't. I didn't lose my cool or anything. She was sitting on the edge of the bed watching TV. When she kept refusing to leave, I put my hands around her ankles and pulled her off the bed. It wasn't like it was a long way down to the floor or

anything, maybe a foot or two. She plopped onto the carpet and looked up at me. She started laughing at first, but she could tell by my face that I was serious. She got up and walked out to the front and that's when we started arguing. I was like, "Leave! Leave!" I'm sure I might have scared her a little bit, but I didn't mean to. Everyone came in and started making a big scene. Then she left. I never hit her like she said. It was a weird night. I look back on it now and just figure it was another step, more trial and error, something to learn from. Coach Self kicked me off the team the next day. That was it for me at Kansas.

## FROM BAD TO WORSE

In terms of basketball, I went from the best program in the country at Kansas to the worst in the country when I transferred to Oregon State. That whole organization was terrible. Jay John may make a good assistant coach somewhere, but he was obviously in over his head as a head coach, because that program was in bad shape. His assistants were even worse. They didn't care about anything. Practice would end, and they would actually beat me to the bars and the clubs each night. That should tell you everything you need to know.

One day one of the assistants was getting on me in practice, and I pulled a card I shouldn't have pulled. But I couldn't help it. I blew up in front of the whole team and said, "You're out drinking and partying all the time when you should be coaching and watching film and getting us ready. You should be more into the team." That was probably a mistake, because after we lost at Washington that January, Jay John got fired. The next day I was called into the coaching offices and told that Kevin Mouton, who they promoted to interim coach, wanted to "go in a different direction." I was off the team after playing just 10 games. They didn't win another game all season and finished 6-25 and 0-18 in the Pac-10.

The athletic director told me to stay in school and that I could rejoin the team the next year when they hired a new coach. But I decided to go ahead and enter the NBA draft. At that point my financial aid got cut off and my roommate moved out. I didn't have enough money to pay the rent on a two-bedroom place, so I actually snuck into the arena and slept in the locker room for four or five nights. A few months later I watched Kansas win the national championship on television. It was good to see guys like Brandon and Sherron and Rodrick get that trophy. I was proud of them, happy for them. And disappointed I wasn't there.

## NOT GIVING UP

I didn't get drafted that year, but I'm still doing my best to make it to the league. I've spent some time with the Lakers summer league team and I've played in Lebanon, Beirut, Qatar, Dubai and Saudi Arabia. Last year I played for the NBDL team in Sioux Falls, South Dakota, and then went to Lebanon. Things haven't always been perfect. I've messed up a few more times. But I'm continuing to mature. I think my best basketball is still ahead of me.

All these ups and downs I've been through are going to make me a better professional once I do get the chance to step onto that stage, because I've learned from all of them. God put me in those positions for a reason. I went through all of that stuff at Kansas and Oregon State and overseas so I could learn from it and conduct myself the right way when I become a professional, because I know I'm a professional-caliber player. Don't be surprised if you hear about some NBA team signing a 26- or 27-year-old rookie.

# CHAPTER 19

# 2001/02 - 2005/06
# JEFF
# HAWKINS

Jeff Hawkins is a Kansas City, Kansas native who arrived at Kansas along with Wayne Simien, Keith Langford, Aaron Miles and Michael Lee in the fall of 2001. Hawkins redshirted his first season and later became an integral player off the bench for the Jayhawks. Hawkins' crowning moment at Kansas came in the 2006 Big 12 Tournament, when he swished four 3-pointers to catapult his team to a victory over Texas in the championship game. Hawkins, who was an all-state guard at Sumner Academy, is now the head coach at Perry Lecompton High School.

## IN JEFF'S WORDS

I remember walking down the hall during the fall of my senior year at Sumner Academy. This guy stopped me and said, "Did you hear? Aaron Miles just committed to the Jayhawks." I was so disappointed. For the rest of the day all I could think was, "Dang! I guess I'm not going to Kansas." Coach Williams had told me all along that he only had one more scholarship to give and that he was waiting on Aaron to make a decision. He said if Aaron wanted the scholarship, he was going to get it because he had been recruiting Aaron longer than anyone else. I had some other offers from places like Indiana State and Wichita State but, obviously I wanted to be a Jayhawk. At that moment I figured my chances were gone.

Later that day, though, Coach Williams called and invited me and my family to the game that night. I thought he was going to give me a farewell speech. Instead he called us into his office after the game and told me that he liked my family and thought I was a good kid. He said he wanted to offer me the chance to come there and redshirt. I didn't even know what redshirting meant. He explained it by saying, "Do you think you'd be a better player your first year or your fifth year?" That sold me. I was like, "I'm coming!" I was on academic scholarship my first year and athletic scholarship the next four.

## GETTING NOTICED

The first recruiting letter I ever got was from Steve Lavin at UCLA. Earl Watson was a Wyandotte County kid who was playing there at the time, so he may have had something to do with it. I just remember being called to the office at Sumner Academy, and the lady said, "You've got some mail." It was this big FedEx package. I went back to art class and the teacher and all the students gathered around. I opened it up and there were all these brochures and questionnaires and stuff. When you get your first call from UCLA, you feel pretty special. Still, I was hoping to go to Kansas.

Wayne Simien is probably one of the biggest reasons I ended up in Lawrence. The summer before my junior year of high school I started playing AAU ball with the Kansas City 76ers. Lafayette Norwood and his son, Seth – rest in peace, Seth – were the coaches, and Wayne was on the team. Coach Williams and his staff followed us throughout our whole traveling circuit that summer. We ended up winning the AAU nationals, and I guess I played well enough to make Kansas want to recruit me, too.

## DREW GOODEN: BALLPLAYER, BARBER

I was on two Final Four teams at Kansas, and the thing that sticks out the most about each of them is how well everyone got along. I can't think of any time during those years when there were negative vibes within the basketball program. The players all liked each other.

Drew was the guy who kept everyone loose. He was good at cracking jokes during tough moments to ease the pressure. He could get you to laugh but he also had a lot of strong leadership qualities. Guys really rallied around Drew. He did a lot for Kansas. Drew was the guy you wanted to hang around with off the court and on the court. He'd really bring the best out in you.

One of the funniest stories I remember about Drew involves Michael Lee. Right before the Sweet 16 our freshman year in 2002, Drew was cutting a couple guys' hair in our hotel room in Madison, Wis. Drew was always the one who would line people up before games. He was good at it. That day he had already cut Aaron's hair a little bit earlier, but when he did there was a guard on the clippers. Then Mike walked in and picked up the clippers and was going to cut his own hair. The problem was that someone had taken the guard off, and he didn't realize it. He shaved a big bald strip right down the side of his head. We all started dying laughing. Mike was like, "Don't tell anyone! Don't tell anyone!" So of course I ran out of the room and got everyone. Aaron, Keith – even Neil Dougherty's little son. Within a few minutes we had 10-15 people in the room laughing at Mike. Aaron was rolling around on the floor he was laughing so hard. Drew ended up shaving the rest of his hair off for him. It's funny to look back at those tapes and see Mike Lee bald in the Sweet 16 and Final Four. People probably just figured he wanted to shave his head, but that wasn't the case at all.

## BIG GRAVY

Jeff Graves joined our team the next year. I liked Jeff a lot. On the court he cared – but he didn't care. He played with a mean streak. He's a guard's favorite kind of big man. If you started complaining in the huddle that some dude on the other team was pushing you, Jeff would say "Who's pushing? Which one is it? I'll get 'em for you." It didn't matter if it was a guard or a big man. If Jeff found out anyone on the other team was messing with one of us, he'd take care of it. He was a lot of fun. No one disliked him. He worked hard to get in shape. And once he got in shape he took it to a whole new level.

When it came to effort, though, no one matched Stephen Vinson's intensity in practice. Actually, Kirk and Brett Ballard are all probably in that group. They set an example for everyone with how hard they worked. Kirk just made it look so easy. I roomed with Kirk for two years. He was a quiet dude. He didn't say much, but we still hung out and went out to eat a lot. We mixed well as roommates. For some reason I always vacuumed his room for him. I think he always appreciated that.

## WRITING ON THE WALL

The guys on those Final Four teams didn't spend a lot of time reading the paper, so I don't think the situation involving Roy and North Carolina affected our play when we lost to Syracuse in the 2003 NCAA title game. We may have seen some stuff about it on ESPN during the week but no one was really paying attention at the time.

But I could definitely tell something was in the works after the Syracuse loss. After every away game, we always went back to the hotel to eat dinner as a team. We even did that the previous year after we lost to Maryland. Win or lose, Roy would always eat with us. But after the Syracuse game he wasn't there. I kept looking around the ballroom and I couldn't find him. Then I went out into the lobby and I saw Dean Smith lingering around. . I was like, "Man, I don't think Coach Williams is coming back." That was a pretty solid sign that it was over, in my opinion.

A week later we were all waiting for him in the locker room. He walked in and his eyes had tears in them. To me it seemed like he didn't want to say what he was about to say. You could tell the pain he was feeling was genuine. No one said anything back to him when he told us he was leaving. That's the kind of respect Coach Williams had from us. Once he left, a couple of guys went off. But no one did it while he was standing there.

We got out in the parking lot, and all the media was around. We were acting out and saying some things, but I think that was us putting on a little show for the cameras. It was still an emotional day, though, whether we showed it by tears or not. Roy had a plan mapped out for all of us. Now he was gone and that plan didn't exist anymore.

## SUSPENSION

For all the talk about players struggling to adapt to Coach Self, we did pretty well during his first two years. Coach Self could've easily stuck with his philosophy 100 percent, but he got really creative at times and adjusted some of his schemes to fit the personnel. That was really the case whenever Wayne was injured. I don't think he gets nearly enough credit for winning as many games as he did those first two years in a tough situation.

It was definitely a tug-of-war at times, though, and Coach Self butted heads with some guys. I was one of them. I got suspended in the summer of 2004 – right before my junior year – and wasn't allowed to go on the Canada trip that September. I wasn't allowed to do anything with the team. If I worked out at Allen Fieldhouse, I had to bring my dirty clothes home and wash them myself. One time I called a few of the managers to see if they'd come rebound for me while I got up some shots, but they weren't allowed to work with me. It was definitely a good wake-up call. But at the same time, it was good for me to get away from basketball for a few weeks. I actually had a really good time. Players usually don't get to enjoy the life of a normal college student. I had so much free time. I'd leave class and say, "Wow, I've got nothing to do."

Coach Self gave me multiple second chances. I'll always be appreciative of him for that. This year I had a chance to go to his fundraiser, "The Bill Self Boogie." He says the whole purpose of the charity is raising money to give kids a chance. I'm a firm believer and a witness to all of that. I truly believe he wants to help people and that he's sincere about it, because he gave me chances multiple times. He could've easily said, "Bye Hawk. I don't have to deal with you." He didn't do that. Coach Self always said we'd get along better once I was finished playing. He was right. Our relationship continues to get better and better.

## SEEKING AN IDENTITY

I'd had knee problems prior to my senior year, but I chose to play through them and get shots before each game, which was kind of nuts. But I was playing pretty well and I thought I might get to start. It all caught up with me after college. I went to Germany and played four or five months, but my knee started hurting, and my wife was pregnant at the time. I came back because I wanted to be closer to her. Then I went to Arkansas to play in the ABA. My first week there, I was driving baseline, and my knee kind of gave out. I ended up having surgery. It was a bone-on-bone situation. I didn't have any cartilage there, and my bones were rubbing together and causing some pain, so they went in and shaved my bone down. My knee didn't react as well as I'd hoped so I couldn't bounce back the way I wanted to. I went to some D-League camps but I clearly wasn't 100 percent. I ended up in Hays, Kan. – my wife's hometown – trying to figure out what I was going to do next.

For a while I was working all kinds of jobs. I worked construction and I did some substitute teaching. I worked at a foster house in Quinter, Kan. where I was mentoring kids who had troubled lives. I even worked in the kitchen of a brewery in Hays called "Gella's." Other than watching my dad cook at home, I really didn't have any experience on the grill, so my job at first was to make salads. By the time I left there, though, I could cook anything on the menu. Steaks, salmon, whatever. I took pride in my steaks. The manager always said to take the steak off the grill and put it on a plate and then carry it over to the dish you were going to serve it on. But one time I thought I really had a good grip on it with the tongs. I tried to carry it across the room like that and, sure enough, I dropped it on the floor. I'm not going to lie: My initial instinct was to use the 5-second rule and pick it up before anyone noticed. Those steaks take a long time to cook, and I was scared the customer would be mad if he had to wait a whole lot longer. But I ended up throwing it in the trash and giving the guy a free dessert. He was cool about it.

In my spare time I watched the Jayhawks as much as I could. I missed it. It's Kansas basketball, the best basketball in the country. If you don't miss it you don't have a soul or a heart. It was a tough time in a lot of ways. I was trying to figure out which direction I was going. I wasn't very stable. Part of me was saying, "play basketball" and part of me was saying, "Don't do that. You've got a kid and a family." I decided to approach life the same way I approached basketball: Never give up, keep working hard and good things will happen.

## COACH HAWKINS

My last year in Hays, I was asked to become an assistant coach at Ellis High School. I had a little success there and ending up getting the head job at Perry-Lecompton, where I just finished my first year (in 2011). I love teaching kids and watching as they start to pick up on things. It's rewarding to see them take big strides. My guys would probably say I was pretty laid back during my first season. We were in a weird situation with a bunch of stuff that had gone on the previous year in our program. We're in the rebuilding process, so we were really stressing positive encouragement and building kids up instead of breaking them down. It may be a little different (in 2011-12) now that we have a year under our belts.

I have a long way to go as a coach. I remember watching Coach Williams and Coach Self and how quickly they'd react to situations and draw up plays. There have been times when I've been in our high school huddle during a timeout, and by the time I find the dry erase board, the 30 seconds have already passed. All I have time to do is say, "All right guys, go back out there and play hard." I'm learning from my mistakes. When you play the game you're playing off of your ability. You don't have to think as much. But when you're coaching you really have to break the game down. That's where I'm still trying to grow as a coach. I didn't reach out to Coach Self as much as I probably could've during my first year. I wanted to try to learn on my own. I'll probably call him this season, though. I know he's there if I need him. That's the best part about him.

# CHAPTER 20

**2002/03 - 2005/06**

# CHRISTIAN MOODY 34

hristian Moody joined the University of Kansas basketball team as a preferred walk-on in 2002. The Asheville, N.C., native played four seasons for the Jayhawks, eventually earning a scholarship as a senior. During Moody's junior year in 2004-05, CBS analyst Billy Packer called him the best walk-on in college basketball history. Moody played 22 minutes a game that season and averaged 5.8 points and 4.7 rebounds. Moody is in his third year at KU med school, though he's still unsure of a specialty. He and his wife, Nicole, have a son, William.

## IN CHRISTIAN'S WORDS

There's a profile picture of Roy Williams in the trophy case at my high school, kind of at the top, outside the basketball stadium, near the concession area. I think it's probably from when he first started coaching at KU. All the high school students walk by the trophy case every day either coming in from the gym or going to the gym. He's in a pretty prominent spot.

I remember early on in high school reading about Roy under his photo. I don't remember thinking much of it. I never thought I would get to play for him. I just thought, "Oh, there's a famous coach. It's cool that he went to school here." I didn't ever think our paths would cross.

## RECRUITMENT

In the history of T.C. Roberson — where I went to high school — there have only been three basketball coaches. One of them was Buddy Baldwin, another was Rich Sizemore, and Kevin Keene is the current coach. My coach was Rich Sizemore. Coach Williams played basketball for Buddy Baldwin, and they're still very close. They're like family, father-son almost, I'm sure. They play golf and hang out every year.

And so, late in my high school career, we sent Coach Williams a tape, hoping he could recommend me to his former assistants who had gone on to other Division I programs. I was just looking to play at a medium-sized program like Appalachian State, where Buzz Peterson was, or Vanderbilt with Kevin Stallings or Notre Dame when Matt Doherty was there. We were hoping Coach Williams would make a recommendation for me.

That year, four walk-ons graduated from KU. Coach Williams must have liked the recommendation he got from Buddy Baldwin and Coach Sizemore, and he must have thought that the tape was good enough to offer me a walk-on spot, because he did after we came out to visit.

My high school coach told me in his office that KU had offered me a spot, and I thought he was kidding. It probably took a while for it all to register, because coming out just to visit was an awesome experience. We got to go to Late Night. We got to go check out the locker rooms and meet some of the players. I remember Wayne Simien gave me a Powerade on my first visit into the locker room, because there used to be a fridge of Powerades there. So it was like walking on hallowed ground.

## FITTING IN

My freshman summer, I was so nervous about being on the same court as Nick Collison, Wayne Simien, Drew Gooden, Kirk Hinrich, Keith Langford and Aaron Miles — all the guys that I had spent the last couple of years watching develop into All-Americans. I remember being very scared to shoot when we played pickup. I remember not wanting to make any mistakes, just pass the ball to the guy who was hot, which was usually one of those guys I listed. I just didn't want to make anybody mad out there, because here I was, a little tiny freshman coming in among these giants and pillars of college basketball.

I was so excited to play pickup with those guys that afterwards, I was texting my friends and calling them. I called home probably every day, because my family members are such big basketball fans. My brothers and my dad and mom and sister all wanted to hear what had happened that day — if I had taken a shot or if I had gotten a rebound. They were excited for anything.

Among my brothers and sisters, I'm the oldest, so I was the first to go to college. So it was kind of a new thing for all of us. Being in a basketball mecca, I was telling them stories every day.

## SNACK TIME

I've got a lot of great memories of Coach Williams. On my first road trip, we went to New York for the Preseason NIT. Being a freshman, I didn't really know what was required and what we were supposed to do. I didn't understand how the schedule worked.

One thing on the schedule at 10 p.m. was labeled as "Snack." I thought, "Oh, that's kind of nice. I'll probably go to that." I didn't know that we'd be going over our scouting report while we had our snack.

So I go down there about 9:58, and I did know, with Coach Williams, if you were 15 minutes early, you were on time. If you were 14 minutes early, you were late. But being that I didn't know snack was required, I went in a couple minutes before 10 thinking, "Oh, there's probably going to be some pizza down here."

No. I walk in there, and all the players and managers and coaches are all looking at me, and Coach Williams stands up and he says, "Christian, I am tired of waiting on you. Get your food and sit down." And that was my first road trip experience, my first time getting yelled at. It didn't cause there to be a bad relationship at all. I think it just freaked me out, like, "Oh great, I screwed up on my first road trip." That was pretty scary.

## BIG BOARD

Stephen Vinson and I had a pretty competitive Texas Hold 'Em winner board in our room. There used to be some pretty heated battles going late into the night between Mike Lee, Aaron Miles, Moulaye, Steve, me and a couple of friends. It was all about who could get their name on the winner board, because whoever won for the night got to sign their name as champion for the night. And whoever won would just talk about it the whole time in practice, on campus, until we played another time.

I remember Aaron Miles, if he won at all, he would just talk and talk and not let anybody live it down. He'd talk about dumb moves people would make and would just rub it in our face. Aaron would bring it up in practice. He'd bring it up in team meetings — whenever we were all hanging out. He was good about letting you know that he was the leader for the week.

And we'd also it rub in for whoever wasn't on the leaderboard. I don't think Mike Lee ever made the leaderboard. We'd give him crap about that. Steve Vinson was pretty good. He was probably up there the most.

## "THE PASS"

That particular play – when I threw a blind pass over my shoulder against TCU – I don't think I could do it again. I guess I'm just really happy the ball went to J.R. Giddens instead of into Coach Self's arms and that J.R. made the shot to finish the play.

I think we rotated the ball around a couple times, then it ended up going to Wayne on the right side of the blocks. My job as the other big is to crash toward the basket in case he shoots, which is most likely with Wayne, or if my man goes to double, then he can look to dump off to me for a shot at the rim.

I remember crashing toward the basket. I remember Wayne dumping the ball to me. But also, out of the corner of my eye, I saw J.R. Giddens' man coming at me. He definitely would have been in front of me at the rim had I tried to come down with the ball and go up for a shot.

So I guess I was kind of feeling it that game, and I thought, "Well, J.R.'s over there somewhere." I just flicked my wrist and hoped that it went to him. The ball went to J.R., and he made a great shot, which made the play. Because if he didn't make the shot, then I never would have been on SportsCenter.

I remember Wayne went nuts, and they had to call timeout because the crowd went crazy. J.R. was holding up his jersey. I remember Keith came over and hugged me. Some of my other teammates, like Stephen Vinson and Alex Galindo, they all came over and were hitting me on the head.

I watch that video, and part of me looks at myself, and I'm like, "Why didn't I get more excited? I look too calm. I should have celebrated more." But I probably just get into this mind-set during the game. If I start celebrating, I'm going to screw up, and then I'll just sit on the bench. But it was a really exciting moment, a really exciting play.

## SELF SCHEDULE

One difference between Coach Williams and Coach Self was that, at least during Coach Self's first year, we really practiced a lot. We had some long practices. Coach Williams' practices were about two hours. We were there between 3 ½ and four hours with Coach Self. That was definitely a big switch, but I understand why Coach Self wanted to practice so much. He was totally revamping our entire system – our offense – and he wanted to pound home the way he wanted things done.

There were definitely some long practices, some long days. We'd practice for three hours, and I remember Coach Self, if we couldn't get something right, he'd say, "All right. Go home." And we'd be like, "All right. Yes! Go home!" Then he'd say, "Be back at 11." And that would just drain everybody.

We'd come back at 11 p.m. and practice for another hour that day. Then we'd practice into the night just to start the next day's allotment of hours for practice. It's crazy. I think you're allowed either a weekly number of hours or a daily limit of four hours. So we'd practice for three hours at one point, then one hour at 11 and go into the next day and start a new day.

## BILLY PACKER

I ran into Billy Packer later that year or the next year after he called me the greatest walk-on of all-time on television. I told him that my mom was his biggest fan in the world, because my mom just loved that he said that. I obviously felt very honored that he said that, too, so I thanked him. I think I remember him telling me I played a great game that day, and that I deserved it that day. I still don't know about that at all. I definitely let him know how appreciative I was.

Michael Lee started giving me the nickname, "G.O.A.T." It's cool to get a

nickname at all from anybody. For somebody to call you that as a joke was still pretty cool.

I think I got 300 text messages that night. My phone just was going crazy. That comment has kind of stayed with me. Even when I go to play at a charity game, it will come up. Coach Self always reminds the campers when he introduces me before our alumni game each summer. So that's really been cool to have something like that – even if it's not at all true – stick with you.

## MISSED FREE THROWS VS. MISSOURI

*(During Moody's senior year, he missed two free throws with 0.4 seconds left in regulation of a tied game at Missouri. MU went on to win, 89-86, in overtime.)*

That was a very tough night. It definitely felt like I let my teammates down, let the Jayhawk Nation down. It was definitely a low point for the season, because not only did we lose the game in overtime, but I think we were 1-1 in the conference. Starting my senior year in conference play 1-1 when your goal was to win the Big 12 ... I definitely felt like I'd personally dug us a hole.

It took me a while to get back into the groove and regain confidence and put that behind me. Honestly, that was a big turning point in the season, though, because I think it put the pressure on all of us, being down in the conference rankings, that we had better step it up, because we weren't at the level that we needed to be. That translated into us putting ourselves in the position to win the conference, and we ended up doing that.

I had a lot of people call me, a lot of friends and old teammates call me and encourage me. That was definitely helpful. I had a lot of support through it all. The coaches were very supportive and definitely helped me to get my confidence back.

## FEELING THE LOVE

I got a lot of fan mail after the Missouri game. The support was awesome. But fan mail was awesome all four years. It was amazing how freshman year, you don't think anybody knows who you are, and you're getting fan mail from people you've never met before and who have never even seen me before.

There were a couple kids that were going through chemotherapy that were living in Lawrence. I got a chance to go see a couple of them. It's an awesome thing to go brighten a little kid's day and give them a signed pair of shoes. You see their rooms, and there's Jayhawks stuff all over the place. It's a cool thing to be able to just show up and realize a kid is happy that you're there. And hopefully, his day was better.

One particular kid I'm thinking of, his dad still keeps me updated on how he's been doing. I actually saw (the kid) again at the Rock Chalk Roundball Classic in 2010. A lot of the fan mail you get, if you write them back, they may come up to you at a game and say, "Hey, you wrote me back. Thank you. Here's my son that I was talking about." I think with that little guy, he came to a game, so I got to see him there and meet the family.

## WATCHING NOW

It's really fun to see them run all the plays we used to run, and it's also fun to watch new plays that the coaches come up with and think, "Man, why didn't they run that when we were there? That's a great play." Or to see how Coach Self makes players fit his style of play. It's great to see him run his stuff and win championships with different groups of guys. That's probably my favorite thing to watch is to watch how well the guys run the plays and do what Coach Self wants them to do.

I remember when my high school coach was talking about going to KU, he said, "Would you want to go to Montreat" — which was an NAIA school right near my hometown — "and be able to score a lot of points and probably play a lot, or would you want to go to Kansas, just to be able to wear the jersey?"

Looking back, I definitely made the right decision. It's a dream to know that I got to play at KU. To wear the jersey and be a part of the history is really a special thing.

# CHAPTER 21

# 2002/03 - 2005/06
# STEPHEN VINSON
## 20

S tephen Vinson played an integral role for the Jayhawks after joining the program as an invited walk-on in 2002. The Lawrence High School graduate was nicknamed "The Standard" by Bill Self for his work ethic in practice, and Vinson's teammates routinely credited him for helping them elevate their game by pushing them during workouts. Vinson played in 23 games as a senior in 2005-06. He had six points and six assists in a victory over Cal. Vinson has spent the last five years at Hartford Mutual Funds in Olathe. He and his wife, Anna, have two children: Mia and Cooper.

## IN STEPHEN'S WORDS

Coach Williams called me the summer going into my junior year of high school. He asked me to come meet with him, and he told me the scholarship situation wasn't going to work. But he said, "Even if you tear your ACL, we still want you. Just go have fun playing in high school and use us as a fallback option." He was kind enough to let me bounce the other schools I was looking at off of him, because he knew about the other programs across the country. It was very helpful to me, but I think I knew when I went into my senior year that I wanted to go to Kansas. Of all the offers that I'd gotten, none of them matched what I thought the KU experience would be. There was never really a school that challenged that experience. I didn't decide until the spring, but I probably knew before then.

## DIFFERENCE IN COACHES

I think if you asked Roy Williams, he would want a trapezoid lane. He would want his big guys to look like Drew Gooden and be more finesse players. You kind of see that at North Carolina now with John Henson and some of the other guys they have. They're more finesse guys. He wants a beautiful basketball game.

I remember getting yelled at in practice because I stripped the ball away from Nick Collison as he was going up for a layup. I thought I made a good play. But all of a sudden, I'm getting yelled at because in practice, guards weren't allowed to slap down on big players because Coach Williams was worried about their shoulders or worried about them getting injured.

With Coach Self, you beat the heck out of each other. It was a much, much more physical game. If a player went across the lane and you didn't check him, or if you didn't bump them off their screen or whatever it may be, that's how you got yelled at. It wasn't for being too physical; it was for not being physical enough. It was just a completely different mind-set to adapt to.

Our practices under Roy Williams — and we had a really veteran team — were an hour and a half. They weren't fun — they were very difficult — but it was an hour and a half, and you were done. With Coach Self, his first year there, it was a couple of hours. If he didn't like it, it could turn into another hour on top of that. Then, after that, it was talking for an hour about what we did that day and him just trying to instill his philosophies.

The hours, whether it was actually on the court or just mentally trying to pick up the system, were pretty grinding. You always enjoy playing against other teams who don't know your plays and all that kind of stuff. But gosh, when you get screened by the same guy every single day 100 times, you get tired of it, there's no doubt about it. By the time the first game came around, we were very ready to play against somebody else.

## BILL SELF

Coach Self a great coach. He's a tough coach. He's a guy that wants to break you down and then build you back up. He thinks that if you can't handle a coach, you can't handle playing on the road at Missouri. It's not easy to play for him, but it's certainly rewarding.

There were several guys he broke down when I was there. It starts at his boot camp. It's not like you're done if you make your sprint times. With Coach Williams, all I had to worry about was myself. If I made my sprints, I was going to be OK. But with Self, we weren't done until everyone on the team had made their sprints.

We had a guy, Jeff Graves, who didn't exactly make every sprint. We did a lot of extra running because of it. That'll pull a team apart at the seams when you're tired, and you have to do something like that over and over again.

But probably a better example would be in practice, when you get a young guy that really doesn't know what it means to play hard yet. Coach Self will get all over a guy and try to push him and push him. That player's response will be, "We'll, I'll show you," and they'll have a great three- or four-play sequence.

Then, instead of giving him an, "Attaboy," or, "We need more of that," he yells at them more and says, "You should do that every time." It's all done with the goal in mind of teaching you how hard you have to play, how intense you have to be, how focused you have to be. You can't always do that giving high-fives.

The people that iy worked best for seemed to be the freshmen. I could use Darnell Jackson as a great example. When he first showed up on campus ... if you'd have told me he'd play in the NBA, I mean, my jaw would have hit the ground. And listen, I love Darnell, and he's a good friend of mine, and I enjoyed playing with him as much as anybody. But from a talent standpoint and a skill-set standpoint, there was nothing there that would have made you think when he walked on campus as a freshman that he would be that guy. His role the first couple years he was there was to foul Sasha in practice or to foul our other big guys in practice to give them a realistic look. And all of a sudden, he's on an NBA roster, and he's stuck in the NBA. You can see the development stories.

I can tell you this from going to a couple practices after I was done: The Morris twins, when they were freshmen, were perfect for Coach Self's style of coaching. They are unbelievable players now, getting ready to make a ton of money, but they didn't know what it meant to play hard and were somewhat unwatchable in certain areas that Coach Self expects out of his players. There was certainly a transformation that was going to have to take place there. You learn that you either do it, or you transfer. And there are a lot of guys that don't want to do it, so you get situations like that, too. I think a lot of coaches do this. I don't think Tom Izzo is giving guys high-fives every time down the floor. But listen, the proof is in the pudding. I'm not a stat guy. But I can tell you, I don't think there's been a better defensive field-goal percentage team in the country since Bill Self came to KU. There are certain things that talent helps. Defensive field-goal percentage isn't just talent. That's coaching. That's a mentality. That's a mind-set. In all reality, you're not going to play your best every night, so with his defensive philosophy, you're going to win a lot of games that other teams don't win because you have that mind-set.

## TEAM CHATS

With Coach Self, we would have pretty long talks as a team, just in general. And Coach Self is great in the sense that, everything he talks about isn't X's and O's. It isn't basketball. It's about life. We still joke. He would go around the room and say, "Stephen, if you're starting a company, tell me the three guys on the team that you would hire." And then he would say, "Tell me the three guys that you would not hire." There are things like that. "Stephen, tell me the three guys that you would let date your sister." "Who are the three guys that you wouldn't let date your sister?" The conversations ... he had these crazy analogies, but he was trying to teach us about life at the same time and challenge us for when those things arise in life, so we'd be prepared for them.

It was a unique approach. I certainly don't remember any conversations with Roy Williams like that. That's where they're very different. too. Coach Self's a very personable guy, and pretty open with conversations like that. The common denominator with both of Coach Self and Coach Williams was that you knew both of them cared about you. You can't have tough conversations with people if players don't think you have their best interest in mind. There was certainly plenty of trust from the players to the coaches.

## ROAD TO THE 2003 FINAL FOUR

That week in Anaheim during the Sweet 16 and Elite Eight was just incredible as a whole. As a team, we went and saw the Lakers and the Wizards when Michael Jordan was still playing on one of our off days. So we saw Kobe Bryant against Michael Jordan.

The Duke game, I just remember Nick Collison being unstoppable and how great it was. And I'll say this: That was the happiest I've ever seen Roy Williams after we beat Duke. I'm sure some of that North Carolina-Duke rivalry was still brewing inside of him, so getting his Kansas team to beat Duke was a pretty big deal to him.

He was always pretty good about celebrating wins and letting guys have a good time in the locker room afterwards, but he usually doesn't join in to the extent that he did after that game. I would just say from an emotional standpoint, it was the happiest he's ever been for a Sweet 16 win.

## GUARDING WADE

Unfortunately, coming so close to winning it all in 2003 and losing to Syracuse the way we did, the reality is you look at the stat sheet of that game, and we did about everything that you could do to lose a game, whether it's missing free throws or get outscored at the 3-point line the way we did. We still had a chance to win.

You can't help but remember that whole tournament experience and that whole ride. With as well as Dwyane Wade is playing in the NBA now, my personal memory would be getting to play in the Final Four against Marquette and guarding Dwyane Wade.

I remember getting called in a lot sooner than I expected at the end of the game. I don't remember exactly how much time was left, but typically, I thought I might play the last 2 minutes. We were up by so much. I was certainly gearing up to play.

At first, I was very shocked. Unfortunately, I probably shouldn't say that. Just getting out on the floor and playing in that big of an arena in front of that many people, it's just a different setting than anything I've ever experienced before.

I remember sitting at the scorer's table with Jeff Hawkins. We were trying to decide who we were going to guard, because we were taking both of the guards out. He said, "Let me guard their little point guard, because I want to pick him." So that's how we made the decision that I was going to guard Dwyane Wade, and he was going to guard Travis Diener, who's a pretty good player in his own right. Jeff didn't realize that little point guard was going to play in the NBA for a good six or seven years, too.

First of all, Dwyane was gassed, and they were down 30, so he wasn't as interested in the game as he probably was at the beginning. Still, there were only a couple of players I faced in my career that had that kind of explosiveness. It was on a different level. I just remember him dribbling the ball the first time I was guarding him, just lazy at the top of the key, and he made his first move, and it was a different kind of first step and a different kind of explosiveness than I was used to guarding.

I probably gave him five or six feet the rest of the game. I remember it took me almost all five of my fouls to guard him just for a few minutes. He didn't score, but I did foul him on a 3-pointer. He missed all three free throws, if my memory is correct. He helped me out a little bit. I certainly didn't guard him very well.

Before I was married, the story I told about the game was, "Yeah, I shut Wade down." Afterwards, if I'm being honest, it was, "Yeah, it wasn't very pretty." It depends on who I'm telling the story to, let's put it that way.

## CAREER GAME AGAINST CAL

I remember the game before the California game my senior year. We lost to St. Joe's in New York, and I was furious because, if I thought I could do anything, it was play defense, and there was a guy for St. Joe's that scored a bunch of points on us. I thought I could guard him, but I never got the chance. He was playing against freshmen. It was frustrating for me to watch.

So I remember in practice that next week, I finally got put on the blue team and was excited about the opportunity and was told very clearly that I was going to play and get good minutes against Cal. Then I remember pulling my groin – or I thought I pulled my groin – and slamming the ball down. It was one of those injuries where no one was around me. I was just dribbling the ball up the floor and I just crumbled. I thought my season was over. I'd had the injury before and I'd had to sit out about three months. This time it felt exactly the same. I thought it was bad, but it was actually just deferred pain coming from my back. I've got a horrible back. All of my injuries have originated there. So I got a shot in my back the day before the Cal game. Once we hit shootaround, I ran around and could kind of feel my leg, kind of not. But eventually adrenaline took over, and I played in the game.

I just remember Mario just having the worst game of his life for the first 4 minutes or so, just turning the ball over. We were down 13-3 or something like that – a horrible start. And then I got a chance to play.

Guys like me don't get a ton of chances. I was just trying to facilitate the

offense. I remember that we got on a good little stretch there. I just remember being out on the floor, and every time a guy would go to the scorer's table, I thought it was for me, but it never was. It was a lot of fun.

I didn't have a huge stat game, necessarily (six points, six assists in 25 minutes). But I just remember winning a game that we really needed to win, because we'd just come back from Maui and we'd just got beat in New York. We really needed to win a game. That was a turning point for us to beat a quality team, because Cal was good that year. They had Leon Powe. They had some good players.

I remember Seth Davis said on TV that, "KU has found their point guard." Listen, I know the game well enough to understand that our best team had Mario on the floor. I even remember saying in the postgame press conference that this wasn't going to be a normal thing. The reality is, you could see the talent level there with Mario. We knew he was going to have to play huge minutes for us if we were going to be great.

Still, I remember being the one player that went with Coach Self to the press conference and having a ton of media there. I felt a little out of place, because I was used to being more of a player that was in the background, not so much in the forefront.

## MOULAYE AND THE OREGON DUCK

One of my favorite Coach Williams stories involves Moulaye Niang. We were playing Oregon and we were ranked No. 2 and they were No. 3 with guys like Luke Ridnour and Luke Jackson. They were very good. We were playing them in Portland so we could have a home game for Aaron and Mike. At one point, Moulaye was finally going to get his chance to play. Oregon had just gone on a little bit of a run and we were getting beat. Coach Williams called timeout. He was going to put Moulaye in the game for his first real action against a good team.

During the timeout, their mascot, the Oregon Duck, came out in one of those crazy spandex suits and was doing a dunking show. The fans were going crazy. We knew something was going on in the background because of the reaction. This guy was doing, like, three flips and dunking the ball with a big mat underneath him. All the while, Coach Williams was drawing up a play.

As the Oregon mascot was jumping off the trampoline, you could see Moulaye's eyes following the Duck. And he was watching the mascot right as Coach Williams was telling him what play to run. So he's telling Moulaye what he's supposed to do on the play, and he looks up at Moulaye, and Moulaye's eyes are following this Oregon Duck through the air.

Coach Williams literally grabbed him by the chest, pulled him out of his chair and put Michael Lee in at the power-forward position. That was the birth of Michael Lee getting to play. Mike never got to play before then.

I don't know if you remember the game or not – we lost – but Mike had a really good game. That was his Cal game, in other words, if you wanted to equate it for something to me. That was the game that he gained more trust from Coach Williams for him to play the rest of the year and the rest of his career.

But it started with Moulaye not paying attention because he wanted to see the Oregon Duck. We would give Mike Lee a difficult time about it. He probably would have found another way to play eventually, but it was funny. You don't put a 6-3 guy in at power forward unless you're desperate.

## PICKUP PROS

I'll never forget what happened a year or so ago, when myself, Nick Bahe, Christian Moody and Brett Olson played on the same team as Keith Langford during pickup games at Bill Self's camp. It probably wasn't the team Keith wanted to be on, considering we'd be going up against just about any NBA player you can think of who was back in town for the camp games.

There were about 30 guys trying to play on one court. So if you lost, you had to sit out 45 minutes to an hour. But I'll never forget this: We won eight games in a row. You play to seven, so that was 56 total points. I think Keith probably had 52 of them. We're talking about being guarded by Kirk Hinrich and then help defense coming from Scot Pollard, Greg Ostertag and Nick Collison. Every player you can think of, probably minus Paul Pierce and Raef LaFrentz, was in town that day. There were teams of five NBA players – and then there was our team, with four former walk-ons and Keith Langford. We won eight games in a row. That's as good of a memory as I can remember.

# CHAPTER 22

**2005/06 - 2006/07**

# JULIAN WRIGHT

# 30

J ulian Wright played two seasons at Kansas before declaring for the 2007 NBA draft, where he was selected 13th overall by the New Orleans Hornets. Wright was part of a banner recruiting class that also featured Brandon Rush, Mario Chalmers and Micah Downs. Known for his creative play and flashy dunks, Wright averaged 12 points and 7.8 rebounds in leading the Jayhawks to a Big 12 title and a berth in the Elite Eight as a sophomore in 2007. He now plays for the Toronto Raptors.

## IN JULIAN'S WORDS

The moment I decided to come to KU is something I won't ever forget. It happened in September of 2004, during a home visit with Coach Self and Coach Townsend.

Frankly, I thought they just dropped the ball earlier. I believe Coach Self had some ulcer problems, something that needed to be taken care of immediately; it was in the window of when they could contact us in the spring. Then, the assistant who was recruiting me at the time, Norm Roberts, he got the head coaching job at St. John's.

Players notice who's watching them when they're playing a game. So in the summertime, I would keep seeing Coach Self or Coach Townsend over there after they hadn't recruited me in the spring. And I was like, "Why are they here?" And I felt like I was having a big summer, too. So that was like a pride thing. I think of myself as humble, but even if you're humble, you still obviously have prideful moments. I think pride got in the way. I was like, "Why are they just starting to watch me now, when I'm blowing up and playing well?" I had to put my pride aside. That was pretty much why I wanted to do a visit anyway in the fall, because I gave it some thought. I wanted to allow everybody to clear the air on both sides.

## NO GUARANTEE

After the visit and really just talking, I appreciated their honesty. That's one thing that I really go by, is just being honest and just being straight-forward. I can live with that, whether it's criticism, a compliment or just talking.

One thing was, I didn't want guaranteed minutes. Not that other coaches may or may have not said that, but to hear Coach Self say that he dropped the ball on recruiting me then coming in on a visit and saying, "I'm not going to guarantee minutes," … it was just a sense of realness and him being genuine and honest with me. Those were the types of things that I wanted.

In high school, I played for a coach who was well-known and a hall-of-fame coach in the state of Illinois. He didn't promise me minutes, either. I had to earn them. So that's something I was familiar with, because I felt like if you earn minutes, it's harder for someone to take them from you compared to if someone just gave them to you. I wanted a coach to push me and I could tell that was what Coach Self was going to do.

So right after that visit, I was talking to my mom about it. I told her, "I really, really want to go there." And then she was like, "Well, you just might want to give it some thought," because I had other schools that I hadn't even visited. Then I just started bursting out into tears. Once again, out of nowhere. I didn't expect that, but I just knew, "Man, this is where I want to go."

I called Coach Self and Coach Townsend like 15, 20 minutes later. They were about to hop on the expressway. So I'm pretty sure they had a flight to catch and all that. I called them and said, "You mind coming back for a minute?"

They probably didn't know what was going on. So they came back, and I told them I wanted to come. Coach Self was very surprised. We just exchanged hugs. He waited until I called other schools to let them know I wouldn't be going on visits and things like that before we let it out to everybody. I think my life is like that. It's not scripted. And I think that's kind of the best way for me.

I'd already heard about the program and of course, how prestigious Kansas was. In terms of campuses, I just look at it objectively. A place like that, I know it's going to be great regardless. The proof is in the pudding. It was more about the relationships with the people I'm going to be around the most. So I committed without a visit.

## TEXAS GAME

The game in Dallas versus Texas my freshman year in the Big 12 tournament is one of my best memories at KU. I think that just signified our growth from the beginning of the year, where we started off under .500, leaving the Maui Invitational, to really getting the ball rolling and capping it off by beating a team that had beaten us pretty badly earlier that year.

We were a young team, mainly freshmen and sophomores. I think the light came on for that group of guys, like, "Hey, we could do something special."

I'm always a team guy, so I think about all the plays that added up to that win. Of course, my 360 dunk at the end of the game was personally one of my favorite plays. Honest to God — I can only be honest — I didn't even think I was going to do that. I didn't know what I was going to do. I think Mario tipped it, and Russell got the rebound and threw it to me. I didn't even know where the rim was. So at last minute, I was like, "Oh shoot," and I just did something. It's crazy. I really don't know why I did it, either. Hey, that's what basketball's about. It's just poetry in motion.

I was just like, "Well, you know, this is a team that beat us pretty badly at first, so how can I just kind of add to the excitement?" That's kind of what, I guess, happened in a split-second. The game is pretty reactive, so I just did it, kind of just celebrating.

Coach Townsend, for sure, and Coach Self gave me a hard time. They said, "You know, I've never seen you do that one too much in practice. So we're glad you brought that one out and made it."

## WANNA GET AWAY?

My botched dunk against Colorado — where I fell down — is one of the most memorable things in my career, college and overall.

Put my laughter in the book, too. Put it in the caption. Oh man. It's funny, I always joke about it. I say, "If anything's going to happen like that, let it happen to me. I don't want it to happen to anyone else." What I took away from that was, "This is what happens when you think too much." (laughing)

I got a steal, and I was like, "Man, what am I going to do right now?" And to this day, all my friends, everyone who asks me, they're always thinking I'm lying — it's all good fun — but I'm going on record to say that when I took off, I slipped on a wet spot. No really. Because I took off kind of far away from basket. I wanted to do a windmill. When you do a windmill, you have to start the motion of the arm going up, then you have to go down. And when I realized I wasn't going to make it, I was like, "Whoa, whoa, whoa."

I took off, and my right foot was OK, but it was a two-foot jump, so you have to use both of your feet to jump for the windmill. So I jump up. Right foot was OK, but my left foot dragged. That's what happened.

I was bracing my fall. I couldn't even get a shot up. And so to this day ... I was in shock. I wasn't hurt — like some people thought I was trying to act hurt. I rolled, because it was just more of a shock thing. Then Russ came to my rescue and helped me up, because it was so embarrassing on so many levels.

That's never happened to me in my life, going up for a dunk and not making it. So to be funny, I said, "No publicity is bad publicity." I can joke about it. It's funny to this day.

My teammates gave me a hard time. Someone actually came out with a Southwest commercial on YouTube for it. But I don't care. It doesn't matter. At the end of the day, I'm an entertainer. Not in college, but in terms of now, I'm an entertainer.

What was tough for me ... I was embarrassed. I'm supposed to be a dunk person and dunk all the time. Coach pulled me out of the game. Then he put me back in. He said, "You going to play?" and I said, "Yeah, I'm ready." So a lot of people don't know that I got a dunk in that game as well. In the second half, I came down the middle like, "Don't try to dunk it hard." Of course no one knows about that. (laughing) I remember that. I had to redeem myself, even though no one else remembers.

We won the game, which was great. Coach just wanted me to go home and clear my head, because we had the whole rest of the season with conference play. Why harp on it? He always tells me to have a cornerback's mentality — a short memory. A cornerback might get burned for a touchdown by a wide receiver. They can't think about it. They have to move on to the next play. It's not like they can think about it, because their performance gets worse.

So he helped me with that. He said, "Look, you need to get over it. If the media writes whatever they want to, as long as you get over it, you're going to be able to play." And I started playing some good ball after that anyway. Knowing that just kind of magnified the fact that, "Hey, you'll make mistakes. You'll mess up. But you need to bounce back."

## MANNING MEMORY

One thing about Coach Manning, he would practice with us some days, and he would be killing us. But he wouldn't be moving around with us. It's not like he's in college shape.

He just always made the right play. It was just interesting because now, being in the league, they always say, "Slow down. If you slow down, you'll see the game much better." In college, everything's all pumped up, which is great. But I can tell now, I remember how Coach Manning used to practice and just be killing us, and it's because he slowed down and he could see everything.

He'd make the right pass when he needed to, pump-fake, dribble ... whatever. He'd just always do the right thing, and that's obviously because of his experience in the NBA.

## BOWLING

I guess I can be enigmatic at times. I don't want anybody to think that I didn't take basketball seriously. Coach wouldn't allow that. My teammates wouldn't allow that. They knew how hard I worked. They knew I was dedicated to the classroom and everything.

But I believe in balance. That's me. Some people have their own philosophy. I believe in balance and translating other experiences to what takes up most of your time. I learned a little bit from bowling in terms of translating it to other things in college life.

Bowling was the only sport that I tried to pick up outside of basketball at the time. So people were gracious enough to give me some pointers on some things. And they said, "You've got to follow through." Their terminology, their jargon, it was pretty close to basketball. In basketball, you can't have your elbow out. Same thing in bowling. It will throw your bowling off. So you've got to keep you arm straight, your elbow in, and you have to follow-through. It's like a jump shot.

It's a different way of being competitive, because you're just competing against yourself and competing against the score. That's something that I don't do in basketball. I don't think, "I've got to go out and score 20." But in bowling, it's like, "I've got to get 200." So it's a different way to balance out putting pressure on yourself, and I don't mind putting pressure on myself.

If I do something, I try to take it seriously and have fun. So with bowling, I started getting good at it, because I did it three days a week maybe. I'd bowl three to four games, just to get it in. We'd have an off day or we'd have a day after practice, and that day, you'd have so much energy. So, once I got my studying done and did everything that I had to do, I tried to go bowling.

I'd usually go in the evening, when a lot of people were up there. I just started getting better and better. I started bowling 200. Really, about 185, but I'd bowl 200 every now and then.

To be honest, my bowling has gone down, mainly because I don't have as much energy as I did at 19. When I get done with workouts now, I'm like, "All right, I need to chill a little bit." I'd say I go once or twice a month. Outside of this year, I'd maybe go twice a month my first three years in the league.

## LEAVING KU

I don't regret saying during my sophomore year that I was going to stay at KU, because at the time, that's exactly what my mind-set was. I'm a person that tries not to think too far down the road, because had I had that mentality, I promise you, I think I wouldn't have even had a good season. Because mentally, I'm all about pressure to perform, but pressure to perform in the present. I don't really think about me performing to the point where, "Oh, this will give me this accolade or this will give me that." I'm only thinking about this game or this next game coming up.

So it wasn't that I was trying to dodge those questions. That's exactly how I felt. Honestly, when the season was over, there was more time for reflection. But during the season, I owed it to my teammates and to myself to not think about anything in the future. That's pretty much how I felt then and now.

I won't say there's regrets, because I'm true to myself, and I don't feel like I have to fool myself or fake anybody out. If people would have a chance to be around me, they would know that.

With that decision, I had the support of my team. I don't have too many people in my ear, but it was more for me thinking about some stuff in terms of stock, to be honest. I just felt that with the same team we had, my stock would be pretty much the same. So I figured it would be a good year to come out and explore it. Coach Self even helped out the process in terms of just contacting teams.

The consensus was 10 to 16 — that was kind of the consensus of where teams said they'd draft me on their board. And so, I just felt it was a good opportunity to go. At the same time, I didn't and would not to this day want my teammates or anybody to think that it was anything negative in terms of the support and everything that Kansas had given me in my two years there. It was just, for me, I felt it was a good time to go forward.

Coach Self said he understood. With him being honest, he said that he definitely thought I could benefit from another year, honing my craft and things of that nature. But he just said, "At this point, this is probably the most important decision you've made in your life. If you've given it a lot of thought, all I can do is support that." I really appreciated that.

I believe it was the right decision. I would say it's the toughest decision I've made in my life, to be honest. I know being a man and growing up, you have to make tough decisions, because you can't go down both paths. That's another thing. I get the question about regretting leaving. No, because that's a sign of weakness if you make a tough decision and then you are regretful. If it took a while for you to make a decision, and you go with it, you need to stay with it.

## 2008 TITLE GAME

Like I said, I'm a person where there's nothing scripted. The day of the national championship game, after we got done with practice, I was like, "Let me see what flights they have out of New Orleans to get to San Antonio." We got done with practice at about 1. So I ended up finding a flight at maybe 3:30. It was a flight from New Orleans to Austin, then a short flight from Austin to San Antonio. So I remember driving and getting to the airport. I just brought some toiletries and some other stuff.

I ended up contacting Coach Townsend, and he was able to find me two tickets. It was short notice, so I really appreciate that, too. I don't know how many people contacted him about tickets way before the game, and I'm trying to come to the most important game of your life on game day.

I heard the game as I walked in, but I didn't get to my actual seat until maybe seven, eight minutes to go in the first half. So I'm walking in the arena and still watching, watching.

So I got there and got to my seat. I didn't care what was going on with my phone or anything else. I wasn't doing anything. I was just into the game. It was just very interesting to watch and see. For one, the atmosphere is just so intense.

I was sitting with some of the walk-ons and people on staff, so I wasn't just by myself in the middle of nowhere. So I talked to people during timeouts,

but during the game, I was watching — shoot — every bounce of the ball. Everything.

I was able to watch Mario's shot. I knew it was going in. I didn't want to be loud or anything. I didn't want to say to anybody, "That's going in. Buckets!" or something like that. But I saw the arc. It was high-arching. I was like, "Oh yeah, that's the Mario shot." It's a play that Coach Self drew up my sophomore year against Texas in the Big 12 championship. Similar play, where the ball is handed off and you get them with a quick screen and come off for the shot. I was like, "Yeah, I know that play. That's going in."

One thing that somebody pointed out to me was how on Sports Illustrated my sophomore year, we did a photo shoot together, me and Mario, and he was ducking behind me. And so it was interesting that on that famous photo of Mario's shot, he's the main event making the shot, and I'm in the background like, "Yeah, that's about to go in." When somebody showed me the cover, I was like, "Wow, that's crazy."

I was so excited after they won. Honestly, I basked in the glory, because I understood it. Of course, fans all over the world and the country and Kansas, they've been watching and covering the team. They're definitely faithful to the team. But I had a special bond with most of the guys on the team, so that made it even more of a great experience for me to be there and try to show my support.

The coaches invited me to the stage. They had me on the podium. I was really moved by that, because they didn't have to. That shows a lot of class, and I was really humbled by that.

Then they had me back in the locker room celebrating. I was congratulating everybody. It was one of those things where, at first, I was like, "I didn't start training camp." Of course I was a former player there. But for them to say, "No, you started this with us. You didn't end it, but we know you're family," ... that meany a lot to me. That's another experience I won't forget.

The locker room was bananas. Everybody was just yelling, screaming, throwing water bottles. There was a water fight. Everyone was jumping. Big hugs. Bear hugs. High-fives. Coaches kissing wives. All kinds of stuff. Kissing babies. It was madness. It was amazing, though.

They told me where they were going to be at in the hotel, so I went there with them. I was just like, "Man, this is amazing."

I had to get back to New Orleans for a shoot-around at 9:30 a.m. And I had to get the doughnuts as a rookie. So I had my brother help me by getting some Krispy Kreme doughnuts and meeting me at the arena.

I pulled an all-nighter and had a taxi drive me from San Antonio to Houston. Then I had a flight from Houston at 8. And it got me to New Orleans in 50 minutes, so I got there at 8:50, 8:55. And I had to go straight from the airport to shoot-around, and of course I took a shower after shoot-around. (laughing)

But yeah, it was worth it. I could have got fined. I could have got suspended. I felt like it was necessary, and I went for it, and that's kind of what life is about. I took a couple gambles, and it was worth it, because I was able to have that experience.

## NBA CAREER

The NBA is what I expected. Tough. Ups and downs. At the end of the day, it's about mentally being ready for anything, because what's going on with your situation, it can change. That suits me well, I guess, in that I'm able to make adjustments and I'm not so scripted in a sense like, "Oh, everything's been going this way. Why is it changing?" in terms of minutes, in terms of coaches. You have different teammates every year. You have to get adjusted to anything.

You can't get too familiar with a team or philosophy. Coaches change plays, take out plays. You just have to learn on the go. It's more mental than anything. You're sore. You're hurt. You don't want to sit out, but you want to sit out if you really are hurt. You don't want to sit out too long, because then you get out of rhythm. It's a lot, but it's what I expected. And I knew what I signed up for and that it wouldn't be easy.

If you saw me right now, I have a glow about me. I'm very optimistic. I don't think I've allowed anybody to say that I haven't worked hard or I'm not about winning or any of those aspects that teams look for. But in terms of skill set and things that I know that I have to continue to work on, I'm very optimistic. And, to my advantage, I feel fresher, as opposed to, say, an 18-year-old who got into the league and played six or seven years. I've played four years, and I have a lot left in the tank.

## MUSIC CAREER

Music is something my family's always been a part of. Since I was 4 or 5, I was in choir. My grandparents taught music. My mom loves music, arranges it and is a vocalist. My uncle is a DJ. Another uncle is a choir director and plays piano.

So there's a long pedigree of music.

And it's just something ... I knew I had the talent, but I felt like I suppressed it because of basketball, which I believe is good, because everything happens for a reason. I was in choir until I was 13, then I stopped because of basketball. I had to make a decision at the time, and I was like, "I really love basketball." I'm competitive. It's an outlet as well. I'm not saying I lived in the ghetto, but I didn't live in Mr. Rogers' Neighborhood.

But I believe — I believe a lot of things, as you know — but I believe God has equipped us with more than one talent. I think we sometimes allow ourselves to think that we have one thing we're good at or one thing that we should just focus on. I think that's important, but there are obviously priorities with those talents and skill sets and things like that. I've been able to push it aside, because I knew that wasn't as important for me at that time in my life.

So I started picking up music pretty much my second year in the league. It just went from there. I started just making music, dibbling and dabbling with it rather than being confident that I'm going to do music. I've just eased my way into it and started to say, "Hey, not too bad." I could see myself continuing to do it.

Now, after four years of being in the league, I'm starting to do even more. I want to be a songwriter, singer, producer, make my own music and I want to be, eventually, a sound engineer. So when I do go back to school, I want to earn a degree in music and be a sound engineer when it's all said and done. So that's kind of my next transition from basketball, because it's obviously a small window.

## LOOKING BACK

I'm very blessed for the opportunity that I had. When a coach and a coaching staff and a community like Lawrence takes you in, it makes you feel like family, not just when you're there in the locker room, but that's forever. It's one of those things where ... it's a bond that's tough to break. Almost impossible.

The guys, we were obviously going on different paths, but we all still contact each other and talk and reach out. That just shows for however many years you're there or however many years since you've been there, guys are still in that fraternity. I'm definitely happy to have been and will always be a Jayhawk.

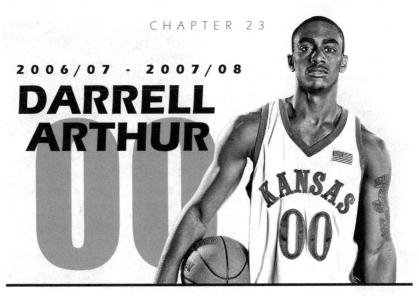

# CHAPTER 23

# 2006/07 - 2007/08
# DARRELL ARTHUR

D arrell Arthur is arguably the most talented player to wear a Kansas uniform during the Bill Self era. The 6-foot-9 forward from South Oak Cliff High School in Dallas averaged 12.8 points as a sophomore on the Jayhawks' NCAA championship squad. Had it not been for Mario Chalmers' heroic 3-pointer, Arthur would've been a shoo-in for Most Outstanding Player honors in the national title game. He scored 20 points and grabbed 10 rebounds in the Jayhawks' overtime victory against Memphis and hit two huge – and difficult – shots to spearhead his team's miraculous comeback. Arthur, whose nickname is "Shady," was the 27th overall pick in the 2008 NBA draft. He averaged 9.1 points and 4.3 rebounds in his third season with the Memphis Grizzlies in 2010-11.

## IN DARRELL'S WORDS

Back when I was playing high school ball in Dallas, I really didn't have any plans to go to college. My thought all along was that I'd jump straight to the NBA. But in 2005, a year before I graduated, the NBA put a rule in place that said kids had to wait at least one year after high school before they could turn pro. Talk about bad timing … I was pissed. All of a sudden, I had to make a decision. I was like, "Damn, I've got to find somewhere to go to school."

Kansas was a place I had known about since my freshman year. Keith Langford and I both played for the same AAU program, Team Texas. I didn't know Keith very well because he was older, but he was still nice enough to invite me up there so I could see the environment. I went to a game with Keith's mom and another one of my friends. Roy Williams was still the coach, and it was rockin' in Allen Fieldhouse that day. It was crazy. The fans were going nuts. That's what really made me want to go there, the fans. It was so loud and so packed. I had never seen anything like it.

## THE BAYLOR SITUATION

As much as I liked Kansas, the school I really wanted to sign with was Baylor. I was this close to going there. People were pressuring me to go other places, but I was convinced I'd be fine if I just stayed close to home and played ball in Waco. My grandmother wanted me to go there. My high school teammate, Kevin Rogers, was playing there. The coaching staff was really cool, and it was a little more than an hour from home. It was the perfect situation.

Right at the end of my senior year, in May, I told Baylor I was coming. I actually called Coach (Paul) Mills, their assistant, and committed over the phone. I told him I thought I could get Damion James to sign there, too. Damion ended up at Texas but, at the time, he had been calling me, because he had gotten out of his letter-of-intent at Oklahoma after the Kelvin Sampson stuff. He was like, "What are you going to do?" I told him, "I don't know. I think I might go to Baylor. You should come, too. We need to go to school together." I was trying to get Scottie Reynolds to come, too, but he really wanted to go to Villanova.

After I called Coach Mills, I scheduled a press conference for the next day. Kevin Rogers drove up for the press conference and I had heard the Baylor coaches might come, too. But I never showed up that day. Instead we put a sign outside that said the press conference had been rescheduled for the following day. The whole thing was freakin' crazy.

## JAZZY

Here's what happened: The day I was supposed to have my press conference, Jazzy Hartwell, the AAU coach I'd been with since about the fifth grade, came to me and said, "You really need to rethink your decision to go to Baylor."

Jazzy had a lot of influence on me at the time. He was pretty much my father growing up – or at least my father figure. I didn't have my dad around. I stayed on Jazzy's team all the way up to my junior year of high school. It really was a family bond type of thing. So he really had a lot of influence on what I did college-wise. He knew a lot more about it than I did. He really didn't want me to go to Baylor. They were just coming off of probation. He wanted me to be on a winning team and to get far in the NCAA Tournament, so I could get a lot of exposure, and NBA scouts would see me.

It wasn't at the point where he could just tell me where to sign and I was going to do it. I was listening to my mom and my grandmother, too. Both of them said, "It's your decision," although my grandmother kind of wanted me to go to Baylor, because she was sick and she wanted me to stay close to home. And my mom was a little pissed off at Jazzy for putting the thought in my mind that I needed to change schools. At the same time, I wanted to win. He didn't call the shot, but he made me think about it. At that point, there were only two choices left: LSU and Kansas.

## DREAMY

I knew I had to figure something else out fast, because another press conference had been scheduled for the next day. When I went to bed that night, my mom said, "Pray on it, because you have to make a decision tomorrow." That's when I went to sleep and had that dream that I was playing for Kansas. I know some people laugh about it and think I made the whole story up, but it really did happen. I dreamed that I was on the court, playing with Mario and Julian. When I woke up, I was trippin'. I was like, "Man, why the hell did I have that dream? That was crazy." But the night before, I had asked God to give me some sort of sign, because I didn't know what I was going to do. So when I had that dream, I was like, "I guess that was a sign that Kansas is where I need to go to school." So I got up and texted Coach Self and told him I was coming. A week later, I was in Lawrence. It all happened so fast. It was really stressful.

I'm a loyal dude. I don't like making commitments to people that I don't end up keeping. So when I committed to Baylor and told them I was coming and then didn't end up going, it hurt me really bad. I never even called their coaches to tell them I'd changed my mind. I didn't want that responsibility. I couldn't bring myself to do it. I didn't want to crush them like that. I guess they found out through the media. When we went to play them in Waco that year, those fans were on my ass. They were like, "Are you serious? You had a f---ing dream? You should've come to Baylor!" I understood why they were upset, but I had to do what was best for me. We ended up winning a national championship at Kansas, so it's hard to argue with Jazzy's advice.

## ON MY OWN

When I moved to Kansas, my mom stayed with me for the first week. When she finally left, I burst into tears. I had never been away from home for a long amount of time. I'd never been away from my mom or my family. My grandmother was sick, and I didn't want to leave. I just had to get used to it.

Mario and his family really took me in. They took care of us. It was a family environment. They'd have Mario and I over and buy us groceries and cook for us or whatever. Coach Self invited us to his house for dinner sometimes, too. It was cool to get those home-cooked meals. Coach Self's wife made this really good buffalo chicken dip, wing dip. Sometimes they catered in food from Longhorn Steakhouse, which was one of my favorite places in Lawrence. They had those Firecracker Chicken Wraps, the little enchilada-looking things with spicy chicken and cheese inside. I loved those things. Mario's mom used to make soul food, some green beans and mashed potatoes and candied yams. It was cool. After a while, I was really starting to enjoy myself.

My mom got to where she loved Kansas, too. She and my grandmother made the drive frequently, every other week or so. They'd drive 7 ½ hours from Dallas for a game. They'd watch me play and then drive back. They loved to come up there. They had fun. My mom always liked going to Jefferson's for wings. She always talks about how she needs to go back up there just so she can go to Jefferson's.

## FRESHMAN SEASON

Physically, my first year at Kansas was probably the hardest thing I've ever had to go through. I showed up weighing about 205 or 210. I gained 20 pounds really quick. I got all the way up to 230. Coach Hudy, our strength coach, put that weight on me fast. I thought I was going to die once I started doing the conditioning. I wasn't really in shape. Every suicide we did, I felt like I was going to throw up or die. You can ask anyone there. I was probably in the worst shape of anyone on the team. Even Matt Kleinmann had me beat. I was behind him in all the drills. Coach Hudy gradually got me on a good weight program and things changed. I wasn't weak or anything. I was benching 225 when I got there, but Hudy took me to a whole different level. She's a hard-ass. She made you respect her. She made us get our work done. She put us through hell. Some days we had to run about 20 100-yard sprints outside on the football field. Some days we had to run the stairs in the gym. Some days we had to run outside. She got me in the best shape I've ever been in during my life.

Boot Camp was the worst. One day, we had to do 30 suicides, and I stripped out of my whole uniform. We were halfway done, and I sweat a lot, so my shorts and my shirt were drenched. I felt like they were weighing me down, so I took my shirt off first. After about three more suicides, I took my shorts off, too. I was running in my tights and shoes. Everyone was just laughing at me. They couldn't even finish their suicides because they were looking at me and laughing so hard. After every suicide, I'd go straight to the ground, like I was about to die. As soon as Coach Self blew the whistle, I'd hop back up and run. It was probably the hardest time I had at Kansas, but probably the funniest time, too. I never threw up from running, but if I did get last in the sprints, Coach Self would get mad and make me do more conditioning in the pool. One time I finished last, and Coach was like, "You're too tired. We need to get you in better shape." So, after a three-hour workout, he made me get on the underwater treadmill for extra conditioning. I remember Hudy turning the jets on 100 percent, and then she put the treadmill on full blast. I was running on that thing, and I slipped. My feet came out from under me and I just started swimming. I said, "Forget all this running. I'm tired. I'm swimming." She started screaming at me to get back on the treadmill. But I couldn't do it. I didn't have anything left.

## RIVALRIES

Coach Self wasn't on me as hard as he was on a lot of the other guys. I tried to make sure I did everything right. When he did get on me, he was tough. One time we were getting ready to play Texas and Kevin Durant. He was talking about how Durant was having this great season and doing this and that. Then he was like, "Shady, what the hell are you doing? What the hell have you done?" He kept going on and one about Durant, and finally I was like, "Man, f--- Durant!" I was so happy we beat their ass – twice. Those were probably two of the best wins I was ever a part of. Texas had us down by about 16 or 18 points each time and we came back and won.

Missouri was supposed to be our rival, but we usually didn't have much trouble beating the hell out of them. But Texas ... those games were close. Those games were fun, because they were up and down, nothing but running. Big-time players played in those games: Durant, A.J. Abrams, D.J. Augustin – guys that can really play. The time we played them for the tournament title in Kansas City was phenomenal, too. I liked both of those games. I wasn't a very big fan of the University of Texas. I didn't really like their coaching staff. If I didn't go to Baylor, I didn't want to go anywhere else in Texas. Any school from Texas, I wanted to beat them, beat them bad.

## SHERRON COLLINS

Sherron's a competitor. He's going to go out there and try to bust someone's ass. He hates other people getting credit. He wants the credit. He wants to be the man. I like that. He shows a lot of leadership. He'll get in your face and cuss you out. He doesn't take any bulls---. I remember him and Darnell getting into it one time. Sherron actually picked Darnell up and slammed him into the ground. Darnell recovered and flipped him back over and started wrestling with him, because Darnell is a beast. Still, I was like, "Damn, Sherron picked up Darnell and slammed him like that? Wow." Sherron and Rodrick Stewart were like brothers. They were that close. They were always going places together. I liked that team we had. Everyone got along with each other. There wasn't any bulls---. No one was hating on anyone else for scoring a certain amount of points. We just wanted to win.

## DARNELL JACKSON

Darnell can be really quiet and emotional sometimes. But he's got a flip side, too, where he can be really fun to be around. Sometimes he gets down on himself. When we were in school, his grandmother passed, and one of his cousins got shot before the Oklahoma State game. His life was really hard. He had to take care of his mom and his brother and sister at the same time. His mom passed after college. You start to wonder how much one guy can take. We always used to comfort him. I'd let him borrow my car whenever he needed it. We all tried to keep a watch on him, because he could've cracked any time. He actually left school one time. Coach Self had to go down to Oklahoma City and bring him back. He had so much stuff going through his head. He just couldn't take it anymore.

On the court, he was the most hard-working player I've ever played with or against. He had a knack for getting rebounds. He was so physically strong that he was hard to get position on in the paint. We used to have these drills where you had to get three rebounds and then you could come off the floor. I was in there battling Sasha, Darnell and Matt Kleinmann. All of those guys were 20 or 30 pounds heavier than me. I was trying to throw them out of the way, but Darnell was getting every rebound, sometimes four or five in a row. Whoever didn't get the rebound had to run sprints. I started screaming, "F---! This is some bulls---!" I didn't want to run those sprints. Darnell was a beast.

## PAINT PRESENCE

When I first got to Kansas, I remember Coach Self telling me that the practices were going to be harder than the games. He said, "You're going to have to practice like you play. If you don't practice hard, your ass is going to be on the bench." So every workout, I had the mind-set that I was going to try to bust the next dude's ass, or I wouldn't be playing. The problem was that basically every big man we had on the team was probably an NBA-caliber player. And if they weren't when they got there, they turned into one eventually. Cole Aldrich is a great example.

For a while, Cole loved to talk trash. I remember the first week Cole got to school, we played a pickup game, and I dunked on him the first three possessions. And I mean I dunked it hard. After a while, he stopped taking that noise. He started coming into his own. He started blocking shots. He started getting physical. His work paid off against North Carolina. I think all of the other big guys took a little bit of pride in the way he played that night, because we felt like we helped prepare him for that. He played better than I thought he was going to play. He stepped in and played some huge minutes. He blocked some shots and made a couple of key baskets and got in Tyler Hansbrough's head a little bit. He was a game-changer for us, because we ended up blowing their ass out.

## BRANDON RUSH

Brandon was super funny. He's a character. I looked up to him. He's always been a great basketball player. I admired him a lot when he was in high school, playing AAU ball. At Kansas, he and Mario were the guys I hung around the most. Coach Self called us the Three Amigos, because we were always getting into trouble, missing curfew. One summer, we missed curfew, and as punishment, they said we had to either lose 500 calories on the elliptical or run 5 miles. It was up to us, and we had an hour to do it. If we didn't finish in an hour, we were going to start boot camp a week earlier than normal. It was me, Brady, Sherron, Mario and Brandon. We had to do it for two weeks straight, Wednesday through Sunday. The very last Sunday, we got there and realized Brady wasn't there. I finished my workout early and then went and knocked on Brady's window. He opened it and was just laying there, smiling. I was like, "Dog, you just missed the workout!" Brandon and I were laughing at him. He hopped out of bed and raced over to see Coach Hudy. He was like, "Coach Hudy, I'll do anything. just please don't tell Coach Self that I missed that workout." So she drove him way far away somewhere, dropped him off and said, "Now you've got to run back to school." Brady said he just started running and didn't stop until he got back.

Back to Brandon .... Brandon is a good player. But he hasn't been as aggressive in the NBA as he was at times at Kansas. Part of that is probably because Coach Self isn't there to get on him all the time. Coach Self used to always say, "Score the ball, Brandon! Shoot it!" Brandon can be a very passive player. He's a good team player, but he's very passive sometimes. Coach is like, "Man, you're open. You're one of the best scorers on our team. You've got to shoot the ball." Before the NCAA Tournament in 2008, Coach Self sat down with Brandon and Mario and told them they needed to be more aggressive from the 3-point line than they've ever been. That whole tournament, those guys were on fire. It seemed like they couldn't miss. From the Texas game in the Big 12 championship all the way to the national championship, those two guys led us. Now, I'm guessing people aren't pushing Brandon like they were at Kansas. He can shoot the ball better than damn near anyone I've seen play.

## JULIAN WRIGHT

Julian was different than everyone else. He was a loner most of the time. But he was cool to play with on the court. He's a great guy. He played different. His body was a little different. But he had a good basketball IQ. He could handle the ball and he could jump out of the gym. And he had those long, freakish arms. Off the court, he always had his headphones on. He loved to bowl, and he thought he could beat anyone in Call of Duty.

## DANNY MANNING

Coach Manning is a great guy, very smart. I've actually been working with a coach who worked with Danny back in the day, Barry Hecker. He was with the Clippers when they drafted Danny. Coach Manning had more to offer than most college coaches. There aren't a lot of assistants out there who were in the NBA that can tell you what you need to do to get there. He tells you what moves you need to learn, and shows you how to work your position with duck-ins and rebounding position and things like that. He's also a big influence on you off the court. He was my adviser when I was there. He always told me, "Once you get older, it's going to be harder for you to go back to school." He said, "I didn't get a college degree, and my wife came to me and said, 'How are you supposed to tell your kids to get a college degree when you don't have one?' So I went back and got my degree." He told us a lot of stuff to help better our lives. I've got intentions of going back and getting my degree, but it's hard right now because of all the time we spend working out in the offseason and keeping our bodies right and things like that. I'm going to do some online stuff for now. After that, we'll see.

## BILL SELF

He's a great motivator. He's a little bipolar, I think (laughing). No, seriously, he's a great guy. I talked to him last year. He told me to keep working hard to stay on the team. He said not to let some punk-ass rookie come in and take my job. I took that to heart last year and went out and tried to prove myself to people. He came to my grandmother's funeral. That was big time. I sure did appreciate that. Jeremy Case came, too. They all showed love and support. I'll never forget that.

## LOCAL CELEBRITY

The attention we got for being Kansas basketball players certainly wasn't bad. It was actually pretty cool. It was definitely good when it came to girls. That's probably one of the main reasons guys play college basketball, for the chicks, the females. We had some wild nights. I don't want to bring up any details. But I've got some wild memories.

As much as people loved us when we won, it definitely wasn't fun around Lawrence when we lost. We didn't want to walk on campus or anything. The school thrives on us winning games. We really didn't want to show our faces, because we were embarrassed about losing. I remember losing to Oral Roberts my freshman year. That was probably one of the worst experiences of my college career – and the fact that Coach Self used to coach there made it even worse. He was like, "This team is a great team. They're capable of coming in here and beating you guys." He said that before every game, though. We were thinking, "Whatever. We're fixin' to go out there and beat the s--t out of these guys." They ended up coming in there and kicking our ass. One guy scored about 24 on us, another guy had 22.

Coach Self made us come back to the gym that same night for a practice at midnight. Then we woke up the next morning and practiced again. That was as pissed as he's ever been. For the whole next month, our practices would last three straight hours. That was one of the toughest times ever, losing to that team. We lost another tough game to DePaul a few weeks later.

The UCLA game in the Elite Eight that year was terrible, too. Brandon and Russell and Darnell had good games, but that was about it. We didn't play well at all. At the same time, those guys were making 3-point buzzer-beaters right at the end of the shot clock. There was nothing we could do – and we were playing on their home turf in California.

## TREK TO THE TITLE

I had been struggling a little bit entering the NCAA Tournament my sophomore year – mainly because of foul trouble. I had 17 points in the opening game against Portland State, but every game after that up until the championship, I scored in single digits. I honestly didn't care that much, though. We were winning and having fun. That's all I cared about. At the same time, I knew I had to impress NBA scouts, because I wanted to play in the NBA. Still, every time I'd get frustrated with my performance, it wouldn't last long, because I could see how close we were to winning a championship.

Davidson was probably the toughest game we had that tournament, just because of the pressure we had to get to the Final Four. Coach Self had never made it until then. We were playing against Stephen Curry, who had been killing everyone the whole tournament. He had 25 on us and we only won by two points – and they had a last second 3-pointer to win the game. When that shot didn't go in, I was about to rip my jersey off and yell at the top of my lungs. I saw Coach on the ground, just thanking God that we won. They played great defense the whole game. We couldn't get a big lead and pull away from them. We were just glad when it was over.

## NORTH CAROLINA

We were glad when we got matched up against North Carolina, because that was the team we wanted to play the most. We'd been hearing all year about Tyler Hansbrough and Ty Lawson and how good they were. And some guys had their opinions about Roy Williams. I didn't have much of a problem with him. I visited North Carolina. It was my first visit. It was cool. Roy Williams came to a few of my games and did an in-home visit with me. I liked him, but it was really early in the process and I wanted to see everyone else. A week after my visit, Brandon Wright committed to North Carolina. It was done after that.

Still, I was dying to play them. We all were. We just wanted to go out there and beat the hell out of them. Before the game, Coach Self told us that we'd already made him proud. He said there was no reason to stop now. He also said, "We're not going to let them play their transition, fast-paced s---. They're not going to run on us. We're going to be the team that runs. We're going to wear their asses down."

Coach told us to make them pass the ball at least three times before they took a shot. We wanted to slow them down, but we wanted to run back at them on offense and play fast. In other words, we wanted to switch it around on them. We probably practiced harder for that game than any game in the tournament. Those guys got up and down the court so fast. In the first few rounds, Ty Lawson was getting to the rim on everyone and finishing. And they had been absolutely blowing people out. We had a great scheme for Ty Lawson. We were meeting him at the rim every time and forcing him to make a play or make a pass. We didn't want to let him finish. Cole had a few blocks on him. That win was for the whole state.

## MEMPHIS

I was nervous before the Memphis game, but I was nervous before just about every game at Kansas. I wanted to come out and play well. You never know how you're going to play. When we were coming out to run through the tunnel, Memphis was talking noise. Memphis was supposed to run out first, but Pierre Niles said, "Let those bitches go first." I don't know why he did that. It just put an extra chip on our shoulder.

Luckily, I had one of the best games of my career at just the right time

(20 points and 10 rebounds, including eight points after the 3:30 mark of regulation). One thing I remember was looking across the court into the stands. My little brother, Juicy, was crying. He was only 6, and later my mom told me he was saying, "We're not going to win it, are we momma? We're not going to win it, are we?" That was with about 2 minutes left in the game, and I'm sure a lot of people were probably thinking the same thing. Our team, though ... we never lost confidence that we could get it done.

I made two shots during our comeback against Memphis that I'll never forget: an 18-footer with a hand in my face and a turnaround jumper from the baseline that rattled in. Coach Self told me later that I should've taken a step back and shot a 3 instead of the 18-footer, but I didn't even look down. I just shot it. There were 2 minutes left, and I was trying to help bring us back. I had an open shot and I just took it. Coach Self called a timeout after that. He said, "We've got to keep believing. The game isn't over. We've got to keep believing, keep playing." We went back out there and kept trying.

A few plays later, Sherron stole an inbounds pass and got it to Russell under the basket. I was screaming at him to shoot the ball. Shoot it, Russell! Shoot! But he saw Sherron in the corner and passed it to him, and Sherron made the 3. We got another stop, and then I came down and made the baseline shot that made it a two-point game, 62-60. Then we fouled Derrick Rose, he made 1-of-2 free throws to put Memphis up by three. After that is when Mario hit his big 3-pointer.

We knew we'd win after that. Joey Dorsey had fouled out, so they didn't have anyone big inside. We just said, "Let's attack them. Let's kill 'em." The only thing I remember Coach Self saying is, "Believe. Don't give up!"

When the game was over the confetti started coming down, the first person I hugged was Matt Kleinmann. I don't know how it happened. I just ran up to him and hugged him. There was a big picture of us in the paper. After that I hugged Coach Self. Then I ran over to my mom and hugged her. My dad was in the stands. I hugged both of them. Tears were coming out of my eyes and out of their eyes. We easily could've lost that game. But we ended up winning because we didn't give up hope, we didn't give up on ourselves.

That night we went and hung out with a friend in another hotel. We didn't go to sleep at all that night. The whole team stayed up all night and kicked it and had fun. We were so excited. We were tired as hell on the plane the next day. We slept on the flight and then drove to the football stadium after we landed. All the fans were out there. It was fun. The next week was the parade. That was the most people I've ever seen on one street. People were running up to the car, taking pictures of you. It's one of those memories that will never go away.

## BETTER LATE THAN NEVER

One of the things I'll remember the most about the NCAA title game is that my dad was in the stands, watching me play. It was the first time he had ever been to one of my college games. My dad wasn't really around when I was growing up. He got into drugs when I was about 6 or 7 and moved to Houston. I hardly saw him after that. When he showed up at the national championship game, it was the first time I had seen him in more than two years. Since then, he's been making an effort to do better.

I loved playing in front of my dad that night. Around Dallas, he was a pretty big name when he was younger. I remember he had all these trophies and medals and things. When I was growing up, people would say, "Your dad used to be the man around here." His nickname was "Grasshopper" because he could jump so high. That's why I started playing basketball, to impress him. His name is Anthony Arthur. He played at South Oak Cliff, just like me. Before he moved to Houston, I used to go to his mom's house, my grandmother's house, and I'd see all his trophies. I'd be like, "Man, daddy, you won all these trophies and things?" He'd be like, "Yeah, those are mine." I remember pointing to one of them and saying, "I want to win me a big one, just like that." Well, that night in San Antonio, we the biggest one there is to win, and he was there to see it.

## BAD PRESS

*(Shortly after he announced he was entering the 2008 NBA draft, a Dallas television station reported that some of Arthur's grades in high school had been altered so he could remain eligible to compete at South Oak Cliff as a sophomore and junior. Arthur led his team to the state championship in each of those seasons but, after an ensuing investigation, those titles were stripped. These are Arthur's first extensive comments on the issue.)*

After we won the national championship, things got a little rough for a while. Just as I was beginning to go through my NBA draft workouts, all that stuff came out about my grades being changed in high school. It was a complete shock to me and my family. I didn't know anything about that. I'm being 100 percent truthful. I had honestly never heard anything about it. Every report card I got in high school said I had passed everything. When all those stories came out, I was like, "I didn't even know y'all were (changing my grades), so how are you going to put it on me?" If they changed stuff, I didn't know about it. They were trying to say that I didn't have any grades in one math class for the whole semester. Seriously ... how could anyone get by without going to class for a whole semester, a whole year? I don't know how they got all those records and stuff. It was bulls---. It felt like people were attacking my character, which didn't seem right. I don't know if anyone changed my grades or not. But no matter what happened, it shouldn't be on me. I didn't have anything to do with it. I was just a sophomore in high school, a 15-year-old. How was I supposed to know what was going on?

## DRAFT NIGHT

*(Arthur was projected as a top 15 pick in the 2008 NBA draft. But he fell to No. 27 after*

*rumors surfaced on draft night that he had kidney problems. Those rumors turned out to be false and may have ended costing Arthur millions.)*

When I went to the pre-draft camp, I was sick. I was taking Claritin, because my sinuses were messed up. The next day, someone told me something was wrong with my kidney levels. The doctors asked me if I'd taken anything, and I told them about the Claritin. They said sometimes that can affect your kidney readings. So I took another test in Washington a few days before the draft, and they said my kidney levels and everything came back fine. But they didn't send those test results out to everyone else like they were supposed to, so on draft night, everyone thought my kidneys were messed up. Memphis was one of the teams that had the most recent results. They were like, "There's nothing wrong with this kid. Let's pick him up." It was a blessing. I think everything works out for a reason. I got there and got a chance to play right away. I was able to acclimate myself to the NBA early. Still, I was mad as hell that night. My grandmother had flown up there and she was all sick. I was the last guy in the green room that night. When they finally picked me, Juicy was sitting next to me, asleep.

## MORE PROBLEMS

*(In September of 2008, Arthur and Mario Chalmers were fined $20,000 apiece and sent home from the NBA rookie symposium in New York after security detected the scent of marijuana coming from their hotel room. No drugs or drug paraphernalia were found, but two women were with the players in the room, which violated the no-guests policy.)*

What happened in New York … that was probably the worst day of my life. No one was supposed to be in our room, but we snuck some girls up there. Mario knew them. One of them was his cousin. They had some weed with them. Someone came and knocked on the door, and my heart just dropped. Boom! I was like, "F---!" It was the lowest feeling I've ever had.

One thing led to another until there were about 20 people, 20 security guys, in our room: the NBA security, the hotel security, all types of people. Mario and I were in there and Michael Beasley was hiding in the closet. He was literally in the closest for about four hours. They never knew he was in there. He ended up telling on himself, from what I heard. He started telling people how he got out and how he got away. But I didn't say anything. My general manager even came up to me and asked if Beasley was in the room, but I didn't tell on him. It was crazy, but the whole situation made me into a better person. It was a wake-up call. It was time to put my childish days aside and turn into a man. That helped me out a lot as far as becoming a better man.

I've tried to spin the situation into a positive. I'm trying to live my life on the straight and narrow. I hardly even drink anymore. I might on occasion, but as far as going out every weekend and partying and clubbing, I don't do much of that anymore. I usually just stay at home and play video games. You're not going

to see my name out there like that again.

One of the worst things about the situation is that it kind of hurt Mario's and my relationship. Since then, we haven't been as close as we were in college. It sucks, because he was one of my best friends. He was probably the coolest guy out there, out of everyone I was with.

I'm not as close with any of the guys as I was in college, just because I'm not around anymore. I try, but it's not the same. It's not like when we were all at school, hanging out in the dorms and spending so much time together. Now we're on our own, doing our own thing. It's unfortunate. I miss it.

## RETURNING TO KANSAS

I haven't set foot on Kansas' campus since we won the championship. The only time I've been back in town was to renew my driver's license but, even then, I didn't go near the school. Ever since all that stuff happened in the NBA at the rookie orientation deal, I've been embarrassed. That's the reason I haven't been back. A few months after we had that great accomplishment, I went out and got in trouble and spoiled things a little bit. I don't know what Kansas fans think of me now. I want to go back, though. I want to see everyone again. I'm sure I'll probably get back there soon. It'd be cool to see everyone again.

I want Kansas fans to know that I'm sorry for what happened after I left. I loved my time at Kansas. The two years I spent at Kansas were the best two years of my life, and the fans were the main reason.

# CHAPTER 24

# 2003/04 - 2007/08
# JEREMY CASE
# 10

Jeremy Case spent five seasons at the University of Kansas from 2003-08. A 6-foot-1 guard from McAlester, Okla., Case had his best game on Senior Night, posting career-highs in points (nine) and three-pointers (three) in KU's 109-51 victory over Texas Tech. Along with an NCAA title ring, Case graduated from Kansas with a bachelor's degree in Communication Studies in May 2007 after notching a 4.0 grade point average his final semester. He is entering his third season as an assistant coach at Southeast Missouri State.

## IN JEREMY'S WORDS

Bill Self and my dad actually played at Oklahoma State together for two years. They became pretty good friends, and I guess just maintained a relationship after those two years. Then they both got into coaching afterwards. I didn't really know Coach Self then. He knew me as a baby. I guess my mom was always bringing me and my sister up there to see my dad in the dorm. I guess Coach Self would be around, and he actually held me when I was a baby. I don't remember, but that's what they say. It's pretty ironic. I was actually really surprised that they would remember that.

## ROY'S DEPARTURE

I was stunned when Coach Williams left. I was shocked. I heard it from a bunch of different people. I was actually working out at my high school, and then when I was on my way home, people were calling me saying, "Coach Williams is leaving." I was like, "No, no, no," because I didn't hear it from him. I didn't really know what to do. It just hit me out of nowhere. I didn't think he would leave Kansas at all. It didn't cross my mind before that.

I think he called me that next day after he announced it and talked to me about it. He just kind of explained his situation and apologized for putting me in that predicament. He was really sincere about it. I told him there were no hard feelings. I understood that he did what he had to do, regardless of how I felt or how anyone else felt.

I see him out on the road recruiting, and I'll go give him a hug, and we'll sit and talk for a little bit. We still have a good relationship. Coach Robinson and C.B. McGrath and all those guys — I still talk to those guys when I see them.

## STICKING WITH KU

When Coach Self first got the job, I was thinking about not going to KU. I was talking to my dad, and he said, "No, you need to stay. Coach Self's a great coach. He's a great guy. He's somebody you can get better from, somebody you'll want to learn from." My dad's relationship with Bill Self is really what made me stay and want to go there after Coach Williams left.

Transferring to North Carolina crossed my mind, but Coach Williams, he didn't put that out there or say, "If you want to come with me, you can." He said, "UNC has signed all their guys, and they're going to go that way. And you signed with KU. You didn't just sign with me." He kind of explained it to me as far as, "You need to go ahead and stay here. You don't need to follow me." I was good with that. I agreed with him. It wasn't just Coach Williams that I signed with. I signed with the University of Kansas, and that's what I basically based my decision off of.

The whole reason I signed with Kansas and with Roy Williams was because of their style of play. I thought it definitely fit my style of play to a T. Who's to say I would have actually been able to do a whole lot more if he would have stayed? I don't know. I don't really like to think about it, because I'm happy with my decision and haven't really given it a whole lot of thought.

I don't wonder about what would have happened if Coach Williams would have stayed. I used to. When I was in college, I used to be like, "Man, would I be getting to play 20, 25 minutes a game or this and that?" But not any more. I don't think about that any more. I'm happy with the outcome. I'm happy with my decision. I don't regret anything.

## THE NEXT JEFF BOSCHEE?

I don't know if I was the best shooter on the team. I think if we were just out there shooting around, I think I would most likely win, but Brandon Rush was a big-time shooter. He made a lot of big-time shots. If we were just sitting there shooting, I probably could beat him.

I could see people comparing my style of play to Jeff Boschee's. We're both about 6-1, both really good shooters. I would like to say I could do a little more than shoot, though. (laughing)

Boschee's a great shooter. I don't know if I could actually do some of the stuff he did. I wouldn't have minded trying, and I wouldn't have minded actually trying to fill his shoes.

I know when Boschee would come back to play pickup, I would always kind of try to go after him a little bit. I went after Boschee just because, in my mind, I felt like I could do what he did. It was kind of like me trying to prove that I'm as good as him type of thing — just being young and being a competitor. But yeah, it would have been nice to have the chance like he did to showcase my talents.

## J.R. GIDDENS

I didn't know a whole lot about J.R. before we went to KU. We played AAU together, and we went to two different high schools. I didn't see him until we started playing AAU with him. But he was a great guy, very competitive. He wanted to work hard and wanted to get better. He was a good guy, a good friend of mine.

I kind of heard about the Wal-Mart thing late. *(Giddens was arrested his senior year of high school after attempting to steal nearly $4,000 worth of electronics from an Oklahoma City Wal-Mart.)* It was kind of weird. I didn't think he would do anything like that. And I know he was kind of surrounded by some people he shouldn't have been around. I was definitely surprised by that.

If I'm not mistaken, when J.R. was on his visit, I called Coach Williams and committed to him while he was actually on his visit. That's what Coach Williams told me. Then right before he left, J.R. committed. So we almost committed at the same time.

I didn't think J.R. was a bad guy at all. I felt like he could make the right decisions. He knows right from wrong. He's not out there to do bad things or anything.

J.R. was my roommate for the first few years at Jayhawk Towers. We basically spent every day together. Our classes were almost the same. I remember every time we'd go to class, we'd play "Juicy" by Biggie (Smalls, the Notorious B.I.G.). We'd have it on repeat when we'd drive to class. It'd be 8 in the morning, and we'd just put it on blast. This was our freshman year. We were just so happy to be there. That was probably one of my favorite memories, driving to class and listening to Biggie.

J.R.'s an interesting guy. One minute, he would try to be a clean freak and make sure everything was clean and neat, and then the next minute, all his stuff would be everywhere. It was kind of up and down that way. Sometimes he was loud, and sometimes he liked to talk about himself a little too much. It was OK. I was used to it.

A lot of people just really didn't know how to deal with him, and I was around him enough to understand it. It was almost like he didn't get enough attention when he was in high school, and he was trying to get some attention at Kansas. It wasn't him trying to be cocky; it was him wanting some attention, wanting somebody to talk to him. He was always one of those guys that wants to be on the phone, or wanted to do something all the time. A lot of people really didn't understand that, didn't understand him. But overall, he's a great guy. He'll look out for you just like he'll look out for his family.

## MOON BAR INCIDENT

It was kind of a freak deal. We were playing pickup that afternoon. Everything was OK. We went back to the dorm. I think it was actually finals week. I had a test early in the morning. J.R. decided to go out. I didn't. I regret that I didn't go out, because I maybe could've prevented something like that. Because we would always go out together. We'd always look out for each other. And that night, we didn't go together.

I wake up at 5 in the morning, and I've got, like, 20 missed calls. And everybody's wondering what happened, and I've got no idea. They're calling me because we're usually together. And I don't even know what's going on. And the next thing I know, he's in the hospital. It was kind of like a bad dream.

I wish it hadn't been finals week, and I wouldn't have been trying to be ready for my test, because I definitely would have went with him. I had a car, so I would have been driving. We would have left together, and everything would have been fine. If he would have gotten into an altercation, then we would have left the scene. From what I understand, he left and then came back. I don't know the full details, but I feel like if I was there, I maybe could've at least tried to prevent that.

We knew each other well. Sometimes we would get into altercations, because, you know, we had targets on our backs, especially him. He was big-time at KU. He was a starter. Everybody knew him, and everybody wanted to talk to him. He had a big target on his back, just like most of the KU basketball players do. We kept each other out of trouble. We tried to avoid trouble the best we could.

If somebody's kind of jealous of you or jealous of what we have — because we get a lot of attention and things like that — they might try to start stuff or be inappropriate toward us. Everybody's not on your side. One of us might look at somebody's girlfriend, and they might not like it. Something little like that that other guys – or other athletes – might get jealous of, we'd take ourselves out of that situation and leave.

There was always a certain group of football players that didn't like us. It wasn't all of them. It wasn't the whole team. But when I was there, there was always a group of football players that didn't like us and had a problem with us. But we tried to avoid that as much as possible. I think it's always been around. I think some of the football players — I don't necessarily want to say they were jealous of us — but as most people know, KU basketball is the main event there. It's kind of obvious that they would be jealous. If they were, they had a right to be.

## RESERVE ROLE

A lot of people think that the guys on the bench aren't very good. And what a lot of people don't understand is that the guys that are playing in front of the guys on the bench are pros. Everybody on the team is not necessarily a pro, and people may look at it as, "Well, they suck," or, "They're sorry," or something like that. But that's not always the case. But I wasn't worried about it. I don't care what other people think.

After my sophomore year, when I thought about transferring, it was just really hard to actually think about not being at KU and not being in front of 16,000 people every night. I didn't want to feel like I gave up or like I couldn't play there. I didn't want to leave. I wanted to keep trying and keep pushing forward.

In my heart, I believed that I was going to get to play, and I was going to get to play 20, 25 minutes. In my heart, that's what I believed. And I enjoyed it so much being at KU, it was just hard to leave.

When I was thinking about leaving, it was more like, "Where I can get closer to home?" I thought about schools in Oklahoma or Texas. I was looking at SMU. I was looking at maybe going Division II. I was looking at some mid-major type stuff. I wasn't real sure. My dad was just kind of throwing things out there.

I think the closest I was to leaving was right after the season had ended. It didn't end the way we wanted it to end, and it was frustrating. I was probably angry. It was me thinking, "I want to play in the NBA. I want to do this. I want to do that. I want to be an All-American." It was kind of like, "Would I do better at another school?" It wasn't Coach Self. It wasn't KU. It was just me being kind of selfish for myself, wanting to prove to everybody that I could play on this level. It wasn't like, "I don't like Coach Self," or anything like that.

It was a really tough decision. I remember, I would think back to when Coach Williams left, and before I even got there, I remember getting all types of fan mail saying, "Please stay. Please come to KU. We still want you." It was kind of like, "Man, I can't leave here. This is why I came here, for the fans and to be loved like that. To be a part of something great." I can say I was part of a top-three program in the country, and a lot of people can't say that.

I think my mom actually kept almost all my letters. She kept them in shoeboxes and stuff. I was into it, but she was really into it, because she had never experienced anything like that. There was so much – I don't necessarily remember just one – but there were so many letters that just said, "We still want you here. Please come back." It was unreal. And I hadn't even been there yet.

## COACH SELF

As far as me coaching, I'm going to do exactly the things Coach Self does. On offense, I'm going to do a lot of the same stuff we did, as far as ball screens and high-low and mixing it up a lot. I think a lot of coaches know this, but one thing I learned from him is that you've got to adapt to your players. You can't just always do the same thing, because your players aren't always the same.

I remember when we had Wayne Simien, and all we ran was what we call, "Two game." It's the high-low. That's all we did. And then once Wayne graduated, we turned it into ball-screen stuff. It was just kind of interesting to see how our offense evolved based on our players and our style of personnel.

Coach Self and I had our ups and downs. It was kind of where I just completely disagreed with him not playing me. The thing that I've come to realize as a coach is that you can't please everybody. He has 15 guys to please, and I know I was low on the totem pole. But now I realize that, I don't know if I was ready. In my mind then, I thought I was, so at that time, I was kind of angry with him. I thought, "I'm not getting a fair chance." That was just me thinking selfishly.

## COACH TOWNSEND

It's always funny with Coach Townsend. He's always cracking a joke on somebody. He's always making fun of somebody. I would be standing by him in practice, and Coach Self would be talking, and he would whistle or something or say something, and I could hardly hold my laughter in. I'd start laughing, and Coach Self would look over, and I'd try to hide it. But I tried to avoid going around Coach Townsend during practice, because he was always saying something funny.

One of the managers was named — I can't even remember his real name — but Coach Townsend would call him "Frankie." And Frankie's not even his name. I can't even remember his name. I just know him as Frankie. Isn't that bad? He would always give the manager some kind of name and actually believe that that was their name. I don't know where he got Frankie. Nobody knows where he got it. We just know he started calling him Frankie, so everybody started calling him Frankie.

## COLLEGE LIFE

Away from the court, I probably partied a little bit too much. There was always something to do, whether it was a Tuesday night going to Quinton's or a Wednesday night. During my first year, J.R. and I would go party Thursday, Friday and Saturday almost every week. Thursday, Friday and Saturday – unless we had games and stuff like that. But we were always out doing something.

The negative from that was being at practice and being dead tired, or having class at 8 in the morning and being sleepy in class. I remember the summer I got there, we had a class at 8 in the morning. Man, I was struggling so hard to stay awake in there. It was terrible. J.R. and I had it together. I know the teacher probably thought I was an ass, but I couldn't help it.

## SENIOR NIGHT

I wasn't even really nervous for the game. I remember being extremely nervous to actually speak in front of all the fans. I was kind of like, "Dang, I'm going to forget what I want to say. Should I write stuff down, or should I just go off the top of my head?" I really didn't know exactly what I wanted to do. And that's kind of what I was worried about. I didn't want to just get up there and start stuttering or saying "uh" a lot. I knew I wanted to thank a whole lot of people, and I didn't want to be up there for too long.

It ended up being a really great game for me, and not only just for me, but for the team. We beat Texas Tech pretty bad. I think everybody on our team scored. It ended up being a really great night.

It was a great feeling, just to hear the crowd scream when you make a shot. It's electrifying, being able to affect the crowd like that and to be a part of something that great. It was just so amazing how loud the crowd got when I hit a shot — or not just me, people on my whole team. It felt great with my family being there, and I was able to actually put on a good show for them and actually do some good things on the court.

## DAVIDSON GAME

When we went into the locker room, everybody was kind of sitting there like, "Damn, we're about to go to the Final Four." Nobody was really celebrating, and everybody had their water, and everybody was like, "Do we pour water on Coach Self?" Everybody was kind of scared to do it.

We kind of thought he would get mad at us or something, because it wasn't like it was the championship. But we were like, "Man, forget it. We don't care. We're going to the Final Four."

Me and Russell looked at each other like, "Uh, yeah we're going to do it." So we all got our water bottles. Everybody got a water bottle. It was a long walk, and so Coach Self could see us the whole time. So we had three or four people on the side to come up from behind and pour it on him. We had people hidden out, because the locker room was huge. The best thing ... Coach Self came in, and we poured water on him and everything. He jumped up and down. He was as happy as we were.

## ICE-BREAKER

When I go on my recruiting trips, I like to slide my championship ring on. It's a really good ice-breaker. A lot of people want to see it and talk about it and talk about my experience with that. I don't wear it too much. I usually have it with me for home visits, or if I go see a player at a game. I'll have it on just so I can have a good conversation piece.

One of the guys that we signed this past year, Corey Wilford from Connors State Junior College ... he was one of our big recruits. He was all into that. He said, "I remember watching you play." He was amazed that the ring was so big. He talked about it a lot.

When I look at it, I think about all the hard work that it took to get there. I was at KU for five years. I redshirted one year. It was so hard to actually get there. We went to the Elite Eight, Sweet 16, all of that. All of the fighting, all of the sweating, all the tears. It's just so hard to get there, and when we actually won it ... it just makes you think about all the boot camps, all the ups and downs I had at KU. It just makes it all worthwhile.

# CHAPTER 25

# 2005/06 - 2007/08
# MARIO CHALMERS
## 15

Mario Chalmers' 3-pointer to force overtime in the 2008 NCAA title game against Memphis is regarded as the greatest shot in Kansas history. Chalmers, a guard from Anchorage, Alaska, played three seasons at Kansas before entering the NBA draft. He is currently the starting point guard for the Miami Heat. Chalmers averaged a career-high 12.8 points during Kansas' championship season, when he was chosen Most Outstanding Player at the Final Four. His 283 steals rank second in Kansas history. Chalmers has a son, Zachiah, who is 3.

### IN MARIO'S WORDS

I had been a fan of Coach Self when he was at Illinois. I liked his coaching style and the way he ran his team. Growing up, though, I was a North Carolina fan, mainly because I lived there for a while during elementary school. I wanted to be a Tar Heel really bad.

I met Coach Williams at an AAU tournament. He was still at KU at the time, and I think I was in the eighth grade. He told me he liked my game. He said, "Just keep getting better, and you'll have a spot at Kansas." I kept working, and he kept sending me letters. When he went to North Carolina, he was still watching me. I remember one game when we played Bobby Frasor's team. We beat them, and I was killing Bobby. But after that Coach Williams said, "The only way you can come to North Carolina is if Raymond Felton goes pro." A week or two later, Bobby Frasor announced he was going to North Carolina. Coach Williams obviously didn't tell Bobby and me the same thing. From there, I was like, "I don't like Roy Williams. I don't like North Carolina. I don't want anything to do with the Tar Heels."

It didn't really matter, because Coach Self and Kansas were on me hard.

Coach Dooley was the guy that they'd send up to Alaska most of the time to recruit me. Coach Dooley and I developed a good relationship. He'd send me text messages all the time and call the house. I told him, "I like Kansas, but I'm going to take a visit to Arizona first."

I liked Arizona a lot, too. I visited there before I visited Kansas. My hosts were Andre Iguodala and Mustafa Shakur. It was during the season. Still, something just felt kind of weird. I went to a game, and it seemed like there were a bunch of old people in the stands. People always say that Arizona is a place where you go to retire once you're done working. That's what it felt like to me. I was thinking, "How am I going to have fun? Nothing is really around here." It was a good school, and a lot of their guards had gone to the NBA, which is the main thing that had me interested. But it didn't seem like a place where I'd have a lot of fun.

When I went to Kansas I had six or seven different hosts, guys like Aaron Miles, Jeremy Case, J.R. Giddens, J-Hawk and Darnell. I even went to an actual class with Darnell. He had 11 a.m. class and I went with him. Everyone made me feel like I was their little brother, like I was one of them already. I had a lot of fun. The other thing that helped was that, when I went to Arizona, I was kind of by myself. When I went to Kansas I had C.J. and Micah Downs. Then I came back for Late Night, and it was me and Julian. I was sold from there. I saw the crowd. I went to a club that night. I was like, "Oh yeah, I'm coming to Kansas."

## GROWING PAINS

I struggled really badly when I first got to KU, mainly because I wasn't willing to listen. With my dad being my coach in high school, I had free reign. I could tell him what I wanted to do. He put the ball in my hands and let me control the whole team. At KU, I wanted to do that right off the bat. But I had seniors in front of me. I felt like things should be given to me because I was the No. 1-ranked point guard in the nation. I felt like no one could mess with me. I was cocky. I didn't want to do anything. I didn't want to work. I was just like, "Give me the ball." Coach Self didn't like that, so we bumped heads.

We got embarrassed in the Maui Invitational that year. The only team we beat was Chaminade. We lost to Arkansas and Arizona. After the Arkansas game is when I really started to think about transferring. I hit two 3's and – bam! – he took me out. He put me back in, and I hit another 3. Then he took me right back out again. I didn't understand at the time why he was taking me out, but I know now that it was because I wasn't playing any defense. I was just worried about offense. My man was just cruising by me, breaking me down and getting other people shots. I started playing less and less and less. I couldn't figure out what I was doing wrong. Eventually I realized this was a defensive team. I had to play defense to stay in the game.

## HAWKINS TO THE RESCUE

Pretty soon after we got back from Maui, I was on my way out the door. I wasn't even going to wait until the end of the semester. I had decided I was going to transfer right then and there. Coach Self wasn't playing me. It wasn't that he thought I wasn't good enough. He was just mad at me. He was trying to break me. I don't even think my dad knew I wanted to transfer. But my mom did. I called her and said, "Mom, I want to leave. I don't like this place." She just said, "Relax and pray about it. Whatever your decision is, I'll support you."

The thing that kept me at KU was Jeff Hawkins. Jeff came and picked me up about 12:30 one night after a late practice. I had told Jeff a few days earlier that I was leaving and he was like, "We're going to talk." I told him there wasn't anything he could do to change my mind. But he called me that night anyway and said he was on his way to get me. He basically said, "Hey, when I first got here I was stubborn and hard-headed just like you, but I stuck it out. If you stay here, I guarantee Coach Self is going to make you a great player, a great person. He's going to get you where you want to go." I was like, "Man, I don't believe that. I'm transferring." He said, "Please, if you don't listen to anything I ever tell you again, listen to this." I started thinking about it and realized, "He's a senior. He's been through it all. He knows a lot, and he and I are alike in a lot of ways. Maybe I should trust him." That changed my whole mind-set. I thought, "Maybe I'll see how things work when I'm not acting stubborn." Once I bought into Coach Self's system, everything started turning. My playing time increased, me and Coach Self started getting along, and everything started getting better. From that point on, I loved it. So I owe a lot to J-Hawk for talking to me that night. We just drove throughout the streets of Lawrence for about three hours. By the time I got back to the room it was about 3:30 a.m.

## BRANDON RUSH

I was at home in Alaska the summer before my freshman year when Coach Self called me. He said, "I've got Brandon Rush coming in. I know you guys are close. I want you to be his host." I said, "OK, just schedule it for when I get back." I came to Lawrence a few days later, and they brought Brandon in. He stayed for three days, and we just kicked it.

I've known Brandon since I was 13. I first met him at ABCD camp, when we played against each other. He made the all-star team and I made the all-star team. It was me, him, Andre McGee, O.J. Mayo and Tasmin Mitchell. We were the big names that year in the younger group. Guys like Dwight Howard, Josh Smith and J.R. Smith were in the older group. After that, I stayed in contact with Brandon. We'd call each other every now and then. Then we saw each other in Denver. We had the USA Basketball thing. We worked out together and went and took extra shots at night. Ever since then we've been close.

I think it's safe to say that Brandon had a lot of fun on his visit, but I think his decision was deeper than the fact that we just went out one weekend and had fun. For one thing, his family was close by – and there was no one at his position. We also wanted to go to the same college. I was like, "Look, your home is right down the street. I'm here. All these other good players are here. You're not going to find a better situation. We're all here for you. We're all freshmen and sophomores. We're all going to be working together. We're all going to grow up together." That was the main thing, the chance to grow up together. There wasn't going to be that one person that acted like they were above everyone. The team that was here before us ... what I heard was that, even though they were close, there were cliques within the team. With us, we were always together. When we went out you'd see the whole team, from the starters to the walk-ons.

## MICAH DOWNS

Micah and I were both from out west. We took our visit together, and he really liked it. But then Coach Self signed Brandon really late. Micah felt like, "They're sh--tin' on me. They're acting like they don't need me anymore." Micah went and told Coach Self that he should be starting over Brandon. That wasn't a good idea. Micah didn't like that. He had wanted to go to the NBA straight out of high school. He wanted to be a one-and-done player. Since he wasn't getting his opportunity he transferred. Micah was cool. I got along with him fine.

## RIVALRIES – OR NOT?

When I was a freshman we lost to Kansas State and Missouri in the same year. The Kansas State game was at home. The Missouri loss happened in Columbia, when Christian Moody missed those free throws at the end. We had both of those games won. We shouldn't have lost either of them. Even when we lost, we weren't really worried about them after that. We were like, "They're not going to be much of a problem anymore." We dogged both of those teams for the next two years. We didn't consider those schools huge rivals because we beat them so bad all the time. Our bigger rivals at that time were Texas and Texas A&M. They were more on our level. Texas had Kevin Durant, and Texas A&M had Acie Law.

I guess there was the one other time when K-State beat us. It was the year we won the championship, and they had Mike Beasley. I've known Mike since he was 14. I'm two or three years older than him. Mike and I didn't like each other when we first met. We hated each other. We were both big names trying to come up. He felt like he was better than me, and I felt like I was way better than Mike. At tournaments we would always go at each other. We were the top two leading scorers at camps. One time, we played in this invite-only camp, and they put us on the same team. We talked and started being cool. Ever since then I've treated him like a little brother. When he went to K-State it was nothing. We were still going to be cool. When we both went to the Heat everyone was like, "How are they going to get along, being from KU and K-State?" It wasn't like that at all.

## TOUGH ENVIRONMENT

Kansas State had a really tough home court when Beasley and Bill Walker were there, but the toughest place to play in the Big 12 is Oklahoma State. At most arenas, the stands stretch outward and wide. At Oklahoma State, they go straight up. When we're on the court it feels like the fans are on top of us. The whole arena is rattling, rattling, rattling, the whole time. Rattle, rattle rattle! I was like, "Would y'all shut up so we can play ball?" I couldn't hear anything. Whistles, horns being blown, timeouts being called, my teammates and coaches talking ... nothing. It's probably the toughest place I've ever played.

## TROUBLE IN SIN CITY

When I was a sophomore we played Ball State and Florida in Las Vegas. Florida had won the national championship the previous year – and they ended up winning it that season, too.

The Ball State game, we didn't cover the spread. Coach Self was hot at us. He was cussing us out after the game. The last five minutes we were up by about 20. We let them come back in the last five minutes and cut it to eight, I think. Coach Self was livid. We watched the film and he was like, "Y'all didn't play hard for the last 5 minutes. What if they would've come back and beat us?" When you have a team up, that's when you have to have a killer instinct and step on their throats. We were like, "Coach, we still won the game." He was really upset, though.

We were on the elevator going to our rooms and I said something like, "Dang, I can't believe Coach Self was trippin' on us like that. That's some bulls--t." Julian said something like, "Oh Rio, shut the hell up. You were out there bullsh--tin' the whole game" or whatever. So I felt like he was coming at me. We got off the elevator, and I just snapped. I tried to charge at him, but Russell and Darnell were holding me back. They put me in my room. After I calmed down, we had a team meeting later that night. We asked Coach Self, "Why are you so mad at us about the Ball State game when we're playing Florida, the No. 1 team in the nation, tomorrow night? Why are you nitpicking?" He basically told us, "It's not about nitpicking, it's about trying to make y'all better and make y'all realize that, when you have a team down, you can't let them come back. I've been in too many situations where we were up and we let a team come back. We took Bucknell lightly, and they came back and beat us." Once he did that we kind of understood where he was coming from. Me and Julian apologized to one another and made up. After that we beat Florida, and everything was cool.

## JULIAN WRIGHT

Julian had all the talent in the world, but you never knew what he was going to do. I loved Julian to death. That's my guy. He was my roommate my first year. We were cool. We always kicked it. Julian loved to go to the gym, but he would work on the wrong things. He'd work on "and-one" moves for, like, two hours. I'm like, "Why would you do that?" He'd get to the game and try to do something crazy like that and mess it up or turn the ball over. Coach would take him out and, when he came back in, he'd dominate.

Julian is one of the most dominating-undominating players I know. He can dominate a game, but in college he didn't do it nearly enough. No one should've been able to stop Julian when he was at Kansas. A 6-foot-8 guy with length who can dribble like a guard and shoot it a little bit … no one at the college level should be able to stop a four-man like that. But Julian held himself back. To this day, anyone in the NBA will say, "Julian Wright holds himself back." I still think a lot of it is because he goes to the gym and works on the wrong things. Like I said, "and-one" moves and shooting 3-pointers with his left hand. Stuff you wouldn't do during a game.

## JEREMY CASE

No matter how good your starting five are, your team won't be any good unless you have a good practice squad. I think that's what made us so good – our practice squad. We had shooters like Case and Conner Teahan and Stephen Vinson. They may not have played a lot, but in practice they were nice. People always see those guys that aren't playing in games and think they're not that good. But they're there for a reason. It's just that some guys are better than them. That's the reason we won. Our practice squad was strong.

Defensively, Case would get after you. That's also what Stephen was really good at. He'd pick you up full court in practice. That's the type of stuff you need coming in. I used Case to work on my defense. I would try to guard Case in practice every time, just because I knew he was a shooter and that he was going to be coming off screens. That's how I got better and better at running through passing lanes coming off screens. I'd slow down and wait until the pass was thrown and then I'd take off at full speed. That's how I got better, by chasing Jeremy Case off screens every day in the gym.

## SHERRON COLLINS

Having Sherron on the team really helped. Me and Russ had to guard Sherron, who was as good as any point guard we'd face. Sherron was tough to guard. He's so little, and he's really, really fast. He's got crazy handles. That's what makes him so good. He also brought a little extra toughness. His attitude was, "You're not going to show me up. I'm going to get the last laugh." That was my mentality, too. My mentality was that I was going to shut you down the entire game. I was going to be in your face and be in your ear as much as I could. Sherron is the type of player that when the going got tough, he was going to get tougher. He was going to rise above it all. Brandon was the type of player that was just going to be solid and do the little things and knock the shots down. He was the solid, stay-in-front-of-you defender. Me and Russ worked the passing lanes and Sasha, Shady and D-Block were the shot blockers. The thing with Shady was that he could defend a guard on the perimeter. That's what made our team so special.

Coach Self was very hard on Sherron. He would gain weight so easily. If Sherron lifts weights, he gains weight. Anything Sherron does, he gains weight. They had to put him on a special diet just to help him with his weight. He didn't eat all that bad. It was just in his genes. When his weight would get up, he'd have knee problems, injury problems. We couldn't have that on our team. For our team to be where we wanted to be, we needed Sherron to stay healthy and keep his weight down. Coach Self put all of us in charge of helping Sherron. Russell and I would run extra with Sherron, just to make sure he did it and went hard.

## RUSSELL ROBINSON

There was no tension between Russell and Sherron. I don't think people realize how bad Russell wants to win. He's very competitive. He's not going to let you get the best of him. But at the same time, he wants to do what's best for the team. He was the leader of our team. I'm telling you: Russell Robinson was the leader of our team. We followed Russell. However Russell was playing, that's how we were going to play most of the time. If Russell was energetic on the court, the whole team was all over the court.

## DARNELL JACKSON

I think D-Block was closer to me than anyone on the team. We've been through similar things. His grandmother died, and my grandmother died. Both of our families have been in car accidents. The same bad things were happening to both of us.

Before every game, we'd get in a huddle in the locker room and jump around and get hyped. When he was a senior, we played Boston College on the one-year anniversary of his grandmother's death. So while we were all jumping around, I looked over at him and he was by his locker with his head down. I went over there and he was crying. I said, "What's wrong, man? We're about to play a game. Get your mind right." He was like, "Man, just stay right here and talk to me for a second." So we let all the other guys go out and start warming up and we hung back for a few minutes.

He said, "It's the anniversary of my grandmother's death. I don't know how to handle it. It's tough." I said, "I know how you feel, man. My grandmother died, too. But I had a decision to make: Either go to her funeral or go play in an AAU tournament. I chose to play in the tournament because I know that's what she would've wanted me to do. When I played in that tournament, I killed it. I averaged almost 40 points a game, and that was the tournament that really helped me get my name out there. I know she was looking down on me smiling. Your grandmother is going to be doing the same thing today. We're going to go out there, we're going to have fun, we're going to play this game, and we're going to win." D-Block had one of the best games of his life that day (25 points, nine rebounds).

## FAMILY AFFAIR

My dad didn't really play a role in me choosing Kansas because I had already signed when he decided to take the job. I know everyone likes to say that it was a package deal and that it was pre-arranged. But it wasn't. That situation didn't present itself until months and months after I had signed.

Even with my dad at every practice and every game, Coach Self didn't hold back at all. My dad yelled at me sometimes, too. Even though he was there, I didn't want him to help me out. I didn't want him to say anything if Coach Self yelled at me. There have been times when Coach Self and I have yelled back and forth at each other, face-to-face. I thank Coach Self for everything he's done for me. He's one of my greatest mentors. I have the utmost respect for Coach Self. He's one of my favorite coaches all time that I've ever had.

## NEW ADDITION

Midway through my senior year, I became a father. We were playing Nebraska when my son, Zachiah, was born on Jan. 26. The mother of my child was cool. She knew I didn't have a lot of time and what my schedule was like. There were times she wanted to do something, and I'd be like, "Bring Zachiah over and I'll watch him for the night." Or if we had a day off I'd go spend time with him. I did as much as I could, but she understood that I couldn't be there for it all. It's excellent now. I love being a father. It's a lot of fun. It changes your life a little bit. It made me wise up and realize I can't go out and do the things I used to do.

I've got a son now. I've got to be able to provide for him and make sure his name doesn't become a bad name because of something I did. He lives in Lawrence. I get to see him all the time. I'll fly my mom up there to get him and pick him up and then fly him back down here to Miami.

## ON A MISSION

My first year, we lost to Bradley in the NCAA Tournament. Yeah, we were supposed to beat them. But they were pretty good, and we were a young team. We learned from that. The next year we got to the Elite Eight and lost to UCLA on what was basically their home court in San Jose. I had a terrible game. I was 1-for-7 with 2 points and eight steals, eight assists and seven turnovers. That whole summer, when I was working out, I kept telling myself, "I will never have a game like that again." Not in a big moment like that. They overpowered me. They put Josh Shipp on me, and he was physical with me. I couldn't get to where I wanted to get. I couldn't get to my sweet spots. Every time I started getting near one of my spots, he'd give me a little bump and throw me off balance and block my shot. That whole summer I just worked out with Coach Hudy in the weight room and got bigger and stronger so it wouldn't happen again.

That next year, we were ready. We knew it was our chance. The seniors were graduating. Brandon, Shady and I knew we were probably leaving. We were like, "This is for us. This is our last chance. Let's go get it."

## A LITTLE PAYBACK

People like to talk about the North Carolina and Memphis games, but one of the biggest wins for us during the NCAA Tournament was against Villanova.

That game was personal, because Jay Wright – the Villanova coach – had also been the head coach of the USA Basketball team that represented the country in the Pan Am games the previous summer. Jay Wright cut both Sherron and me from that team and kept his own player from Villanova, Scottie Reynolds, who had clearly been the worst player at the entire camp. He led the whole camp in turnovers. Sherron didn't play all that well, either, because his knee hadn't recovered from the previous season. But for me, I felt like I did everything right. I led them in steals, I had a lot of assists and I barely had any turnovers. But I wasn't shooting the ball very much. They used one of those international balls, so they were different. I didn't like the ball. I shot maybe six times.

When they cut me, they told me it was because I didn't score and that they wanted a scoring point guard. I was like, "Why do y'all need all these scorers? What do you need a scoring point guard for when you've got all these other scorers?" They had Alonzo Gee from Alabama and guys that could already score. I was just trying to get other players involved. When they cut me, I was hurt. I was like, "Oh, you wanted me to score and you didn't tell me that?" They had told Coach Self they just wanted a guy to distribute the ball, but Jay Wright cut me and kept his own player.

So when it came to the Villanova game, Coach Self called Sherron and me into his office and said, "How do you feel about this Villanova game?" I said, "Coach, this is personal to me. I don't like Jay Wright." He was like, "I understand that, but keep it out of the media." So when the media asked if it was a personal game, we'd say, "No, it's not personal. It's just another game." But during the game we were talking all kinds of s--t to Jay Wright. We'd run by him and tell him, "Sit your ass down! We got this!" Another time we said to him, "This is what you get for cutting us. We're about to dog you!" Anytime we were throwing the ball in from the sideline, when he was standing up trying to call a play, we'd tell him to shut his mouth and sit down. There was one play where I threw a lob to Shady on an inbounds pass and he dunked over Scottie Reynolds. Right before I threw it I looked at Jay Wright and said, "Watch this!" That game was definitely personal for Sherron and me.

## ELITE EIGHT

The Davidson game was a different type of game. That was the game that everyone wanted us to lose. It was a tough game for me. The first half, I was killin'. I had 11 points and was the only one who was really knocking down shots. Then, in the second half, I hardly touched the ball. I might've had two points on one shot. It was like, "I'm the one that kept us in this game. Why am I not getting the ball in the second half?" Even though I didn't show it on my face, because we were winning, I was still mad. I was hot that first half. Why am I not getting the ball anymore? The ball was sticking. It wasn't swinging. Everyone was trying to get theirs. In the end, I guess it didn't really matter. We were going to the Final Four. It was our moment.

## TROUBLE IN TEXAS

What really changed our mind-set in San Antonio was when Rodrick Stewart got hurt. We were just messing around, dunking. I was going to be the next guy to dunk after Rod. When he hurt his knee, I was like, "Oh no!" Rod was a senior. I started thinking about all of the things he'd been through. His cousin was shot, his little brother got shot. Then you throw in all the stuff that happened with D-Block's family and stuff that happened off the court with guys like me and B-Rush and Russell and Sherron's son dying. We were like, "We've all had problems. We might as well put those problems aside, win these six games and deal with these problems afterward, when we're the champs."

When that happened with Rod, he was crying, and we were helping him back to the hotel with his kneecap broke. We were like, "This is a sign. Rod, we're going to win this for you." I can remember talking to him right after he got hurt. I went to his hotel room and he was lying there in bed with ice on his knee. I was like, "Rod, we're going to win this tournament for you. Mark my word. We're going to win it for you." He was crushed. He was really starting to play a lot. He was our eighth man behind Sherron and Sasha.

## NORTH CAROLINA

Our team had a vendetta against North Carolina when we played them in the Final Four. There was my situation about not getting recruited there, and then the deal that happened with Roy Williams and JaRon Rush and the Rush family. So Brandon wanted to get them. Darnell did, too. When D-Block first started getting interested in KU, Roy Williams was here. Something happened, and they fell out. That was just a big moment. In some ways that game meant more to people at KU than the Memphis game, even though that was for the national championship. A lot of people were hurt by Roy Williams leaving. A lot of people were upset. Leading up to that game, we had so many moments when we'd talk about that kind of stuff. Coach Self would say stuff about it, too. He just did it all behind closed doors. I'm not going to tell you what he'd say, but he was obviously really motivated. Anytime we were around each other, we were like, "We're going to get North Carolina. We want them. We want them." It was a little more explicit, but it was generally stuff like that. We were happy when we got matched up with them. The other motivation we had was that the analysts were saying we were the worst No. 1 seed that year. We took that personally.

Even when we were up 40-12 on North Carolina, I didn't care. I just wanted to dog them. That was my whole mind-set. Just think about it like it's 0-0. Every time they score, we score. That's what I kept telling the team. I was in foul trouble that game. Whenever I was on the bench, I kept yelling, "We're still down. We're still down." Then we just kept going and going.

## MEMPHIS

There was almost a fight before the national championship game. Memphis' players were in the tunnel, waiting to be summoned on the court, and we walked up doing our little chant. They were like, "Shut the f--k up, you gay-ass Jayhawks." Then one of the arena guys asked Memphis' players, "Are y'all ready to go on the court?" Pierre Niles was like, "Hell no! Let those bitches go first." I was the first one to say something back. Some people started shoving, but it ended pretty quickly.

Toward the end of the game, when they were up by 9 points with 2:12 left, Coach Self called a timeout. We came back to the huddle with our heads down. Coach Self said, "Everyone look up." We all looked at him, and he just said, "Believe! We worked too hard to get here for us not to win. Believe!" So we believed. From then on, every timeout or every time there was a stoppage in play, Coach Self kept looking at us and saying, "Believe!" Anytime your coach is giving you that confidence – and you've already got a little confidence in yourself – that goes a long way.

## MARIO'S MIRACLE

For about two years after I made "The Shot," I would replay it over and over in my head. I remember it really well, starting all the way back to the huddle a minute or two before the play.

In the huddle, Coach Self had asked everyone, "Who do you want the ball to go to?" And everyone was like, "Mario!" Maybe the guys didn't actually say my name verbally – at least not all of them – but when he asked that question, all of their heads just swiveled and turned right toward me. I said, "Wow! If y'all believe in me like that, I'm not going to let you down. I'm going to make the shot. This ain't nothin'." I just told Sherron to get it to me anyway he could.

Sherron said later that he heard Calipari yelling for a foul. I couldn't hear that because I was already down the court. We ran that play all the time at the end of games. Sherron was supposed to be more toward the sideline but he cut to the middle to get past D-Rose. When he stumbled I got worried. I was just thinking, "Sherron, just get me the ball, and I'll make the shot." Somehow he tapped the ball to me and I got it in my sweet spot. I had perfect form on the shot. It felt good from the time the pass hit me in the hands. I could've turned around and thrown the ball between my legs and it would've gone in. That's how confident I was feeling in that moment. It's a great feeling to have. So, no, I wasn't surprised when it went in. I had known the whole time that I was going to make it.

## MEMORABLE MOMENT

My favorite picture from that night is the one of me hugging my mom. The two of us had talked about that ever since I was little – me hitting the big shot to win the national championship. For that moment to actually come true, I was like, "Mom, all the work that we put in when I was younger, all that stuff you used to tell me, all those times you worked me out, it finally paid off."

My mom used to rebound for me and motivate me when I was younger. From about the fifth to the seventh grade, my dad wasn't around because my parents had split up for a while. He came back when I was in the eighth grade, but he was coaching at the high school so he was really busy all the time. My mom was a schoolteacher at Romig Middle School in Anchorage. My eighth-grade year I transferred there to be closer to my mom. She had to be there early in the morning, so I'd go with her and work out in the gym, take a shower and go to class. After school, while she was still there for parent-teacher meetings, I'd go back in the gym and shoot some more. When she was finished with her responsibilities, she'd come in there and help me.

It'd just be me and my mom working out. She used to always tell me, "The game is on the line, 3-2-1 shoot it! 3-2-1 shoot it!" All that hard work, all the late nights and early mornings in the gym, it all paid off.

## END OF AN ERA

About a week after we won the title, Brandon, Shady and I had a meeting in Shady's and my apartment. Brady Morningstar and Sherron were there, too. We said, "What are the pros and cons of going and staying?" The cons of staying were: boot camp, class, cold winters and playing for free. If we left, we were thinking about how we'd already won a championship. We'd spent three years here, and Brandon and I only had 20 hours left toward our degrees. We could always come back and get those. Also, if we left, we'd get paid and put our family in a good position. In the end it was like, "What else is there to do here?" We weren't going to have the same team. Even if we would've come back, we would've missed Russ and D-Block and Sasha and Case, who was a really big part of our team even though he didn't play much. He helped all of us so much in practice. Case would kill us in practice and make us work. With those guys gone, we didn't want to take the chance of not winning as much, so we made the decision to go.

Coach Self was a little upset about me leaving. I don't think he was necessarily mad. I just think he was kind of worried, because everyone left. The seniors were gone, and the big three left early. All he had was Sherron and Cole. He really didn't have a good recruiting class because he didn't realize what we were going to do. The only person he thought was leaving was Brandon. We flipped the switch and all three of us left, so he was like, "Wow, what are we going to do?"

Before we announced, he sat down with the three of us and said, "Shady, you're going to be a high pick. I encourage you to go. Brandon, you're going to be a lottery pick. I encourage you to go." Then he told me they were projecting me as a late first-rounder or an early second-rounder. When I heard that I was like, "OK, I'm going to test the waters and work myself up." My first workout

Marketing, knowing the right people ... just how to be more of a people person. The NBA is an all-out business. You really need to know how to market yourself.

It can be crazy playing on that team, with all of the attention and the hype surrounding those guys. But it's fun to me. You either enjoy it or you hate it. I try not to get too deep into it. When they go out, a lot of the time I'm not with them. I'll stay at home or in the hotel room. A person like me, who really doesn't have a big name like that, people will see me in the club with them and be like, "What's he doing here?" The good thing is that they pay for everything (laughing). They take care of everything.

## FINAL THOUGHTS

When I was at the ESPYs a few months after we beat Memphis, I was in the back, and I heard someone yell, "What's up, Jayhawk? What are you doing here?" I turned around, and it was Paul Pierce. I had never met him before. I didn't even know he knew me. I told him they nominated us for Best Comeback and he said, "Yeah, I bet a lot of money that y'all were going to win. You did your thing." I was happy to get that kind of recognition from such an established guy like that, especially one that went to KU.

It's like that all around the league. Every time I see Kirk or Nick, they're like "What's up Jayhawk?" Every time I see Drew or Paul Pierce, it's "What's up, Jayhawk?" We've got a connection like that.

It's a good feeling to actually know that I'm going to be remembered not just for what the team did, but for what I did. Not to be selfish, but it's nice to get recognition for what you did. Who wouldn't like that?

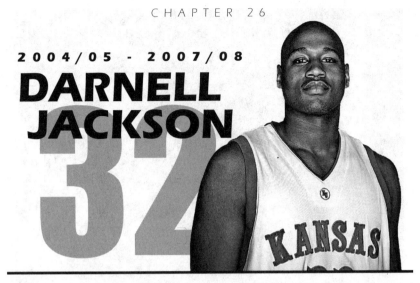

# CHAPTER 26

**2004/05 - 2007/08**

# DARNELL JACKSON

**32**

D arnell Jackson was a starting forward on the 2007-08 Kansas squad that won the NCAA title. A fan favorite, Jackson averaged 11.2 points and a team-high 6.7 rebounds that season. He had eight points and eight boards in the championship game against Memphis. Successful as he was on the court, Jackson will also be remembered for his perseverance off of it, as the Oklahoma City native excelled despite a series of family tragedies that could have easily caused him to lose focus and drive. The Miami Heat selected Jackson with the 52nd pick in the 2008 NBA draft and then traded him to Cleveland, where he was teammates with Shaquille O'Neal and LeBron James. Jackson has also played for Milwaukee and Sacramento.

## IN DARNELL'S WORDS

I think about Kansas almost every day. I always think about the fans. I think about walking up that hill and going to class and going to The Hawk at night. It was a lot of fun. The thing I miss the most, though, is running through that tunnel. We'd be in the locker room, and Coach Self would give us a speech. Then we'd say a little prayer and everyone would line up in the hallway. Then we'd burst through the door, and the fans would be lined up in the concourse, high-fiving us as we ran by them. As soon as we came through that tunnel, newspapers and confetti would be flying everywhere. You'd hear the band playing, and once we got to the other end and started the layup line, you'd look up to the right and see your family and friends in the stands. It was just a great feeling. It was like nothing else mattered in the world except being on that court and performing for the fans. That whole experience would give you goosebumps.

## FROM OKLAHOMA CITY TO LAWRENCE

I wasn't a huge Kansas fan growing up, but I was a Drew Gooden fan. I used to watch Drew Gooden and Wayne Simien play on TV all the time. I remember after Kansas won the Big 12 title, I watched Drew do an interview on TV. I was like, "Man, I want to go to Kansas." But I never thought I'd get the opportunity, because Coach Williams wasn't recruiting me, and Coach Self was at Illinois. That's where I would've ended up if he wouldn't have switched jobs. But once I heard he took over at Kansas, I thought, "Man, I might get to go to KU!" I remember he came to my high school pretty soon after he got the job and said, "You want to come to Kansas?" Of course I said, "Yeah!"

I hung out with Aaron Miles, Mike Lee and Keith Langford on my visit. It was one of the best experiences I'd ever had in my life, just being with those guys that night. I'd been watching them on ESPN for a few years, so I was kind of star struck. They got me in trouble, because they didn't get me back to the hotel in time. My mom had given me a curfew that night, and when we got back, she was standing outside the hotel, waiting on me. I was like, "Man, I'm about to get it." But getting in trouble was worth it that night. We went to a big house party. I loved hanging out with those guys.

## THE EARLY YEARS

My first season at Kansas, the team wasn't as close as some of the other teams I played for. The freshmen had so much to learn, and the older guys had been there and done it before. It was hard for me to get used to it. I had never done anything like that before.

*(Note: The NCAA suspended Jackson for the first nine games of his sophomore season in 2005-06 for receiving impermissible benefits from KU booster Don Davis, who had been a close friend and mentor to Jackson for years).*

Because I was suspended, I didn't get to go to the Maui Invitational with my teammates my sophomore year. Every game they played, I watched on TV. I told Coach Self, "Make sure you bring me some sand back from Maui." He didn't bring me any, though. It was me and Rodrick Stewart, sitting around back in Lawrence. He wasn't playing yet, either. So we were hanging out every day, talking about how hard we were going to work once we got eligible.

It was hard not to be negative. It was hard to stay positive all the time. It was hard not to get down on myself or blame anybody. I'm sure a lot of people formed an impression of me. They developed their own opinions of what I was like. But no one knew what was really going on. I didn't do anything wrong. People didn't realize that Don Davis was there from the beginning. He and I were close long before I ever became interested in Kansas.

## J.R. GIDDENS

J.R. and I grew up together in Oklahoma City. From AAU to high school ball,

J.R. and I were together almost every day. I always knew he was going to play in the NBA. People don't understand that he wears his emotions on his sleeve. He's so competitive, and he loves the game of basketball so much. Some people think he's being arrogant, but he loves basketball so much that sometimes people mistake his passion and his talking for arrogance. All he wants to do is play. He wants to play against the best players, the best teams. I loved hanging out with him, but a lot of people were like, "Man, he's rubbing me the wrong way." I was like, "Man, he's not doing it on purpose. That's just how he is. If you spend some time with him, you'll see that he's a great person. He'll help you out. He'll pick you up." When he was out here in Sacramento for training camp, he and I were in the gym every night after practice. We'd go back and get more shots up. We were cheering each other on, and some of the other guys on the team were like, "Man, this guy is crazy." He was speaking all the time and yelling. I kept telling them that he wasn't crazy. That's just how he shows he loves the game. I guess no one understood, though, because it didn't work out.

I know J.R. was really upset when Coach Self kicked him off the team. He left one of the greatest schools in America and ended up at New Mexico, so obviously he wasn't going to be happy. When it all came down to it, none of it was his fault. It was just something that happened that shouldn't have happened. I hated to see him go.

## OFF THE COURT

I lost my grandmother in a car accident the summer before my sophomore year, and that same accident left my mom with some injuries that made things really difficult for her. I also had an uncle that was killed, and later on a friend and a cousin. All of it caused me to deal with a lot of emotions, a lot of pain and guilt. Sometimes it was tough to focus.

Mario and Rodrick talked to me a lot. If it wasn't for those guys – my teammates and coaches – I would've never made it. I was always thinking negatively. I was like, "Why is all this crap happening to me?" I didn't want to play. I didn't want to practice. Coach Self just told me, "God has a plan for you. I don't know what it is. You can't beat yourself up about something you can't control. You'll drive yourself crazy." When I finally got to the point where I could go talk to somebody and get it all off my chest, it helped me. I had been holding everything in. I never wanted to talk about anything. I always had an attitude about everything. Coach Self would always say, "What's wrong?" I'd tell him that I was cool, that I was all right. But he knew I wasn't. He finally sat me down and asked me how I could be so angry on the inside. At that point I had to get it off my chest. I just let it all go.

Coach Chalmers played a big role in my life at that time, too. He and Mrs. Chalmers would come and pray over me. That helped a lot. I wasn't really into church like that. But Coach Chalmers would call and say, "You want to come to

church with me?" And I'd say, "Yeah, I'll go to church with you." It helped me a lot. Having that male role model in my life was big. He'd let me hang out with him. We'd sit in his car for hours and he'd talk to me. He helped.

Still, there was one time when I felt like I just couldn't take it anymore. One night, around 1 a.m. in the winter of my junior year, I packed up some of my things and drove home with my brother and my ex-girlfriend. It was a long, quiet ride. I did the driving. There wasn't really any talking, because they slept the whole way there. When I finally got home it was about 6 a.m. I walked through the door, dropped my bags on the floor and crawled into the bed with my mom.

When I didn't show up for practice the next day, Coach Self knew that something was wrong. He found out I was in Oklahoma, so he and Coach Chalmers got on a plane and came to talk to me. We were in my living room with mom and my uncle, Edred, and I asked Coach Self if I could talk to him outside. I was like, "I'm tired of seeing my mom go through this." She was in all this pain from her surgeries. She wasn't working because of that, so the bills weren't getting paid on time. It was everything. I told him I thought if I left and came back to Oklahoma City, all the bad stuff that was happening to me would stop. He grabbed me and gave me a hug. I started crying. I just broke down. I didn't know what else to do. Having him there helped me understand that he had my back. He said anything I had ever wanted or dreamed about was about to happen for me. He was like, "Come back home." Once I got back, my attitude really changed. I'll never forget what Coach Self did for me that night.

## THOUGHTS ON TEAMMATES

Even when I was a senior, I never considered myself much of a leader. I was just a guy doing dirty work for my teammates. If I needed to set a good screen to get Brandon or Mario open, I'd set a good screen. Everyone played a role. Everyone was a leader. If one person spoke, everyone else listened.

I loved playing against Sasha, Shady, Cole and those guys every day in practice. Those guys were great. My whole mind-set was, "I've got to defend these guys to the best of my ability, so when they get into the game, scoring against other opponents will seem easy for them." I think I did a pretty good job of holding Sasha and Shady and Cole on defense. I'm sure one of the reasons I'm in the NBA right now is because I had the experience of battling them every day.

Mario wasn't scared of anything. He was never timid. Whoever was in front of him, he went after every game.

Brandon was funny. He was a quiet assassin. We were roommates for a while. Every time he came back to the room, he'd knock on the door and say, "I'm home, big daddy" or something crazy.

Cole was always talking nonstop. He loved to talk, loved to have fun. Shady was competitive. He brought it every single day in practice. Sasha was the strongest guy on the team. You couldn't push him around.

Sherron brought a little bit of everything. His attitude was great, especially for a guy that was running the point. He was the captain out there a lot of times, the guy calling the plays. He kept everyone in line with his intensity off the bench. He hit some big shots for us.

Russell did it all, man. He put in the time. He was the best defender on the court. He just knew what it took. When Russell played hard, everyone else played hard. Russell led by example on and off the court.

## FINAL FOUR

The thing I remember the most about the Final Four is the fans. When we pulled up, all we saw was a bunch of Jayhawks T-shirts. We saw a bunch of red and blue. The band was playing when we walked into the hotel. It was crazy. I was like, "Man, this is like a movie. We're only going to experience this once."

It wasn't hard to stay focused. Coach Self threatened us before we got down there. He said that anyone who broke curfew or got into trouble wouldn't play. He was serious when he said that. Plus, we knew what we had to do. We knew we had to keep our minds right if we were going to win.

Before the North Carolina game, Coach Self was like, "Let's go out here and kick these guys' butts and then we'll come back in here and celebrate after the game." That was basically it. We went into that game with the mind-set that North Carolina's players thought they were better than us. In my opinion, we had the better players. I think North Carolina thought they had the game won before they ever stepped on the court. We came out there and put it on them really quick.

## MEMPHIS GAME

Against Memphis, I can still remember walking in the tunnel toward the court. I came around the corner and I didn't know what the holdup was. Then I heard

Joey Dorsey and Pierre Niles talking a little noise. Niles was like, "Let those girls take the court first." I was standing behind Sasha and I said, "We'll see who ends up talking noise once we get on this court." From the beginning, we knew it was going to be a battle.

When we were losing near the end, the thing Coach Self said that stood out the most was, "Stay calm! Those guys are tired. We're going to win this game." I also remember Coach Manning coming up to me during a timeout and whispering in my ear. He said, "Don't worry about it. We're going to win. We're going to win." I looked at him like, "Yeah, right. How do you know that?" He said, "Trust me. We're going to win the whole thing." Sure enough, Mario made that big shot a few minutes later. I looked over at Coach Manning. He just smiled and nodded and gave me his little wink, like "I told you so."

I was standing underneath the basket when Mario took his shot. When he shot it, I thought it was going to be an air-ball and that I was going to have to rebound it. But it just curved. It was like someone just grabbed the ball out of the air and guided it straight to the rim. It was like a curveball. It was just crazy. It was as if someone up above wanted us to win that game, after all we'd been through.

When the game went into overtime, we knew we were going to come out on top. By that point, Memphis was down to five or six players. They were tired. They were worn down. My whole career, the biggest thing with Coach Self had always been conditioning. We all felt fresh. It was like, "Man, let's go out here and win this game." And we did.

I definitely gained a lot of respect for Memphis after that. They fought hard to get there and came so close to winning it. They wanted to win, and we wanted to win. It all came down to Mario. But as far as them talking … now they know who has a championship ring and who doesn't.

I'll never forget the parade a few days after we got back to Lawrence. I just sat there and took it all in, like I was a fan. I kept thinking, "I'm never going to experience something like this ever again." It was neat to see our fans so excited. The fans are more competitive than the players. They want to see us do so well and win every game we can. It's almost like, if we fail, they fail. It's like we're on one big team. So it was good to see them have the chance to yell and to go a little crazy.

## STILL GOING STRONG

*(Darnell's mother, Shawn, died on March 25, 2010, after overdosing on pain medication. She had endured more than 10 surgeries in the three years following the car accident that also killed Darnell's grandmother, Evon.)*

I'm out here in Sacramento on my own, but the Jayhawk Nation is really big. It's amazing how many Jayhawks are out here. Considering all that has happened, I think I'm doing pretty well. I try to keep myself busy. I go to the gym each morning and workout from 10 to noon. I box two times a week. I'm a free agent right now, so whenever I get my next opportunity, I want to be ready. I had so many people standing behind me and depending on me. If I would've ever quit, I would've let them down – and I definitely would've let myself down.

I have a 1-year-old daughter named Evonna. She looks just like my mom, and I named her after my grandmother. I think about them every day when I wake up. I have a picture of me and my mom and my grandmother right next to my bed with my daughter's picture right in front of it. Every day I wake up, I say a little prayer. Everything I do, I think about them.

My mom's death was obviously really hard for me. I was so angry. Every little thing that happened to me, I'd get so mad. I was pissed. I even talked at the funeral about how mad I was. It was a whole bunch of bullcrap. I was mad at her. I was mad at her for quitting. She quit. There's nothing else to say about it. She quit. I'm still dealing with it. I try not to think about it. When I do, sometimes I get a little upset. But I understand why she did it. I know why she did it. Nobody knows but me and my little brother. Everyone thinks she did it because she was on all of those pills because of the surgeries and the car accident. But there was more to it than that.

I've got "Suicide Is Not An Option" tattooed on my right wrist. Other than my forearms, my body is almost completely covered in tattoos. My whole back, my entire chest, the left side of my ribs … I've only got a couple of open spots left. Every tattoo on my body means something. Some of them symbolize me or my family or God. I don't have anything stupid on me like big dollar signs or money bags. Everything I have on me means something to me.

## PAID TO PLAY

My first three years in the NBA have been great. I really enjoyed my two seasons with LeBron James in Cleveland. Being around those great players, it was crazy. It was like playing with those guys in a video game, except now you're actually there with them in practice, seeing how hard they work every day. They kept telling me, "You've got to work twice as hard as you've ever worked. You've got to keep yourself in shape." So I just took that advice with me to Milwaukee. I had to work hard and put in overtime. I did the same thing in Sacramento. It's all about business in the NBA. If you don't handle your business, you don't play.

Playing at Kansas has helped me a lot in the NBA. Knowing the game of basketball and having things beat into your head every day in practice by Coach Self, it gave me an edge over a lot of guys – especially when it came to playing defense and knowing how hard I had to work. The things I learned at Kansas will stick with me for the rest of my career.

When I see guys like Mario and Brandon, I'm always like, "Man, can you believe how far we've come?" I sent Mario a picture a few days ago of this poster that he gave me when we left. He signed it for me. I was like, "Man, can you believe I've still got this?" It's crazy how long it's been since college, but we're all in the NBA now, doing what we love to do.

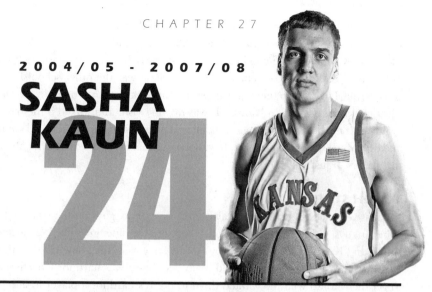

# CHAPTER 27

# 2004/05 - 2007/08
# SASHA KAUN

Alexander "Sasha" Kaun was a member of Bill Self's first recruiting class and a key figure in Kansas' run to the 2008 national championship. The 6-foot-11 standout from Tomsk, Russia averaged 7.1 points and 3.9 rebounds that season and was the hero of the Jayhawks' victory over Davidson in the Elite Eight, when he made all six of his field goal attempts in a 13-point effort. Kaun attended high school at Florida Air Academy in Melbourne, Fla. He arrived there as a ninth-grader knowing zero English. Kaun was selected in the second round of the 2008 NBA draft by the Cleveland Cavaliers. He now plays professionally in Russia. Kaun is married to former Kansas soccer player Taylor Blue.

## IN SASHA'S WORDS

Coach Self started recruiting me just before he left Illinois, and it continued once he was hired at Kansas. On one of his first days on the job, he flew to Florida to see me. I knew my high school coach at Florida Air Academy, Aubin Goporo, was a big, big fan of Illinois and Coach Self. And I mean a big fan. Every time I walked into his office, he'd bring up Illinois. He had an Illinois backpack, and there were always articles up about Illinois on his computer screen. His girlfriend lived in Chicago, so whenever he visited her, he'd drive to Champaign and go watch Coach Self run practice and then come tell me stories about it. But somehow he had never met Coach Self in person until he came to visit me at Florida. The minute Coach Self walked into the room, I pointed to Aubin and said, "You know this guy is one of your biggest fans, right?" I think I embarrassed him a little.

There were so many great schools recruiting me. I don't think I could've made a wrong choice wherever I had gone. They were all great academic schools with great basketball programs. I knew that I wasn't going to go to Duke. With the way Duke plays, I don't think it would've been good for me. I know they've had some good big guys in the past, but around that time they just seemed really guard-oriented. Michigan State was the other school I was considering. I liked it up there quite a bit. I went back and forth on it. In the end I just couldn't say "no" to Kansas. It was my first visit, and I liked it the most. Wayne was my host. I remember walking around and going to the football game and everyone knowing who I was. It was obvious that everyone cared a lot about the players. It just felt right.

## TOUGH START

My first year at Kansas was very awkward. Five or six guys on the team – the younger guys – were recruited by Coach Self. But the older guys like Wayne and Aaron and Keith and Mike were Roy's guys. They were still going through that awkward transition stuff. You could really see that it was hard for Coach Self to get them to do what he wanted them to do. It's hard for a player to accept someone else as a mentor or a leader when they were so loyal to a different person. You could see there was some tension. It didn't feel right. It didn't feel natural. The team was split. The older guys treated us nice, but we never really hung out together. The older guys did their own thing, and the younger guys did theirs. There wasn't any unity.

That second year, after all those guys graduated, and J.R. Giddens left, it was a whole new young team, especially with Brandon and Julian and the rest of that class coming in. We became one team, one union. I think Coach Self probably had a little more fun coaching. He had a young group of guys that didn't know anything and wanted to be coached. They did what he told them to do instead of trying to go their own way.

## TROUBLE IN PARADISE

There was so much hype around that 2005 recruiting class with Brandon, Julian, Mario and Micah. We knew how good those guys were. We heard all the talk about the Fab Four. A few weeks after practice started we went to the Maui Invitational and got a good eye-opener. I just remember thinking, "Wow, we really suck." Those freshmen were talented, but as a team, we were really, really bad. Against Arizona, our guards couldn't get past half-court. Like I said, we knew they were good. They had great, great talent. But they needed something like that to show them that it takes a lot more than great talent to win. We needed to work. We were ranked in the preseason top five, but after Maui, we were done. We had to work ourselves back into the poll. Even though we lost in the first round of the NCAA Tournament (to Bradley), the job that was done over the course of that season was amazing. We won the Big 12 championship and we won the Big 12 conference tournament. Overall it was a great year for us.

## HARD-NOSED HAWKS

One thing Coach Self is good at is getting us to play tough. It's not something most people are used to when they get to Kansas. They think they're tough, but they're not. Loose-ball drills are the worst. Coach Self will stand in the middle of the court and roll the ball across the floor. We have to sprint to it and dive on it. We'll do it for 10-15 minutes. There are definitely some bruises after that practice. People just hate it. After a few years it gets into your head: "Hey, dive for loose-balls!" If we have a bad game where we didn't dive for loose balls, we know we're going to have a loose ball drill at the next practice.

Coach Self's boot camp is harder on you mentally than physically, just because you know you have to go through it. You've got to run a lot, but you can do it. What's tough is going to class afterward and also being expected to show up in time for tutoring and stuff. You have a lots responsibilities for two weeks.

## BIGGER AND BETTER

Coach (Andrea) Hudy was one of the biggest reasons I was able to improve during my time at Kansas. When I first heard we had hired a female strength coach, it was weird. It was strange to hear that. But looking at her resume, with all of the national championship rings Connecticut won when she was there … it speaks for itself. She has a very good motor. She's always energetic. She makes you want to work. She's always reading and going to seminars and upgrading her knowledge. I'm really thankful for her.

One of her biggest pet peeves was music in the weight room. When the football team was working out with us, they'd have music playing really loud. She hated it because people would sing and dance and they wouldn't stay focused. As soon as they left she'd turn it off. She was very strict in the weight room. No one talked back to her. If she got mad she'd make you work even harder. It was all business with her.

The other benefit was having Danny Manning as our big-man coach. Danny was a great NBA player, and he would've been even better without all of his injuries. He stayed in the NBA for 15 years and he wasn't always 100 percent. A lot of players would've said, "I'm done. I can't play anymore." But he didn't. He wasn't a great jumper. He wasn't the fastest guy or the strongest guy. But somehow he managed to play 15 years. That tells you how high his basketball IQ was and how smart he is about the game. That's what he passes on to the guys. He knows so many little things that he teaches his players: How to seal, how to post up and use your body properly without fouling – things that separate good players from great ones. I can't remember him ever cursing or screaming. He's very quiet, very organized. Watch him in games, and you'll always see him writing things down and observing everything around him. He's going to be a great head coach someday.

## THOUGHTS ON TEAMMATES

There were times early in our freshman year when I thought Russell might take Aaron's job. He was scoring and running the team really well. But in practice Coach Self really started to get on him. He'd say, "Stop being careless! Stop being careless!" I guess he was turning the ball over too much. From there things kind of escalated between those two. I'm sure there were times when Russell was thinking, "Why did I come here?" But I'm glad he stuck it out and stayed until the end. He eventually found his way and ended up playing a huge role.

C.J. was one of the biggest talents we ever had during my time at Kansas, but he ended up being a waste. I don't know what the reasons for that were. Maybe it was his mind-set. Maybe it was the people around him, the people that were telling him stuff. The things he could've done with his athleticism and his abilities were limitless. Seriously, he could've been unbelievable. He's one of the most athletic big guys I've ever played against. He was 6-foot-11 and could jump and run like crazy. He just never got to the point where he could produce at a high level. It was unfortunate. He was a nice guy who had the right intentions. He was never mean to any of his teammates. He would never do anything to screw us. We all liked him. He just did some stupid things.

Brandon was a good teammate. He really cared about everything. He wanted to get better, without question. He was funny, too, always cracking jokes. I think he could've been more of a leader. He wasn't much of a leader. He came in and did his thing. He got his points and rebounds. But he wasn't a true leader who went into the huddle and said, "OK guys, let's get it together. Let's go!" With his talent level, he could've done that. He could've been a strong presence, because he was so good, and people respected him. But that wasn't in his personality, which was fine. It's not for everyone. There wasn't anyone on the team that didn't like Brandon.

Sherron hardly ever worked out with us in the weight room because they didn't want him to get any bigger. When the team was lifting he was usually upstairs running or doing the elliptical or the Stairmaster. Every now and then we'd give him a hard time about his weight. Hudy sometimes called him "Pork

Chop" or "Meatball." He knew he needed to be careful.

Cole was a freshman when guys like Darnell and I were seniors. We definitely made it hard on him. When he came in we knew he was good because he was so highly recruited. Not being as physical as we were and not having a college body took a toll on him that year. We could do whatever we wanted to against him in the paint. He couldn't stop us. When we got the ball in the paint, it was done because he wasn't strong enough to do anything. That drove him and made him get better.

Darnell made a huge leap between his junior and senior year. During the summer Coach Self would tell us, "Darnell is down in Oklahoma working hard." I guess he had some people watching over the practices. Before then Darnell was a little bit softer. I don't mean physically soft. He just might not have had the drive to go hard every time. After his junior year he went hard after every possession. Maybe the tragedies in his life drove him and gave him more motivation to do it for someone other than himself. I'm not sure what it was, but we were all happy for him.

## NATIONAL CHAMPIONS

After we lost at Oklahoma State my senior year, we all got together at Henry T's and talked about what we needed to do better. We knew we were good. But we needed to get to the point where we could win a championship. We knew this was our chance. Guys were leaving. The five seniors were graduating, and we knew Brandon and Mario were probably leaving. During that meeting we all said, "Let's do everything we can to make sure we can play our absolute best these next few months." We never lost again.

My best game of the NCAA Tournament was in the Elite Eight against Davidson (13 points in 20 minutes on 6-of-6 shooting). I didn't sleep the night before the game. I thought about the year before, when we had lost to UCLA in the Elite Eight. It was a bad memory. The next day I was just looking and making sure everyone was focused during warm-ups. I wanted to make sure everyone was on the same page. I knew it wasn't going to be easy, especially playing the underdog. I know how that happens in the tournament. If you compare it guy-by-guy, there was no way they could beat us. But they were hot. That's all that really mattered. We won, but it wasn't easy.

A few days before we played North Carolina in the Final Four, we all turned on ESPN, and they were saying, "How is Kansas going to keep up with North Carolina? They're so fast. How can Kansas keep up with their speed and guard them?" I remember Coach Self saying the day before the game, "Guys, don't worry about that stuff. If anything, North Carolina should be worried about how they're going to keep up with us." That was good motivation for everyone. It wasn't about them. We have fast guys, too. We came out so fired up.

When we won the championship, I think Coach Self was really happy for the seniors. Our class meant a lot to him. That was the first class that he graduated. If you looked at his career from Oral Roberts to Tulsa to Illinois, he'd never been in a place more than three or four years. He never actually had a chance to recruit a class, bring them in for four years, coach them and graduate them.

## REVELING IN THE AFTERMATH

When we had our parade through downtown Lawrence, I felt like I was on top of the world. Here you are, in college, you've just won a national championship, and all of these people are cheering for you. It was really cool. Three years later I can still see how much the championship means to people around here. When I'm back in town people in stores still come up and say, "Thanks for the championship. Thanks for 2008."

I think winning the title helped my professional career. I don't know if I would've gotten some of these opportunities otherwise. Who knows what would've happened to me? The attention that I got afterward and all of the agents that were contacting and me telling me I'd be a good pro … I'm not sure any of that would've happened if we didn't have so much success.

When people in Russia found out about me, they started contacting my agent. They knew it'd be a great market for me: A young, hometown guy with a Russian passport who had just graduated from college.

## MOVING ON

There is such a difference in style in overseas basketball. There are so many other aspects to the game you have to learn. It's all about being at the right place at the right time. It's so much more structured. In college you've got five players out there that are usually on the same level, unless you've got one huge superstar. Overseas it's a little bit more of a thinking man's game.

I've still got one more year in Russia. Maybe I'll sign an extension, I don't know. We like it there. My wife (former KU soccer player Taylor Blue) enjoys it there, for the most part. There are things she hates, but there would probably be even more things she hated if I was in the NBA, and I'm mainly just talking about the lifestyle. We don't travel as much as NBA teams. Our road games are like college road games. We leave the day before and come back immediately afterward. It's easy on her. She doesn't have to worry about where I am and what I'm doing. Plus, I'm contributing to the team. I'm a big part of it. If I came to the NBA who knows how it would all turn out?

The good thing is that we still get to spend the offseason back in Kansas. We've got a place on The Plaza. This is definitely always going to be one of our homes. We always want to come back and visit and go to the games and be a part of everything. Kansas definitely left a big mark on my heart. It's a special place for me.

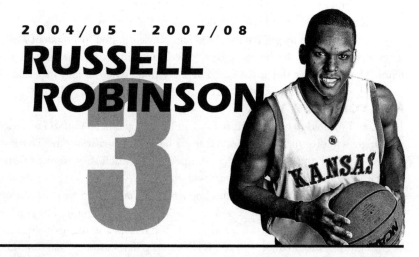

# CHAPTER 28

# 2 0 0 4 / 0 5 - 2 0 0 7 / 0 8
# RUSSELL ROBINSON

R ussell Robinson was the starting point guard for the 2007-08 Jayhawks squad that won the NCAA championship. The New York, N.Y. native became a member of Bill Self's first recruiting class when he signed with Kansas in the fall of 2003. A defensive stalwart, Robinson owns four Big 12 title rings and was known as the team leader during his final two seasons in Lawrence. Since graduating in 2008, Robinson has enjoyed success in the NBDL and overseas.

## IN RUSSELL'S WORDS

Being a part of Kansas' basketball program changed my life. It's the best thing that ever happened to me. Every now and then, though, it causes problems. Or at least it did for me when I was playing in the NBA D-League.

A lot of people looked at me and said, "You think you're all that just because you went to Kansas." They weren't joking, either. They resented me for being a Jayhawk. The first D-League team I played for was the Reno Bighorns. We had a lot of good talent, but most of the guys came from smaller programs or programs that simply weren't that good – especially compared to Kansas. I was making the same paycheck as everyone else, yet because I went to Kansas, people expected different things from me. They thought I was going to be above and beyond everyone else. I caught a lot of heat from guys on my own team.

At Kansas, we were coached a certain way. There was a certain level we were used to playing at. Not everybody is fortunate enough to have been taught that way I was taught. Not everyone played for the same caliber of coaches. I was out there trying to lead and do my job as a point guard, and some people took offense to it. They thought I was acting like I was better than them because I went to Kansas or that I was trying to do things like we did them at Kansas.

There were a lot of conflicts because of that. Guys would be out of position or they'd forget the play. I'd correct them and they'd get mad and say, "You're not in Kansas anymore." I was just like, "Man, I'm just trying to win games." It's amazing how many guys at that level have always gotten by on talent alone. They never learned the importance of sacrificing things for the sake of the team. That's what we did at Kansas. There are times when I really miss that.

## NEW YORK, NEW YORK

I realized I wanted to come to Kansas when I took my official visit to Lawrence as a high school senior. The football team beat Missouri that day. The fans rushed the field and tore down the goal posts, and when they went to throw them in Potter Lake, I was right there with them.

Excited as I was to start school, I knew Kansas hadn't had a ton of players from the East Coast and from New York. I wondered how I'd fit in. I remember calling Norm Roberts, the assistant who recruited me, and asking his permission to get a tattoo. Not too many guys on KU's campus had tattoos at that time, and I didn't want to do something that was going to make anyone mad.

Even though he was from Oklahoma, J.R. Giddens was the closest thing they had to a New York kind of guy. I felt more comfortable coming to Kansas because J.R. was there. I thought, "If they can deal with this guy than they can surely deal with what I have to offer, because he was so off-the-wall." They loved J.R., so I figured I'd be fine because I wasn't as crazy as him.

## FRESHMAN FRUSTRATIONS

Being around Coach Self for four years, I learned that he always chooses someone to pick on, whether they're playing well or not. My sophomore year it was Julian, my junior year it was Sherron and my senior year it was Cole. My freshman year it was me. If I'd had known Coach Self made a yearly tradition of singling someone out, I might have handled it a little better. But this was the 2004-05 season – just his second year at Kansas – and no one had quite figured him out, so they didn't know enough about him to warn me.

The season actually started out on a pretty good note. I was the backup point guard for most of November and December. I had 13 points against Nevada and came up big at the end of a close win against South Carolina at home. But then things took a turn for the worse. My minutes started going down and I didn't understand why. I was playing well and doing some good things. I thought I had found a nice rhythm. I didn't know I'd eventually have to deal with certain elements as far as guys being seniors and stuff. I figured the best guys would play and we'd go from there. Whether you were a freshman or a senior, I didn't think it would matter as long as we were winning and playing well. That's not how it always goes. With the way I was playing, there's no reason I shouldn't have been the sixth man on that team. I definitely felt like I was our best defensive player, even better than Keith, but I was having a hard time getting into the game.

Maybe Coach Self was trying to toughen me up and prepare me for the future. But if that was the case, no one told me that. Coach Roberts was the guy who recruited me, the guy I had built the best relationship with. But he had taken the St. John's job during the offseason, so he wasn't there to translate any of that to me. I just decided I'd figure out how to deal with things by myself. So I did what I did best: I went back to my New York ways. My attitude came out. For a Midwest guy like Coach Self, that didn't go over too well. I came across as arrogant, like I was stubborn and nonchalant and didn't care. I can definitely be stubborn – but that same stubbornness and toughness is what had made me a good basketball player. With me, you've got to take the good with the bad.

## TEMPERS FLARE

My frustration reached its peak the day Coach Self called me a "New York bitch." Back home, there are certain things you say and certain things you don't say. That word "bitch" is a trigger word. It's a word that leads to fights. I guess he didn't really know how I got down.

It happened during a practice. I was copping an attitude. Everyone was fouling me, and I was turning the ball over. Coach Self was trying to get me ready for Big 12 and how physical it was going to be. I was mad at Stephen Vinson and all those guys for fouling me because they couldn't guard me. Coach Self was saying, "Hey, you're going to have to play through this kind of thing on the road." But I was looking at it as, "These guys can't guard me. How can you let them foul me this hard without saying anything to them?" I was obviously mad. My attitude starting taking over, so he called me out and yelled at me and said, "You're just a little New York City bitch."

At that point it wasn't about basketball anymore. I looked at him and said, "Is this personal? Because if it's personal, we can do that, too. I don't have a problem with that." I took my jersey off and starting walking toward him. Guys were holding me back. I told them, "Don't touch me. If you want to fight I'll fight you, too. This is between me and Coach Self right now." It lasted a good 30 seconds before I snapped back into reality and said, "This is my career, and he's just my coach. He's trying to make me a better player." After it was all over I think he respected me, and I certainly respected him. He never called me that again.

That stuff happens all the time where I'm from. I didn't think it was any big deal. It's just part of being a team and growing as a family. All families fight. We went through it and moved on.

## BUCKNELL

In some ways I felt like we had the Bucknell loss coming to us because of the way things were handled with the seniors and certain guys getting more playing time than others. I just thought our team was destined for that because we didn't do things the right way. When we lost that night I was upset but I wasn't surprised. A reporter from New York came up to me in the locker room and asked me how I felt, and I said, "I don't really care." I was mad because I thought I could've helped change the game, especially defensively, but I never even got off the bench.

Our team wasn't very close that year. The seniors had never really gotten over Roy leaving. They were still hurt. Some of the guys tried to be professional about it, but deep down they still wanted to do things Roy's way. They tried to do things the way Coach Self wanted them to, but I'm not sure they ever fully embraced it. Aaron was the main guy trying to bring us all together, but at the same time, he knew it was his last chance to try to make it to the NBA. Keith was probably the biggest piece in all of it, the most important player, but you know how Keith was. He didn't always care. Mike Lee was a good player and a good person, but he wasn't better than me. He just wasn't. I thought I should've been playing ahead of him. Once I stopped playing I actually started practicing a lot better. But it didn't equate to any playing time.

After the season a lot of people thought I was going to transfer to St. John's to play for Coach Roberts. Loyalty was a big thing with me. Kansas was by far a better option than any school I ever thought about going to. There were a lot of reasons I wanted to come here. I wasn't going to let one bad season affect me. Alex Galindo was my roommate. I wasn't going to let his negative energy affect my decision, either. We were both going through some stuff at the same time. I didn't want his emotions to rub off on me. I made my own decision. I decided to stay. He decided to leave. I didn't even look into transferring, even though I probably could've transferred to a couple of places and been OK. I wanted to finish what I started.

## THAT'S MORE LIKE IT

Things completely changed for me my sophomore year – mainly because of my attitude. My life off the court was great. I was happy. The fans in Lawrence treated me great. They reminded me of why I came to Kansas in the first place. Whatever problems I was having on the basketball court, I figured they'd be easy to fix.

The main thing I did was change my relationship with Coach Self. I came in and separated myself and became more of a leader. I played well and did some good things. I just looked at it as, "I'm going to do everything he asks me to do, and I'm going to go as hard as I can go." As tough as he was on me as a freshman, I realized there are probably coaches out there that would've given it to me even worse. I decided to focus the rest of my career on making up for that one bad season.

That was also the year that we brought in the hyped-up recruiting class of

Brandon Rush, Mario Chalmers, Julian Wright and Micah Downs. Brandon was the exact opposite of what I thought he'd be. Instead of being all cocky and arrogant, he was one of the funniest guys in the locker room. He fit in great. Julian was probably the most talented teammate I ever had at Kansas along with Darrell Arthur. Mario didn't let pressure get to him. He wasn't scared of anything. He had a confidence that carried over to the entire team. Then there was Micah. They assigned him to be my roommate since Alex Galindo had transferred to Florida International but, after the first semester, he ended up leaving, too.

It only took a few practices with Micah for me to get excited about his potential. He was one of the best players in the preseason. I thought he would start. After about five games I realized it was only a matter of time before he was going to quit or break down or something.

Micah thought things were going to be handed to him because he was so talented. Whenever things didn't go his way, he'd fall into the tank. His girlfriend was a long way away in Seattle, so that didn't help the situation. He isolated himself from everyone, and that made it hard for anyone to help him out. I was in a situation similar to his my freshman year, so I tried to talk to him. I told him things would get better, but I knew it was only a matter of time until he left. A few days before Christmas, he knocked on my door early in the morning and said, "I'm out." I was half-asleep. I just said, "OK, man, stay in touch." He left a lot of his stuff behind. I was just happy to have the apartment to myself.

From the beginning of the season to the end, our team probably improved as much as any team in the country. Most people will remember the first-round loss to Bradley in the NCAA Tournament. But I'll remember winning the Big 12 regular-season title and the Big 12 tournament title, too. For a team that was starting three freshmen by the end of the season – Brandon, Mario and Julian

– I thought that was a pretty big accomplishment. With everyone coming back, we knew big things were in store.

## ADDITION BY SUBTRACTION

A few weeks before the start of my junior year in 2006-07, Coach Self kicked C.J. Giles off the team. C.J. was an incredible talent, but he made too many mistakes off the court. I played against C.J. in high school and hung out at camps with him. I always thought he was cool. When I came on my Kansas visit, C.J. was supposed to be there with me. I remember Coach Self calling him and C.J. said, "I got sick so I had to stay home. I can't make it." I found out later that he was in Florida visiting the University of Miami that weekend. The coaches found out about it, and I figured there was no way C.J. would play here. I never thought Kansas would take someone who did something like that. During recruiting, my circle of people back in New York would always say, "Watch what you do. Watch what you say. There are a ton of great players out there. Coaches will cut you off real quick if you mess up or if they don't like you." So after what C.J. did, I didn't think he should be playing at Kansas. Sure enough, Kansas signed him, and he showed up and started doing all the same stuff that C.J. has always done. I wasn't surprised. The coaches knew before he got here that he was capable of doing that kind of stuff. He didn't do anything spitefully. He was a good guy. He's not a bad person. I like C.J. He just moves to his own beat.

## SHERRON & SHADY

Losing C.J. didn't hurt all that bad because we added two pieces that year in Sherron and Shady (Darrell Arthur). Coach Self picked on Shady a lot, too, and Shady didn't respond very well. He didn't talk back or anything. He just wasn't really motivated by that kind of stuff. I think he was happy here, though. He and Brandon and Mario were all really close. I think people had the wrong perception of him sometimes. Shady didn't come in here with the mind-set of "I'm going to use Kansas to get to the NBA." I think he genuinely enjoyed it while he was here. He was a good teammate. If we wouldn't have won that championship, he may have actually come back.

Sherron was a Chicago guy. We related to one another because we were both from the inner city. We had a mutual respect for one another. We helped each other out. We made each other better. There were times his freshman year when I could've really, really put him under the bus. He was overweight, and Coach Self had been getting on him for it. He wasn't playing that well. I could've really separated myself by going at him in practice and just blowing by him and getting to the basket. It would've made him feel even worse. But I didn't do that. I pushed him through that period and helped him learn the plays and stuff. New Yorkers usually don't do that. A lot of people back home wouldn't have understood that decision. They'd say, "You've got to get yours. Don't worry about him." But at the end of the day, he was my teammate. And I also remembered how no one did that for me my freshman year. My biggest goal when I came to Kansas was to win. And I wasn't blind to the fact that we needed Sherron to win. I also think a lot of his weight issues were genetic and not completely his fault. He was actually a very hard worker, especially if he had someone next to him working with him. If you asked him to do it all by himself, he may not have gone as hard. But if his boys were with him, he was intense. He won us some games, I know that.

## INCHING TOWARD THE TOP

We lost to UCLA in the Elite Eight my junior year and, a few weeks later, Julian declared for the draft. You'd think that would've hurt us down low, but Darnell Jackson caught everyone by surprise. Darnell went home to Oklahoma City that summer and came back a different player, a different person. Everybody deals with family issues, but he dealt with a lot more of them than most people. I think a lot of that stuff made him stronger. By the end of his career he had a different attitude, a different swag, a different energy. It showed in his game. Once Julian left, it opened up the gates for him to blossom. Darnell is definitely hard to read. Of all the hiccups on the team, Darnell had the most as far as arguments in the locker room and things like that. But he's a good guy. He's a grizzly bear on the outside and a teddy bear on the inside. He looks like a beast, but he's really a soft, sensitive guy.

Darnell was actually one of the people who got everyone together for a team meeting late during our senior year. We had just lost at Oklahoma State, which marked our third Big 12 road loss. Even in some of our wins, we didn't look as dominant as we should've. So we all met up at Henry T's in Lawrence and talked it out. That meeting came at a good time. It was late February and it needed to happen. As far as the actual meeting, I don't think anything was said that hadn't been said before, but it got everyone's attention. Everyone acknowledged that we needed to turn things around and go in the same direction. It wasn't like anyone said anything earth-shattering, but it caused us to refocus.

## THE TREK TO THE TITLE

Everyone will always talk about the 2008 Final Four and how all four No. 1 seeds advanced. And they'll always remember us beating North Carolina and Memphis. But when it came to pressure, those were the easy games.

The hardest games we played that year were UNLV and Villanova, games we ended up winning by 12 or 13 points. When you're playing against teams that have nothing to lose, those are the hardest games. We played at a high level when we played other high-level teams. When we played against North Carolina, there was no scouting report. They didn't have to tell us about Ty

Lawson. Everyone knew all about Ty Lawson and what he can do. The same thing went for Memphis and Derrick Rose. The scouting report on that game lasted 10 minutes. Against Portland State, the scouting report lasted 45 minutes. Coach Self made their players out to be a lot better than they really were. It got our attention.

The thing I'll never forget about the North Carolina game is being up 40-12. Everyone was shocked and gasping for air. Not just them, but us, too. We knew they were going to make a run. When you go against good teams you come to expect that. With some of those other teams, you don't know where a run is going to come from. But we knew those North Carolina players had it in them. We got to the locker room after we beat them, and everyone was so excited. It was Coach Self's job to come in there and say, "Hey, hey, hey. What are you so excited for? You've got one more game."

Coach Self was so good that whole weekend. When we were playing Memphis, and Derrick Rose hit that 3 off the backboard, I thought that might be the dagger. But Coach Self never allowed us to get down. I didn't always listen to what he said in the huddle, but I always paid attention to how he was saying it. That night he never panicked. He was real confident that we were going to make plays and that it was going to work out. He was calm, and that poise spread throughout the whole team. In the end, Mario was the perfect guy to take that shot. You still see it when you watch him in the NBA now. He has no fear.

## AFTERMATH

Winning the championship that night was fun, but what followed was even better. Out of everything – winning the game … cutting down the nets … everything – the parade was the best part. We got to see firsthand the lives that we impacted by us winning. It was cool to know that I played a part in making people's lives a little better. We were each riding in a car through the streets of downtown, and everyone was rushing up to us. They were getting so close that I'm shocked no one's feet got run over. There was so much love in the air.

Another cool thing was getting all the text messages the night we beat North Carolina. People were sending us pictures of the celebration on Massachusetts Street and people were calling us all drunk and to congratulate us. It wasn't annoying. It made us feel good. The bad part was sitting in the hotel, because I wanted to be right there with them. We missed a hell of a party.

That summer we all got to go to the White House to meet President Bush. Just being able to say I went to the White House is cool. Most people will never, ever get the chance to meet the president. He actually talked to us for about 20-30 minutes. Someone said the New York Giants had been there a few weeks earlier, and their whole ceremony lasted 8 minutes. We were surprised he talked to us that long in the Oval Office. If the election would've been that day, he would've gotten my vote. The main thing I remember him telling us was about how, at that time, a lot of people thought he was a bad president and that his approval rating was terrible. But he said Abraham Lincoln's approval rating would've been pretty bad back in his time, too – especially after he abolished slavery. But now Abraham Lincoln is viewed as one of the best presidents in history. You won't be able to tell if Bush was a good president until all is said and done and you look back on it. There were a few Secret Service guys in there, but I thought there would be more security than that. There were probably a few players who didn't think going there was that big of a deal. But they'll appreciate it when they're older. They'll look back at those pictures and relive those memories. That's when the magnitude of what we did will really set in.

Three years later, everyone still identifies me with winning the title. No matter where I go in the world, someone always recognizes me. Sometimes I get mistaken for Mario, but they still know I was on that team. Even though I've done other good things since then, that doesn't bother me. Everyone tells me they'd trade everything to have a championship. I don't promote it. I don't wear my ring and throw it in people's faces. But if people recognize me and want to remember me for that, that's fine with me.

## STILL CHASING A DREAM

I spent my first two years out of college in the NBA D-League and then played the 2010-11 season in Spain. It's a high level of basketball over there. Not a lot of people realize that. If the NBA never works out, I want to be able to play overseas. I had to start somewhere and I figured Spain was the best place to do that. I got lucky. I lived in Barcelona – right across the street from the beach – and I started every game. Everybody I talked to said I was fortunate to have that as my first experience. It was a culture shock at first. The basketball philosophies are different. But I was having fun and enjoying life.

If I had solid options overseas I might take that over the NBA right now. It's not just about job security. It's about lifestyle. Barcelona is a lot better than Indiana. I was right by the beach. The gyms were packed, and I was actually playing. If I make the NBA, I'm probably not going to play much. Overseas I actually feel like a part of the team because I have a role. Keith Langford told me something about a year ago that I agreed with. He tried the whole NBA thing and eventually said, "I want to spend my prime basketball years in a place where I'm actually going to get to play." He has a good point.

Still, I'm not giving up on the NBA because I know I have what it takes to play there. I was right on the brink two years ago in Cleveland. I played well in the NBA summer league in 2009 and got a camp invite two weeks later. I was a little nervous at first because I didn't know what to expect. At first it felt weird to be playing with LeBron and Shaq every day and sharing a locker room with them. They treated me like I was one of their teammates. After a while I started feeling like I belonged. I played well enough that I got to start one game. I played against the Mavericks and Jason Kidd. Drew Gooden was on that team, too. I thought I had carved out my spot on the team. They had a poll on the Internet asking fans to vote for whoever they thought should get the last roster spot. I had about 60 percent of the votes. Most of that was probably due to Kansas fans voting.

We had a day off after we played our last preseason game. It was a Friday, and I was expecting the decision to be made by Monday because Tuesday was the deadline. I figured I at least had a weekend to go through a few more practices and show my worth. But when I woke up Friday I had three missed calls on my phone. They had left me messages saying Danny Ferry, the general manager, was downstairs. I knew what it was about. I met him in the hotel lobby and he said, "We like what you do on defense. Your shooting could be a little better, but we like what you do on offense, too. We love your work ethic and professionalism, but it's a numbers game and you're not going to make the team." I just said, "OK, cool. Thanks." I didn't know what else to say. I went back upstairs and about 20 minutes later Mike Brown, the head coach, called me. He repeated the same things, and it was over. It was pretty painful. One day I was at practice and the next day I wasn't. There wasn't a big sendoff or anything like that.

From there I went back to the D-League. I was frustrated I hadn't made the team in Cleveland, so I started trying to score as many points as I could. I had some good games, some 30-point games. Still, I felt a little bit out of character. I'd never been a score-first point guard. It just didn't feel right. My numbers all increased, but overall I think it hurt my route to the NBA.

Wherever I end up, I'll always find my way back to Kansas during the offseason. There's no way I'll ever be able to stop coming back to Lawrence. It's part of me now. No matter what team I'm playing for or what city or country I'm in, I always have a pair of Kansas shorts and a KU hoodie packed in my bag to remind me of my college days. I go back to New York and people say I'm not the same. They say, "You're from Kansas now." They're referring to my mind-set and my swag and everything that I do. I'm more relaxed. The Midwest thing has really rubbed off on me. So when they joke about me being a Kansan now, it doesn't bother me. I just smile and say, "Hey, I like it there."

# CHAPTER 29

# 2005/06 - 2007/08
# BRANDON RUSH 25

Brandon Rush led Kansas in scoring and earned first-team All-Big 12 honors in each of his three seasons at Kansas. He sparked the Jayhawks to the NCAA title in 2008 and also helped them win three conference championship and three Big 12 Tournament crowns. A Kansas City native, Rush is the younger brother of former UCLA star JaRon Rush and former Missouri and NBA standout Kareem Rush. The Portland Trail Blazers selected Rush with the 13th overall pick in the 2008 NBA draft and then traded him to Indiana. In three seasons with the Pacers, Rush has averaged 8.9 points and 3.6 rebounds. *Note: Some of the excerpts in this chapter were obtained during an interview with Rush at his apartment two weeks after the NCAA title game in 2008.

## IN BRANDON'S WORDS

When I was growing up, I never had any intention of going to college. I always figured I'd go straight to the pros. I entered the NBA draft straight out of high school and, even though I had to pull out at the last minute, I still felt like I was ready for the league. I just decided that going to school for a year would be the best way to improve my draft status. Even after I enrolled at Kansas, the plan all along was to only stay for one season. But then something happened that I wasn't expecting. I fell in love with Lawrence. I fell in love with Kansas. I fell in love with being a college student.

## FIRST VISIT

I let my AAU coach handle my entire recruitment. I had known him for a long time, since I was really little, and he had dealt with my brothers and their recruitment, too. He knew how it all worked as far as setting stuff up with different colleges and scheduling visits and getting kids into school and stuff

like that. I don't regret letting him help me at all. I wouldn't have known what I was doing otherwise. Recruiting could get kind of dirty at times. We got offered a bunch of stuff – money and gifts and stuff like that. I don't want to go into a bunch of details, though. It's over now. There's no reason to discuss it.

For most of my recruitment, Kansas wasn't even on our list. Then, all of a sudden, I found out they were on the list. I don't know how that happened. I talked to Coach Self in July, the day I was going to visit Oklahoma. I was on my way to the airport and he called my coach. My coach handed me the phone. He said he wanted me to come to Lawrence for a visit the day I got back.

When I went on my visit, I stayed with Mario, who had just moved down there that summer. I knew him from the AAU circuit, and I knew Julian, too. I had a ball that night. We went to a bar and then over to some chick's house. We were everywhere. Even after my visit was over, I kept driving back out there to hang out and chill with everyone. I didn't want to leave Lawrence. At that point I knew that Kansas was where I wanted to go. I loved it out there.

## WISE CHOICE

Signing with Kansas was one of the best decisions I've ever made in my life, and not just because of basketball. I became a man at Kansas. I did a lot of growing up during the three years I spent there. I definitely came a long way from the days of getting suspended all the time in high school.

I was always in trouble at Westport High School (in Kansas City), but it's not like it was ever for anything serious. Usually it was for being late for class, goofing off in the halls or talking while the teacher was talking or not turning in assignments. I just messed around a lot and was never very serious about anything.

I remember the principal there telling my AAU coach that my life would never amount to s--t. I kept getting suspended. I didn't want to tell my mom. She'd drop me off in front of the school each morning and I'd walk toward the door — even though I knew the security guards weren't going to let me in the building. Then she'd drive off, and I'd find somewhere to go or something to get into. One suspension would end, but then another one would come. Eventually, near the end of my sophomore year, it became a permanent deal, and I was kicked out of Westport for good.

Looking back on it now, what happened there was probably a good thing because it got me out of Kansas City. I went to Mt. Zion in North Carolina and started to mature a lot there, and after that it was Kansas.

I know I had a bad reputation when I got to Kansas. People said I was selfish and uncoachable and that I didn't play defense. On the road, fans would taunt me. They'd hold up signs that said, "Rush Can't Read." All those people that said bad things about me ... none of them knew me or had seen me play. Those people didn't know what type of person I was.

## FROM SELFISH TO SELFLESS

The main reason Kansas was good for me was because I needed to be coached. I didn't realize it until I got there, but I had never really been coached before. Before I got to Kansas, I didn't really care about winning and losing. I was just trying to do everything for myself and reach my goal, which was to get to the NBA. At Kansas I learned about X's and O's and weight training. I developed good practice habits and I learned how to take coaching, how to take criticism. All of that has helped me in the NBA.

I also became a more team-oriented player. The results of the games actually mattered to me for once. I wanted to play well because I didn't want to let my teammates or our fans down.

If we lost a big game – or any game – it was rough. I didn't even want to show my face on campus the next day. I did that a few times. I wouldn't even go to class or anything. I didn't want anyone to see me. If I had a girlfriend, I'd tell her not to come over. I took losses hard. All of us did.

On the flip side, when we won, things couldn't have been better. We'd go to eat at a restaurant, and a lot of times the manager would refuse to let us pay our bill. We'd go out to the clubs, and everyone knew who we were, and all the girls wanted to talk to us. In school, if we had been on the road, the teachers would give us an extra day to study for a test. We definitely got a lot of attention. I'm not a guy that really likes a ton of people coming up to me, just because I'm kind of quiet and like to stay in the background. But I certainly appreciated the love.

## BILL SELF

Every player has frustrations with their coach at some point in their career. But, overall, I don't have one bad thing to say about Coach Self. I grew up watching as all these people tried to get at my brothers and take advantage of them. They were young kids, and sometimes young kids make wrong decisions. It was tough on them, because they were like pieces of meat, and everyone wanted to take a bite. Before I came to Kansas, there were times when I felt like that, too.

I showed up in Lawrence not trusting anyone. Three years later, I left knowing that I had people in my life that really cared about me and wanted what's best for me. Coach Self is one of those people. I realized that more than ever after I hurt my knee. He was calling or texting every day to check up on me and telling me to call him whenever I needed to talk. He had already treated me well, but I think our relationship got even better at that point. I know it did on my end.

That's not to say that Coach Self couldn't be mean. At halftime of the Nebraska game in the Big 12 tournament, he called me out like I've never been

called out before. I'm pretty sure you can't print the word that he called me in front of the entire team – and I actually didn't think I was playing all that bad. Luckily I've always been good about not letting stuff like that get to me. If it affects me at all, it's usually in a positive way.

## COMMON CRITICISM

Throughout my whole career, people were always critical of me because I didn't shoot more. They said I wasn't aggressive enough, that I was too passive. Coach Self was on me about it, the fans, the media ... it got annoying. Why should I have shot more? We were a great team. We went 37-3 and won the national championship. I didn't need to take any more shots. I always had good players around me. Everyone was happy. If I'd have started taking 20 shots a game it would've messed up our chemistry. Who knows what would've happened then.

Coach Self even set up a treadmill each day in practice that was just for me. No one else used it. He'd make me run for not shooting the ball enough in practice, for passing up shots. If I passed up a shot I should've taken, I'd have to run. I kind of pissed me off, to tell you the truth.

Everyone was doing anything they could to get me to shoot more. Midway through my junior year, a dude that I've known for a long time – a family friend – started paying me for every basket I made. I'd get a little bit for a layup, a little more for a 3-pointer and a little more for a dunk. It wasn't very much money at all. I think he just wanted to give me incentive to be more aggressive so the scouts could see what I could do, because obviously I wanted to be drafted high. I don't know if I played any differently because of it, but the guy that was paying me ... he cared about me. He was just trying to help. Even today in the NBA, people say I don't shoot it enough. But I think I've done pretty well for myself.

## RANDOM THOUGHTS

I used to hate playing against Stephen Vinson. He would go so hard in practice. He'd play the toughest defense. He was doing everything he could to get some playing time. Whenever he was guarding me, practice was harder than the games. He made me a lot better.

Shady is a jokester. He's the one that's always cracking all the jokes on everyone. He's fun to be around. I never could tell if he liked Kansas. I think he was homesick a little bit. He liked playing with everyone, liked all the guys. I just don't think he was feeling the campus or something. If he had problems, he didn't bring any of them to the court.

Coach was always on Sherron for his weight. He and Coach Self would go at it all the time. He talked back to him. Sherron isn't the type to hold his tongue.

I loved playing Texas when Kevin Durant was there, because I always had to guard him. He brought out the best in me. Mike Beasley was fun to play against, too. He was always yapping at the mouth.

I think Julian should've stayed another year. But he was a lottery pick, so what the hell. On the court, we didn't know what Julian was going to do. That was probably because he didn't know what he was going to do. He was out there. You never knew what you were going to get with Ju-Ju.

## FINAL FOUR

The Final Four was one of the best experiences of my life. Beating up on North Carolina felt good, but it had nothing to do with the fact that we were playing against Roy Williams. I know the media made a big deal out of that situation, but I honestly don't think any of us thought about it. Coach Self didn't mention it one time. There were some things that happened years ago with Coach Williams and my brother, JaRon, that upset my family a little bit. People kept asking me what I thought of him, but I don't have anything to say about the man because I don't know him. It's obvious that he's a great coach, and he seems like a great person, too. After we beat them he came up to me in the handshake line and said, "Good luck." Then, after we got through the line, he came and found me again and said, "I mean it. Good luck. I want you to win this thing for you and your family."

It's kind of funny, because now I play with Tyler Hansbrough on the Pacers. Tyler barely even speaks. You can only get a few words out of Tyler. Still, any time I bring up that game, he says, "F---you, man." He just laughs and shakes it off. I like Tyler a lot. He's a good dude and he's a really good player, too. He's got that midrange shot down. It's money in the bank.

The Memphis game was crazy. I thought we may have let it slip away, but Mario hit the shot for the ages. Afterward people were throwing water all over each other in the locker room and hugging each other. We went back to the hotel and stayed up all night partying. There was a big party on the 22nd floor with everyone: Coaches, administrators, players ... lots of people. After that the players went to the 11th floor and got after it all night long. Most of us didn't go to sleep before 8 a.m. We were all pretty tired the next day when we got back to Lawrence and went to Memorial Stadium for Welcome Home rally.

## NEW PERSPECTIVE

Who knows where I'd be right now if I didn't go to Kansas. I probably would've ended up in the D-League or something like that, but at least I would've gotten paid a lot earlier (laughing). I know Kansas was good for me. I'm always going to go back there. I miss college. I miss it a lot.

The NBA is a full-time job. I'm having fun. But it's still a job, still a business. Right now things are a little frustrating. I think I should be playing better, but I'm also in a tough situation in Indiana. I'm trying to get back on the right road. My story is still being written.

# CHAPTER 30

# 2005/06 - 2007/08

# RODRICK STEWART

Rodrick Stewart transferred to Kansas from USC – where he played with his twin brother, Lodrick – in December of 2004. He became eligible one year later but played sparingly until his senior season in 2007-08, when he worked his way into the rotation for the Jayhawks' NCAA championship squad. Stewart averaged 2.8 points and 2.2 rebounds in his final college season but, unfortunately, he was unable to participate in the Final Four. The day before Kansas played North Carolina, Stewart fractured his kneecap while attempting a dunk during the Jayhawks' practice in San Antonio. He cheered his team on from the bench against North Carolina and Memphis before undergoing surgery in Lawrence. Stewart was given the Danny Manning "Mr. Jayhawk" Award at the team's postseason banquet. He has continued his career overseas. Stewart's daughter, Aleena Mae, turned 2 in September of 2011.

## IN RODRICK'S WORDS

Things were weird when I first got to Kansas. I came from a school, USC, where football was everything. People at USC kind of knew who I was, but it wasn't the same. Going to Kansas … I know what celebrities go through now. When you're a basketball player at Kansas, you're viewed as a celebrity, whether you're a starter or a walk-on. When you drape that Kansas Jayhawks jersey over your back and you run through that tunnel for the first time, you've become a celebrity, whether you like it or not. I really don't like attention like that. I love to laugh and have fun. But I hate attention. I don't like things being all about me. I've never been that type of guy. I'm not saying the situation didn't have its perks. It did. But at times, it was like, "Man, this is crazy."

## JAYHAWK TIES

One of the main reasons I transferred to Kansas was Kurtis Townsend, our assistant. Coach T was one of the assistant coaches when I went to Southern California. He ended up taking a job at Miami as soon as my brother and I arrived on campus in Los Angeles. The situation didn't work out for him in Miami, so he ended up at Kansas.

I looked at Coach Townsend like a father figure. I always looked to him for advice. I'd known Coach Townsend since I was in the sixth grade, before I ever even thought about playing basketball. I met him through Jamal Crawford, who went to my high school and played at Michigan. Jamal is like my big brother. He's in the NBA right now. I was around Jamal all the time, so I'd see Kurtis around a lot and talk to him. I always thought he was cool. I thought he knew a lot about life. He could make anyone laugh. I've been through a lot in my life, and he kept my spirits high no matter what I was going through. It's good to be around people like that.

The other thing that sold me was that C.J. Giles was here. C.J. was one of my high school teammates and one of my best friends. With him at Kansas, too, I just felt like it was going to be the perfect situation for me. If I was going to leave my twin back at USC, I had to go to a place where I was going to have someone that I was close to. C.J. was that guy.

I was happy with the college experience at USC, but I had really high goals for myself coming out of Rainier Beach High School in Seattle, being one of the top players in my class. It was nothing against Henry Bibby, the coach at USC at the time. He was a great coach. But he's kind of old school, at least more old school than I was used to. I was used to a more up-tempo kind of system. The way he wanted his players to play didn't fit my game at all.

## LEAVING LODRICK

Transferring was, hands down, one of the hardest things I've ever had to do in my life, because it meant leaving my twin behind. I remember it just like it was yesterday. My brother was standing outside on the sidewalk as I pulled away from the apartment, looking down at the ground. Our plan was to pack up my stuff and try to make me leaving as least sad as we could. But we couldn't do it. He was so sad he couldn't even ride to the airport with me. I don't think he felt like I turned my back on him, but I was accused of that by some people. I think at times he felt like I left him there to dry. But that was never the case. I just needed a better situation for myself.

Lodrick and I came into this world together. We had been together since Day One. We knew there was going to be a day where we were going to have to play basketball without each other. It was definitely hard. It took a while for me to get used to being by myself. You get so used to having your twin there with you. We had all the same classes and everything in high school and at USC.

When I got to Kansas, I didn't even know how to act. I stayed to myself at first. I was real quiet. It took me a long time to make friends. It was so hard for me, just being Rod and not being a twin. Everyone at USC just called us "the twins." I was used to hearing people say, "Lod and Rod." So just hearing people say, "Rodrick" and nothing else was an adjustment. I was nervous just to walk across campus by myself. Those are things the average person wouldn't be scared to do, but I was. I'd be sitting in class, wanting to look over and talk to my brother, but I couldn't. People don't know what it's like to have that best friend/twin next to you at all times. It was a new experience for me.

## C.J. GILES

I've known C.J. since he was in the ninth grade. I remember when he walked into school for the first time. He had on some big, thick glasses. He looked like a nerd. No one wanted him to play on our team the first day he came for pickup. I thought, "This little skinny guy isn't going to help us." I didn't see him that whole next summer. He came back for his sophomore year, and he had grown about 5 inches. He was a totally different person. I was like, "OK, we could probably use him."

C.J. was one of my closest friends, so obviously I hated it when things didn't work out for him at Kansas. At times, I think C.J. should've been a little more mature. It's easy to get caught up in being a KU athlete. You start thinking, "I'm a Kansas Jayhawk. I can do anything." In reality, you're no different than anyone else. I always had to remind myself of that. C.J. got reminded of it, too. I just wish he would've been a little smarter.

At the same time, I don't think people realize how much pressure C.J. was under once his dad moved to Lawrence. He went from the playful, fun C.J. to the serious C.J. He felt like he had to play well – or else. He tried so hard to impress his dad that it actually affected his game in a negative way. He just had so much stress on him that no one ever knew about.

There is only so much you can ride your kid. There is only so far you can push him. Every parent wants greatness for their kids but, at the same time, you have to know when to push them and when not to. It can't be push-push-push all the time. I think C.J. felt like that's what was happening with his dad. I remember talking to him one time, and he said, "Basketball isn't even what I want to do. I just feel like it was something that was forced upon me because I was tall."

If I'm ever blessed enough to have a son, I'm never going to push him into playing sports. Whatever my son wants to do, I'm going to respect it and stand behind him 100 percent. I would never push him to where he didn't love the game anymore. In my career, if I ever questioned my love for the game, that would've been the day I put down the basketball forever.

## IMPACTING LIVES

One good thing about being on the team is that you realize you have the power to affect so many people. You can change someone's day just by smiling at them or shaking their hand. Just seeing how excited a little kid gets just to see you, or to see the look on kids' faces when you wave at them ... those are memories that stick with you for a long time.

When I was at Kansas, there were these twin girls, Mary and Sarah, who went to all of our basketball camps. They were always so nice to me. They were nice to everyone. I was like, "Man, these little girls love basketball so much. They're two of our best fans ever." All the other players thought the same thing about them. We loved them. After a game one time, I went into the locker room and grabbed a pair of shoes. I gave each one of them a shoe. They still remember it to this day. Three years later, they hit me up on Facebook all the time and ask me how I'm doing. They check up on me. It just shows you how loyal KU fans are. Just little things like that get me through the day sometimes, especially if I'm having one of those days when things aren't going right. When you hear from someone like that, it feels good, because it reminds you how many people out there actually care about you and want you to better yourself. That and family ... that's all I need to keep going.

## RODRICK'S ROLE

I knew if I could bring anything to Kansas' team, it was toughness. I've always been that type of player. I'll never back down. I don't care if I was guarding someone who was 5-10 or 6-10. I was going to go at them. When he recruited me, Coach Self said he wasn't going to promise me anything. He said anything I got at the University of Kansas was going to be because I worked for it and deserved it. I told him, "I'm definitely going to try to be the toughest player on the team." I felt like I accomplished that. I felt like I was that person.

When I say "toughness," I'm mainly talking about defense. It's being the guy that comes in there and locks people down. It's being a vocal leader. It's being the guy who dives on the ground before anyone. If there's a fight or a skirmish that breaks out, it's being the guy that gets in there and gets his nose dirty. I felt like that's what I brought to the table every day. Not just in games, but in practice.

Our practices were actually harder than the games. Our practices are where we had all the fights, all the talking. That's where the real competitiveness came out in our players. Any KU player from that season will tell you that the games, most of the time, felt like our day off. They were easy compared to the practices.

## RUSSELL ROBINSON

I remember one practice, we kept having to run as a team because one player – I think it was Darnell – made a mistake. Everyone was mad at him because we

had to run because of his mistake. Russell said something to Darnell, and they started fighting. They got into a fistfight. When it broke up, Russell screamed out that he wanted to go home. It was the only time I ever heard him say something like that. He said, "If we're not going to bust our tail and give 110 percent every day, then we shouldn't be here."

I gained a lot of respect for Russell that day. All he cared about was winning. If he saw a guy slacking, he was going to step up and say something. I guess he felt like Darnell was loafing, so he said something and got his point across. They fought like brothers do, because we all looked at each other as brothers. They fought and made up – and it took our team to another level.

After practice that day, I remember thinking in the back of my mind, "We're going to be fine. I know we're going to win it. This group I came in with ... we're definitely going to get a championship." I felt that way because of what Russell said. I could tell he was sincere when he said it – and I could tell that everyone on the team agreed with him. When you have so many winners and so many people making the type of sacrifices coaches can only dream about ... it was the perfect situation.

## SHERRON AND DARNELL

Another time in practice, Coach Self came up to me and was like, "Guard Sherron. Guard Sherron. Don't let him score." I was using my chest and my size. I was bodying him up and turning him. Finally, it got to the point where we both got so tired and fed up that we tried to fight each other. We gained so much respect for each other just by going at it and making up afterward.

That's how Sherron and I got to be so cool with one another. We have a lifetime bond now. It's the same thing with Darnell. Those are my brothers forever, no matter what happens. We're going to be 60 or 70 years old, looking back and talking about all the funny stuff and the good times we had at Kansas.

They're the type of people I like being around. We all come from pretty much nothing. We didn't have rich parents or the best situations. But we always had a smile on our face. I noticed that about Darnell when I first met him. He could walk into a room and light up a room. Sherron could, too. They're like my dad. My dad has been through a lot, losing his brother and his mom – and then losing his grandmother three days later. But you'd have never known it by looking at him. He's just so positive about life.

Darnell and I were roommates for two years. That was the best thing that could've ever happened to me. Being around a person that's been through almost identical situations as you in life really helps you. We'd sit up late at night and talk about things we want in life and about how we wanted to be remembered. We knew our tough backgrounds could actually be a blessing for the team. That's why that 2008 team was so good. It was the only team I've ever been on where every person who picked up the ball understood and accepted their role. That's what it takes to win. Every team has good athletes. Every team has players who can jump, dribble and shoot. But it's the teams that have players who are willing to sacrifice for the good of the team that are going to win.

## THOUGHTS ON OTHER TEAMMATES

Brandon and Mario were connected at the hip. They were like twins. If one made a joke, the other made a joke. If Mario walked in late to a practice, you knew Brandon was going to walk in late. They were like true brothers. Guys like that made my college experience great. In boot camp, when everyone was mad about having to be there that early or struggling through drills, Brandon would say something to make everyone laugh, even the coaches. Just like that, everyone's mood changed and the workout started going better.

The hardest player to guard was Sherron. He'd come at you full speed, doing moves that other guards would do starting out stationary. It was harder to guard him when he was coming at you full speed. If you made one little mistake, he would get all the way to the basket on you.

Sasha didn't talk a lot, but when he did it was the funniest thing. He looked at basketball like it was his job. He was so focused every day in practice. He was the most responsible person. I don't recall Coach Self ever really having to yell at Sasha about anything. When you see a guy like him going hard 24-7, it's going to wear off on everyone. Whether he was hurt or not, he never made excuses. He just showed up ready every day.

Jeremy Case was definitely the best 3-point shooter on the team, hands down. I honestly believe this: If he would've shot the ball in games even halfway as good as he did in practice, he'd be in the NBA, even with his size. He was that good of a 3-point shooter. He'd miss some in the games, and I'd think, "C'mon, Jeremy. You've made these time and time again." I don't know if it was pressure or what. But he definitely had one of the best shots I've ever seen in my life.

## FINAL FOUR FRUSTRATIONS

If had I to do it all over again – if we went back in time and I had to break my knee again for us to win it all – I'd break it again. If it would give us that extra fire, that extra energy, with players looking over at me on the bench the way that they did during the Final Four, then I would do it again in a heartbeat. It's all about sacrifice. Maybe it did take me breaking my knee for us to really focus and say, "Whatever it takes, no matter what happens, we're going to win this for him."

People don't understand what it's like to break your knee at the Final Four of your senior year. I had been preparing myself for that moment from the sixth grade on. Two-a-days, three-a-days, when I played football just so I could get stronger for basketball … that was all done so I could get to the Final Four someday. When you work your whole life for that moment, and then you achieve it and it gets taken away from you, it's devastating.

Some people ask if I have regrets about trying to dunk in practice the day before the game, but I don't. It was a freak accident. It could've happened in the North Carolina game or in the Memphis game. Throughout the whole NCAA Tournament, I had never dunked during warm-ups. I always just let the freshmen go. But in San Antonio – the day before we played North Carolina – I heard someone say, "All the reserves … go ahead and dunk." I thought, "Why not? It's the Final Four."

My plan was to bounce the ball up in the air and do a windmill – a dunk I've done hundreds of times. I could tell the timing was going to be off, so I should've stopped after the bounce. But instead I thought, "Let's go ahead and finish this off for the crowd." I lost my footing and fractured my knee cap. That was the end of my college basketball career. At first I thought I'd torn my ACL, but then I looked at my kneecap and saw that everything was out of place. I started pointing at it and everyone ran over. All the guys thought I was playing. So did Coach Self. Then he took a closer look at what I was pointing at and he freaked out. He was like, "Trainer, trainer, get over here."

The main thing I remember is that it hurt like hell. It was the worst pain I ever felt in my life. You'd have to experience it to know what I'm talking about. The pain lasted until I got surgery five days later.

They had a machine that actually X-rayed me at the arena. They asked me if I wanted to go into surgery immediately, but I said I didn't want to do anything that was going to keep me away from my teammates.

One of the things I'll never forget is Mario coming into my hotel room the night it happened, the night before the North Carolina game. He came in there just like a brother would. He looked at me and shook his head a little bit. I could tell he was sad. I was in so much pain, but I was happy to see him. I looked up him and smiled. I said, "I'm good, man. I'm good. You guys go out there and do it. Don't let this be a distraction to anybody. When you're out there, just play the game. Any time you need extra motivation, just look at me." Mario said, "We're going to win this for you, Rod. We're going to win it for you."

I didn't sleep at all that night because of the pain. I had some strong painkillers, but I've never been very big on taking pills. I wasn't going to have surgery and be away from my team during the most important weekend of our lives. I just decided to deal with the pain as best as I could and be there to support my team. I got real emotional during the North Carolina game. I was so happy for my teammates and how they came out and played. I was trying to sit there and cheer but, at the same time, I was in a lot of pain. With about 5 minutes left I just broke down. The crowd was chanting my name and the magnitude of what had happened to me started to set in. I was crying in front of everyone, and I didn't care.

Overall, I'm proud of the way I handled it. I kept a smile on my face when I could, but it wasn't always easy. It's just good to know that, in a different way, I played a part in those two wins in San Antonio.

## MOVING ON

Getting hurt at the Final Four made me love the game so much more, because now I know what it feels like to have it taken away from me. No one was there with me during my rehab, when I had to learn to walk on that leg all over again. No one saw that. They only saw me breaking my knee. Most of the fans haven't seen me play since that happened, unless they've gone on YouTube and seen my highlights from overseas. They probably don't realize I'm even playing at all.

I'm not 100 percent now. I'm 110 percent. I actually jump higher now than I did when I was at Kansas. I feel like everyone should do rehab. It made me work on muscles I didn't know that I had in my legs. It definitely helped my game. You're working three or four times harder than people who are actually in shape.

I played point guard in Finland in 2009-10 and averaged 17 points, seven rebounds and five assists. It was a great experience playing in Finland. The people there were so nice. I'm getting to do what I love and seeing the world at the same time. You can't beat that. I sat out last year to spend time with my daughter. But now I'm heading back overseas. I just signed with Estonia.

## NEW ADDITION

My life changed a few years ago when I became a father. My daughter, Aleena Mae Stewart, is almost 2 now. It's honestly the best thing that's ever happened to me – better than anything in my life. There will never be anything that tops being a father. If this would've happened five or six years ago, I would've been like, "Man, I'm not ready for a kid. I don't want a kid." But seeing my daughter's eyes light up when I walk in the room or hearing her cry when I leave, it's just a crazy feeling to know that one human being is depending on you so much. I love it.

No one really knows this, but I had to watch my daughter's birth on Skype. I had to watch my daughter come into this world on Skype. If it wasn't for Skype, I wouldn't have had a chance to see it. I was playing in Finland, and I had my best game that day. I think I scored 30 points. It's amazing I did that well, because I was so excited about my daughter being born that I couldn't really focus. I knew she was going to be born right after the game, because they had induced my girlfriend a little earlier. I just kept looking at the clock. It was the longest, slowest game I've ever played. I wanted it to be over so bad. After the games there, they give a gift to the player of the game, which was me. I didn't care about any of that. I didn't wait around. I ran straight from the court back to the apartment. I just wanted to see my daughter come into the world.

For the next few months I'd see her every day on Skype. She saw me so much on Skype that, when I came home for Christmas, she recognized my face. I was supposed to be home for four days at Christmas, but I got stuck in Amsterdam for two days because of the snow. I was like, "Man, that's two days I'm losing being with my daughter." After I finally got to see her, it made it that much harder to leave. I honestly didn't want to go back. I felt like I was abandoning my family. I was over in Europe, playing basketball and having fun. And my girlfriend was back in Kansas, going to school and trying to take care of our daughter. I felt like I should be back here experiencing that with her. But she made it clear that she didn't see it that way. It made me feel better about going back to Finland. Basketball isn't just a game anymore. I've got a family now. I'm playing for them as much as I'm playing for myself.

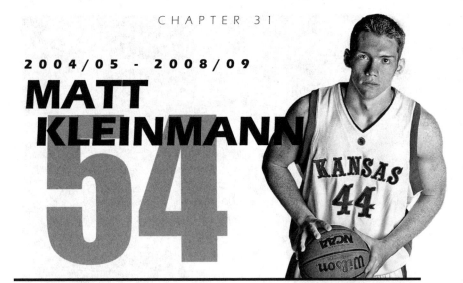

# CHAPTER 31

**2004/05 - 2008/09**

# MATT
# KLEINMANN
# 54

Matt Kleinmann spent five years on the Kansas men's basketball team as a walk-on. After finishing a master's degree in architecture, the Overland Park native moved on to Washington University in St. Louis for graduate school to study urban design. His studies have taken him to China, Argentina, Brazil, Peru and Bolivia in recent months. Following school, Matt began working for Helix Architecture in Kansas City.

## IN MATT'S WORDS

I remember last year, Turner Gill, the KU football coach, caught flak for not letting his guys have cell phones. People don't realize, they took our cell phones away from us for an entire year in 2006-07.

I remember we were all in Maui. We were in the back row as a team at the Maui Invitational at the dinner banquet. And we were all leaning back. We all had our cell phones out and were texting away, because the banquet was boring and they kept going on and on. And I think it was Danny Manning that caught us and brought it up the next day. I'm not sure we got our cell phones back before Christmas. It was a solid few months before we could have our cell phone in a hotel as a team.

The managers would come knock on the door and say, "Drop your cell phone in the bag." They'd walk on to the next room. By the end of the night, they'd have a bag full of cell phones, but I'm sure everybody else had a second or third somewhere in their shoe or hidden away in a bag somewhere.

## SNEAKING OUT

I remember my freshman year, we had a curfew ... we had curfews generally every year, at least for a short period of time. Anytime anything was handled internally as punishment, it's a safe bet that there's some sort of curfew in place for the month or so following.

And I remember it was nothing. It was a small, small little punishment. I just remember we all did our curfew check in our room, then we ran to Nick Bahe's room, then we all got together and we all ran out the basement door. We hopped in the car and took off, just a little bit of freedom one night. And we got caught by a manager. Thank God he didn't say anything, because I think we all would have had to run the next week if we had been caught.

That might have been the one time I knowingly broke curfew, because I was so scared of what would happen after that. Guys got caught breaking curfew maybe once a year, and that was the last time they ever broke curfew when that happened. When they were caught, there was always some sort of creative punishment.

I remember my very first summer, we had a guy named Jonas who was the strength coach for Roy. We had punishment that included us, it's hard to imagine, but us doing tuck-jumps — just jumping and bringing your knees to your chest — for 30 seconds on, then 30 seconds off. So we probably did 10 sets. Some ridiculous number of tuck jumps. Tuck jumps are fine, but when you're jumping on one those blue mats that people land in a track pit — one of those big, squishy blue mats — it's torture.

And I think more people than not threw up that day. It's never punishment. It was a good workout, but gosh, if you broke curfew or you ever broke a rule, it was generally a safe bet that if you weren't in good shape, you were going to throw up the next day or week.

## COACH SELF

If there's anything that Coach Self did that's worthy of applause, it's the way he helped shape guys. Some guys came in there with a chip on their shoulder. Some guys came in needing, for lack of a better term, an attitude adjustment. That's not any knock on them.

I briefly mentioned it in my senior speech, but I think what Coach did with those guys to me is more impressive than any wins or losses. That's what I'm probably most proud of being a part of, just seeing those guys come around.

There are days when Coach intentionally provokes a guy. I don't know if Coach does it personally or not. I'd like to think he does it intentionally, because if not, he's just being mean some days. But he's not a mean guy.

Some guys would crack. They wouldn't break down and cry, but they'd want to call it quits. Some guys tried to. Some guys tried to get in trouble. They tried to be stubborn.

## RUSSELL ROBINSON

The guys I'm most proud of are the guys that it's very clear their lives took a different direction while in Lawrence.

I remember vividly one night we got beat by 21 points by Villanova in Philly at 76ers Arena. So then we're getting chewed out, which is normal after a devastating loss. And we're getting ready to go home, and we got snowed in. So we had packed all of our bags, had gotten on the airplane, had been on the tarmac like an hour, had to go check back into our hotel. So we must have watched the game two or three times that night.

And I just remember Coach just wasn't happy with Russell. Russell played in the first half a little bit, then he got benched in the second half, then he got yelled at. He wasn't playing well, and Coach was trying to motivate him.

But when Coach asked him later if he wanted to go back in, Russell said, "No, Coach, I'm fine. I'm good." That, I think, more than anything, upset Coach. We could have lost by five, we could have lost by 100, but for a guy to say, "Coach, I really don't want to play any more," for him to say that to Coach was kind of like a, "What is this? You're not going to try?"

I think after that night, we all thought Russell was going to transfer. And he didn't. He stuck around.

I remember Russell trying to fight everybody on the team. And I remember Russell fighting Darnell. I remember Russell trying to fight Coach. I remember Russell trying to fight me. And Russell's not the only one. I guarantee one person every year gets picked on, and the reason they get picked on is if Coach can get under their skin, they will learn how to not let things get under their skin. And they'll do so with the help of teammates that are senior leaders who will take them aside after practice.

I remember I'd say this to some guys like Marcus and Markieff Morris. I was fortunate enough to be in a position where I could take them aside and say, "Look, today's your day. Today, Coach is going to say you're doing everything wrong, that you're not breathing right, that you're not walking right. Don't let it bother you, because he's doing it to make you better." I think Russell had one entire year of Coach getting under his skin. It was every day. And he took it in stride like a man and he battled through it and he became a national champion.

Russell was a winner. And by the end of it, he was Coach Self's favorite player. Coach would tell that to us in person: "Russell's my favorite player." And that's just how it was, because he'd been through the most adversity through Coach. Coach came hardest on him, and he responded the best.

## DARNELL JACKSON

When looking back at my time of KU, one thing I think about is having been with Darnell through everything that he went through – everything from being suspended to losing his grandmother in a car wreck. I wasn't there for a lot of one-on-one conversation and stuff, but I was there around him while it all happened.

I remember this did happen: Darnell had his girlfriend at the time, and his brother came up from Oklahoma, and they helped pack him up. And I saw him walking out of the Towers. And I remember helping him move out. And that was one of the toughest things I've had to do, but I was like, "Well, I'm either going to watch him move out or I'm going to help him."

Darnell's in the NBA right now, and he's making a living doing what he loves, and I couldn't be prouder. But I just remember that moment when he was driving away from the Towers, I was thinking, "I might not ever see this guy again." So, moments like that make you really proud. Guys in Lawrence changed. From where Russell came from, from where Sherron came from, from where the twins came from ... everybody that shows up in Lawrence, by the time they leave, they've either matured or they've had to fight to make themselves fit in.

## PICKUP SCUFFLE

One time, we had a pickup game in the volleyball gym, and it was over the summer. I remember Darnell and Russell got into it. Somebody must have thrown an elbow inadvertently and somebody took it the wrong way. Then it just became, "Well, I'm going to get you back. Who's the bigger man?" These are two of the most stubborn guys I've played with, and they're two of the best guys I've ever played with.

But one of them kept saying, "Cross this line. Cross this line." And the other one kept crossing. He'd step behind the baseline, "Cross this line." They'd try to tackle each other, then they'd try to wrestle for a second like brothers do. Guys that are close have a familiar bond to try to prove who's the bigger man. Darnell and Russell was a pretty fun matchup to watch. But I think by the end of it, Russell was laying on his chest or Darnell was laying on his chest and somebody was saying, "I quit. I quit. I'm transferring." We were all just sitting there laughing.

## BRANDON RUSH

Brandon was the coolest cat out there. Some days, Coach would try to faze Brandon. He'd try to get in his head. He'd try to tell him he's not as good as his brother. He'd just try to make him show emotion. We'd always have a good laugh. If we ever watched game film and would see Brandon yell — like he'd actually show a little bit of passion in the game — we'd have to rewind it and watch it again. It was so rare to see.

There's one great clip we always enjoyed. Brandon must have hit a jumper or dunked it and gotten a foul and a timeout happened right afterwards. Mario went up to celebrate with Brandon, and he gave him a big ol' chest bump at half-court, and if you watch Brandon's reaction, Brandon kind of shies away from it. He's getting ready to jump into it, then he kind of turns his shoulder and doesn't really jump. We like to joke that that epitomized how Brandon liked to be. Nothing fazes him, and yet, you get him in a game, and he could go for

20 points and again, it wouldn't faze him.

We used to run out of the tunnel, and I'd tease him and ask him if he was asleep. If you ever watched us running out of the tunnel, I'd always run right behind Brandon because of the height order, and I'd pass him. I'd pass him every single time running out of the tunnel, and I wasn't running fast. I was the slowest guy on the team by far, but I'd pass him running out on the court.

And it was because ... I don't know if he was in the zone or that's just his demeanor. I just think it was just his demeanor. That's who he was.

## PLAYING ROUGH

The two stupidest things I did involved hurting guys that were already hurt or couldn't afford to get hurt.

I remember my very first year, my very first month of practice, Wayne Simien was coming down the lane on a fast-break drill. I was the last guy back, and I didn't know what to do. Wayne was coming at me with a full head of steam. And I love Wayne to death, but I was scared of him at that moment.

I just jumped, and I think I got tangled with him, and I'm not the most athletic guy, as you can tell. I fouled him pretty hard. He came down pretty hard.

I think Coach Self's comment, to paraphrase, was, "What the hell are you doing? You, we don't care about. Wayne, everybody cares about." And he was right. If Wayne would have broken anything in his body that day, I can honestly say I would not be having this conversation with you, because I wouldn't be on the team anymore.

I think Shady (Darrell Arthur) used to get pissed off at me a lot, and Sasha used to get pissed off at me a lot, because I'd foul them. I would intentionally foul them sometimes, because it was just the way my nature is.

And I remember Sasha had a root canal one year. If you would have seen his face, he looked like the Elephant Man. He had a giant lip sticking out of his mouth. He looked as ugly as sin. He was playing a zone defense, and in my defense, I didn't know what Coach was doing putting him in the drill, because he wasn't going to play that game.

But they had him on the baseline, and he's running the offense. This is a walk-through. And my job as a zone offensive player was to turn around and screen. Simple job. We were literally walking.

And I turn around and I put my shoulder in a spot where it should be for a screen and Sasha turns kind of quickly and his lip hits my shoulder. I think Sasha was on the ground crying. I mean, this was probably the most painful feeling you could have ever imagined. His face was oozing puss it was so sensitive. And here I was, throwing my shoulder into Sasha's lip.

It's one of those things, you can't say, "I didn't mean to do it," because you did it. I got a pretty good tongue-lashing from Coach that day, because I had no defense. It was my shoulder.

I just remember feeling like I had to apologize to every single person in the world that day, because Sasha is there looking like hell and crying because he's in so much pain. And it's a walk-through. I think that was the worst, because it came out of Coach Self's mouth. "Matt, it's a freakin' walk-through. What are you doing?"

## LEFT-HANDED HOOKS

People thought I was a left-handed shooter, and I have Coach Jankovich to thank for that. When we would do big-man drills, there would be about seven guys, and the way he'd break it up on baskets is that there would be two guys on each basket. There's three baskets that we had, then one in the middle that's really unsuitable for the drills we're trying to do. So if we split it up evenly, I'm the odd man out.

Sometimes, he'd just say, "Matt, just work on your left-handed hook shot." And I'd work on that shot for a half hour before I'd rejoin practice.

And there were times where I'd say something to Coach Jankovich, and he'd take it the wrong way and get pissed off and say, "Matt, shut the bleep up and go shoot some left-handed hook shots." Those are the kinds of moments, I look back on them now and I laugh. What little career on the court I had, I can honestly say I probably would have scored half the points if I hadn't practiced my left-handed hook shot. Who's honestly going to shoot a left-handed hook shot in a game? And that was the one thing I did pretty well.

## MIP

If you want to say the punishment doesn't fit the crime, I had five years of verbal abuse for a five-minute ordeal.

What happened was, my brother was getting married, and it was my freshman year. From the moment I set foot on campus to about February, I would go out with the guys on the team, and we'd go to bars and we'd drink. It's what college kids did. It's not like I did it every night or anything. But I wouldn't do it every night. School always came first for me.

I think it got to the point by February where I was going to church a lot with Wayne, and Wayne was really instrumental in my life. He was kind of motivating me to be better and have a better legacy than going out to bars a lot. And, as a freshman, you're kind of malleable. You'll listen to whoever will take some interest. So by February, I said, "I'm not going out anymore."

Well, my brother was going to have a bachelor party in St. Louis and he wanted me to come, but of course, I couldn't. So, to make up for that, he and his friends came to Lawrence — he and his law-school buddies. My brother Derek literally said, "Matt, let's go out and get one drink at The Wheel." And I was like, "Well, I don't want to get an MIP. I don't want to get in trouble." It was Sunday night. And he was like, "Look, we'll go at 8 o'clock. Dinner time.

No one's going to care."

So we show up, and I think I'd had one beer, and I had another one in my hand. And we snuck in the back of The Wheel. And I turn around and face the back door, and all of a sudden a cop walks in, and I make eye contact with him. And like a scared little freshman in college, I turned around right away and set my beer down and acted like nothing happened. This cop comes right up to me and he says, "You play basketball, don't you?" And I said, "Yes sir." And he said, "Well, you're not old enough to be here then. Let's go."

So he takes me outside and gives me an MIP — a minor in possession — which basically is a misdemeanor offense, which in the grand scheme of things is about as little as you can get for drinking underage. And I took it like a man, but as soon as I called Coach Self to tell him the news, I was so worried he was going to kick me off the team or that my career was done or he was going to run me until I puked every day for the rest of the year. And he didn't do a thing. He told me years later why. He said, "Matt, we didn't worry about you. You were the most mature kid on the team. And yet, here you were, you were so sad, the only thing we could do was tease you about it, because you were moping around for a month after that. You were so scared to offend anyone."

## MAKING THE NEWS

I think it took me about two to three years before I was able to roll with the punches and give it back as soon as I got it. It's funny now, because I look back on it, my brother paid for my MIP, I got a diversion, nothing happened. I think I showed up in court one day to say, "Yes, I'll take a diversion." And nothing happened, and nobody knew about it until J.R. Giddens got stabbed.

The day J.R. got stabbed was the worst day, because A) we got in trouble, B) J.R. was hurt, and we were really worried about J.R., and C) that was the day that the Lawrence Journal-World decided to run a little paragraph at the end of the J.R. column — the column that everybody in KU has to read — and the very last little blurb was, "Also, a couple months ago — a couple months ago! — freshman redshirt walk-on Matt Kleinmann got an MIP for drinking underage." And I must have gotten 20 phone calls that day from friends and family saying, "What?" They didn't even know about it. I'd forgotten about it. I'd let it be water under the bridge, because I figured, "Nobody knows, nobody cares." And until J.R. got stabbed, nobody knew.

It was like one of those media things where they wanted to make a mountain out of a molehill. So, "J.R. got stabbed, oh yeah, Matt Kleinmann had a beer at 8 o'clock with his brother to celebrate his brother's wedding." It was a funny moment, but I'm glad it happened in retrospect, because if nothing else, Coach Self learned my name pretty quickly, because he cracked jokes on me with the best of them.

## PICKED ON

Coach Dooley and Coach Townsend together would go at me about the MIP. It was kind of a rite of passage, but it was a rite of passage that lasted for five years to the point that I could laugh at myself after a couple of years. The worst thing was, I used to hear this every day from Dooley. And I never really understood what it was coming from, but years later I found out that Steve Vinson and Christian Moody, my fellow walk-ons no less, they were behind my back saying, "Dooley, Dooley, you've got to get him today. You've got to say something." This would be in the huddle — team huddles. They would be standing behind me and they'd be pointing at me and they'd be cracking up, pretending I was drinking and they'd try to make up some jokes when they were alone.

Steve and Christian would be like, "Matt, it's OK, you've just got to deal with it." And then they'd go to Dooley and say, "Hey Dooley, tomorrow, you've got to tell him this about his MIP." That's the kind of stuff I miss.

Coach Townsend would always say stuff like, "You're the biggest criminal on our team. You've got a record. You'll never get a credit card. You can't run for Senate. You can't do anything." And he'd say all these things like they were the end of the world. But Coach Townsend is probably one of my favorite coaches of all time, because he'd say stuff like that, he'd say it in love. He'd say it because he enjoyed talking to you. But he'd do it to the point where you'd just want to tell him to shut up.

I used to do team prayers after Christian Moody left. After he graduated, my role on the team was kind of a minor team chaplain. My job was to do a team prayer and say, "God, protect us and don't let us get hurt today. Let us perform up to the best of our abilities for Your glory." And I would say that kind of stuff, and every once in a while, you get Coach Dooley or Coach Townsend whispering, "We've got an ex-felon here saying this."

Those are the kind of ribbings I got on a daily basis. And I loved it. I think just as a person, that matured me a lot, to realize that some things are worth taking seriously and some things are not.

I will say this: I got my revenge. One nice perk of being an architecture major is you learn how to Photoshop. I took the time to Photoshop every single person in some way or form to make fun of them.

So I had one of Coach Dooley — Coach Dooley sweats a lot, I don't know if you ever noticed. He sweats more than anyone has a right to sweat. I Photoshopped his face onto a Right Guard commercial with his armpits hanging out. I remember Sherron used to give me a hard time about stuff. I got him looking like Frank Thomas the baseball player, something everybody used to tease him about. There were so many little ones. I remember Quintrell Thomas, everybody used to tease him about being thirsty. It was a saying we used to have. I put him in a Gatorade advertisement, a printed advertisement saying, "Quench Your Thirst." And I put these all up the very last week of practice, and I put them all in the locker room hallway. And I think practice started like an hour late that day because everybody was too busy laughing at each other.

## ONE-LINER

The only other good joke I had ... I don't think anybody else thinks this is very funny, but I thought it was pretty good. I showed up late one day to a shootaround before a game. We were playing DePaul in the Fieldhouse. It's a 9 a.m. shootaround — there's no exercise, but normally, it's an hour-long practice. But at a 9 a.m. shootaround, there's 20 minutes of just going over scouting report basically.

I don't know what I'd done, but I slept in that morning and I didn't get to practice until 9:17. So three minutes before walk-around ends, I show up. And I felt like crap. I even got into a little fender-bender pulling out of my garage because I was in such a rush.

I was scared to death, and I ran in there scared to death, chills sent down my spine. And they didn't say anything to me. And they didn't do anything, until the game.

The game comes around, and I would have probably played a minute or two. I probably would have played two minutes, because we were up by 20 with two minutes to go. Everybody else played but me.

We get to the locker room, and Coach goes through his postgame stuff, says good job. And then he looks at me and says, "Matt, do you know why you didn't play?" And I said, "Yeah, Coach, I understand." I had no hard feelings.

Coach Self had walked out of the locker room. Usually after the game, every assistant coach comes in and has a one-on-one conversation with each player just to say, "Good job" or "Bad job." But Coach Townsend, of all people, gets up to me and says, "Jesus, Matt, you must have been drunk last night. You must have been drunk this morning, got another MIP." Just giving me grief.

I was in good nature, and I was ready for it, so I think I came back with the quick comment, "Well, yeah, I could have got a speeding ticket, got my car towed, got arrested and maybe broke up a bar fight and you guys would have started me."

No one that heard it laughed. Everybody's eyes widened, and Coach Townsend said, "You'd better not say that around Coach Self."

My teammates probably all had that happen, and I wasn't singling anybody out; it's just one of those things I'd prepared in advance for when Coach Townsend or Coach Dooley got after me. It was just the right time. I think Coach Townsend chuckled a little bit, but I think he was kind of scared that if I would have said that around Coach Self, I would have gotten in a little bit more trouble for it.

There was one game — it was the next game I think — where we were worried Brandon was going to get pulled off by a state trooper when we crossed the Kansas-Missouri line because he had unpaid parking tickets. And we were playing Missouri. So they thought there was a threat out there — a rumor — that some Missouri state trooper that was a Missouri alum was going to get on our bus and take Brandon to jail. And that kind of stuff happened maybe every year — somebody got in trouble with a parking ticket, or somebody got in trouble with something. So my comment was, "I showed up 17 minutes late, and I regret that, but I'm pretty sure two minutes wasn't the end of my world."

So I like to tell that story, but I don't know if Coach Self ever heard it.

## FLORIDA GAME

I remember we played Florida in Las Vegas in 2006, and the game before, we barely beat Ball State. We were in the hotel that night, and we were getting chewed out. Coach was so pissed at us that he said, "Look, we're not going to talk right now. I'm too mad too talk. I want each of you to come up with one thing that you think we as a team do right, then come down and tell me in two hours."

So we go up to our hotel rooms, and everybody's pointing the finger at everybody. We're getting ready to play Florida, the defending national champion, the next day. And not one guy on the team could look at another guy and smile. Everybody wanted to fight everybody.

I remember Mario and Julian got into it. I remember we had to separate Mario and Julian because they were blaming each other for the previous game's poor performance on both their parts. We got them into their separate rooms, and guys on the team talked to them individually. I think I talked to both of them. Guys were just frustrated. Nobody wanted to lose by 50 points the next day to Florida, and at that moment, we all thought we were going to lose by 50 points, because we could barely beat Ball State. How are we supposed to beat Horford, Brewer and Noah?

We came back, there was a team meeting that night, and I think I was the only one that did not get a bad answer from Coach. I remember guys said, "We play hard defense." Just standard material. And Coach was like, "No, you don't." And he'd point out exact examples of guys not playing hard defense. The next guy, "We shoot the ball well." "No, you don't." And he points out exact examples. "We try hard." "No, you guys don't." And he'd say exactly what happened. I think the best one was, "We show up to practice on time." Coach Ballard says, "No, you don't. Mario and Brandon have shown up late every day this week" or something like that.

Nobody could get a word in. I think mine was the best only because I put a lot of thought into it. I knew going in he was going to tear us apart for whatever we said, because he was probably going to be right. And my answer was, "We get the ball out of the basket quickly when the other team scores."

I think everybody just kind of laughed, because nobody expected that. "Great, Matt. The best thing we do — the only thing we do well — is when the other team scores, we get the ball out quickly." I think that was kind of the best moment of laughter that night.

Nobody went to bed thinking we were going to win, and then we came out and killed them. Well, we didn't kill them. It was a close game, but if you watch that game, we smoked them. They kept the game close because they're really, really good. We weren't really, really good yet. But Julian played the game of his life. Mario, Brandon, everybody on that team performed excellently. And we smoked them. If you watch our reaction, we know that we should not have won that game, and we won it.

I still remember 'Spoon — Brad Witherspoon — running through the court and popping his Kansas jersey, and that made it on SportsCenter Top Ten that night. It was just those kinds of moments ... those are some of the best moments. We didn't win a national championship for another couple of years, but if you'd have asked any of us at that moment what it felt like, we felt like we were the national champions. Outside of the Memphis game and the North Carolina game and the Davidson game, that was probably my favorite game ever to be a part of the team, because 24 hours earlier, nobody gave us a chance. And we won.

## OUTSIDE LOOKING IN

I'm actually back in Kansas City now. But even when I was watching KU games in St. Louis, it's tough to watch them lose, but you can't get mad at them, because you know that the pressure is so high, and the expectations are so great. I watched as a fan growing up, watched as a player on the bench, I've played on the court, and now I'm watching as a fan looking back. You definitely get a different perspective. You don't live and die KU basketball anymore. At least I don't. But at the same time, I understand what everybody's going through.

# CHAPTER 32

# 2007/08 - 2009/10

# COLE ALDRICH

C ole Aldrich is a 6-foot-11 center who played three seasons at Kansas before the Oklahoma City Thunder made him the 11th overall pick in the 2010 NBA draft. Aldrich owns a 55-0 record at Allen Fieldhouse and ranks second on Kansas' all-time blocks list with 254. He was a third-team All-American as a senior. Although he was a freshman role player on Kansas' 2008 national championship squad, Aldrich made a huge contribution off the bench in the Jayhawks' semifinal victory over North Carolina, when his defense on All-American forward Tyler Hansbrough helped key the Kansas victory.

## IN COLE'S WORDS

By the end of my sophomore season I knew I wouldn't be at Kansas all four years. Sherron and I actually had a chance to leave right then, but it didn't feel right to either of us. We talked about it in the locker room a number of times that season. We were mad we didn't beat Michigan State in the Sweet 16. There's no way we should've lost that game. We thought if we matured and got better we could do some damage the next year.

There was never that one definitive moment where we were like, "Yeah, let's do it. Let's come back." I just knew he was thinking about it and I was thinking about it. We had to do what was right for ourselves and our families. But we both knew it was a good choice to return to school. We were going to have a good team, and we wanted to leave a little bit of a legacy by getting to the Final Four again.

For me personally, I wanted to leave my own footprints just like Darnell and Sasha and Shady and Wayne and Nick and Drew and all the big men that came before me. I looked up to those guys. I wanted to be thought of just like them and maybe someday have my name in the rafters. Sherron felt the same way.

We looked at each other and said, "That's our goal." We wanted to see another national championship banner in the rafters and, hopefully, our jerseys, too.

## HOOKED

I was in the eighth grade the first time I visited Kansas. One of my AAU coaches said, "Hey, I've got a sister that lives in Lawrence. Do you want to go to a Kansas game sometime?" I was all for it, so we drove down, and the team managers showed us around Allen Fieldhouse. I thought, "Wow, this place is really cool." Six months later they offered me a scholarship. I was only a high school freshman, so I thought that was pretty cool. I committed on my birthday of my junior year. It came down to Kansas, Minnesota and North Carolina.

About a year before that, while I was still looking at other schools, my summer league team was in the Jayhawk Invitational in Lawrence. About 200 KU fans showed up at all of our games to watch me play. I was like, "You guys are nuts. I'm only a sophomore in high school." It was an early taste of the kind of support I was going to get at Kansas.

## "I WASN'T READY"

When I showed up as a freshman at Kansas I wasn't ready to play. I got my ass kicked every day. I had the size, but the game was faster than what I was used to, and those guys were older and stronger than me. It got to the point where I was like, "Man, this isn't any fun."

You name it, and those guys did it to me. Shady dunked on me at every practice. I'd tried to block his shot but he'd throw it down right over me. He was only a sophomore but he played like a senior. Sasha has some of the boniest elbows around, and he was really good at hitting me with them in every place

imaginable. My shoulder, my bicep, my face. Sometimes I was like, "Damn, Sasha, stop! I know you didn't mean to do it or anything, but jeez …" He could definitely push me around. At the time he was the strongest guy on our team. Once I ripped the webbing between my fingers going up for a rebound against Sasha. I had to get six stitches in my hand and the novocaine they used to numb it only worked for the first two stitches, so that wasn't very fun.

Everyone on the team stayed positive with me, though. They were really supportive. I kept on fighting. I treated every day in practice like it was a game, like it was my chance to show I was getting better, because I knew I wasn't going to play in the games unless we were blowing someone out. The work started paying off toward the end of the season.

## FINAL FOUR

When we went to the Final Four in 2008, I didn't expect to play very much. Darnell and Shady were starting in the paint, and Sasha was doing a great job off the bench. I had been taking some of Rodrick Stewart's minutes the last few weeks of the regular season, but I still didn't think I'd play much of a role in a situation like the one we were in. To me it didn't even feel like the Final Four. It just seemed like another big game. Once we started going over the scouting report, though, I could tell I might get the chance to contribute. North Carolina had Tyler Hansbrough, who was an All-American and a really, really good player.

I watched a bunch of extra film on Hansbrough and thought, "Hey, if I get into the game, I know what he'll struggle against. I know what's going to bother him." You've got to be physical with him. You've got to play long because he struggles to shoot over length. You've got to get him out of his comfort zone and keep him off the boards. It didn't take long during the game to tell that he was frustrated. You could see it on his face. We rushed him with four big guys. How could he not get frustrated? He was 6-foot-8. Darnell was 6-8, Shady was 6-9, Sasha and I were 6-10 or 6-11. With all of those bodies coming at him in waves and waves … I mean, it was only natural that he got tired and rattled. I hardly got off the bench in the championship game against Memphis, but I was glad I was able to have a small impact against North Carolina (eight points, seven rebounds and four blocks in 16 minutes).

## AWESTRUCK BY ARTHUR

Mario hit the biggest shot when it mattered most and is obviously a great player. But if I had to choose one guy that was consistent all year when it came to doing big things, it was probably Shady. Even on nights when he didn't play all that great, he'd still score 15 points. He was so athletic. He could run the floor like crazy. In practice he'd put a full-court press on the guards simply because he could. He could run for days. Last year in the NBA, when we played Memphis,

I guarded Shady. It was a little awkward, but you've got to get over it quick. You check in and say, "Hey what's up? You been doing well? Cool. I'm going to try to kick your ass now."

## BIG MAN ON CAMPUS

As a Kansas basketball player you're always in the spotlight. But winning the championship took things to a whole new level. We had no privacy. The only privacy we had was when we were in our rooms at Jayhawker Towers. Even now, I've been gone for a year, and people still stop me on the streets and say stuff about the championship whenever I'm back in town. It's awesome that people remember you and still follow you. It takes some getting used to but you learn to appreciate it.

I hear about it a lot in the NBA, too. There are Jayhawk fans all across the country. We were in Sacramento, and the alumni association from that city had people at our game just because Nick and I were on the team and we were playing the Kings, who have Darnell on their roster. I took pictures with 30 people after the game. While all of it was going on, the other guys on the team just sat there and stared at us, stunned. They're not used to seeing something like that.

## FOREVER LINKED

With five seniors graduating and Mario, Brandon and Shady all entering the draft early, Sherron and I were the only returning players in 2008-09 who had seen much playing time the year before. The assumption was that we were in a "rebuilding year," but neither one of us wanted to settle for that. Sherron and I worked really well together. I think there was a mutual respect there that led to some really good chemistry on the court.

We hung out a little bit off the court, but we had an even stronger tie on the court. In the locker room we always talked to each other and said, "Hey, this is what you need to do and this is what I need to do." There was no bulls--t between us. If he was doing something he wasn't supposed to do, I'd yell at him. I'd cuss him out. If I was doing something I wasn't supposed to do, he'd cuss me out. There was something about Sherron that made people rally around him. He was so talented and he had such a confidence about him. It's hard not to follow a guy like that.

## SOPHOMORE SEASON

A couple of things from my sophomore season stand out. That was the year we got the twins, Marcus and Markieff, who went on to become great college players. They're very close, but they're also really competitive with one another. When they first got here, they thought they knew how to work hard, but they didn't. Once Coach Self broke that barrier, you could see them really, really improve. They were rebellious at first. They always wanted to do their own thing. They went through their struggles, but ultimately, when you look at them now, they've come a long way.

We used to just call them "twin" because we didn't know which one was which. Being around them long enough, you can start to see the difference. Markieff's face is a little longer, and he's a little taller. Marcus is a little quieter.

I know last year they had a few technical fouls, which made people think they played dirty at times. I played with them for two years and I never thought they played dirty or cheap or anything. You're fighting guys to win a ball game, so you're going to be physical. But I've never seen them do anything cheap. You get going in a game, and you're going after a rebound and you accidentally hit someone in the face. It happens. That's how I lost my tooth. It's part of the game. It's part of competing.

My sophomore year was also the season I got one of my front teeth knocked out. It happened early in our home game against Kansas State. I don't even know exactly how it happened or who did it, but I must've been hit pretty damn hard, because I had my mouth-guard in and my tooth still got knocked loose. We were shooting free throws, and my girlfriend was sitting in the family section behind the opponents' bench. I smiled at her and my mouthguard was filled with blood. She had this worried look on her face and mouthed to me, "What happened?" I could feel that my tooth was crooked in there. The doctor came over and said, "We'll probably have to take it out in the morning." I was like, "OK, can I keep playing tonight, though?" He said he didn't see why not.

## MAKING HISTORY

We ended up losing to Michigan State in the Sweet 16, but the game before that, in the second round, I had a triple-double against Dayton with 13 points, 20 rebounds and 10 blocks. It was the sixth official triple-double in NCAA Tournament history and the first in Kansas history, although Wilt Chamberlain probably would've had plenty if they would've kept those kinds of stats when he played. What made it so special was that the game took place in Minneapolis, just a few miles from my home in Bloomington. I actually struggled offensively that game. I felt like I couldn't hit a shot. But they kept on driving into the lane. I'd block their shot and we'd get a little run-out. I was more impressed with the 20 rebounds than the 10 blocks. I didn't think about the triple-double until I came to the sideline near the end of the game. The guys were like, "You got it! You got it! You got a triple-double!"

## TRYING TIMES

All indications after my sophomore season were that I'd be a first-round pick if I left school and entered the NBA draft. I didn't feel like I was ready, and no one was pushing me to go. That includes my parents, who were experiencing some pretty tough times because of the poor economy. My dad was going through unemployment and whatnot. He had been laid off. My mom was an embroiderer and things weren't going well for her, either. They couldn't get cable TV anymore because of the cost. I think they even quit using Caller ID just to save some money. Still, my parents were like, "You've got to do what you think is right. We're not going to tell you to go because things are tough at home. We're not going to pressure you to do it or not to do it. You've got to do what you want to do." I'm fortunate to have parents like that.

During my final season, my junior year, my dad moved to Lawrence and lived with a good family friend of ours. He got a sheet metal job in Topeka and worked there most of the year. It was tough doing the long-distance thing with my mom, but it certainly helped pay the bills. Plus, it was nice to have him here to see all my games. He didn't live with me, though. We would've driven each other nuts.

### OH HENRY

Everyone from the 2008-09 team returned for my junior year, so we knew we were going to have some really good chemistry with Sherron and the Morrises and Brady and Tyrel. We also signed Xavier Henry that spring. Xavier and I got along really well. He definitely helped our team, because we added another guy that was offensively polished. The year before, Sherron and I took most of the shots. If we didn't get those shots up and we didn't score, we probably weren't going to win. So having Xavier really helped. He could've been a Brandon Rush-type of a player if he stayed at Kansas longer. He was really athletic and he could defend and score. If he stayed two or three years he could've really been special. I don't think Xavier did anything to hurt our team chemistry. He's one of the nicest guys I know. He was always smiling. It got to the point where I had to tell him to stop smiling. We spent a ton of time going to dinner and doing this and that. I know he enjoyed his time here.

### NICE JOB, ROOMIE

I lived with Tyrel Reed throughout my time at Kansas. It was really fun watching him improve so much my junior year. He definitely came a long way. His freshman year, he was so nervous. He couldn't do a thing without being nervous. He'd call out a play in practice, and then he'd dribble that ball 50 frickin' times before he passed it. Then he'd get it back and dribble it 50 more times. Coach Self would jump on him and he didn't know how to react. I still give him crap about it.

I used to have some fun with Tyrel once I lost my tooth. I had a fake tooth made that was attached to a retainer. Each night, I'd take it out and place it right next to his toothbrush, so it'd be waiting for him when he woke up each morning. I'm pretty sure it grossed him out.

Tyrel and I created a really strong bond. We still go to dinner and get some shots up or go hang out and play video games. From where he started to where he finished … it's night and day. He puts a lot of pressure on himself. He's a Kansas kid who grew up dreaming about coming here. He grew up watching Kirk and Nick and Drew and all of those guys. He probably never would've imagined that he would've played here and started and accomplished all the things that he accomplished. He just tried to fulfill that dream he had as a

kid. In my mind, he went far beyond what he ever imagined he would do.

## EARLY EXIT

The final game of my college career came against Northern Iowa in the second round of the NCAA Tournament. They were very good. Looking back on it, though, their big guy (Jordan Eglseder) had gone 1-for-9 from 3-point range all year. One of the first shots he took was a 3. I wasn't going to guard him because I knew he wasn't going to make it. He missed it – but then he made his next two. In my head I was thinking, "What the hell? This isn't what they've done all year." Then there was the play with Ali Farokhmanesh. We were making our comeback, and he hit that long 3. I was sitting on the bench as the ball was in the air thinking, "Hey, this is good for us." We had turned them over a few times before that, they were flustered and now the guy was taking this long 3 early in the shot clock. I figured we'd get the rebound and get a run-out and an easy basket. Then he hits the shot and I'm like, "S--t!" It was a play where you know their coach was like, "Don't shoot it! Don't shoot it! Umm, good shot!" But that's how it is. You get a team that gets hot … I mean, they probably should've beat Michigan State in the Sweet 16, but Kalin Lucas hit a game-winner.

People can say we played nervous. But whether we played nervous or not, we faced a team that said, "Hey, we're going to live by the 3 today. We might win or we might get killed by 50 points. But we're going to live and die by the 3. If we can make it a close game, we've got a shot at them."

Everyone was disappointed about it. You work so hard for so long. You know what it takes to get to the final game, but it doesn't happen. Think about it, though: Other than Michigan State the last few years, there's not one team recently that's consistently been in the Final Four over the years. It doesn't happen for the same school every year. People don't realize how hard it is to get there.

## LIFE AS A PRO

My first NBA season in Oklahoma City had its ups and downs. Getting drafted at No. 11, I knew I was coming into a good team. We had Serge Ibaka and Nick Collison and Jeff Green and some others. I knew I was going into a situation where nothing was guaranteed and that it was going to be more of a learning year for me. But it was a lot of fun. The NBA is a lot different. In so many situations, you're on your own whereas you wouldn't be in college. On the road a few guys will go out to eat together. Some guys won't leave the room. There was a lot more free time, which was always enjoyable. If you wanted, you could get up at 8 in the morning and go for a run and get some coffee as long as you're on the bus when they tell you to be.

Having Nick in Oklahoma City has been great. He's been a really good influence on me. We definitely went to dinner quite a bit. Not every team has a guy that's been in the league for eight years that will say, "You're a young kid. I'm going to help you out." He works hard, he's never in trouble, he does the right things … he's just a caring guy, a good guy, a true professional.

From the time I went from training camp until the end of the season, I definitely felt like I made a lot of strides. The game is different, the pace is different. Playing in the D-League for a while was really beneficial. The first time you get sent down, it's tough. You don't know what to expect. Are the guys on the team going to like you? Traveling is different, the hotels are different. When I'm traveling with the Thunder, we have our own plane. You get your own room at the Westin or the Ritz Carlton. I get my own room with the D-League, too. When you're on a call-down, you get your own room and you get to fly first class, even though not every airline we fly has first class. You stay at Holiday Inn Express and places like that. They're not terrible hotels, but they're not what you're used to.

One thing that's really good about Oklahoma City is the fans. They really get behind the team down there. I've been lucky to play in two places that get a lot of support. I get tickets to every home game, but sometimes I just don't have anyone to give them to. In those cases I usually get on Twitter and have some sort of contest where a fan can win my tickets. I'll just get their name and leave the tickets at will call. It's nice to be able to give back.

There are going to be some open minutes next year. Myself, Nazr Mohammed, B.J. Mullens … we're all going to have to fight for them, but there will definitely be some opportunities. I'm in great shape right now. I'm about 241 pounds. I feel quicker and stronger than I ever have. I lifted every day last year and I developed a nice hook shot. I'll keep working and working until I get my chance, just like I did at Kansas.

# CHAPTER 33

# 2006/07 - 2009/10
# SHERRON COLLINS

S herron Collins is a strong candidate to have his No. 4 jersey retired at Allen Fieldhouse after finishing his career as the fifth-leading scorer in Kansas history. The Chicago native also ranks seventh all-time in assists. A tremendous leader on the court, Collins played his best late in the game when the score was tight. He was an unsung hero in Kansas' victory over Memphis in the 2008 NCAA title game and ended his career with a record of 130-19. Collins played most of the 2010-11 NBA season with the Charlotte Bobcats.

## IN SHERRON'S WORDS

The day I left for Kansas, I cried like a baby. I was at Midway Airport in Chicago, and I missed two flights to Kansas City while I just sat there and cried to my friend, Bo. I was so scared. I was actually ready to go a few days before that, but when the time finally came, I didn't want to leave. I had graduated from high school the day before. I wanted to hang around and chill with my classmates and go to Six Flags Great America. But I had to get to Lawrence for summer school. I finally got on a plane and flew to Kansas, but once I got there, I didn't think I was going to make it.

## ALMOST AN ILLINI

There was a time during the recruiting process when I didn't have any intention on even visiting Kansas. I was set on going to Illinois. It was close to home. That's all I cared about. I just wanted to be close to home. I'd talked to Bruce Weber and Dee Brown and Luther Head. They were like, "Coach is going to let you play. He'll let you do what you want to do." That all sounded great to me.

I remember one day, I was outside of Crane, my high school, talking to Tracy Webster, the Illinois assistant who was in charge of recruiting me. He had a letter of intent with him. I called Bo, who was advising me a little bit during recruiting, and told him I was going to sign the paper. Bo was like, "I'll be cool with whatever you want to do." Somehow, though, Coach (Anthony) Longstreet, my coach at Crane, caught word of what was going on outside. Coach Longstreet is a big guy, a heavy guy. I've never seen him run in my life. But he came running through the side of the door screaming, "Noooooo! You aren't signing anything!" He pointed his finger at Tracy Webster and said, "I told you already!" I didn't really know what they were talking about. But Longstreet told me the next day, "When schools like Duke, Kansas, North Carolina or Kentucky offers you a visit, you don't turn them down. You go visit no matter what the situation." So I went on my visit to Kansas, and once I got back, Illinois was out of the equation. I signed a day or two after my visit. Tracy Webster called me. He was so pissed.

Looking back, all that was kind of shady of (Webster), because Longstreet had told him I was going to take four visits. I had already been to Illinois, although that one was unofficial because it was so close that we just drove there. I also visited Georgia Tech unofficially my junior year. I wanted to go there at the time because Will Bynum, who went to my high school, was playing there and really liked it. There were a lot of comparisons between me and Will. But Georgia Tech ended up signing Javaris Crittenton, so they were out. Connecticut was in the mix until they signed Jerome Dyson, plus they already had A.J. Price.

## LURED TO LAWRENCE

When I went to Allen Fieldhouse on my visit, I walked through the tunnel and heard all these applause, but I didn't know they were for me. I didn't know they knew who I was. I finally realized it, so I started walking in and out on purpose, just so I could get the claps. When I sat down, Shady's mom (Sandra Arthur) grabbed me and asked me what I was going to do with my hair. I had braids at the time. She said, "Baby, what are you going to do with this when you come here?" I told her I was going to cut it. My high school coach was always on me about cutting it anyway, but I never wanted to do it.

We all went out that night. We went to Abe & Jake's. My hotel was right there by the bar, so it was cool. The next day we played pickup. I crossed Jeremy Case over so bad that I made him fall. Ever since then, when Brandon would stick me in practice, he'd get scared and say, "Oh s--t!" He'd start shuffling his feet and try not to fall. That was all because he remembered what I'd done to Case.

After that trip, I didn't need to take any more visits. My mind was made up. I was going to Kansas.

## ROOMIES

When I got to Kansas, I walked into my room and I saw Brady Morningstar. I was like, "Oh my God." A few months earlier, I had asked Bo who he thought

my roommate was going to be. He said he figured it would be Brady. I was like, "I don't want to share a room with no damn white boy." But they did it for a reason. I didn't find out about it until I got there, though. I was sitting on my bed unpacking, and Brady brought me some sheets from his parents' house in Lawrence. I started putting them on my bed. The first thing the dude asked me was, "Are you going out tonight?" And then he turned on some Jay-Z. I thought, "All right, I might be OK with this guy." Ever since then, me and Brady have been like brothers.

I'm scared of any dog. But with Brady's dog, Mackie … I wouldn't even go in his house at first. Mackie is a boxer, and the Morningstars have one of those front doors where you can push the top out and leave the bottom closed. The first time I went over there as a freshman, the entire door was open, and Mackie started barking at me and rushing me. I closed the bottom part of the door and told them I wasn't coming in the house unless they put the dog up. I walked back to the car, got inside and closed the door. Brady's mom, Linda, had to walk all the way out there and talk me into coming inside. The first time I was there they put the dog up, but the second time they wouldn't. They said I was going to have to get over my fear. I eventually learned that, if you give Mackie a treat, she'll listen to you. I'll tell her, "Mack, sit!" And then I'll say, "Shake" and she'll shake my hand, and I'll give her a treat. Mackie and I get along great now.

The Morningstars became like a second family to me. They treated me so well. Linda used to fix these big-ass sandwiches that Brady would bring back to the Towers. She'd make them in a pie frame and then cut them in fourths. You should've seen them. They were huge. Darnell spent a lot of time hanging out in our room that year. I think it was because he liked those sandwiches so much.

## FAMILY TRAGEDY

A few weeks after I got to Kansas, I had to rush back to Chicago because I had a son, Sherron Jr., who was born about three months premature. After about 10 days, his lungs stopped getting oxygen, and he died. It was one of the toughest things I've ever had to go through. The girl that I had him by, I thought it was her fault. During the time she was pregnant, she was still going clubbing and this and that. But we found out later that she couldn't have babies at that time in her life, because she ended up getting pregnant later by someone else. This time she had twins, and she lost them just like she lost my son. She had to have some sort of surgery so she could hold the babies for nine months. She's got a son now.

After the situation happened with my son, I wanted to leave Kansas. I wanted to go home for good. I didn't know what I was going to do. But my uncle, Walt, played a big part in me going back, and my mother did, too. She doesn't know the difference between a travel and a double-dribble. She knows nothing about basketball. But the education part was more important to her. She never went to college, so the fact that I was even enrolled in college was important to her. My auntie had a master's degree and my grandmother did, too. She just wanted me to get some sort of degree and enjoy the experience of it all.

Still, if they'd have given me more time to linger around Chicago, I'd have been stubborn and stayed. But they kept reinforcing what the right thing to do was. They were basically pushing me back toward Kansas. Coach Townsend flew up, too, to make sure everything was OK and that I was keeping my head on straight. Coach Self and his wife were great during that time, too. They were there for me.

## BIG MEN ON CAMPUS

Once I got back to Kansas, I learned real fast what it was like to be a basketball player in Lawrence. For one thing, no one lets you pay for your own drink. Everyone tries to buy you shots and tries to get you drunk. You have to be careful, because you could really get drunk if you actually took them all. You just have to say, "Thank you, but I'm not drinking tonight." I'd either do that or give them to my brother. It was like that every night we went out. It's still like that now. It happened last season when I went back during the all-star break. Most of the time you'll pay for the drink if you're actually standing there by the bartender – unless you know the bartender, in which case it's free as long as you tip them. Some nights, if my friends and family were in for a game, I'd have about seven people with me when I went out. We'd all be out at a bar, and just before I was about to pay for all of us, some stranger – a fan – would say, "No!" And then he'd tell the bartender, "Whatever Sherron owes you, just put it on my tab."

After we won the title, I probably didn't pay for food for three months. Every restaurant in town was trying to help us out. Before I'd even order, the waiter or manager would walk up and say, "This is going to be on us tonight, guys. Order whatever you want." It didn't matter if it was fast food or a steakhouse. My brothers didn't even pay for their meals. At the bars, we never had to wait in lines or worry about that kind of stuff. The doorman or the owner would just wave us all in. Even when we went to Power & Light in Kansas City, we weren't even 21 yet, but they were letting us walk past everyone and right into the bar without even ID'ing us.

The attention is going to go to your head regardless. The key is how you handle it. You've got to find a way to be humble. Luckily, because of the attention I got in high school, I was already prepared for it. I started my first few games as a freshman on a team full of seniors. I ended up coming off the bench because the fact that I was starting was f---ing with one of the senior's heads, but that was fine. They all left, and the team was mine my sophomore year. That's when I got noticed. That's when I got big. It all hit at once. Girls and publicity and letters and rankings. I went through it all for a whole summer and let it get to my head. When I got to Kansas, I had already been through it. Some guys hadn't, though, and some people definitely got lost in it for a while.

## COACH SELF

Coach Self has a guy he picks on every year. It was definitely me as a freshman. One time I stood up to him. I don't remember exactly what I said to him, but he got mad at me and kicked me out of practice. I was kicking over garbage cans and everything. He sent me to go find our strength coach – Coach (Andrea) Hudy – and run. I cramped up when I was running for Hudy and had to stop. He heard about it and made me finish it the next day. I knew he was picking on me. So I asked him, "What the helll do you have against me?" He said, "When I stop coaching you, that's when you worry." I thought about that for a couple of days. I realized the guys he yells at the most are the guys he expects more out of. He doesn't get on the lesser guys or the walk-ons nearly as much.

B-Rush actually told me I had it light. B-Rush said he was on his ass more than he was on mine. So I woke up. From that point on, I just let everything he said roll off of me. I started to realize how much he cared about me as a player. There are a lot of coaches out there who only talk about basketball with their players. But if Coach Self saw me earlier during the day, before practice, he'd ask about my mom, my kid, my family situation, how class was going. He was always there for those things. He always had our back. He just wanted you to be straight up with him.

## WEIGHT ISSUES

When I was a freshman, we played Toledo at Kemper Arena in Kansas City a few weeks before Christmas. They had a really quick guard named Kashif Payne. At one point, he made a steal around the free-throw line. I was standing near halfcourt when it happened, and he blew right past me on his way to the other end. Coach Self said I should've been able to contain him better in transition. After the game he called me into his office. He said, "You're being lazy. I guarantee you that your weight right now is affecting you." He told me he wasn't going to play me until I got down to 205 pounds. The next two weeks were the worst of my life. Absolute hell. I had to eat every meal with Hudy. I had to eat with her in the morning and at lunch, too. And I had to tell her where I was and what I was eating at night. Those two weeks turned out to be great for me. I got down to 205. And the whole month of February, I was the best player in the league. That's when I couldn't believe how much hype I was getting. I was like, "OK, I've made a name for myself. Now I've got to live up to it."

## MORE ON HUDY

Coach Hudy is one of the craziest chicks I know. The story I heard was that, before I got there, she tore her rotator cuff doing an incline bench press. She was maxing out and she tore it on the third rep, but she still finished out her set of 10. She and Coach Dooley are two of the craziest people I've ever met in my life. They probably have zero body fat, but they still run all the time. I used to tell her that I could hang with her on a bike workout. So the two of us and Coach Dooley all went riding together. I didn't know a bunch of hills would be involved. They were leaving me so bad that they ended up waiting for me two blocks ahead at a light. There was this one funny moment during that workout I'll never forget. I was pushing and pedaling so hard, and all of a sudden some skinny-ass girl cruised right past me on this old-ass bike. Hudy and Dooley started dying laughing and then just went on without me. I went to Russell's house and grabbed something to drink. I said, "F--- that. I quit." I almost threw up and everything. I told Russell about it. He went and tried it, too, and he quit at the exact same spot that I quit at. We both told Hudy that we were never going on a bike ride with her again.

I love Coach Hudy, though. I always called her my second mom. She helped me. She'd always say, "I know you don't want to do it now, but you'll be smiling in a couple of years." Every time I listened, I got a good result.

## RELATIONSHIP WITH RUSSELL

A lot of people thought Russell and I should be at each others' throats because we played the same position. But I think that's one of the reasons we won all the time. We had players that were willing to sacrifice. They didn't care about anything but winning. It didn't matter. We bought into Coach Self's system.

I'm not saying we didn't bump heads a little bit when I first got there. He used to foul me all the time real hard. I was a freshman, so he was like, "All right, I'm a junior. F--- you. You're not getting any calls, you little freshman." I didn't care about getting calls anyway, because that's how I'd always played in Chicago. I never cared about getting fouled as long as Russell didn't call them when I did it to him. Me and Russell never got into altercations. He just fouled me hard, and I fouled him.

Russell used to always talk to me and try to tell me the right things to do on the court. Sometimes I thought, "Should I be listening to this dude? We're going for the same position." I don't think he really cared. He just wanted to win games. I truly think that's the main thing he cared about. And of course he wanted to start and have his position, but that was fine with me. I went to Coach Self and said, "I don't care about starting. I know I'll play."

It actually helped me coming off the bench. I could see what Russell wasn't doing, so I could come in and try to correct it. That was the easy part. Coach Townsend would sit next to me and point things out. He'd be like, "See, you've got to attack in that situation," or, "He should've pulled it back right there." Then I'd go in and correct all the things the coaches were telling me Russell was doing wrong.

I looked at Russell like a big brother. He helped me out a lot. For a while I thought Coach Self was picking on me a lot. Russell could tell it was bothering me, so he would always stay after practice and talk to me. He'd always said, "Let it go." I used to hold a grudge against Coach Self all the way to the next practice because I would be so mad. I'd see Coach Self the next morning and I'd mean-mug him. He'd just smile and say, "Are you all right? How's your day going?" He had already forgotten about it. I just hadn't learned how to deal with him yet, but Russell helped me through that. He was a great teammate.

## BRANDON RUSH

B-Rush is one of the goofiest guys I know. When you were around him, you couldn't help but laugh. Every day in practice, B-Rush had something about going left baseline. Seriously, he wanted to go left baseline every time. Instead of shooting a pull-up jumper or an open jumper, he'd put the ball on the floor and go left. Coach Self used to tell him he had a magnet in his left nut that pulled his hand down toward the floor and forced him to dribble. He kept making fun of him for it, too, because Brandon has that short arm that he broke when he was little. Coach Self used to mimic him by walking around with his arm dangling all crooked-like, just like Brandon. He'd say, "Here's what you do. You get the ball, and you put it down on the floor with your little short-ass arm, and then you go to the lane." Coach Self got so frustrated that he set up a treadmill on the baseline especially for B-Rush. Every time he passed up a jump shot and went baseline ... before he ever made it to the basket, Coach Self had blown his whistle and said, "Treadmill!" B-Rush would have to run.

I've never seen B-Rush get into an argument with a teammate. As a matter of fact, I've never seen B-Rush get into an argument with anyone on the court, not even an opponent. He probably never said anything back to Coach Self. B-Rush is just laid back all the time. He really didn't have any problems. He's always in a good mood.

B-Rush could turn a bad situation into a good one on the court without even trying. Coach Self would be hollerin' at everyone, but then he'd look over

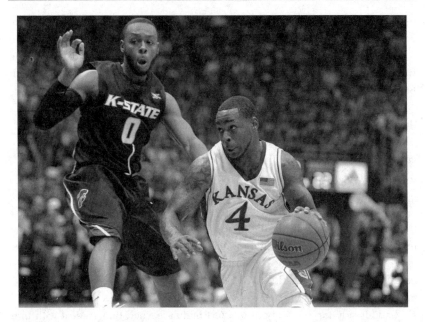

at B-Rush, and he'd have this stupid look on his face. Then Coach Self would start laughing, too. He couldn't get serious. He'd be like, "What, Brandon?" B-Rush would say, "I don't know what you're talking about. I'm just listening."

The other thing about B-Rush is that he never lied. Coach Self would be like, "Did everyone make curfew last night? If you didn't make curfew, raise your hand." All of us that broke curfew kept our hands down – except B-Rush. He'd raise his hand and tell on himself. Coach Self would ask him why he didn't make curfew and he'd say, "Because the club was crackin'!" Everyone would laugh, and he'd make B-Rush run a little bit.

## MARIO CHALMERS

I had a good relationship with Mario. Mario and Brandon were together a lot. They were carrying the load before I came. It was funny, because when we would go out, whatever B-Rush was wearing, Mario tried to wear the same thing. If Brandon put on a polo and khakis, Mario would do the same thing. I always teased B-Rush about it. He was like, "Man, Mario needs to stop that." Mario was cool to me, though. He helped me a lot.

A lot of people in Chicago were mad at me during the playoffs because I picked the Heat to beat the Bulls. I wore a LeBron shirt on the day of the games. Everyone would say stuff on Twitter about Mario. There was one game when Mario hit about three 3's, and I kept tweeting, "There goes another one. There goes another one. There goes another one." People kept asking me why I wasn't going for the Bulls and I told them, "Because my teammate, my boy, plays for the Heat." I'm proud of Mario.

## JULIAN WRIGHT

Julian is a different dude. We used to always tease Julian because he played high school ball in the suburbs, but he was actually from the city. We always joked that he was from the suburbs, and he'd get mad. Julian was tough to figure out. One day Ju wanted to go to the club, the next day he wanted to go to the bowling alley. I think Ju probably wants to be a professional bowler when he's done playing basketball. He's just a different type of dude. He dresses different, he acts different. He's a music fanatic. I heard he's singing now. I haven't heard his stuff yet, but once I do, he'll get a call from me.

Julian is the reason I used to be ready for games my freshman year. He had this thing called "beast mode." He used to come in the locker room before games and say, "Beast mode, Ron-Ron!" He used to call me that all the time. He could really get me and Rodrick Stewart going. Our lockers were all right next to each other. He was always saying, "Beast mode!" We'd start jumping around, and Coach Self would have to come in and calm us down.

## RODRICK STEWART

Rod and I didn't take anything from anyone. I think Coach Self liked that. My freshman year, I never liked playing on the same team with B-Rush and starters at practice. I didn't like playing with the blue team. I liked playing with Rod and them. It was more competition. It evened things out on both ends. We used to try to beat the starters every time. This one time, one of the starters started cramping, and Coach Self put Rod on the blue team, and he ended up having to guard me. Rod fouled me really hard, and it pissed me off. I fouled him back on purpose, and we just about got into it. It took the whole team to keep us apart. Coach Self couldn't stop it. It was like a street fight was about to break out. It wasn't like when Mario and Case got into it, where all he had to do was say, "You two, sit down and stop it." Once we got into the locker room everything was cool.

## NCAA TITLE GAME: THE BUILDUP

The Final Four is something I'll never forget. There are four teams left, and you're the center of attention. You can't go anywhere without security escorts. They have the hotel on lockdown. It feels like you're in the pros already.

The night before the Memphis game, I stayed up until 4 or 5 in the morning. I couldn't sleep. I was ready to win. My brother was in the same hotel, but he was on a different floor, and we weren't allowed to leave. So I talked to him on the phone, and my mom, too. Everybody was awake. Tyrel Reed was my roommate, and he goes to sleep earlier than anyone I've ever known. But even he was awake. The game started late on Monday night, so we had to wait all day long. We got up and ate breakfast. We couldn't read the papers because Coach Self had told the hotel people not to deliver any papers to our room. He wanted us to keep the TVs off. But of course, it's hard not to watch ESPN the day of the big game. You want to hear what everyone is saying. So everybody watched it.

Later, when we were in the locker room getting ready, everyone had something to say about what we'd heard on TV. People were like, "Did you hear what they said about us losing?" A lot of analysts picked Memphis. We were pretty pissed. I think we did a great job of handling the big stage. There was a lot of pressure, but I like pressure. Pressure is something I laugh at.

There was almost a fight in the tunnel before the game. Memphis was supposed to run out first, and we were supposed to run out second. We were all standing there, and the big dude for Memphis, Pierre Henderson-Niles, stepped out and said, "We ain't going first. Let those bitches go first." Darnell Jackson said something back to him. Some people started shoving, and the police had to come back there and separate us. That set the tone. From that point on, we were ready.

When we were in the layup line warming up, people were talking s--t across the court. Big Joey Dorsey and Sasha were going back and forth. Of course, I never could understand half of what Sasha was saying, but you could sure hear him. I don't know if it would've been smart for Dorsey or anyone to go after Sasha. He's a strong dude. I wouldn't want to go at the big fella like that.

## GUARDING DERRICK ROSE

Coach Self kept messing with me all week. He'd say, "Memphis has that good point guard who is 6-foot-3. I don't know who to put on him. Russell might be too slow. I don't know who is going to guard him." He kept saying that in front a group of people, but he made sure I was always nearby. I finally exploded and said, "F--- that! I'm guarding him. You can stop saying all that because I'm going to guard him. He's from Chicago, and I've been guarding him all my life. I'll guard him." He looked at me with a little grin. I think he liked that. I guarded Rose pretty well until we went to that 2-3 zone in the second half. He didn't get off on us until we changed what we were doing defensively.

## MAKING A COMEBACK

With about 2 ½ minutes left, I made a move to the basket, and Robert Dozier blocked my layup off the backboard. At that point we were like, "Damn, it's not looking too good. We can win, but everything is going to have to go perfect." Then I hit some crazy-ass layup. Then Shady hit that 18-footer. A few seconds later, in the huddle, Coach Self told Shady that it was the worst shot he could've taken. He could've taken a step back and hit a 3. He was right on the line. The next play is when I got the steal on the inbounds pass and hit the 3. I knew it was good. If you listen to the tape closely enough, you can hear me yell, "Boom!" after the ball left my hands. Right after I hit the shot, I ran into B-Rush's shoulder as I was running down the court. My jaw felt like it locked. I fell to the ground right as Memphis was calling a timeout. My jaw was stuck. I had to work it back into place. I was too excited to feel much pain, though. After I hit that 3, I knew we could win.

## MARIO'S MIRACLE – THE UNSUNG HERO

Once D-Rose missed that first free throw with 10 seconds left, we all lit up. We knew there was still a chance. He made the second free throw to put Memphis up by 3, so there was time for one final play. When Darnell threw me the ball inbounds, I paused for a second so I could hear what John Calipari was yelling at Rose. He was on the sideline screaming, "Foul him! Foul him! Foul him!" At that point, I made a crossover move to get D-Rose leaning the wrong way so I could get by him. The play was initially set up for me to come down the sideline, but instead I went to the middle and then toward the sideline. That's what made the play so hard. D-Rose was on the right side of me, just riding me and riding me and riding me. Then somehow he got behind me, and I lost the ball. I tried to put the ball in front of me so he wouldn't tap it, but I put it too far in front of me so I had to dive to toss it back. I didn't know where D-Rose was at. I saw Mario's blue shirt over my right shoulder. I just flung it toward his shirt. I was so sweaty that, as soon as I hit the floor, I slid five or six feet across the court and didn't even see Mario take the shot. I just heard the crowd scream, so I knew it went in. On the way to the bench, I passed by Chris Douglas-Roberts, or maybe it was Dozier … one of them said something, and I was like, "It's over now. You'll never win." Memphis wasn't supposed to lose. They were shocked. In some ways, I think we were shocked, too – not that we beat Memphis, but just at how it all happened.

Looking back on it, I know how fortunate we were. I don't know how I got that pass to Mario. D-Rose pushed me – fouled me – as I was losing the ball and diving for it, but I still managed to make the play. It was probably the hardest pass I ever had to get off. I don't know how Mario caught it.

Do I get mad when I hear Mario getting all the credit for that win? Hell yeah, I get mad (laughing). I made that steal in the corner and then hit that 3. Without that play, there's no game. And then I passed Mario the ball at the end. Give me my credit, please. I'm just kidding. It is what it is. It's been long enough. I say things like that jokingly, but I never really cared. We all played a big part in that win. We won and we all got rings. That's all that matters.

## RIVALRIES

I really liked playing against K-State. Jacob Pullen, Denis Clemente, whoever they had, it didn't matter. That was a good rivalry. I liked playing them in Manhattan better than I did playing them at home. It was so loud there, but when you come out on top, everyone shuts up. K-State's players are cool. Missouri … ummm, no. But we all got along with Kansas State's players. Pullen used to come to Lawrence to hang out with us. He'd drive up, stay at my apartment and then leave the next day, him and Denis. No one bothered him. Our fans were really respectful. I don't think Kansas players could drive to Columbia and go out without anyone saying something or starting something. But no one in Lawrence said anything to Pullen except, "You're a good player."

## 2008-09

My junior year was the best year for me. I probably should've left after that season. Everybody counted us out. People had us finishing third in the Big 12 or something like that. We went undefeated at home, and the big fella (Cole Aldrich) really emerged. We took being an underdog personally. Brady was knocking down shots. My big thing was I tried to make everyone feel like they were good on the court. I tried to boost their confidence. I'd tell them, "Don't worry about Coach Self. Don't worry about nuthin'. Just make shots and guard."

I didn't have to say too much to Cole. But before every game, I'd hit him in his chest, and he'd punch me on the shoulder and it'd be like, "OK, let's go." Cole said a lot of stuff I never thought he would say. In the huddle, I didn't have to talk all the time. Sometimes it helped. I couldn't tell bigs certain things because I'm not a big. Sometimes he'd tell the big guys, "Stop being so soft and letting them push you over." Then you'd see the Morris twins start to fight down there. I had all the guards doing their thing. We were clicking. Everyone bought into Coach Self's system.

The NCAA Tournament was huge for me. I had 32 points against North Dakota State and 25 against Dayton. Everyone kind of excused that Michigan State loss because we were supposedly rebuilding and expectations weren't as high for us that year. But, hell, we wanted to win and we should've won. We'd have beat Louisville in that Elite Eight game and gone to the Final Four. Coach Self even said it. We'd have beat Louisville. I still blame myself, because I gave that 3-point play away to Kalin Lucas right at the end of the Michigan State game. I should've fouled the hell out of him, and he'd have only gotten two points. Then we just would've needed two points to tie it at the end instead of three. He got me in the air, and I pulled my hands back instead of fouling the hell out of him. It ended up being a three-point play that made it 63-60 with about 40 seconds left. We couldn't come back.

## ONE MORE YEAR

Even though we lost, I still went to the Final Four in Detroit that year because I was a finalist for the State Farm Player of the Year award that Blake Griffin won. I was at the banquet and, after it was done, Coach Self was like, "Have you decided what you're going to do yet? I'm not trying to pressure you to do anything. But do you know what's going on?" I told him I was coming back. He stopped in his tracks and said, "What? Wait, wait, wait. Are you serious? Can I tell people?" He didn't believe me. He called me about three times that night just to make sure. I was like, "Yeah, I'm coming back." It was that simple.

The main reason I came back for my senior year was because of my mom. She had been getting sick and wanted me to finish my degree. She had breast cancer throughout most of my college career. Luckily, they caught it so it never got too serious until my junior year. She had to have surgery and get some lumps removed a few days before the NCAA Tournament. Our first two games were in Minnesota that year and then we played Michigan State in Indianapolis. She drove both places. I wasn't going to let her fly.

After we lost to Michigan State, I went and talked to my mom in her hotel room and she told me she wanted me to go back to school. I thought about it for a week and then I said, "OK, I'm going back." I was the first male in my family to get a degree.

Looking back on it ... sometimes I still feel like I should've left. My senior year didn't go quite like I wanted it to go. But I also became Kansas' all-time winningest player. A lot of accolades came along with that, which was cool. Overall I don't regret coming back. I don't regret it at all.

## OH HENRY!

About a month after the season, Coach Self signed Xavier and C.J. Henry. Their father (Carl) came out with these quotes in the paper about how his sons – both of them – were better than me. He put his sons in a bad spot, because we were going to take what he said out on them. I stood up and said that in the locker room, and everyone was like, "We're with you. Who are these dudes?" At the same time, we had to remember that Xavier and C.J. weren't the ones that said that stuff. It was their dad. Still, they weren't there all summer while we were there working. We heard they were back in Oklahoma City working out, but that didn't mean anything. They weren't there working with us. So they were already coming in on a bad note.

They finally got to school, and it was time for pickup games. I told Coach Self, "I'm gonna be on C.J. for 94 feet, since he's supposed to be better than me. I'm gonna guard them all 94 feet (of the court)." The second he touched every ball, I was on him tight. Our whole team was going hard at them at first. After the first couple of days – after we got a feel for Xavier's personality – we were like, "He wasn't behind all that stuff his father said. He doesn't think those things." Xavier was a cool guy. C.J. was a little cocky. He had played pro baseball a little bit. It was different with him. It was like, "All right, man, we're going to bust your ass and let you know how things are. We know Kansas recruited you way back in 2005 or whenever, but things are different now." He was pretty rusty. I scored on him at will and got a little rough with him. After a week or two, things were normal and everything was cool. We never went back and told them, "Y'all may not have realized it, but we were after your heads at first." It was their pop's fault. I actually saw him in Lawrence a couple of days after he said that stuff. He tried to shake my hand and talk. I just nodded my head and walked past him.

## XAVIER'S ROLE

Xavier showed flashes sometimes. But he worried too much. He was worried about the wrong things. It may have messed up our chemistry a bit, but not too much. Any freshman that comes in and starts is going to mess up chemistry. The only thing he messed up was a chance for everyone else who had been waiting. Guys like Mario Little and Travis Releford … the guys that were ready to step in play, he messed it up for them. But that's recruiting, that's college basketball. At times Xavier really helped us.

There were also a lot of games when he just shot so much. I was like, "Daaaammmmnnn! Come on, dog! Seriously?" The Memphis game in St. Louis, he was clipping the hedges. Every time, he was clipping them off. Coach Self had to take him out. At the same time, he probably had a little chip on his shoulder playing against Memphis. I could understand that, because if I played Illinois, I probably would've done the same thing.

A lot of the time, I thought Carl should've left Xavier alone. Xavier was under a lot of pressure. We never knew he was under that kind of pressure until he told us one day. He said when he had a bad game, his family let him know about it. We used to get mad at him because he was always pouting on the court and crying and this and that. We played UCLA on the road, and his father was standing behind the rim at Pauley Pavilion, telling Xavier not to pass the ball, just shoot it every time. I told Coach Self, and Coach made him move into the stands and leave Xavier alone. That's what he went through all year, but he didn't tell us about it until we were going into the Big 12 tournament. We had one game where we were up by about 30, and he was still pouting. I went off. I was like, "What's your problem? We're up by 30. It doesn't matter if you're having a bad game. We're winning." I snapped. Coach took him out. When we got to the locker room he told me what the deal was, and I went and told Coach Self, "Man, his father is f---ing with him." I felt bad because I was on his ass all year, but I never knew what he was going through.

## FAMILY MATTERS

We knew the coaching staff must've been haggling with Xavier's family, because all of a sudden in December, C.J. Henry started playing a lot more than he normally played. Most of the time, he only got in when we were up by a lot toward the end of the game. Then all of a sudden, there was a game or two when he brought C.J. in before he brought in Tyshawn. Later on, Coach Townsend told me the Henrys threatened to pull Xavier off the team if Coach Self didn't start playing C.J. more. The thing is, once the second semester starts, you can't transfer. You're stuck. So when the second semester started that year, I remember Coach Self standing in the locker room, pointing at them and saying, "I don't have to play you f---ers now. You're stuck."

## FOOTBALL vs. BASKETBALL

The fights with the football team were all about jealousy. The football players never could get the attention that we were getting. We overshadowed them. There were even a bunch of football players who used to walk around telling people they were better basketball players than the guys on our team. They honestly believed it, too. So we played them five-on-five at the rec and absolutely blew them out. After we beat them we told them, "We'll never play y'all again. We'll never give y'all another game." I'll admit, though … a few of them could play. Marcus Henry dunked on some people. Raimond Pendleton was good. My team was me, Chalmers, Brady, Darnell and Shady. We killed them. We were throwing lobs all over the place.

There were three girls from Chicago that went to Kansas that I knew. We'd hang out sometimes, but we were just friends. They were like family. The football players didn't know I knew them so well. I'd walk into a bar with one of them, and a football player would come up to her and say, "Are you really here with Sherron Collins? Do you know how many girls he's been with? Why are you with him?" She'd come back and tell me what they said. I was like, "Wow, really?" There was always something going on like that.

The day the fights happened on campus, it was over girls. There were two girls who were messing with a couple of players on our team. And they were also hooking up with someone from the football team. There was a he-said-she-said thing, where they were telling one group of guys what the other one was saying about them. They ended up clashing.

Whatever was said outside the Burge Union that day was between Thomas Robinson and Johnathan Wilson. But Marcus (Morris) went up to Wilson and said, "Man, we don't have time for this." Johnathan Wilson was like, "All right. It's all over with. It's squashed." Then someone just came up and sucker-punched Thomas Robinson for no reason. I wasn't there, but I heard about it. He said he was standing there, and some little dude came up and punched him for no reason. He got a concussion from it. It was crazy man. If you caught one of those football players by themselves, they'd say, "What's up?" and speak to you like nothing was wrong. But when they all get together, they try to act all tough.

All of the football players weren't like that. All the big names you hear like Darrell Stuckey, Kerry Meier and Todd Reesing … they never did anything. It was always the young guys that weren't playing, the guys that redshirted or whatever.

The football-basketball fights didn't end with the one on campus. The big lineman they had, Cesar Rodriguez … he had a little brother (Jose) that was a dummy. Coach Self put us on punishment for something that was totally (Jose's) fault. Me and Tyrone Appleton were shooting pool at Wayne & Larry's and (Jose) walked up and moved all the balls across the table. He was like, "I'm getting really tired of all you basketball players thinking you're this-and-that. If you ever mess with my brother ...." He was saying all kinds of stuff. I was like, "If you don't get out of my face, I'm going to knock you across the head with this pool stick." He was drunk and talking all crazy. He pushed Tyrone in the face.

There ended up being a brawl, because the Morris twins had Ty's car that night. When they came to pick us up, there was a fight. The dudes – Jose and his friend, another lineman - followed us outside as we were leaving, and they wanted to fight. There were about six of us: Me and Ty and the Morris twins and their two cousins. It was crazy. I told Coach Self, "Do you really think me and Ty were going to walk into a bar and start a fight with two dudes that weigh over 270 pounds? Are you serious?" Everyone knew what had already happened with Tyshawn and Thomas Robinson getting that concussion. We asked Coach Self, "What's it going to take for you to realize that we've got to protect ourselves?"

## NO PLACE LIKE HOME

Senior Night was sweet and bitter. I was thinking about all the memories I was going to leave behind: The tunnel and running out in front of all those fans, the coaches and teammates I'd built relationships with. Some of the young fellas were telling me, "I don't know what it's going to be like without you here next year. It's going to be different. It's not going to be the same." All that stuff was going through my head. My family was there. They were proud of me. It all hits you at one time when you're making that speech.

## NORTHERN IOWA

Everything about the Northern Iowa game felt different. Everything went wrong. First of all, we weren't used to being down by 10 points. We were down by 10 points for most of the game. We weren't used to playing from behind. Being down by a few points is OK – but not double digits.

When we got into the locker room at halftime, everyone was arguing, including myself. Tyshawn said something to me about a loose ball that I didn't get. I was like, "Shut the f--- up. Why don't you start guarding Farokhmanesh so he'll stop scoring all over your ass." Coach Self came in and flipped a table over and screamed, "Shut the f--- up!" All the 3's we were hitting the day before against Lehigh weren't falling. We couldn't hit anything. We finally got back in the game, and then Farokhmanesh hit that crazy 3. No one knew it was coming. I never thought for a second that he'd shoot that 3. They were up by one point with 40 seconds left. Who is going to take that shot in that situation? You're supposed to pull back, run some clock and let the other team foul you. But he swished it on us. You've got to give him credit.

There was something different with Cole that game, too. Anytime he faced a big 7-footer or somebody that's supposedly decent or good, he got timid a little bit. Their big fella (Jordan Eglseder) set the tone for them. He came out and scored seven points in the first few minutes of the game. He hit two 3's that game and had that left hook. We were like, "Damn, Cole, we told you to be ready to get out there and guard him." That was always our problem with Cole, getting him to guard on the perimeter. We just didn't make the adjustment. We didn't help him like we usually help him. It didn't help that the refs dicked us on a charging call late in the game.

The loss didn't hit me at first. I didn't cry in the locker room. Everyone else was crying. I just remember looking at everyone crying and shaking my head. I went around to all the young guys and said, "Don't let this happen again. Y'all still have some time, but this is it for me. It ain't a good feeling." I got back to Lawrence the next day, and my whole place was quiet. My brothers were there. They hadn't made it to Oklahoma City for the game because they figured we'd win easily and then they would just go to St. Louis for the Sweet 16. That's when it all hit me. I flew to Chicago the next day.

## EXCUSABLE ABSENCE?

I was in Chicago right before the team banquet. Coach Self got in contact with me and I told him I was going to try to be there, but I was in the midst of trying to find an agent. I just felt like that was more important than the banquet. I signed with my agent that day in Chicago. I was going to try to get back, but by that point the only flight I could get on was at 5 or 6. Coach Self and Coach Townsend knew I wasn't coming. Cole called me, and I told him why I wasn't coming. He was like, "OK, I understand. Handle your business. That stuff is important." Tyshawn or Mario called me and said Xavier and his family were saying stuff about me not being there. I thought that was bulls--t. I went back to Kansas after that because I had to finish a paper. I saw Coach Self, and he mentioned it again. He was like, "I think you should've come even though you had a bunch of stuff going on, but whatever." Then everything was back to normal.

## NBA DRAFT

I knew there was a chance I would be drafted – but I also realized there was a strong chance that I wouldn't get picked, which is exactly what happened. The thing that changed my whole draft night was Michael Jordan calling me personally. He had actually been calling around looking for me for a while that night, and I didn't even realize it. Larry Brown was trying, too. *(Jordan is part-owner of the Charlotte Bobcats, and Brown was the head coach at the time.)* I never answer calls from numbers I don't recognize. Then my agent called me and said, "Is there a 215 number calling you and a 704?" He told me to answer them next time because it was Michael Jordan and Larry Brown. Eventually I talked to

Jordan, and he told me they were going to pick me up in Charlotte and sign me as a free agent. He told me, "We just got a steal. Be ready to work."

I thought I did well in Charlotte, although I thought I could've played a lot more than they played me. I felt like every time I got in the game, I did exceptionally well. What hurt me was the coaching change. With Larry Brown, I cracked that shell with him by losing the weight and playing well. After I got back from the D-League, I played 22 minutes against Oklahoma City. I had four assists. In the postgame press conference he was like, "We've got to start playing the young fella more. He's throwing passes that these guys haven't seen in a while." Everyone was complimenting me and stuff. Two days later, he was gone. They made a change. Just like that, I was back to square one. I had to prove myself to a new coach (Paul Silas) and a new staff who already had their favorites. They already knew Jarrett Jack because he had played under them at Golden State. If you don't have anyone fighting for you, it's hard. I had good days at practice, where I felt like I was killing the two guards in front of me. But then I was inactive for the next five games. It was hard to stay motivated. It's like you're a whippin' child. Then (Silas) would say, "Be ready, you're going to play tonight." But I wouldn't play. Charles Oakley was always going to bat for me and telling them to play me. But he wasn't the head coach.

My agent called me and told me they were going to cut me and then sign me to a 10-day contract. Even Jordan told me, "We're going to bring you back." But then the chance came, and I didn't go. I just thought they were going to string me along. I felt like they were going to string me on until the end of the season and then let me go. I think there were only 12 games left. I just felt like it was kind of bulls--t. Still, thinking about it now, I should've gone back. It was a learning experience.

## WEIGHING IN

After I left Charlotte, I had a few months where I didn't do a whole lot. I put on some weight and got up to about 245 pounds. I don't eat like people probably think I do. I'm just the type of guy who can lose and gain weight faster than most people. I've just got to discipline myself to do something every day – cardio in the morning or whatever. I'm already down to 225 (as of July 2011) and I'll be right back to about 210 when I sign somewhere to go overseas. That's the weight I played at when I was at Kansas.

It's frustrating because everyone makes my weight into this big deal, and I don't think it's a huge thing. People talk about it all the time, though, and it makes them forget about my game and the things I can do on the court. Coach Self always acted like I had knee problems because of my weight. But the only time I had knee issues was when I was hurt. I had patellar tendinitis and I had microfracture surgery. I was injured in those situations. It wasn't because of my weight.

Being out of shape is different than being overweight. Being out of shape means you didn't do anything over the summer but party, and then you have trouble getting back into the flow. I'm not in tip-top shape, but I'm in better shape than I was a month ago.

## FINAL THOUGHTS

I always viewed Kansas as an escape. In Chicago, nothing ever changes. Yet for some reason, I was always in a rush to get back here in the summer. When it came time to go back to Kansas, I didn't want to leave. I'd usually show up on campus late. I don't know why I was like that. There is nothing here but problems. Every time I come home there are more problems, more people wanting something. When you're away, you really don't hear from people, except for the people who really care about you. When I'm away, it's an escape, because I don't have to deal with the s--t I've dealt with my whole life, the s--t I'm dealing with now.

With everything I've been through up here these past few months, I'm ready for anything. I'm talking about family issues and friends stealing from me and stuff. I had a dude I grew up with for 10 years steal from me. He messed my whole credit card up. I gave him my information to book me a hotel, and he kept it and started buying stuff. They caught him. It's a learning experience. Every time I come back it's the same s--t, the same problems. It hasn't changed at all. That's why I love going back to Kansas. People don't judge me there. People respect me and treat me well. I miss it.

# CHAPTER 34

# 2009/10
# XAVIER HENRY

X avier Henry became the first one-and-done player in Kansas history when he left school after his freshman season and entered the 2010 NBA draft. The Memphis Grizzlies selected him with the 12th overall pick. An Oklahoma City native, Henry averaged 13.4 points and 4.3 rebounds during his one season in Lawrence in 2009-10. He was the eighth-ranked player in the Class of 2009 and, at one point during his senior season, was ranked No. 1 on the ESPU 100 list. Henry is the son of former Kansas basketball players Carl and Barbara Henry. His older brother, C.J., also played for Kansas in 2009-10.

## IN XAVIER'S WORDS

Seeing your name in the recruiting rankings and hearing you have a chance to go to the NBA can be exciting – but it can also make a kid fast-forward his life sooner than he probably wants to. Things start coming at you really fast, and you have to take advantage of every opportunity. It's tough to keep going that fast when you want to just be a kid and do your own thing for a while. But that's just how it is. I'm not complaining.

I really didn't think about the NBA until after my freshman season, when everything was over. It was a tough thing to predict, because during the year I played really well at times, and other times I struggled. My draft status was going up and down. People were like, "Maybe you should stay" and others were telling me I should go. After everything happened, and it was time to make a decision … I mean, it was a hard decision. I wasn't sure what I wanted to do at first. I had Coach Self talk to some people for me. They all said that it was the right time, based on my potential and how young I was. I just went ahead and took their advice and left. It's worked out pretty well so far, but sometimes you want to be back in college with your friends and teammates and stuff like that.

Every chance I got last season, I watched Kansas games.

## CHOOSING A SCHOOL

My recruitment dragged on for a while, because I was already committed to a school (Memphis), but then the coach (John Calipari) left for Kentucky. Just like that, the process started all over for me. I liked Coach Calipari, but I didn't want to just follow him.

I just didn't want to be the guy that follows a coach to whatever school he went to. That's not a good look, and it's not who I am. I was going to make my decision based on where I wanted to go, not where a certain coach was. I took my time and thought everything over and made the decision to go to Kansas. I nearly committed there a few months earlier when I chose Memphis. Both of my parents played there, and I really liked Coach Self.

No matter what other schools I was looking at, Coach Self never changed anything he was saying. He never said anything bad about Coach Calipari or Kentucky or anyone else. He always just talked about Kansas and how much fun we could have and how much better he could get me and what we could do as a team. When you're contending for national championships and you're preseason No. 1 and you've got guys like Sherron and Cole there ... it's a pretty attractive option. Plus, Elijah Johnson was there. Elijah was one of my best friends. We'd been saying we were going to go to school together since we were young. I didn't think it would actually happen. When I finally told Coach Self over the phone that I was coming, he was like "OK, let's roll. Let's get this started."

## WRONG PERCEPTION

A few months before I got to Kansas, an article came out (in the Kansas City Star) that portrayed me and my family really badly. It caused some tension between us and the guy that we let come into our house and do the interview. He turned around and made us look like prima donnas. Once we got to Kansas, people got to know us, and they realized that wasn't the case. We thought the article was shady. There was just a lot of stuff in it that wasn't true. We couldn't do anything about it, though. We just forgot about it and moved on with our lives.

There were probably some people that didn't understand why my brother (C.J.) and I didn't work out in Lawrence the summer before our freshman year. There were just a few people – fans or whatever – that were like, "Why wasn't he here this summer?" or "What was he doing?" or "I can't believe he didn't come down here and work out with the guys." But that summer, I had my braces taken off. I had, like, four root canals, and I had my wisdom teeth removed. My face was hurting, my head was hurting, my body was tired. It was a tough summer.

When I finally got to Lawrence, it was great. Everyone acted like they were excited to see me. It was so fun, because everyone knew who I was. Everyone was coming up to me and talking and taking pictures with me. You could fall in love with the attention quick. The best part about it was that I was always with my teammates. We were experiencing it all together.

## COLE ALDRICH

The thing I remember about Cole was that he would always take his fake tooth out, wherever we were. When I first met him, I had no idea that he'd gotten his real tooth knocked out the year before. One time Cole took me out to dinner for a talk. I hadn't been playing well, hadn't been shooting well, and I was pretty down. We got to the restaurant and, before we sat down, I went into the bathroom. I came back and sat at the table, and he started ordering his food. I glanced at him, and it looked like he was missing a tooth all of a sudden. I couldn't tell for sure, but I kept looking at him, and finally I said, "Man, this may sound weird, but are you missing a tooth or something?" Then he smiled and showed me the whole thing. He had taken his (fake) tooth out before I'd gotten back to the table. He loved smiling really big when he had that tooth out.

## ELIJAH JOHNSON

Elijah is one of the funniest people I know. He makes up a bunch of words out of the blue, just makes up his own little language. After a while, everyone starts saying what Elijah says. He'll use the dumbest words you'd never think of – something like "shadookie." It'll sound so funny that everyone starts laughing. For the next few months, people will be saying "shadookie" all the time.

I've known Elijah since middle school. We met in AAU, but we were set on going to school together. We tried to get him on my AAU team in high school, but they said there were some boundary rules that said he had to at least live in a state connected to me to play. We were trying to do everything we could to play together, and when we couldn't, we talked about playing in college together – and it actually happened.

## TYSHAWN TAYLOR

I think Tyshawn can easily be the biggest leader they have. Not only because he's about to be a senior, but because when I was there, he was only a sophomore, and he was one of our leaders right along with Sherron. He's definitely a vocal leader. He's already got that down. He has no shame about speaking up and telling someone what they need to do. The big deal with him is that, in practice and off the court, he has to show he's as committed as everyone else, that he's working as hard as everyone else. He needs to set a good example for all of those young guys who look up to him. And I think he will. Tyshawn wants it. He works hard.

## SHERRON COLLINS

Sherron had that killer instinct. He's one of the toughest players I've seen. He's 5-11 and a little thicker. He just has that will to win. We won some games just because Sherron said, "Forget all this. I'm about to take it to 'em and win this game for us." He did that for us a couple of times. That was big. I hope he's doing OK. I'm surprised he's not in the league. I know he's had weight problems that might not all be his fault. If he can get that under control and keep a good head on his shoulders, he'll have to be in the NBA. Sherron is too good of a player not be playing somewhere. Everyone knows that. Everyone has seen him play. He just needs to get in shape and keep his weight down and keep his head straight.

## BILL SELF

Coach Self was pretty hard on me at times, but I loved playing for him. He did everything he said he was going to do. He tried to make me the best player I could be. He took care of me. We just had a lot of fun. He's a great guy. That's the best thing about him. He's really genuine off the court and a great coach on the court. I had a lot of fun with Coach.

## STAYING FIT

Staying in shape takes a lot of work. You really have to be dedicated to conditioning and keeping your body strong. That's not to say I didn't go out to eat sometimes. I love to eat. If I eat really badly, I've got to work real hard the next day. It's not fun. But that's what you've got to do if you eat a bunch of bad stuff. I used to love going to that Italian place in Lawrence, Paisano's. And I liked Henry T's, with the wings and those big buckets of chicken fingers. And I always liked going to the Underground before or after class with the guys.

I'm not like T-Rob. He can eat anything and still look all cut up. I can't do that. I saw T-Rob at the Adidas Nations deal this summer. We took him to eat, and he was eating everything. He has the highest metabolism ever. I got a little plate and called it a night.

## PRESSURE

I've always felt pressure. I put more pressure on myself than anyone does on me, just because I want to play well for my family and for the people that helped me grow up and play and taught me stuff. They deserve it. I feel like I'm showcasing my talent based on what they taught me. I feel pressure to play good for them. It's not like they're getting mad at me if I don't play well. It's just that I don't want to go out there and play terrible, because they taught me so much better.

My mom stays with me in Memphis. She's gotten to see all of the games. My dad is still in Oklahoma City. He been to some of them, but he has to work a lot, so he has the NBA package thing for his television.

## NORTHERN IOWA

I definitely didn't expect my one season at Kansas to end like it did, against Northern Iowa. Personally, I think we walked the ball up the court too much. When we used to blow teams out, we'd play really fast and score a bunch of fast-break points. That game, for whatever reason, we walked the ball up the court a lot and took our time with everything. If we would've just run at them they wouldn't have been able to do anything to stop us. We had too many good players on our team. Still, even after all of that, I still can't believe that kid (Ali Farokhmanesh) made that last 3-pointer.

I've been in some tough locker rooms before, but never after a game that was played on that big of a stage. We knew we shouldn't have lost that game. We just had to live with it. We just sat there and didn't say too much, but it was hard. Most of the time, we were quiet. But there were guys in the locker room that would stand up and yell, "We shouldn't have lost." Then a couple of other guys would stand up and scream, "We've got to come back strong from this. We've got to do better next year," and blah-blah-blah. Not everyone had next year. Sherron didn't have next year. We were hurting for Sherron. We knew Sherron wanted one bad. He deserved it. We all put the work in. We all tried.

## NBA LIFE

Things were going well in Memphis until I got hurt. I hyper-extended my knee at the end of December and strained a couple of ligaments. I wasn't able to get healthy until now (August 2011). It's been a battle. Shady (Darrell Arthur) is one

of my best friends on the team. He's a cool guy. He's really funny. We both went to Kansas, so we always have each other's backs. It's definitely great having him on the team.

It's been a different experience, going through the NBA with new teammates in a new city. It's not like college. There are definitely a lot of things that I miss. Playing in the NBA can be pretty fun. But at Kansas, you have all those avid fans and you're around a bunch of college kids. You just have a better environment. In the NBA, it's really a business. At Kansas, it was more of a family environment, a friendly environment. We were having a lot of fun. Playing in the NBA isn't so bad, though. You get to play against the best guys in the world, the guys you watched growing up. It's cool to be able to play with them.

It was tough moving on from Kansas. I had one of the best years of my life there. But I can't look back on it now. I'm in the NBA and I'm trying to make the best of it. I've got to get healthy and get back to playing. That's all that really matters now.

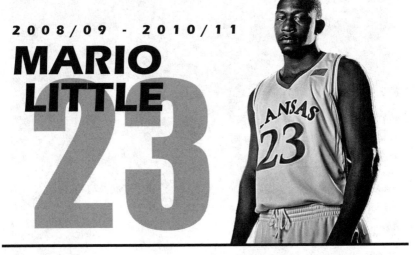

# CHAPTER 35

# 2008/09 - 2010/11
# MARIO
# LITTLE
## 23

Mario Little spent three seasons at Kansas after transferring from Chipola (Fla.) College, where he won National Junior College Player of the Year honors in 2008. Little averaged 4.7 points as a junior before redshirting in 2009-10. As a senior in 2010-11, Little averaged 5.1 points and 2.9 rebounds in 32 games. A Chicago native, Little chose Kansas over Illinois and Kansas State.

## IN MARIO'S WORDS

Meeting Michael Jordan was an experience I'll never forget. I never really had a real relationship with him or anything. If he still remembered me, I'd be thankful. It was just something that happened in high school. I went to his house and played with him, and I played really good.

One of his nephews knew one of my coaches. My coach came and got me and kind of surprised me. He told me, "Get your stuff ready. Bring out your A game." I didn't know where I was going. We had talked about it before, but I really didn't think that this could happen, so I never really set my mind to, "Hey, I'm going to play with Michael Jordan." We pulled up in front of the house, and I was like, "Wow."

I was playing to impress. I wasn't going out of my way and doing dumb stuff and exaggerating everything, but I was playing hard. I was wanting to play really good. I didn't want to get caught up into playing with Michael Jordan. He liked how I played and invited me back.

The school that I wanted to go to — because I was such a big Michael Jordan fan — was North Carolina. So I asked him about that, and we were talking about that. He said he liked my game and for me to get my grades together, because I told him my grades weren't good. I wasn't going to lie to him.

I don't know if he'd remember me or not, but it was a good experience for me. I don't worship him, but I really like Mike. I grew up in Chicago, not really watching basketball except for the Bulls. So it was a mind-blowing experience for me. It was probably one of the best times of my life.

When I played basketball as a kid, I tried to imitate his moves like everybody else in my neighborhood. He was basically the reason I played basketball. Growing up, I witnessed him at his greatest time in Chicago. Some people in Chicago don't even realize Michael Jordan's not from Chicago. That's how big he is.

Growing up in that era, watching playoff games ... I was amazed by it. It's hard to explain. I can't put it in words how I feel about what he did for the game and the respect level I have for him.

As a kid, I owned a Michael Jordan book. I don't even remember where I got it from. It was a Sports Illustrated book. It was all about Michael Jordan growing up while he was younger, all the way up to maybe 1998. But I had a lot of stuff. I had so many Michael Jordan cards and shoes and jerseys. Growing up in Chicago, it's not hard to find Michael Jordan stuff.

## JEFFREY JORDAN

Both of Michael Jordan's sons play for Central Florida. I don't know Michael Jordan's younger son (Marcus) that much, but I know the older one (Jeffrey) pretty good. We're cool. I talked to him and texted him when I was in Tampa this summer, and he was in Orlando. I got to know him just through basketball and when I came to his house. We played on the same team: me, him, his dad and two other people.

When I visited Illinois, Jeff was playing there. That was before he transferred (to Central Florida). I drove with him everywhere. He wasn't my host. I don't remember who my host was, actually. They really wanted me to come there. I was the only recruit there that week. It was pretty fun. He drove me and my two friends and my cousin around. He was basically my recruiting chauffeur. And he was younger than me. We just drove around campus, meeting the coaches or going to a coach's house, going back to their apartments and all that.

They knew how big it was for me even being around anything that has to do with Jordan. That's probably why Jeffrey was going to be my roommate, because he already had a roommate, and they were going to exchange him for me. So yeah, they probably tried to use that as bait. But I already had my mind made up on Kansas.

There was a lot of stuff that went into my decision. I wanted to be focused. I didn't want to be at home, because the University of Illinois is like two hours from Chicago. My friends and family probably wanted me to stay close. I didn't think it was a good idea. I felt like I was focused down in Florida at junior college, so I felt like I needed to stay that way so I could do my best.

There weren't distractions around my family, but I knew there could be. I just didn't want to make the wrong decision. I didn't think I should be close to home. At home sometimes there's just trouble — stuff I don't need to get into with friends, partying and all that kind of stuff.

On my visit to Illinois, I already knew I was coming to Kansas. I just wasn't being real with myself and anybody else. I already knew what I was doing. I just took my visit anyway. It was a good visit. I liked Illinois. I liked what they had to offer, but I just thought Kansas had more, so I came here.

## KANSAS STATE

I visited K-State, too. The coaches were so cool. Frank Martin … he's hollering and all that on TV, but off the court, he's a great guy. The team was pretty cool. They had great fan support. The same fans who were booing me at Kansas were the same fans that were chanting my name at the football game. I was walking on their football field. I forgot who they were playing, but their whole stadium was just chanting my name. It was something that I never really experienced. It was fun for me at the time. They really, really did show me love.

But it's funny now that I think about it, because the same fans cursed us out and were saying bad things when we beat them. But I enjoyed each visit I went on.

If I wouldn't have already had my mind made up that I was going to pick Kansas, I don't know what would've happened. It probably would have made my decision really hard. Kansas just had a little bit more to offer me. Great players came before me. A lot of stuff I learned on my visit I didn't know. It was kind of a no-brainer because of the history and how big basketball is.

## FIRST MEMORY

The first day I got here to KU, I had to do a lot of stuff. I got here late. They wanted me to play in the camp game. I was too tired to play in that. I didn't know there was going to be all the fans there.

I flew from Florida. I didn't have much anyway, but that stuff I did have, I didn't want to pack all that stuff up. It was all old stuff from high school and stuff I really wasn't going to need, like a TV and posters. So I just packed what I needed. I either gave away or threw away the rest of my stuff. I knew I didn't need it where I was going. I came to KU with one bag. It was my grandmother's suitcase, actually, that I'd brought down to Florida. I just had clothes. It was stuff that I needed.

Brennan Bechard was my roommate. I don't think he saw me that day or that night. So I just went to my room and put my stuff up. Brennan didn't really know I only came with one bag. That night, I went to Wal-Mart. I had a scholarship check, so I had money to get stuff. I got some pillows and sheets. That's it.

## "MOUSE IN THE HOUSE"

I remember one time Coach Self called me a mouse, because I was playing the four position. I was guarding Cole, and he kept saying, "Mouse in the house. Mouse in the house." Standing next to Cole — I switched up on him — and everybody kept saying, "Mouse in the house." I kind of took that personal, so I blocked his shot and started screaming, saying I was a big rat. After I said that, everybody started laughing. I didn't really mean to say it like that, like I was cracking a joke. I was just reacting, and everybody thought it was funny.

Coach never really said something that could get under somebody's skin, unless he was mad. Then he didn't care what he said. As far as joking and having fun, he doesn't say anything personal. He knows how we feel about certain things, and he doesn't want to embarrass anybody or anybody to feel bad. He's a good guy.

Every coach snaps. But when things aren't going well, when we come in lackadaisical at practice, he's going to try to make sure everything is tight. He wants everything to run smooth. He believes in doing things for 19 days in a row, saying that it will become a habit. So if he doesn't feel like we're going hard enough to get better, he's going to tighten things up.

When he snaps, he just usually ends up screaming and making us run. Nobody likes to run, especially when we do so much running during practice. Extra running is not really needed. Sometimes he'd get extreme. Sometimes, he'd just give us a little wakeup call – something light – then we'd pick it up.

## NORTHERN IOWA

*(After the Northern Iowa loss in the 2010 NCAA Tournament, TV cameras captured Little – who was redshirting that season – crying while crouched on the court.)*

I just thought we were going to win a championship. I just felt bad. It was just tough, because I felt like we worked so hard. I know every team works hard, but I can say that we worked hard every day. We never had a day off.

We never had any time when we went to the gym and didn't go hard. All of that was running through my mind. Me and Sherron were really cool. That was his last game, so I just had mixed emotions going in and out of me. That was just tough.

People gave me a hard time about that, but I don't care. I'm true to myself. I don't like sugar-coating things. People can say whatever, but I'm comfortable with what I did. It wasn't about TV ... I wasn't thinking about the TV. I was just thinking about what just happened.

## LEARNING FROM A MISTAKE

*(Little was arrested in December of 2010 on charges of battery, criminal damage and criminal trespassing following an altercation with his girlfriend and another man. He was suspended six games before returning to the team.)*

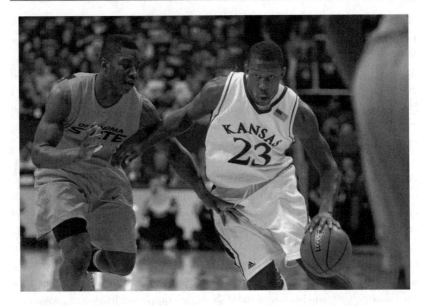

It was a situation that lets you know that just because you play basketball, you can't get away with doing stupid stuff. It was tough for me. I felt like I deserved the punishment that I got. I don't want to say it was blown up, because at the end of the day, I did dumb things that I shouldn't have done. That's all behind me. I don't really want to elaborate on that negative stuff that I did in the past. I just try to move on from them and do what I need to do.

The people who mattered didn't treat me any differently afterwards. A lot of people like my teammates, fans, coaching staff, family, friends — the people who matter know who I am as a person and they know people make mistakes. I'm not saying I'm an angel. I made mistakes. And I felt like the people who mattered forgave me for what I did. And the people who don't, if they're still thinking about that, I can't do anything about it.

At the end of the day, I can't ... you're not supposed to touch women. I never had a problem with that, especially being raised by my grandmother and respecting women so much. But, I mean, I lost my head, you know, in a matter of seconds. So, I mean, I didn't really have time enough to think. But I don't want to plead my case, because it's over. And I don't want to bring anything back up. Being able to tell my side is not really important. It's important that I was able to finish the season and graduate and just do what I love — play basketball.

Coach Self didn't take my side by any means. It was a knucklehead move I made. But he didn't give up on me, and my respect level went up more for him, once he let me know that he had my back and he wasn't going to leave me out to dry.

I didn't know what was going to happen. I knew I made a big mistake, and if I had to get kicked off the team, I would understand, because Kansas has got a history of off-the-court issues. So I knew I let a lot of people down. If I got kicked off, I wouldn't have been like, "Oh, they did me wrong." I'm grateful that they didn't.

## PLAYING AS A BIG

Once I got back on the court, I didn't play as well as I wanted to play, but I played hard. That's one thing I felt like I did. I played hard, and I tried to do what Coach wanted me to do.

There was stuff that I didn't want to do, but I still tried. I played power forward for Kansas. But I felt like that's something that a lot of people can't do, playing power forward against Wally Judge at 6-5, 210. That type of stuff ain't easy. I feel like I didn't accomplish my goals here, but I feel like I learned a lot and established relationships that I don't think will ever be broken.

A lot of people ... even Marcus felt like he was a guard. But I mean, the season's over with. I was here for three years. I enjoyed every minute of my time here at Kansas. I would have played anywhere just to be able to play. If Coach wanted me to play point guard or play center, I would have played, just so I would be able to be a part of something like this.

I didn't have free will to do whatever. I never really did like power forward. I wasn't backing down or things like that. It didn't matter which position group I went to in practice. I could go with the guards, I could go with the forwards. It really didn't matter once I got in the game. I just had to perform. It didn't matter if I was at the 4 or the 5 or the 2 or the 3.

Coach and I never really bumped heads about that. He knew I wanted to play on the perimeter, and I knew he felt like I could help the team more at the 4. It wasn't like I was mad. It was not a mutual agreement, but I could play it. It didn't really matter where I played.

I've been asked if I would have been more comfortable at KU if I was a guard the whole time. I mean, personally, maybe so. It didn't happen. I performed OK at the 4. I held my own. I didn't just get killed. I didn't let anybody just score on me any time down there. I felt like I played good, to be playing against 6-10 guys. I felt like I played good enough.

Some guys were easy to stop. Some guys, it was a little tougher. I had to be more focused and mentally prepared. The Big 12 is a tough conference. Every guy is able to do something, so you've got to keep your focus and be ready.

I don't regret anything I did here. I'm fine with how I left, minus not winning a championship. If I would have gone to Illinois or K-State, I wouldn't be as close with the people I am now. Like I said, I'm grateful for everything.

# CHAPTER 36

# 2006/07 - 2010/11

# BRADY MORNINGSTAR

Brady Morningstar spent five seasons at the University of Kansas from 2006-11, red-shirting during the Jayhawks' national title run in 2007-08. Known as a strong defender and a good spot-up shooter, Morningstar played in 116 games at KU with 68 starts. He averaged 7.3 points as a senior and led the conference with a 4.4 assist-to-turnover ratio in Big 12 play. The son of former KU standout Roger Morningstar, Brady earned honorable mention all-conference honors as a senior and was also named to the Big 12 All-Defensive team. Morningstar graduated from Free State High School in Lawrence in 2005. He spent a year at New Hampton Prep in New Hampshire before enrolling at Kansas.

## IN BRADY'S WORDS

I remember when I was in prep school, and Coach Dooley and Coach Self came down to see me, because they hadn't really spent much time recruiting me. They came for four or five hours and walked around. I showed them the campus. I told them, "Don't waste your time on me. If you offer me a scholarship, I'll come. If not, I'll find somewhere else."

I don't know if the coaches had ever had someone tell them to not recruit them. But I just knew if they offered me, I was going to come there.

I had some other schools recruiting me, but I didn't take many visits, because I had my heart set on Kansas, because I wanted to play here. I wanted to be in a winning program, a winning tradition. I wanted to play at one of the most elite colleges in the country.

They left, and later they said, "Yeah, we want to offer you a scholarship. Do you want to come?" I said, "Yeah, I'll take it. I'm coming." It wasn't like, "I'll think about it."

That night I called some recruiting website around 10 at night, and they released it at 11:30. My dad was like, "Dang, you should have waited till the next morning, because you'd have gotten more press, more pub." I wasn't worried about it, though. I just wanted to get it done with and get on with my prep school season.

## SHERRON COLLINS

I still remember the first day I met Sherron. We were in Horejsi practice gym playing pickup, and Coach T was like, "Hey, your roommate's going to be in here while you guys play pickup. His flight gets in late, but he'll be here."

Sherron walked in wearing a big ol' chain and was kind of big — a lot bigger than I expected for a little guard. After the game, I went up and shook his hand and said, "Hey, Sherron." He didn't have any sheets, so I ran home and got some sheets and some pillows for him.

The first week he was in town freshman year, his son, Sherron Jr., passed away. I didn't know what to do. I didn't know him real well. I knew he had boys back home calling him and stuff. But no one really knew him real well here except for the coaches. Obviously you comfort him and whatnot, but we didn't know his situation.

That's the first tough thing we'd been through together. I saw tears from him, man. Tears. He lost someone he loved.

I just stayed in the room with him, took him wherever, stood by him, played video games with him. There's not much you can do to help someone grieve about their lost son. What can you do, right? I've never been in that situation before. Something like that happens, and it's as serious as it gets. So it helped me grow up a lot, too, realizing like, "Hey, you can't take anything for granted." He's already been through this, and this is his first week of college? That's crazy.

Ever since then, I just knew where he was coming from was super-serious, because he's 18, 19, and he had a baby boy who just passed away. That doesn't happen to a lot of people. I mean, it does, but not to a lot of people you know, especially that young. You just see a different side of him when you're around him more instead of just the Sherron on the court.

## TOUGH DAYS

From then on, I know Sherron trusted me. He went to me for anything. He would tell me a whole bunch of stuff that he said he never told anybody else, expect for his mom. He didn't have a lot of people down here at the beginning that he wanted to share his business with, because he had so much going on in his life, and he didn't know if they wanted to hear it.

People had no clue. Family matters, family issues that weren't in the paper that he had going on with people back home. Life in Chicago is crazy where he's from. Killings, murders, drugs and all that stuff. And growing up in that situation, even though he left, he was still a part of it, because he still get phone calls from people back there to let him know what's going down. It's a tough situation to leave Chicago and to leave the ones you love to come play ball in Kansas — the middle of nowhere.

He had a lot of friends pass away. I wouldn't say a lot, but four or five friends when he was at school got shot. It's just a different world. It's normal out there to hear someone gets killed, because it happens all the time.

He told me every single time one of his friends died. He'd go back to the funerals. He'd leave for the day and come back that night. You've got to go pay your dues, pay your respects, and coaches understood that. Some were tougher than others, but they were all tough.

I think everyone perceived Sherron to be super-tough, hard-core, inner-city Chicago, which he was. He was that. There's nothing around that. But also, he had a big heart. He loved helping people. He had emotion. And unless you knew him real well or you were around him a whole bunch, you didn't really get to see his different side. You got to see his side on the court where he was talking s--t, like, "I'm the man out here. I do this. I play ball." But then after the game, he's got a son. He's got a daughter. He's got a family.

## SHERRON AND THE BOXER

The first time Sherron knew I had a dog was when my parents were out of town, and I needed to bring my dog to the apartment, because I didn't want her at home all the time.

Mackie's a boxer, a harmless little dog. I put her in the room, and I left. I didn't Sherron was afraid of dogs, so I didn't tell him a dog was in the room.

So he walks in, and Mackie comes running up to him and scares the s--t out of him. He's like, "Hey, hey, hey, hey, hey! Stop!" I come back, and he's in his room with the door shut, like, "Is that your dog, man?" And I'm like, "Yeah, yeah." He's like, "I don't do dogs, man. You've got to get that out of here."

He got attacked by a dog in Chicago when he was younger. I swear they all say they got attacked by dogs, but he showed me the scars. He was doing something on the ground at football practice, and a dog came and attacked him at football practice. He said that ever since then, he was afraid of dogs. But the more and more he was around Mackie, I was like, "Yo, she's not going to do anything. She's just a little dog."

I remember the progression with Sherron and Mackie. At first it was like, "Give her a treat. She'll be all right." It was funny. My mom was laughing, because my mom is, like, the littlest person in the world, and she was OK being around dogs. You'd think Sherron, the toughest dude ever, would be OK being around a dog, too. That was one of the funny things I remember about him.

The first couple times he came to the house, he'd be like, "Yo, keep the dog upstairs." And then more and more, he just got used to it. At the end, he was playing with her, playing fetch. He was like, "Come here," showing people he wasn't afraid. He was proud to say, "I can pet this dog now. I used to lock myself in the room."

That resembles his career since he's been here, just how much he's grown from his freshman year all the way to his senior year. He just took giant steps.

## MESSAGE BOARD CHATTER

I really didn't read comments or message boards. Maybe after an article written about me, someone would say, "Hey, you should check this out. This is a good article." I'd read it. Then you'd scroll down to read two, three, four comments, just to see.

They make you laugh. Honestly, it makes you laugh. But no more than a couple times have I ever read a message board, because I know those people have no clue what they're talking about. They really don't. As much as they sound like they do to other people, they're idiots in my book, especially if you're not going to put your real name up there and talk. I think that's foolish. If you're going to say something, be proud to say it. If not, then hide behind a screen name and talk your s--t pretty much.

I'm sure a lot of people on there are from other schools and whatnot, but I don't know how that stuff works. I don't even know how you get on there. But like I said, if you're hiding behind a screen name running your mouth, that shows the type of person you are. It could have gotten me going if I had thin skin, but I don't have thin skin. I'll take that all day. It's nothing.

## RACE ISSUES

People have a perception that, because you're white, you probably can't play at a major Division I school and get major minutes and make an impact and do some things I did. But if you think about it, every team pretty much has a guy like me or Tyrel that did certain things their needed them to do. We can play ball, too.

I know these other guys are more athletic and their style might be a little prettier and all that, but we can play ball, too. That's not a question. We weren't worried about that, and I wasn't worried about coming in here and playing, because when I was in prep school, I was about the only white guy on my team or in the league, playing good and starting and scoring 22 a game. I wasn't worried.

Anyone who's not from Kansas thinks that you're so country. It's just like, "Where do you guys live? What do you guys do in Kansas?" I was like, "It's a college town, man. It's about as good as it gets. You'd be surprised." That's the funny thing. People really do think that Kansas is just dirt, weeds and shacks. That may be true in some parts of the state, but other parts are big. They think I'm a cowboy, until they see us play, then they're like, "Damn, he's got a little bit of game."

When I got to prep school — because everyone there is from out East or from the West Coast; no one from the Midwest really goes to prep school – they'd be like, "This white boy's going to Kansas? You're playing at Kansas next year?" I'd be like, "Yeah." They'd be like, "Pfff. All right."

I heard that all the time, from people in the stands, from other crowds. I knew they were probably just doing that to get under my skin and stuff. It's all fun and games. But some people were being serious, like, "You're really going to play at Kansas? I have to see that to believe it." It happened all the time. But that's the fun part, because when you do compete and you get out there and you make something happen and make plays and hit shots and score points, it feels good, because you know other people are watching, because we're always on TV.

I think in some sports, you have to prove more when you're white. Tennis, probably not. Hockey, probably not. But in basketball, I think yes, the majority of the best players are African-American. It is what it is.

I think people, for the most part, respected players on the court that played for Kansas, because they know we're not pushovers. If he's out there for Kansas, he's obviously doing something right.

## DUI

*(Morningstar was suspended for the first semester of his junior year after being arrested on suspicion of driving while intoxicated on Oct. 3, 2009.)*

The people that were closest to me in my life since I was growing up all supported me. I probably got 150, 200 phone calls between my mom, my dad, friends I haven't heard from in a while, just reaching their hand out, being good friends, good people. It was just a crazy situation, something that I never thought would happen.

I was just coming home and got pulled over. It was just terrible timing, a stupid decision, but you learn from what you do, and other people learn from what you do, too. It's definitely a lowlight in my career at Kansas, but I can't do anything about it. I just had to take my medicine and go.

The suspension was tough. I embarrassed my family, embarrassed my school, my coaches, my teammates, myself. But that next Monday, I got up and went to class. I walked with my chest out and my head up. I didn't show people that I let it bother me, even though I was going home mad, crying.

When you're given an opportunity like this to play at a school like this, you can't put yourself in a position like that. It was a tough situation, but there was a ton of support from my friends and family and even my coaches. They knew it was a mistake, but through all the stuff we'd been through that year with the fight with the football team and stuff, everything was going to be magnified. The next thing you do is magnified. And that was the next thing that happened. It

was all over the place, and Coach Self had to do something about it. He had to show the country, "Hey, I'm going to discipline my players, because they're screwing up right now."

I respect Coach Self to the fullest. I think he and I have one of the best relationships out of any of the players he's had on his teams. I don't knock him at all for suspending me for a semester. It was his decision.

Coach Self was upset. I don't know who told him, but I was in shock. I didn't want to tell anybody. I didn't know what to say. I didn't know what to do. It was by far one of the worst nights of my life, just because you know you screwed up so much. You know you're going to get in trouble. You know it's going to get out to the media. You know the media's going to blow it up. You know for the next two, three years in college, every fan — even if they have a DUI; I don't know if they have one — they're going to come at me.

We got a bunch of laughs and smiles out of it. We'd go warm up for our pregame shooting for away games, and we'd come back in the locker room, and Coach Self would be there, drinking his Diet Coke. "Are the fans good?" "Hell, yeah, they're good." "What are they saying?" We had to tell him what they were saying, tell him what the signs said. We'd start laughing. "So they're getting on Sherron pretty good?" "Yeah." "They getting on you, Brady?" "Yeah." "What are they saying?" He liked to hear stories, because it gave him a laugh, because he knew we were going to go out there and get a win. Because no one in the Big 12 was able to hang with us. That was always the best feeling, knowing that.

It's all laughs, then when the game starts, it's all business. And we used the business that the fans were giving us warming up ... we took it out on their team, which was a good feeling.

## MORE ON SELF

Coach Self and I would go back and forth in practices. We have a really good relationship. I'm a smart ass. He's a smart ass. We'd go back and forth being smart asses. That's what friends do. He's my coach, but he's my friend, too. I love the guy to death. He's done so much for me. He's so well-respected around here, how could you not like him? He's bigger than life, but he doesn't act like it.

I'd crack back at Coach in practice all the time. Like, if I missed four shots in a row from 3, and on my fifth shot, I'd bank one in, I'd say, "Yeah, Coach, you like that one?" Then I'd run back down the court. There were just some stupid instances of me being a smart ass, yelling some stuff out, trying to make people laugh and lighten the mood. What's he going to do? Yell at me? Make me run? All right, I'll do that. It's all fun. Playing ball is serious, but you've got to have your laughs and you've got to have fun at the same time, especially in practice.

One of my favorite memories is of jumping around in the locker room after Big 12 championships. Coach Self would try to get everyone in the middle of the room to start jumping, and we'd start drilling him, hitting him hard to see if he could take the hits. I know the walk-ons especially would be like, "Yeah, come on!" POW! They'd try to hit him and stuff, because he was in the middle. That was our chance to act like we were excited, but also to get a little shoulder shrug on him to see if he could take it.

## JERSEY BOY?

Obviously, Tyshawn's from New Jersey, but we'd bug him because he's really from Florida. He lived in Florida when he was younger. Tyshawn would always rep like he's from New Jersey.

Coach Dooley — he's from the East Coast — would always be like, "Tyshawn, you're from Florida, all right? Get the Jersey s--t out of your system."

Tyshawn would laugh, but I know he kind of hated hearing that, because he wants to be the Jersey boy. But he grew up in Florida, so we always used to give him a hard time about that.

## VCU LOSS

I just think we let everybody down. We had such an opportunity to do something special in my last year. We probably knew it was going to be the twins' last year, Tyrel's last year. You've got such an opportunity in front of you to do something special, and you just let it trickle down your leg. It's like, "Damn, man. Why did we come out missing shots? Why did we come out not defending them, and them knocking down everything?"

We learned our lesson against Northern Iowa. We should have learned our lesson. For the most part we did, until VCU came out hitting shots. It was tough to stop. We made our comeback to get to one, but boom. You've got to catch a break, and we didn't catch a break.

You've got to give VCU credit, but I think we were the better team. I think nine out of 10 times, we're the better team. But that one afternoon, man, they got the best of us, and that was tough because we were supposed to be in that Final Four. I know we were.

It was a perfect draw for us. But a lot of people say, and sometimes I think about it, that maybe we would have been better playing Florida State. They're a defensive team, but they couldn't score like VCU was scoring in the tournament. They're a hell of a defensive team, but maybe we would've matched up better with them. They've got bigger guys. We've got bigger guys.

But hindsight's 20-20. You can't sit back and think, "Who should we have played?" or who you wish we'd have played. We had a chance to play VCU and we had a chance to beat them, and we didn't. We screwed it up for ourselves, although we had a hell of a year.

That night after the loss, I came back and stayed up for a while. I just sat in the room with Conner and Mario. Some of my boys came over, and ... I don't know. It was tough. There's not a specific thing we did. Just sat back there and knew we should be celebrating. We shouldn't be sitting at home quiet without the TV on, not wanting to watch SportsCenter knowing we got upset. We should be the ones coming back to a full house at the Fieldhouse like we did in '08, hearing everyone cheering, "Final Four," then in a couple of days leaving. It should be big time.

## NO PARTY

All I wanted to do my whole career was be part of the reason why (students from my senior class) got to party on Mass Street. The people that were down there in 2008 said that was the most fun they'd ever had in their lives. I was a part of the '08 team, but I wasn't the main part. I wasn't on the court. So I wanted to be the reason that other kids got the chance to do that. I felt like we as a team – and myself – let our students down, because they had an opportunity to rush down to Mass Street and fill that thing up and start partying, because we were going back to the Final Four. And that was the tough thing. I wanted that to happen.

We're doing it for ourselves first. I want to win. We want to win for ourselves. But it's about more than ourselves. It's about our fans that represent us. We're good because of the people that support us. If we had no support, no boosters, no money, no recruiting, we might still be good, but it's tough to keep up in the game with everybody else who's blowing past you with money, new facilities, new arenas. But we've got the best of the best, so I think our fans deserve the best of the best. They deserve to see championships every year.

## GETTING PROPS

The best compliment I got was, "You're a hell of a player." Everyone gets spoiled here. We all get compliments from people that Coach Self brings in, his old coaches. Coach Brown comes here. Obviously, they're going to give us compliments, because they love Kansas, love Coach Self. They're going to love his players, even if Coach Self is pissed at us.

I shook hands with a lot of coaches after games that said, "Hey, you make this team go. I know you don't get a lot of chances to score and all that, but you're a big part to this team." I had a lot of people come up and say that to me. And that felt good. It didn't go to my head at all.

Pat Knight of Texas Tech was one of them. He went to New Hampton, where I went to prep school. Coming through the line, he was like, "Hey man, you're a hell of a player. Keep that s--t up." Something like that.

## EARNING HIS SPOT

I think I proved that Kansas recruiting me wasn't a mistake. I think I proved that I could play at Kansas. I think that was the biggest knock on me, like, "Why did they give him a scholarship? Is he really going to play here, or was it because his pops is doing something for Coach behind the scenes?"

No coach is stupid enough to give a player a scholarship because of his dad or because his dad played there. You might give a kid a walk-on spot for certain reasons or whatnot, but if you give a kid a scholarship, that's one less that you can give to another player that you want to recruit. So coaches don't have to just give up a scholarship just because their parents are nice or because their parents went to KU. But I think people really believed that's why I got a scholarship at first, and I heard it all the time, especially freshman year when I wasn't playing and the next year when I red-shirted and I still wasn't getting any run.

I would hear people. You just overhear people talking. I'm good at that now. I'm good at looking in one direction and hearing what's going on in another. I'm good at knowing someone's staring at me when I'm not even looking at them, because it happens all the time.

But I just think I proved I was capable of playing here at a high level. And everyone that thought I wasn't able to, I don't think they have anything to say now.

CHAPTER 37

**2007/08 - 2010/11**

# TYREL REED

**14**

Tyrel Reed ended his Kansas career in the spring of 2011 with more wins than any player in the history of the program. The Jayhawks went 132-17 in Reed's four seasons. As a senior, Reed was the only player to start all 38 games for a squad that won its seventh straight Big 12 title before reaching the Elite Eight. He ranked third on the team with 9.7 points per game. Reed was also honored as a first-team Academic All-American as a senior. The Burlington, Kan., native married his longtime girlfriend, Jessica, in July of 2011.

## IN TYREL'S WORDS

When I was a freshman and sophomore, I didn't really feel that comfortable around Coach Self, just because I didn't want to make him mad and I was just kind of nervous around him. If he'd make fun of me, I didn't know if I should take it personally or if he was just trying to make a joke.

I didn't really talk much around him, which was kind of awkward. But finally, one summer, I got used to talking to him, which made me a lot more comfortable. I should have been that way the whole time.

Eventually, I was just like, "You know what? You're getting older. You're going to have to be around this coach all the time." I really embraced that and kind of just started to understand his personality and made my personality work with his. But he's a great person, a fun person to be around. Extremely demanding, but that's what makes him such a good coach.

## TEAMMATES

I was really close to Darrell Arthur my freshman year, when I first got here. The first thing that comes to my mind with Darrell Arthur is him giving me my nickname right when I got to KU.

B-Rush was B-Rush, Mario was 'Rio and I was just Tyrel. I didn't have a nickname. We were in the locker room one day, and he came up with T-Squeeze, and it stuck ever since. All the guys on the team still call me it to this day. He just said it sounded good. He said it flowed well, so that was pretty much it.

The first time I met Cole, I was in the Big Jayhawk tournament here at KU during high school. I remember meeting him and seeing how goofy he was. But that's what makes him appealing to people, and that's why I enjoy being around him so much, because he has a free-flowing personality and we just have such a good time together.

Cole and I have so many good memories from being in the dorm together. He was my roommate for three years. We had a little basketball hoop in our room, a little Nerf hoop. I can't remember how many times we would have a game of "P-I-G" or "H-O-R-S-E" in our room and bet a dollar or bet who was going to buy lunch the next day. We did that many times and had some heated battles. It was a good matchup.

For a big guy, he could shoot a Nerf ball pretty well. It was set up in the middle of our room along the brick wall of the Towers. You could shoot from the kitchen. You could shoot and try to make it off the wall – pretty much anything you could think of. I can't say that one of us won more than the other. It was pretty even. We bought lunch for one another multiple times.

Seeing Josh Selby go through what he did this year ... some fans don't see it the same way we do. We're with him every day. Most of the time, he had a great attitude. I loved being around Josh. He's a fun kid. There's something about Josh, something about his personality, that made me really enjoy being around him. When he was hurt, I was hurt, so we were always on the sideline together working out because we couldn't be on the court playing basketball. Coach Hudy had us going through workouts. He had a great attitude about getting through workouts together. Me and him were kind of in the same boat, both injured and trying to have the best attitude we could. And he had a great attitude through it all.

## BONE BRUISE

My foot injury my senior season was pretty bad. It happened after I twisted my ankle. I didn't do anything any different, but there was just this extra bone I had in the back of my ankle that, for some reason, must have gotten injured and gotten knocked loose a little bit. It really started bothering me. That's when the doctors noticed that I had it – and needed to get it taken out.

The reason I said it was like a rock in my shoe is because it was always nagging. It didn't feel like there was a rock in my shoe, obviously. It wasn't my heel that bothered me or anything like that. It was just further up my ankle, kind of around my Achilles. It was just shooting pain through there the whole time. It felt terrible. I don't really know how to explain it, but I'm just glad it's over with now.

The injury made it tough to get going. It was tough to warm up. That was probably one of the hardest things, just going through warm-ups at the beginning of the game. When everyone else was out trying to dunk, that was probably the most painful time for me, just trying to get it going and moving a little bit. I really couldn't jump off of one foot. That's why I tried to jump off two feet or jump off my other foot.

I'm not going to blame anything on the injury. I played through it, and whenever you're playing, you've got to go out there and produce. It was just one of those things that really nagged at me, one of those things you usually don't have to deal with throughout an entire season.

You'd rather, if you could, deal with it or sit out a little bit of time or whatever it takes to come back playing 100 percent. But no matter what I did, that wasn't going to be the case. I'd have to sit out for an extremely long period of time, but surgery was probably the better option.

It's just one of those things ... my senior year I was excited about how we were doing and how we were playing, and I didn't want to miss any time. I was just fortunate enough to have coaches and teammates that understood that. They were fine with me sitting out a few practices and then practicing the day before the game. They knew I was trying my hardest to be prepared and ready.

I could tell the difference after surgery. I'm still a little sore. It's a little different having my bone gone. But I'm getting used to it now.

## RIVALRY GAMES

The times we played Missouri or Kansas State really stick out in my mind. I loved going over to Columbia and beating Missouri in their building. Going to Bramlage ... I think Bramlage is probably the toughest arena that I've played in. Their fans really came out and showed support for them when they played us.

One of the things that sticks out in my mind is when we beat Kansas State my junior year, when Sherron hit that last-second shot against them. That was really a fun game to play in.

My senior year, I hit a big three in the last 2 minutes to help us beat Missouri in Columbia, and afterwards, I screamed toward the MU student section. It was just a spur-of-the-moment thing. I didn't yell anything in particular. I wasn't singling anybody out. I just kind of screamed and yelled and was excited about making the shot.

Coach told me that they were going to run a little play, and he told me to knock the shot down, and I told him I would. It just all worked out. I think Marcus was the one that set the screen for me to get open in the corner. Give credit to him. Playing against Missouri, there are always those kinds of emotions. Just excitement.

## SELF STORIES

Coach Self never really got too mad at me. I tried to always be doing what I should be doing and work as hard as I could. I remember a time when we played Colorado out in Colorado. The first half I was absolutely horrible. At halftime, he said, "I expect a better half. Quit playing like a high school player. Play like I know you're capable of." I think in the second half, I had 12 or so points. Him challenging me was good motivation to help me play a lot better.

We also got in trouble one time, and Coach Self said we needed to shave all of our facial hair. He wanted us clean-cut and everything. I remember coming in one morning from boot camp, and Marcus' and Markieff's faces were shaved. Marcus and Markieff looked like they were 17 again. It's probably the maddest I've ever seen Markieff in my life. That's just who they are. They've always had facial hair. They've always been clean-cut. It's probably the maddest I've ever seen him at Coach Self, because it kind of took something away from them. That's who they were. I could tell Markieff was mad because of his body language and some of the words he said about having to do what he had to do. He was pretty upset with the coaches making him shave his face.

## END OF A CAREER

The night after the VCU loss was kind of a blur. Getting over that loss ... it obviously was the last game of my career. It was a culmination of my four years, and it was just saddening for it to happen that way, because I had such high expectations for that team, and I think if we just had a better shooting game and played a little differently, we would have won that game.

It's kind of a haze. I don't remember much of it. I was just really disappointed and sad that it happened, but still proud of what I did all year.

I have no regrets. I had a great four years playing at the University of Kansas and having the opportunity to be a Kansas kid and fulfill his dream. Now, I'm going to hopefully continue to play basketball. Without playing at Kansas, I wouldn't have had that opportunity.

# CHAPTER 38

**2 0 1 0 / 1 1**

# JOSH SELBY

**32**

J osh Selby played one season at Kansas before entering the 2011 NBA draft, where he was selected by the Memphis Grizzlies with the 49th overall pick. Selby – the No. 1-ranked recruit in the Class of 2010 by Rivals.com – played in just 26 games for the Jayhawks and made 11 starts. He averaged 7.9 points during a freshman season that began with a nine-game suspension by the NCAA and ended with a nagging foot injury that hampered Selby's play throughout February and March. Selby is a Baltimore native who earned McDonald's All-American honors in 2010. He averaged 32 points and seven assists as a high school senior.

## IN JOSH'S WORDS

I never really got into trouble with the law when I was little, but growing up in Baltimore, I was always out in the streets. When my grandmother told me to come in, I didn't come in. Some days she or my mom couldn't even find me. I'd stay out all night and wouldn't come home until the next morning. Stuff like that was normal for a kid living in the atmosphere I grew up in.

In one month alone when I was 15, I had six friends who were shot and killed. A few years before that, one of my friends got pistol-whipped while we were walking home from school. He's lucky he didn't die. There were gangs running around everywhere, violence, drugs, killings. I've never been shot at intentionally, at least I don't think I have, but I've been (on the scene) for a couple of drive-bys.

With all that stuff going on … I was just angry all the time. I was mad – mad at the world. Not depressed, just angry and mad all the time. I felt like the world was against me, and I was against the world. I felt like I was by myself.

## MOMMA'S BOY

I grew up without a father around. I never knew the man. Luckily, I had my mom. I owe everything to her. The thing I appreciate about her the most is that she never gave up on me. My mom had me when she was 17. As a single parent, it wasn't easy for her at all. I put her through some rough times. I was always out running wild, getting into fights and other dumb stuff, just acting like a little thug. But she never quit on me. She never neglected me. I appreciated that about her the most.

I've never had a stable home. Ever. My mom and I had to move around a lot, and sometimes I'd live with other people. I'd go back and forth from my mom's place to my grandmother's place to my uncle's place. When I was living with my grandmother, my mom would get off work around 12 or 1 in the morning. Instead of going home, she'd come to see me – I'd still be up – to make sure I had eaten a good dinner or that I got to bed OK. Other times, she'd take a pay cut so she could stay home on certain days to make sure I was good and taken care of.

My mom was a good basketball player, too. I couldn't beat her in one-on-one until I was in the ninth grade. One time we were playing, and I busted her lip open on accident. I thought she'd want to end the game right then, but she wanted to keep playing.

There were times when I wanted to break down and just quit – quit school, quit basketball, quit everything. She'd keep pushing me. She'd tell me, "God has given you a gift that a lot of people would love to have. Don't waste it." If it wasn't for her, trust me, I wouldn't be playing basketball.

## WHO'S NO. 1?

Once I started getting good at basketball, a few people in my family became Internet experts. They were on the computer all the time, reading about me and all these different players. When Rivals.com listed me as their No. 1-ranked recruit, my phone started ringing like crazy. They all saw it on there before I did.

Sometimes recruiting rankings and things like that can put pressure on a kid. But that ranking actually made my life a lot easier. Before that, I couldn't go anywhere in Baltimore and feel comfortable. But after I got that ranking, I could go anywhere I wanted and feel safe. Everyone knew me. Everyone was looking out for me. All the hustlers and dealers and people in my neighborhood, no one wanted to see me get hurt.

The other good thing was that I was able to travel. Other than me, no one in my family had ever traveled beyond two states. They couldn't afford it. They never had a chance. But I was getting to go to all these tournaments across the country and see all these different places. It was truly a blessing to be in that situation. So, yeah, I liked that ranking. I didn't mind it at all.

## SWAGGER

Even though a lot of people were talking about me, I still didn't feel like I was getting the respect I deserved from people – from opponents or media or whatever. I also had some uncles who were sarcastic. They'd be like, "You're No. 1 player in the country, but you're not averaging as many points as this guy," or, "You haven't done what that guy did." So I always kept myself humble. I've never been cocky at all, and that's not going to change.

Now, if we're talking about on the court ... people take the way I play as cocky. But that's just how I play. I'm confident on the court. When I'm on the court, I don't feel like anyone can stop me except myself and God. That's just how I feel. They take my cockiness on the court and think I'm like that off the court. That's not how it is.

It wasn't until this summer (in 2011) that I truly felt like I had a gift from God. I was playing in a summer league here in Baltimore, the Melo League, against a bunch of NBA guys like Michael Beasley and Gary Neal, who plays for the Spurs. My team was in the championship game, and we were down by eight points with 1 minute left. I scored eight points during that minute and hit a 3 in Michael Beasley's face with 1 second left to send the game into overtime. That's when I knew I had a gift from God. (Note: Selby finished with 51 points in that game was selected as the league's Most Valuable Player.)

## RECRUITING

Before I decided to come to Kansas, I was committed to Tennessee for a long time. I had developed a good relationship with all of the guys there, all of the coaches. So it was really hard for me to back out of that commitment.

Looking back, I committed to Tennessee too early. At the time, they were recruiting me so much harder than anyone else. Other schools kept saying, "Why didn't we get a chance?" I was like, "I didn't know y'all wanted me." So I decided to open it up and give everyone a fair chance, because I didn't give them a fair chance before.

I took my visit to Kansas for midnight madness. If you go to midnight madness at Kansas, trust me, you'll want to commit there. They've got the best midnight madness ever. Just watching the introduction video is going to get you. It gave me chills. It was like, "This is where I want to be." After that, I didn't have to tell my mom that I was going to Kansas. She told me. She said, "I don't know about you, but I'm coming here."

I was trying to get Terrence Jones to come to school with me. I'm kind of glad it didn't happen, though, because the twins were unbelievable. Terrence might not have gotten to play very much. I don't know how it would've worked. He wanted to go to Kentucky to play more of his game. He's a wing forward. If he would've come to Kansas, he probably would've played more on the block.

## LIFE AS A JAYHAWK

*(The NCAA suspended Selby for the first nine games of the 2010-11 season for accepting impermissible benefits from Robert Frazier, the business manager for NBA star Carmelo Anthony. Selby and his mother said that Frazier has been a longtime family friend.)*
I felt like I got screwed a little bit on that suspension, like it wasn't fair. But I also felt lucky, because at first they weren't going to allow me to play at all. That's what I was worried about the most. I was just happy when they said nine games instead of the whole season. That whole time I was sitting out, my attitude was good. I was just looking forward to the day I got to play. *(That day came on Dec. 18, 2010, when Selby scored 21 points and hit the game-winning 3-pointer in a victory over USC in Lawrence.)*

Just seeing the smiles on the faces of my mom that day – plus my teammates, my coaches and the fans. That's what I'll remember the most. It had been a long road to get to that day. I'll also remember how my grandmother got to watch my first game on TV. She wasn't there in person. She doesn't fly. But I talked to her after the game, I called her. She was proud. She was crying.

## RISKING IT ALL

I pretty much knew all along that I wasn't going to be at Kansas for more than a year. I actually knew that before I ever got to campus. That's why I kept playing when I probably should've stayed off the court. Not long after that USC game, I hurt my foot and things were never the same. To be honest, I should have sat out the rest of the season. Coach Self was begging me to shut it down, to take the rest of the year off so I could rehab and come back stronger as a sophomore. The doctors were giving me the same advice. It was that bad.

That's what I don't think people ever understood. I was risking my career just to put on a Kansas uniform. I knew it was probably going to be my only chance to ever play in college, to ever play at Allen Fieldhouse, with all of those good fans. So I just kept trying as best as I could. I had already missed nine games. I didn't want to miss any more.

One thing that was tough was that I had to wear this really big brace. I went from a size 12 to a size 13 ½ because of that brace on my foot. So I'm playing with a brace on, an extra sole in my shoe, and a steel plate in my shoe – which was nearly two sizes bigger than what I normally wear. I was slow, I couldn't jump and it was hard for me to get past anyone. I just couldn't move very well.

I definitely wasn't 100 percent out there but, even then, I still wanted to play more. It was a learning process. I got a little frustrated. But it was hard to get too down, because we were winning. The guys on the team were happy, the fans were happy, because it looked like we could do something special. It's not like I was going to complain or act mad during a situation like that. It wouldn't have been right. I just wanted to do whatever I could to help my team. Whatever I needed to do for my teammates, I was going to do.

## F.O.E.

My teammates were like brothers to me. That's why we were always saying "F.O.E." – Family Over Everything. We had that strong of a relationship. I loved them. I'll fight for my teammates any day, any time. Every last one of them, from the first option on the bench to the last option. I loved my team.

You'd always see me, Tyshawn Taylor, Mario Little, T-Rob, the twins, Elijah Johnson, Royce Woolridge, and Niko Roberts together. If you saw one of us, you saw all of us. We stayed inside a lot and played video games. We went to the club every now and then. After a big win, we'd go celebrate. It was a brotherhood. Our connection was unbelievable. That's why that VCU loss hurt so much. I think we took them for granted. They were VCU, and we were Kansas. We probably didn't respect them like we should have. In the locker room, it was very emotional. Very emotional.

## BACKLASH

Coach Self was pretty emotional when I told him I was leaving. I told him during a meeting I had with him. I just think he was disappointed, because my season hadn't gone like we'd all hoped it would go. But life goes on. He understood my situation. He understood my background. He knew I needed to take care of my family. Hopefully, when I return to Kansas, Coach Self and I will talk and our relationship will be good, just like the relationship he has with his other former players. That's what I want. There are no hard feelings. I love Kansas. My mom does, too. She was disappointed that I got hurt and with how things worked out. But she loved Kansas. You'll never hear her talk bad about Kansas.

The frustrating part about leaving was that there were some fans that just killed me for it – just people making comments on Twitter and Facebook and stuff. I was very disappointed in that. Everyone can have their own opinions, but if they were in my shoes or if they had lived my life, they might have a better understanding of why I did what I did. I want people there to like me and think good things about me, but life isn't always like that. I don't have any regrets about going there. I learned a lot about the game and was part of a great team. I just did what I thought was best for me and my family.

## MOVING ON

On the night of the draft, I had a little party for my family at this lounge in Baltimore. Once the draft started, me and my uncle went outside and sat in the car. I didn't want to deal with everything going on inside. When I got picked, I heard everyone inside going nuts. They were going crazy. That's how I found out I'd been picked. Once I heard everyone yelling, I broke down and started crying.

I was disappointed that I went so low (No. 49, to Memphis), because every workout I went to, I thought I did good. Every coach was telling me they liked my game and that they'd love to have me. So I was disappointed. At the same time, Memphis is a great place. I love Memphis. I love the team that's there and I love the city. Memphis is my new home.

Will and Antonio Barton, my cousins, play for (the University of) Memphis. And I'll be with Xavier Henry and Shady (Darrell Arthur) from Kansas. It'll be like the Kansas Alumni Association. It's the perfect fit.

A few days after the draft, I had a meeting with one of the GMs. I was pretty nervous. He told me they picked me because of my high school career and not my college career. He told me they liked me and that he thought I'd fit in really well. But he told me they wanted me to mature off the court. I looked at him and said, "I got you."

I think people look at what happened at Kansas and think the reason I wasn't playing had to do with immaturity or because there was some sort of problem. It had nothing to do with that. It wasn't because of a bad attitude or anything like that. I was hurt.

I'm just looking forward to getting a fresh start. It still hasn't hit me yet that I'm in the NBA. I still feel like a regular kid who grew up playing ball in the streets and somehow fought his way out.

# CHAPTER 39

# 2009/10 - Present
# THOMAS ROBINSON

0

Thomas Robinson will enter his third season at Kansas in 2011-12. As a sophomore, he averaged 7.6 points and 6.4 rebounds while playing 14.6 minutes per game. After learning of the death of his mother, Lisa, on Jan. 21, 2011, Robinson still played eight minutes in KU's game the following day — a 74-63 loss to Texas. Two days after Lisa's funeral, Robinson returned against Kansas State, scoring 17 points on 7-of-11 shooting with nine rebounds in a 90-66 KU victory.

## IN THOMAS' WORDS

I picked KU because I wanted to come to a school that would help me prepare myself as a person and as a basketball player. Kansas has all those tools to do that. And also with the staff they have and the history they have surrounding the school ... that definitely helped out.

During my visit, I decided I was coming here. I realized how easy I was connecting with the team. I saw how my teammates and I were so alike, and I thought it'd be good to be around people who were similar to me off the court, and on the court also. I thought that definitely helped me get comfortable when it came to adapting to basketball.

When I got here, I immediately connected with the twins and Tyshawn. They're all from the East Coast. We live in similar cities. They came from a similar type background that I came from. And they were working for the same thing that I was working for.

I'd be in a car with them, and they'd play a song, and I'd like it. They'd talk about places they've been and foods they like and certain games they play. Each time, I was like, "Yeah, I do the same thing." It was an easy connection.

We all had the same goals, the same dreams. We're always trying to find a way to provide for our families, coming from the inner city. They were on the same page as me.

## FUNNY TEAMMATES

Mario (Little), he's a fool. The Morris twins, they're funny in their own way. Like when they try to dance, it's the most hilarious thing ever. They can't dance to save their life, but it's the funniest thing ever. Mario cracks on people, and Elijah is just goofy all the time. Those are definitely the most memorable things I think about when I think about this team.

There are so many times — so many funny moments — I can't think of them all specifically. But I would say a majority of them involve Mario and Elijah having moments that just make you laugh.

All of our coaches joke around. The funniest is when Dooley and Mario go at it. Mario will tell him that he looks like a mafia boss. Those two go back and forth at it every day before practice. It's just funny.

## TYSHAWN

Tyshawn is always arguing on the bus. Whoever he's arguing with, he doesn't like to be wrong. So he can argue about anything. When he's arguing on the phone ... we can come back from a road trip at like 2 in the morning, and everybody's knocked out and the lights are off, and you just hear Tyshawn out of nowhere, in the background yelling. He's got his Jersey accent, so everybody's lifting their head up like, "Man, oh my God, be quiet." But with Tyshawn, it's pretty funny. That's one of the memorable things for him.

## COACH MANNING

A funny thing about Coach Manning is that he knows everything. And I literally mean everything. We could be in line for food or something, and somebody will leave a little bit of ketchup in the bottle. And he'll just come out and be like, "Don't act like you didn't use to scrape that ketchup up when you were home, when you were little," or say something like that.

You just feel like he's been through everything you're going through, because he has. He's been in our footsteps. He's been in our situation. He knows what we're going through. He's been exactly where we are right now, and he knows everything we're thinking. He relates to us well, so that's why we respect him so much.

## DEALING WITH TRAGEDY

It was beyond words, the support I received from the whole country. From all of Jayhawk nation especially, but from other people reaching out to me, too. It definitely was an amazing feeling to see that that many people actually cared about me.

I can't count all the letters. There's no way I could count them. It's impossible, unless they go through a number scanner or something. There was

a lot of stuff I received. I don't want to say I have a favorite (item), but a lot of people sent me a lot of stuff. It was way more than I thought it would be. People reached out to me from the NBA. Coaches reached out to me from the NBA. I got letters from little kids and people I don't even know. It was pretty amazing.

## TEXAS GAME

During the first Texas game, I was really emotional, but I wanted to play. That was pretty much it. My teammates were really shocked that I decided to play. But I didn't want to sit around. Before the game, I told Coach Self in the locker room that I didn't want him to treat me any differently. I've seen situations dealing with death, and people get treated a certain way. I didn't want that. I'm still out here. I'm still going to play. So if I'm on the floor, I'm good enough to play.

I don't have that many losses at KU, but one of the toughest ones was Texas. I feel like they kind of hit us and ran. It was kind of a sneaky attack, and we weren't ready. They just got us and ran with it. It hurt because we didn't know if we were going to see them again.

## COMING BACK

My best memory was me returning against K-State at home. I checked into the game, and it just went bananas. I definitely remember that. I felt like the crowd was with me every moment. When I shot the ball, it felt like someone was directing it through the rim. I felt like I couldn't do anything wrong that game. I had everybody on my side. It was 16,300 against five.

Every time I shot, I felt like it was going in. I felt great that game, and it was because of the love I received for coming back. It was amazing.

## ANOTHER YEAR

The support I received from KU fans had a lot to do with my decision to come back this year. I'm happy about that. That showed me a lot, so I feel like I owe something to them. I feel like I can't lose. I'm in a win-win situation, because I know the support that I have behind me. No matter what — if I have a bad season, an awful season — no matter what, they're still going to support me.

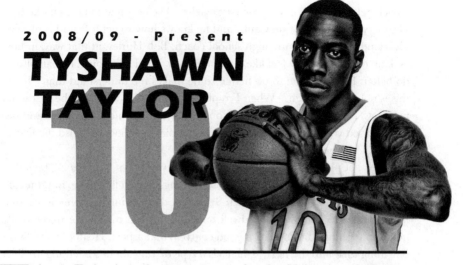

# CHAPTER 40

## 2008/09 - Present
# TYSHAWN TAYLOR

Tyshawn Taylor is a three-year starter for the University of Kansas, averaging 8.7 points and 3.6 assists per game in his career. In 2010, he was selected as one of 20 Bob Cousy Awards finalists, an award given annually to the nation's best point guard. Taylor will be a senior for KU during the 2011-12 season.

### IN TYSHAWN'S WORDS

I made my final decision to come to KU while watching the 2008 national championship game. I was not committed to Marquette at that time, because I had just come out of my commitment, so I was watching the game, and it was between Kansas and Georgia Tech for me. So that next morning after the game, I hadn't told Coach Self yet, but I called Coach Hewitt from Georgia Tech and said, "Coach Hewitt, I slept on it for a couple weeks now. I've been thinking about it. It's been a big decision. But I think I'm going to go to Kansas. And I just wanted to call to let you know."

I came on my visit and was like, "There's no way I can pass this up." Then I went home and committed. It was April 29, on my mom's birthday.

Coach Self came to my high school, and we had an open gym. I remember Coach Self texted me like, "I'm at the gym. Where are you?" And I was like, "I'm coming. I'm rushing to get my mom some balloons." And he was like, "Balloons?"

My mom was there at the gym. I showed up with all these balloons, like 30 balloons. It was a bunch of balloons and a teddy bear. I just gave them to her and said, "Happy birthday, Mom. I'm going to Kansas with Coach Self." I was like, "Coach, I'm coming to Kansas, man." That's how that happened.

## COACH SELF

Coach Self, I think, is one of the best teachers I've ever had as far as basketball. He knows exactly what he wants, and he knows how to get it from his players. He's kind of similar to my high school coach, Bob Hurley, in that way, in how he kind of makes a guy feel like, no matter how good he's doing, he can always do better. He wants me to do better, so he makes me understand that, "Look, this is not good enough." When I'm playing good, Coach Self is the first to let me know. He's the first to smack me on my butt, smack me on my head and say, "You played your ass off." But when I'm not playing good, he's also the first to let me know I need to change some things.

He's got plenty of ways of how he breaks you down, and it's happened to me a couple of times. A lot of yelling, screaming, explicit language. But, I mean, he gets his point across, and Coach Self is good at getting his point across and moving on. He doesn't really dwell on situations too much. He never really holds on to things. I think he's a good coach in that aspect. He doesn't really let one thing turn into the next. If he feels a type of way about something, he'll let you know, then it's over.

Coach Self has got some weird sayings. Some of them are inappropriate; well, most of them are inappropriate and are locker-room talk, but he's got a lot of sayings that always stick with me and that we always use as a team. I always ask him, "Coach, where did you hear this from? What philosopher told you this stuff? Where did this come from?" He says the funniest things. He and Coach Hinson have got the weirdest sayings. Coach Hinson calls me a goober. "What is that, Coach? A goober? I don't know what you're talking about."

The best compliment I ever got from Coach Self was probably when he told me this summer that he thinks I'm the best guard in the country. Coming from him, that means a lot, because if my coach has confidence in me, if my coach thinks I'm the best guard in the country, why shouldn't I? Why shouldn't I act like it? Why shouldn't I play like it? Why shouldn't I train like it? That meant a lot to me.

## TOUGH MATCHUP

Recently, I think Jacob Pullen has been one of the toughest guys I've had to guard. I had a couple matchups with him. He's just good, man. He's been consistent in most of those matchups. He's just one of those guys, if he gets hot, it could be a long night for you. He got hot against me a couple times.

Jake is one of the funniest guys that I've met. He's a jokester. He gets in a room with anybody and can make people laugh. And that's kind of how me and him started being cool, him just being mad funny, and I'm just laughing at him like, "This kid's a clown." He's one of those guys that kind of just says whatever he's thinking.

I think our team and K-State are a lot closer than anybody thinks. We work camps with each other in the summer. I just came back from a camp with Jordan Henriquez and Jamar Samuels and Rodney McGruder. Those guys are cool, man. They're all from the East Coast. It's just one of those things that, we played against each other when we were younger before we were at Kansas and Kansas State.

## DIFFICULT DEFEATS

I've had a couple of tough losses while at KU. Definitely the VCU one. That probably has to be the toughest one, just for the simple fact that we were so close, man. We were right where we wanted to be. Like right there. I felt like if we get that game back, we'll win seven out of 10. I honestly feel like that. Not to take anything away from them, of course, because they had a heck of a season, but I just felt like that was for us to win.

Northern Iowa was disappointing, but when I was watching their highlights and watching their edits, I was like, "This team is a team that could beat us if we don't come to play." It was a surprise, but it wasn't a surprise, because I knew that if we were off our game a little bit, that they would come out and beat us.

Coach had planned for us to go eat at The Cheesecake Factory after the VCU game. I don't know if he was just like, "All right, we're going to win, we're going to eat, we're going to go to the airport and leave." But we lost, so we went to The Cheesecake Factory, and it was one of those things where everybody was sitting around, "Really? Are we here now? Why can't we just go home?" Nobody wanted to be there. It was one of those things like, "Oh, man, is it really over? Seriously?" It was a bad feeling. It was a feeling ... I hate losing so much, especially when I felt like, for us, this is our game. There's no way that we would lose this game. There's no way. To lose like that when you know you're just kind of weren't on your game like you should have been, it sucks.

Brady probably took the loss the hardest. He just had a lot of tears, man. He was really emotional that night, which is very understandable. It's his last year and feeling the same way, like, "We were this close, man. We were this close." I feel like Northern Iowa wasn't so bad, because it was like we couldn't see the finish line. When you see the finish line, then you're just like, "Oh man. Dang." That was pretty sick.

## FACEBOOK INCIDENTS

Early in my career I got into trouble for some things I posted on Facebook. My Facebook account was one of those things that I honestly never really paid too much attention to before, and I never realized how big of a deal it was before. After I got in trouble for it is kind of when it dawned on me that, "Wow, this is important to people. People really care about what I'm saying. They care about it and are actually watching to see what I say." And so, after I did what I did on there, it was one of those things that was like, "Don't say what you're saying.

Modify what you're doing." And I never meant to be harmful or disrespectful or anything like that. It's just one of those things that I've always been doing.

I listen to music, and if I hear something I like, I just throw it on Twitter. Because I listen to music that goes with my mood and how I'm feeling at the time. That's how I listen to my iPod. There are 10 different playlists for how I'm feeling. And so, when I hear something, I'll be like, "Oh, this is cool. I'll throw it on Twitter. I'll throw it on Facebook." A lot of people that follow me on Twitter or watch me on Facebook don't really understand it. They either think it's coming from me personally or something like that. But 75 percent of the stuff that I write on there aren't my words. So it's just one of those things where I've got to watch what I say, because I understand that people are watching me.

It's not really a big deal. I learned my lesson right after I got in trouble for it. I never really thought that it was that big of a deal. I still don't think it is, man, because now that I think about it, it's just Facebook. I'm a 19-year-old kid that cursed on Facebook. I mean, how many 19-year-old kids curse on Facebook, you know? That's what made me realize that this is pretty big, like, "Wow, they actually care what I'm writing, care what I'm saying."

## UPS AND DOWNS

A couple of times, I was like, "Coach Self has to be fed up with me right now. He has to have had it up to here with me." But Coach Self has been really patient with me, man. He has. And I'm thankful for that, because I've been through a lot at Kansas, and Coach Self has pretty much been there every step of the way. Everything I've been through, he's been there, as far as my family ... anything. So he's been really patient with me. I feel like I owe him a little bit. I owe him to go hard, to do what I can to make my team better.

I've been in situations where my judgment wasn't that good. I think it's just me being young. If you ask 100 19-year-old kids if they got in fights in this past year, I can guarantee you most of them would say, "Yeah," you know what I'm saying? I'm in a situation where people are watching me, and what I do really matters and is a big deal. So I've just got to make better decisions. I've got to be a better decision-maker, I think, on and off the court.

A lot of coaches would have kicked me off the team under the same circumstances. I feel like it shows that Coach cares about me more than just a basketball player. He cares about me as a person. I honestly feel like Coach Self wants me to succeed. He always tells me, "You could, and you can, if you stay out of your own way." That's his favorite words to me: Just stay out of your own way. And that just shows me that he believes in me. He sorta, kinda trusts me in his own way. I feel like he trusts me a little bit, even though he might not tell me that.

It just means a lot, because like I said, a lot of people would have given up on me, and he easily could have and would have had every right. Nobody would have argued with him about it. For him not to do that says a lot about him and how he feels about me.

## FAMILY MAN

A lot of college kids can get a phone call from home, and their mom's not doing too good, and they stress about it and they get upset, but they're away at college, so they've got their friends and they've got their books and they're not really worried about it too much. They don't have to deal with those family issues, because they're away. And my family's here, so when my mom is hurting or crying, she's at my door. My sister is the same way. I'm the only male in my family, and so I've got two younger sisters and a mother who, if anybody knows my mother, knows that me and her are more big sister/little brother than mother/son. So, she kind of leans on me the same way my little sister does — both of my little sisters.

So it's one of those situations where, my family was going through some stuff last year, and I have to deal with it head-on. I can't say, "OK, Mom, I'll call you later." Or, "I'll talk to you later about it." It's one of those situations where I've got to deal with at the moment because it's relevant at the moment. It's not something that I can escape. That's one of the biggest things, just trying to make my family happy, and when they're not happy, it weighs on me, and that shows sometimes on the court when I'm not in a good mood or if I'm stressed out.

My mom knows that how she feels and what she's going through affects me. So what my mom tries to do is not to bother me with it, but I know my mom, so if something's bothering her, she really can't hide it from me that well. I can kind of read her. And I always ask, and I'm always worried about my mom, so I want to know if something's wrong. So I ask, and if something's wrong, she won't lie to me about it. It's never been, like, the day before a game, the night before a game, but there are times we've been in a hotel room a couple days before a game that I'm like, "Coach, I've got to send my mom money," or, "Coach, I've got to talk to my sister, because she's doing this," or, "Coach, I've got to do this," and Coach Self, he's good with me. He's good with my family. He's good with my family and dealing with my family and trying to help me deal with my family.

## FUNNY STORY

I remember one time, we had a game at the Fieldhouse, and Jordan Juenemann's girlfriend was getting introduced on the court during one of the timeouts. So Coach was talking and drawing up a play, and he saw a couple guys looking out, so he was like, "Everybody freakin' look at me right now."

So, Jordan's girlfriend's name gets called, and everybody's in the huddle, and the fans clapping, so I look over — and I'm not in the game, so I'm wandering a little bit — and I see Jordan clapping. And I see Coach T like, "What are you doing? What are you doing?"

So after the game, that's the first thing that they want to talk about once the game is over in the locker room. So Coach comes in and is like, "Oh, so Jordan Juenemann wants to clap during the timeout for his girlfriend." So now, anytime Coach says anything, he always brings up the story about, "Everybody pay attention to me in the locker room in the huddle, because if I see anybody clapping for their girlfriends, I'm going to be really upset." He says that all the time, and it's so funny, because Jordan just puts his head down.

## MANNING ADVICE

My freshman year at K-State, I fouled out. And you know, when you walk to bench, they do the, "Left, right, left, right, sit down!" So I'm walking back to the bench. "Left, right, left, right." Coach Manning whispers to me — Coach Manning's always got the inside scoop on everything — he's like, "Here's what you do. Sit down when he shoots, so everybody says, 'Sit down' as he's shooting."

So I'm standing up, standing up. And they're like, "Waiting, waiting!" Denis Clemente goes to shoot, and I sit down, and everybody says, "Sit down!" And he missed it. And I start cracking up. And Coach Manning looks at me. "I told you that s--t was going to work."

Every time I get fouled out, schools happen to do that now. I fouled out this year at Mizzou, and they did the same thing. And I always look at D. He's like, "I told you. I told you." It worked again at Mizzou this year. It works all the time.

I don't think the fans know what I'm doing. And this time, at Mizzou, I just kept jumping up and down, and they were like, "Left, right, left, right." I'm like, "Are y'all that stupid that you're going to do this chant while I'm jumping up and down?" They did it, and the player missed, so it worked.

## THOMAS ROBINSON

The day Thomas' mother died, I remember being in my room, and my little sister texted me, like, "I'm about to come to the Towers, me and mommy." I was like, "Why what's up?" She was like, "You didn't hear?" "Hear what?" She was like, "I think something happened to T-Rob's mom."

So I instantly go downstairs and I see T-Rob, Marcus and Markieff and Elijah in the hallway, and T-Rob was just crying, crying. I was like, "What happened?" T-Rob walked away, and Elijah told me. I was like, "What? No. No. We just saw her. She just talked to him."

It was one of those things where you didn't know what to do. You didn't know what to do for him. You didn't know what to say. This happened at like 11 at night, and we've got a game the next day at 3 in the afternoon. And I didn't go to sleep at all. We had shootaround at 9, and I didn't go to sleep at all. I was up all night crying, just sitting in my bed, thinking, "What if that was me? What is he going to do now? How can we help him? What do I have to do to be strong for him and the rest of my teammates?"

It was a bad situation, man. It was a bad situation that I think T-Rob handled really well and is handling really well. Because I don't know how he's even walking around now. I don't know how he had energy to play in that game the next day. I don't know how he can sleep through the night without, like, tripping, because me, I would be going crazy. It would be hard for me to keep pushing like how he is.

## TEXAS LOSS

I remember the whole game, in my head, all I'm thinking about is, "How is T-Rob not crying right now?" I'm holding back my tears, because he's not crying. So I want to cry, but how can I cry if he's not? And the whole game, this is what I'm thinking about. Of course, I'm thinking about the game and making plays, but in the back of my head, I'm just thinking ... I'm looking at T-Rob. I just keep looking at him, keep looking at him, just to see what's on his face, how is he feeling, to see if I can read him. And he had a poker face the whole time. Nothing.

I think before the game, what T-Rob said to Coach was, "Coach, I want you to come out here and I want you to coach me. I don't want anybody to baby me." I was like, "Damn." I mean, I probably wouldn't tell Coach to baby me, but I definitely wouldn't have said not to baby me. Like, this is kind of crazy how he's handling this. He's handled it well.

I don't think my opinion of Thomas changed; I just kind of feel like I understood him more. I get the kind of person he is. I knew him before, and we were cool. That was my man, of course. But I think that took our relationship from really good friends to like a "brothers" kind of thing. Because now, it's like we're the only people T-Rob's got for real, know what I'm saying? We're the only ones he's really, really got and that he can depend on. That meant a lot to me, because if I was in that situation, man, I'm sure he would be worried about me just like I was worried about him.

I remember there being a lot of people there at the funeral. I remember his friends from home getting up on the mic and talking about how they're there for him and how they appreciate everything he's doing and how he's staying focused, and they're proud of him. And I think that was good for him to hear, because when you feel like you've lost everything and everybody, for people to express how they really love you and truly care about you, I think that helped him to keep pushing. Like, "You know, I've still got people in my corner, even though it's not the people that I would hope to be there, but I've still got people in my corner, people that love and care about me." It was an emotional day, but it was good for T-Rob in a way, just to see how many people really cared about him and his family.

## THOUGHTS ON TRANSFERRING

It's never, ever, ever been something that I've talked to Coach about, that I've talked to any of my teammates about, my mother about. I don't even think it's been a thought that I've ever thought about twice in my head. Like maybe it's been something where I was like, "If I was at this school, I could do this," or, "If I was at this school, maybe I could do that." But, if I was at another school, I wouldn't be playing in front of 16,300 people, no matter who I'm playing. It wouldn't be like this.

This atmosphere is nothing like anything I've ever seen. I've never, ever, ever in my three years being here wanted to transfer, wanted to go to any other school. Never. When I watch college games and see different offenses and see how coaches coach, me and my teammates sit around and are like, "If we were here, we could do this. We could to that." But I'm, like, 95-13 or something like that over three years. I could have went to any other school and probably averaged five or six more points, but I wouldn't be 95-13. I guarantee that. It's not something that I've thought about or would think about, because it won't get any better than this.

I've had ups and downs here, but I know my ups will be a lot higher than anywhere else.

Compiling a book in three months – and, in some cases, working around the busy schedules of high-profile athletes – requires a lot of flexibility. Whether it's driving to Dallas on a whim to interview Darrell Arthur or walking away from the dinner table to take a call from Kirk Hinrich, you have to be willing to do just about anything. That's why the first person I'd like to thank is my lovely wife, Jennifer, who hardly flinched when I took on this project in May – two weeks after the birth of our second child. Each time I felt overwhelmed, I opened my office door, listened to the commotion in the living room and glanced at the toys strewn across the floor. It was a subtle reminder that I was the one who had it easy. So thank you, Jen, for the support – and for making all those late-night Diet Coke runs. I love you.

I also need to express my gratitude to Jesse Newell, who conducted 12 of the 40 interviews in this book. I've long considered Jesse a rising star in the journalism profession. Even though the words in these chapters come straight from the players' mouths, someone still had to ask the right questions. And they had to do so in a manner that made the athletes feel comfortable with sharing stories that, in some cases, had never been told outside of the Jayhawks locker room. I couldn't have picked a better person to help me with this venture.

A sincere "thank-you" also goes out to Beau White for designing the front and back cover of this book as well as the inside pages. In July, Beau asked me to list five or six players I thought should appear on the front cover. I came up with 13 names and then asked him to make the final cut. So you can imagine my surprise a few days later, when Beau e-mailed me a stunning design that featured all 13 players, plus coaches Roy Williams and Bill Self. Beau is a true talent – and so is Steve Puppe, who provided all of the book's photographs. Steve has been a staple on the Allen Fieldhouse baseline for more than a decade.

Equally important were the folks who either helped proofread chapters or served as a sounding board during one of my many moments of frustration. Gerry Ahern, Mike and Susan Fitzgerald, Derek Samson, Sam Mellinger, Dow Tate, Piotr Zygmunt, Michael Ashford, Brett Hunter, Dan Wetzel and Jason Whitlock ... thanks for everything.

Finally, I want to recognize a group of people that became a special part of my life during my days of covering Kansas athletics. Gary Bedore, Tom Keegan, Ric Anderson, Kevin Haskin, Kurt Caywood, Bob Lutz and Rick Plumlee all worked at competing news organizations, but that didn't keep us from going out for a beer or seven after a road game in Austin, sharing a rental car for the long drive to Ames on icy roads or from having each others' backs when times were tough. I truly consider myself lucky to have been surrounded by so many great journalists, and great people. I'm better because of it.

**- Jason King**

I'd like to thank my parents, Dennis and Barb, who always supported me and were proud to collect every sports article I wrote growing up. Also, thanks to my bosses at the Lawrence Journal-World for allowing me to help with this book, especially Tom Keegan, Jonathan Kealing and Dennis Anderson. And lastly, thanks to my wife, Erika, who stayed upbeat and positive through these past few months, even when I had to make my fifth trip of the week to Allen Fieldhouse. I love you.

**- Jesse Newell**

# INTERVIEW INDEX

- Cole Aldrich interviewed by Jason King at Allen Fieldhouse, 6/16/11
- Darrell Arthur interviewed by Jason King at Bob Knight Fieldhouse in Duncanville, Tex. 8/12/11
- Luke Axtell interviewed by Jason King over the phone, 6/7/11
- Nick Bahe interviewed by Jesse Newell over the phone, 5/26/11
- Brett Ballard interviewed by Jesse Newell over the phone, 8/19/11
- Jeff Boschee interviewed by Jason King at the Holiday Inn in Pittsburg, Kan., 6/23/11
- Jeremy Case interviewed by Jesse Newell over the phone, 7/13/11
- Mario Chalmers interviewed by Jason King in Salina, Kan., 7/20/11
- Eric Chenowith interviewed by Jason King over the phone, 7/7/11
- Sherron Collins interviewed by Jason King at Portillo's in Chicago, Ill., 7/13/11
- Nick Collison interviewed by Jason King over the phone, 7/6/11
- J.R. Giddens interviewed by Jason King over the phone, 6/22/11
- C.J. Giles interviewed by Jason King over the phone, 6/26/11
- Drew Gooden interviewed by Jason King at Allen Fieldhouse, 6/15/11
- Jeff Graves interviewed by Jason King at Noodles & Company in Lee's Summit, Mo., 6/9/11.
- Jeff Hawkins interviewed by Jason King at 23rd St. Brewery in Lawrence, Kan., 6/10/11
- Xavier Henry interviewed by Jason King over the phone, 8/23/11
- Kirk Hinrich interviewed by Jason King over the phone, 7/8/11
- Darnell Jackson interviewed by Jason King over the phone, 8/15/11
- Sasha Kaun interviewed by Jason King at Starbucks on Kansas City's Country Club Plaza, 6/26/11
- Matt Kleinmann interviewed by Jesse Newell over the phone, 6/1/11
- Keith Langford interviewed by Jason King at the Oread Hotel in Lawrence, Kan., 6/19/11
- Michael Lee interviewed by Jason King over the phone, 6/12/11
- Mario Little interviewed by Jesse Newell over the phone, 7/21/11
- Aaron Miles interviewed by Jason King at International House of Pancakes in Lawrence, Kan., 7/5/11
- Christian Moody interviewed by Jesse Newell over the phone, 7/1/11
- Brady Morningstar interviewed by Jesse Newell at Allen Fieldhouse, 8/4/11
- David Padgett interviewed by Jason King over the phone, 6/30/11
- Tyrel Reed interviewed by Jesse Newell over the phone, 6/10/11
- Russell Robinson interviewed by Jason King at Sullivan's Steakhouse in Overland Park, Kan., 6/15/11
- Thomas Robinson interviewed by Jesse Newell at Allen Fieldhouse, 6/12/11
- Brandon Rush interviewed by Jason King at Fiorella's Jack Stack Barbecue on Kansas City's Country Club Plaza, 7/10/11
- Josh Selby interviewed by Jason King over the phone, 8/23/11
- Bill Self interviewed by Jason King at Allen Fieldhouse, 8/8/11; and over the phone, 8/19/11
- Rodrick Stewart interviewed by Jason King over the phone, 8/17/11
- Wayne Simien interviewed by Jason King at 23rd Street Brewery in Lawrence, Kan., 8/8/11
- Tyshawn Taylor interviewed by Jesse Newell at Allen Fieldhouse, 6/4/11
- Stephen Vinson interviewed by Jesse Newell over the phone, 5/31/11
- Roy Williams interviewed by Jason King in Las Vegas, Nevada, 7/24/11
- Julian Wright interviewed by Jesse Newell over the phone, 7/15/11

*Numerous attempts to interview Marcus and Markieff Morris were unsuccessful.*